Wheeler, Burton K. (Burton Kendall), 1882-1975.

Yankee from the West; the candid, turbulent life story of the Yankee-born

YANKEE FROM THE WEST

YANKEE FROM THE WEST

Burton K. Wheeler *with*
Paul F. Healy

The candid, turbulent life story of the Yankee-born U. S. Senator from Montana

DOUBLEDAY & COMPANY, INC.
Garden City, New York
1962

Library of Congress Catalog Card Number 62–15909

Printed in the United States of America

First Edition

Dedicated to my beloved wife, Lulu M. Wheeler, without whose devotion, courage, and unwavering loyalty to me and to her convictions, the career outlined in this book would not have been possible; and to my daughter, Frances, who, prior to her death in 1957, devoted long and patient hours to much of the research that underlies this book.

CONTENTS

INTRODUCTION

The career of former Senator Burton K. Wheeler is a favorite for analysis by the writers of Ph.D. theses. He was an influential protagonist in a great many of the most bitterly fought elections, investigations, and legislative battles of this century. As a giant in the age of giants in the Senate, Wheeler also attracted writers in general. *Time* magazine called him a "senator's senator." Hamilton Basso called him "Burton the Bronc." William Hard said Wheeler would have made "a great bucko mate quelling the crew of an old New England China clipper."

Since there are certain things a man cannot very well say in his autobiography, I am taking the opportunity as Wheeler's collaborator to set down a third person view.

As one who has written magazine articles on scores of senators and other national personages, I find the Wheeler story irresistible. It has everything. Approaching a senator important enough to be profiled, I always hope he will be abundantly endowed as a subject with what I call the "three c's," that is, that he be as colorful, controversial, and candid as possible. These qualities are present in Wheeler more than in anyone I have ever studied.

Wheeler is properly regarded as a prototype of the sturdy Western progressive, but what makes him more interesting to me are the many aspects of our national character he reflects.

He has the moral indignation of his New England heritage; the self-reliance gained from working his way through law school—and successfully wooing a farmer's daughter—in the Midwest; and the two-fisted—and cunning—recklessness he refined on Montana's last frontier. It seems natural for Wheeler to have started his career by losing his shirt in a poker game in the tough town of Butte, Montana. Wheeler is a born gambler, always willing to risk long odds and then go all-out to win.

Except for Andrew Jackson, it is difficult to think of another Democrat in American history who succeeded for so long—thirty-six years—while being controversial. He has every element of the successful American politician except one—caution. I had never interviewed a first-rank senator or ex-senator who would let his hair down on the record. Surprisingly few senators write their memoirs and those who do are in a mellow mood which precludes handling old antagonists harshly. Wheeler himself was not eager to refight old political battles but when he did decide to tell his story he characteristically refused to short-change history. Nobody who should wear horns appears in these pages with a halo.

In setting the record straight, Wheeler is not acting vindictively. He names names but holds no grudges. Intolerant of injustice, he is tolerant of men. His only concern is that he may sound self-righteous. "I'm no paragon of virtue," he frequently protests.

One key to his success as a politician is a rare fusion of pugnacity and affability. In the Senate, he was at once greatly feared and greatly loved. President Kennedy, when he was a congressman, once said to Wheeler that President Roosevelt told his father, Joseph P. Kennedy, the only two men in the Senate he feared were Huey Long and Wheeler. Yet all the evidence available to me is that FDR liked Wheeler. The two were strong-minded men—a "king" and a "baron"—and it is perhaps inevitable that they fell out, made up, and fell out again.

A wealthy but much less successful Montanan once remarked to Wheeler: "If I could smile like you while calling someone an S.O.B., I'd give a million dollars." All politicians profess to "like people," and most of them probably do, but I have never before met one who all but embraces friend, enemy, or interviewer on sight. Wheeler's shrewd light blue eyes glitter behind his octagonal spectacles and the crinkling grin which permanently wreathes his wide mouth grows even more disarming.

This instinctive reaching-out—which amounts to instant communication—was vividly illustrated for me when I was working with Wheeler on this book at his summer cabin in Glacier National Park. The local Democratic Party was holding a picnic one Sunday afternoon at Kalispell, thirty-five miles away, and the former senator had been invited to attend. Wheeler had given up active politics fifteen years before, and he feels no blind loyalty to his party. There was no reason for him, at age seventy-nine, to take the trouble to accept. But he could not resist a chance to pass the time of day with a group of Montanans, most of whom would be strangers.

It rained and we got a late start. Though Wheeler burned up the highways driving to Kalispell, we arrived just as the picnic was breaking up. The coffee was stale, the baked beans were cold, and the benches and the departing party members were soggy. Yet for nearly an hour Wheeler hung around, exchanging views and gossip with the party workhorses who were cleaning up. This was more than an old politician reminiscing; it was the picture of a man enjoying life.

Having chatted with these Montanans and many persons in Washington who worked for and against Wheeler (and having seen him needle an opponent in the Senate in his later years), I could better understand the engaging masculine appeal which this man of action projected in his prime.

He was a broad-shouldered six-footer in a comfortably rumpled suit. His trade-marks were a dented Stetson, a thin cigar clamped in his slash of mouth, expressive hands, and a shambling, purposeful stride. He was about as easily cowed as a grizzly bear. He was never an orator or a polished speaker but his natural force and his gift of idiom made him a highly effective one. His straight-from-the-shoulder style apparently shot across from the platform as directly as it did to me in many hours of conversation.

Effectiveness in a senator is a much more unusual quality

than the public realizes; a senator can become famous in ways which have nothing to do with legislation—through speeches, glamour, or even by accident.

"Wheeler was a great legislator—there was none better," says Thomas G. (Tommy the Cork) Corcoran, the Washington lawyer who was FDR's able lieutenant on Capitol Hill and has been in touch with it ever since. Corcoran says the keys to Wheeler's greatness were "a first-class mind" and an intuitive understanding of his colleagues.

Wheeler's effectiveness was best described in a book about the Court-packing fight, *The 168 Days*, written by Joseph Alsop, the syndicated columnist, and Turner Catledge, now managing editor of *The New York Times.*

"His great forte was legislative fighting," they wrote. "His suspicions gave him a peculiar prevision of the enemy's next moves. He was energetic and tireless. He knew every twist and turn of the legislative game, and he was not above using its brutal expedients if they promised to be helpful. Although he had his own good share of vanity, he knew how to soothe the vanities of others, and he worked well with his team."

In accepting an invitation to lead the fight against the President's Court-packing bill, Wheeler had clearly risked his political future—and ended up dealing FDR his only major defeat.

Wheeler fought bigness, whether it took the form of a power-hungry President or the domineering Anaconda Copper Mining Company. His other principal fight was against those who would corrupt and weaken the democratic system. The embodiment of this to him is still Harry M. Daugherty, President Harding's crony and Attorney General, whom a freshman Senator Wheeler drove from office.

Wheeler's life is the stuff of which melodramas are made. In 1939 the movie, *Mr. Smith Goes to Washington,* starring James Stewart, was based on the script, *The Man from Montana,* which in turn was based on Wheeler's exposure of Daugherty's "Ohio Gang."

Political scientists who insist on neatly classifying politicians are puzzled by Wheeler. The common conclusion is that he is a liberal who turned conservative. The confusion here is over the fact that during the first two-thirds of his career Wheeler's fights ranged him alongside those called "liberal"; during the rest of it, he was generally lined up with the "conservatives." Actually, while the times changed, the nature of the issues shifted, and the labels grew fuzzy, Wheeler stayed essentially the same. The wonder is not that he changed so much but that he changed so little.

In 1939 Senator George W. Norris of Nebraska, the patron saint of modern liberals, wrote in a letter: "I have never lost faith in Senator Wheeler . . . I think his courage and fearlessness in the work he has done commends him to all lovers of human liberty." In 1940, Norris endorsed him for the Democratic presidential nomination (in the event FDR did not run for a third term) with the words, "Wheeler is fully qualified to be President." That was the year Wheeler spurned repeated overtures from White House emissaries seeking to make him Roosevelt's running mate. He rejected the opportunity with the simple explanation that he could not say he agreed with the President (on the war issue) when he did not agree. A different answer would probably have put Wheeler in the White House in 1945. It was an actual case of a politician saying, "I'd rather be right."

Above all, Wheeler wanted to remain free—and he did. He once told Democratic leaders who criticized him for having bolted the Democratic Party to run as Vice President on the National Independent Progressive ticket in 1924: "I will not bend my knee and I will not mend my ways." As a symbol of the individualist in politics, he may well be the last of a vanishing breed.

Here I want to express my deepest thanks to Mr. Wheeler for the pleasure of working with him and to the members of his family for their invaluable help. I owe a special debt of gratitude to Frances Wheeler (Mrs. Allen Saylor) who before her untimely death compiled the basic research for her father's story.

Paul F. Healy

Chapter One

THE PRESIDENT AND THE PLAN

Controversy has sparked my public life from start to finish. My opponents have ranged from the giant Anaconda Copper Mining Company to the leaders of both my own Democratic Party and the Republican Party. The names I've been called run the gamut from Communist to Fascist and include a great many other derogatory terms besides. I have been accused of almost everything but timidity. My opponents taught me self-reliance—and that the best defense is a good offense. After all, they were not fighting according to Marquis of Queensberry rules.

All the principal episodes of my career carried overtones of melodrama but in none of them was the stage as large as it was in my second and last battle with Franklin D. Roosevelt. In 1937 I had successfully led the Senate attack on his bill to pack the United States Supreme Court. Within two years this rupture between two close political associates had largely healed but I was becoming uneasy about his attitude toward the war that had broken out in Europe.

I knew little more than any senator could read in the newspapers until one day late in May 1940 I was sitting at my desk in the Senate Office Building when my secretary told me an "Admiral Hooper" was asking to see me. I was curious, since I was not a member of any Senate committee that would normally concern an admiral and I had never posed as a military authority.

The admiral turned out to be a short, pudgy man wearing civilian clothes. He introduced himself as Rear Admiral Stanford C. Hooper and mentioned a previous meeting with me which I did not recall. He said he had to talk to someone and knew he could talk confidentially to me. Then he came to the point.

"The man at the other end of the Avenue is going to get us into the war," he said.

I told him I didn't believe that about the President.

"Senator, I know what I'm talking about," he went on earnestly. I replied that I was not a military or naval expert and wanted to ask some questions. I pointed out first that FDR claimed to be much worried about the security of the United States. The Nazis were overrunning France and the President in his defense message to Congress on May 16 had warned of the dangers we faced if Hitler conquered all of Europe. He had pointed out that "the islands off the west coast of Africa are 1500 miles from Brazil. Modern planes starting from the Cape Verde Islands can be over Brazil in seven hours." Germany's military effectiveness, the President had said, "surely . . . made clear to all our citizens . . . the possibility of attack on vital American zones." He had talked about Hitler bombing New York, Philadelphia, and, as I now recall, he included New Orleans, St. Louis, and Denver. I asked the admiral, "What about Hitler's bombing of American cities, as suggested by Roosevelt?"

He said, "The Germans haven't got a bomber that can fly more than a thousand miles—five hundred miles out and five hundred miles back."

"What about their going down to Dakar and then over to Brazil and cutting up to the United States?" I asked.

"When they're in Brazil," he pointed out, "they're farther away from New York than they were in Berlin, and by the time they crossed the rivers and jungles and got up to Texas, what do you think we'd be doing?"

As the conversation went on, the admiral convinced me that FDR was using the spectre of a Nazi invasion of the United States as a pretext for our joining the allies. I hated to see us slide into a war, as we had done in 1916–17. I asked the admiral what I could do about it.

"You can stop it," he said.

"How?"

"You can't stop him by making one speech," Hooper replied. "You've got to go out and make a lot of speeches. You licked him on the Court issue and you can lick him again."

The admiral said he wasn't against getting into the war because of any fear on his part as he was too old to go. When I asked him how the rest of the officers in the Navy felt, he said, "Most of the older heads feel as I do—that we should keep out—but a lot of the younger men who look forward to promotions think the President knows more about the Navy than we do."

I had already made a number of speeches against an administration program which I felt might entangle us in the war but I didn't believe that the President actually wanted to get us into war. I knew he was most friendly to England and like every good citizen hated what Hitler was doing. My position was the same as it had been in the first war. While I am of English ancestry and was always pro-ally, I felt that this was not our war. When I was U. S. District Attorney for Montana during World War I, the hysteria over possible invasion even in that remote area was so great that I had to resist pressure to prosecute for sedition Montanans who were guilty of nothing more than having a foreign name. I wanted to see the American people keep their heads this time.

I asked the admiral to give me some facts. He said he would. He subsequently sent me a one-page handwritten memo about the Nazis' capacity for launching an air invasion against us.

(Roosevelt's so-called "geography-lesson" speech of May 16 was debunked in Hooper-like terms early in 1941 by Hanson Baldwin, military analyst of *The New York Times*, in his book, *United We Stand*.

"The author does not know of a single responsible military or naval officer or government official who believes that this nation is threatened by direct invasion, even if Germany wins," Baldwin wrote. Asserting that the United States Navy was capable of meeting the combined fleets of Germany, Italy, Russia, and Japan in its own waters, he added: "By air the problem is even more difficult. Colonel Lindbergh, as all military observers know, was perfectly correct when he said that the United States could not be invaded by air.")

Soon after the admiral's visit, I began to make more vigorous and more frequent speeches and to warn more seriously against the policy of "all aid to the allies short of war." "'Short of war' *means* war," I said. This was the opinion of many other senators and the majority of Americans. Whatever his intentions might be, I feared the steps the President was taking might lead us into war. And so I was plunged deeper and deeper into a bitter battle with the White House.

Several years later, Admiral Hooper had me to dinner and wryly recalled that he was the one who had gotten me into "all this trouble," meaning vilification by the interventionists. Hooper (who died in 1945) subsequently was decorated for his pioneering work in radio, sonar, and radar. He had been the original fleet wireless officer in the Navy in 1912 and had won the Navy Cross for his combat service in World War I. Later, he had set up the Navy's first world-wide chain of land stations linked to the fleet.

My first speech after the admiral's visit occurred on June 7, 1940, before a massive rally of the peace-minded in Washington, D.C. That night the Nazi Panzer divisions were forty-eight miles from Paris. I said that "a mad hysteria grips many of our people—a hysteria produced in New York and Washington." I urged my listeners not to be panicked by "bogey stories about air bases from which giant hordes of planes will bomb New York, St. Louis, and New Orleans."

The talk was carried over a radio network and brought a cascade of telegrams and letters asking me to speak in many parts of the country. It also inspired another visit by a military man. This one was to involve me in 1941 in the disclosure of a document which rocked the government with cries of disloyalty on the one hand and duplicity on the other. My key role in exposing the most secret plan in Washington at that time has not been revealed until this writing.

The day after the Washington rally an Army Air Corps captain who was a stranger to me showed up in my office. He was in uniform, and clean-cut and intelligent-looking. (I will omit his name, inasmuch as he may well be a senior officer in the Air Force today.)

The captain sat down and asked immediately: "Are you going to keep up this fight?" I said I certainly was. He asked me if I wanted some facts. I said yes.

"We haven't got a single, solitary plane that's fit for overseas service," he told me. "You've got to have three things—armor plate, self-sealing fuel tanks, and fire power. We haven't got a single, solitary plane that has all three. Some of them have one of those essentials, some have two, but not one has all three."

He said our aircraft were good enough to fight in Cuba or Mexico but not against the modern German Air Force.

"What are you talking about?" I asked. "The administration says we have over four thousand planes ready for combat service, twenty-six hundred of them in the Army Air Corps."

The captain said that any official who gave out such a statement either was misinformed or was "lying to the American people."

Now I was persuaded that we were not only not in danger of being invaded by the Nazis but that we were in no condition to fight in Europe. I extended my speechmaking tour to the Midwest. On July 1, I addressed the Keep America Out of War Congress in the Auditorium Theater in Chicago. Afterward, a group of students from several universities came to my hotel room and said they wanted to organize a new group dedicated to keeping the nation at peace. They asked me if I would head it up.

I advised the students to choose someone outside government and politics. Among others, I suggested retired Brigadier General Robert E. Wood, the eminent chairman of the board of Sears Roebuck & Company in Chicago. I later learned I was not the only one to recommend General Wood. He became chairman of the America First Committee when it was organized on September 1, 1940.

The Democratic National Convention was due to open in Chicago on July 15 and the political pot was boiling over. Much as it may surprise some persons today, I had long been considered a leading possibility for the presidential nomination if FDR did not choose to run for a third term—or as his running mate if he did. For six months I had received an extraordinary buildup by a variety of newspaper and magazine writers as the one proven Democratic liberal most likely to appeal to conservative voters. In February, Doris Fleeson, writing in the New York *Daily News* and Washington *Times-Herald*, had reported that I was "riding high" in the White House as the probable vice presidential nominee.

The President knew me well. I had been the first prominent Democrat to come out for his nomination back in 1930, I had worked for his nomination at the 1932 convention, and, as chairman of the Senate Interstate Commerce Committee, I had done yeoman service for him on the Public Utility Holding Company bill of 1935 and the Transportation Act of 1940. Of course, I had not helped my chances by announcing on June 13, 1940, that I was prepared to bolt the Democratic Party if it was in fact becoming the "war party." But the President was concerned about losing votes among the potent "peace groups" and so I continued to receive overtures behind the scenes about running for Vice President even after the convention was under way, as will be related in another chapter.

My overriding concern as the convention approached was the framing of the foreign policy plank in the Democratic platform. Along with several other non-interventionist senators, I wanted this direct pledge adopted: "We will not participate in foreign wars and we will not send our armies, navies, or air forces to fight on foreign lands outside the Americas." We got this through the subcommittee, of which I was a member, but the full committee was a more difficult hurdle.

I arrived at the first meeting of the full committee a few minutes late. Senator Matthew M. Neely of West Virginia was on his feet reading a long tract against dictators and saying that every farmer, working man, professional, and businessman and banker had to be fitted into his particular "niche" during the emergency. I had made a note—"this *means* dictatorship"—but before I could say a word Senator David I. Walsh of Massachusetts said "this means totalitarianism." I asked Neely who sent the paper in and he said, "the President." All members of the committee looked shocked. FDR wanted the statement as a plank in the platform but we took a vote and everyone on the committee, with the exception of Secretary of Agriculture Henry A. Wallace, voted against it. Leslie Biffle, secretary of the committee, promptly tore the paper into little bits.

Later, it was suggested that we use the statement as a preamble to the platform, but that too was thrown out.

Spokesmen for William Allen White's interventionist citizens group were in the full committee and they wanted a virtual declaration of war written into the platform. The debate behind locked doors got hot. At one point, Mayor Edward J. Kelly of Chicago said he had made a survey of the city wards and had found that the people were very anxious to stay out of the war. After a speech by Senator Claude D. Pepper of Florida, the arch-interventionist, I remarked that he didn't represent the President—that the person closest to FDR politically was Kelly. The hard-fisted boss of Chicago blushed like a schoolgirl.

Another time, Senator James F. Byrnes of South Carolina, whose job it was to protect the administration on the peace plank, slipped over to me and asked in an aside if I couldn't soften our plank because Secretary of State Cordell Hull felt it would "interfere with his operations in the Orient." "What 'operations'?" I asked suspiciously. Byrnes threw up his hands disgustedly and walked away.

A few minutes later, I headed for the lavatory and found Byrnes, Pepper, and Kelly with their heads together in an anteroom. I surmised that Kelly was being worked on.

"What are you burglars up to?" I asked jocularly. Byrnes said he had just talked with the President and that he might not run unless we amended the foreign policy statement in the platform.

"The President will not only run," I told Byrnes, "but he wants to run and will run on any platform we draft. If you delete our language, I will walk out of the convention."

"You wouldn't do that, would you?" Byrnes asked.

"Certainly I would," I told him. He walked off. Kelly waited a minute and then reached over and shook my hand in congratulation.

Byrnes went directly to the telephone, I learned later, and put in another call—his third—to the White House. The last thing the administration wanted was a fight on the convention floor over the peace issue.

When Byrnes returned to the committee, he told us that if we agreed to add the phrase, "except in case of attack," FDR and Hull would go along with the wording of our plank. We had no objection to this proviso and the amended plank was ratified unanimously, first by the full committee and then by the convention.

FDR was nominated according to plan and chose as his running mate—to the surprise and distaste of a great many delegates—Secretary of Agriculture Wallace, an interventionist. At their convention in Philadelphia in June, the Republicans had nominated Wendell Willkie and I had denounced him as a tool of Wall Street and an interventionist.

The 1940 presidential campaign soon settled into a phony contest to see who could most reassure American fathers and mothers that their boys would not be sent off to fight a war. Willkie kept calling FDR a warmonger and the public reaction finally got under the President's skin. The late Robert E. Sherwood, a Roosevelt ghost writer, has written that on a trip through New England on October 30 FDR was flooded with telegrams "stating almost tearfully that if the President did not give his solemn promise to the mothers, he might as well start packing his belongings at the White House."

For this reason, Sherwood explained, the President that night in a speech in Boston spoke those unforgettable lines: "I have said this before, but I shall say it again—and again—and again—your boys are not going to be sent into any foreign war."

According to Sherwood, FDR rejected a suggestion by another speechwriter, Samuel Rosenman, that he add the phrase that was so important to him in the platform—"except in case of attack."

The President's campaign promises did not square with an impression I was getting from insiders. In October, Vice President John Nance Garner called me into his room off the Senate floor. He had just come from a Cabinet meeting.

"Go pour yourself a drink and pour one for me," he said. After a while he said, "Go pour yourself another and pour one for me." He obviously had something on his mind. This time, when he held up his glass and sighted through it, he remarked, "You're a gambler."

"What makes you think so?" I asked.

"Oh, all you fellows from out West like to gamble," he said.

"What's on your mind?"

"I'll bet you a grand," the Vice President went on, "that we're in the war by June first of next year."

"Jack, I won't take you," I said.

"I'll make it April first," he countered.

"I still won't take you," I said.

"Well," he said flatly, "we're going to be in the war after the election."

Garner paused, ruminating, then added: "Hull is more anxious to go to war with the Japs than the Chief is." I asked why.

"Because he thinks we've got to go to war with them sometime and we might as well do it now," the Vice President said.

"That's a hell of a reason," I said. Garner agreed. Later, I mentioned Garner's report of Hull's attitude to Chairman Tom Connally of the Foreign Relations Committee and he grunted, "That's right."

The evidence that Hull wanted to go to war with Japan is overwhelming. Senator George W. Norris, the great liberal independent, knew it and once innocently assured me we would not lose any soldiers in a war with Japan.

In November 1940 my stand on the war was put to a popular test. I was up for re-election to my fourth term in the Senate. My opponent, E. K. Cheadle, a Shelby, Montana, lawyer, was commissioned as a lieutenant colonel in the Army shortly after he was nominated on the Republican ticket and said he was too busy as a soldier to campaign. I met this clever political maneuver by saying that I wouldn't campaign either. I was busy in Congress, which stayed in session until the end of the year.

I was re-elected by a majority of 114,000 votes, carrying every city and county in the state. It was the most lop-sided victory ever won by a candidate in Montana history. In contrast, FDR carried the state by only 54,000 votes. I made no speeches for the Roosevelt-Wallace ticket because I never supported hypocrisy.

In the election, I voted for Norman Thomas, the Socialist candidate, for President because I thought he was the ablest candidate running and was genuinely interested in keeping us out of war.

Immediately after the election, I took a restful trip to Hawaii. Pausing in San Francisco on my return, I read that Roosevelt would ask Congress for authority to lend-lease all sorts of aid to the allies. It would be a revolutionary law giving him tremendous dictatorial powers to further our intervention—something he would not have dared to broach before the election. I said at once that I would fight the bill.

When I arrived in Washington, D.C., Senator Ed Johnson, a Colorado Democrat who shared my sentiments about the war, said he felt I could not prevent its passage, since the leaders of both parties were supporting the bill.

"The skids are all greased and the Republican and Democratic leaders are all for the bill," Johnson said. I told him I would fight it even if the only vote I mustered was my own.

"When you pass this bill, it means war," I told my colleagues. All the Democrats speaking for the administration said the bill meant peace.

"If it is our war," I said on January 4, 1941, "how can we justify lending them stuff and asking them to pay us back? If it is our war, we ought to have the courage to go over and fight it, but it is not our war."

When the bill was before the Senate that month, I debated it on Theodore Granik's "American Forum of the Air" radio program. Among other things, I said: "The lend-lease program is the New Deal's triple-A foreign policy; it will plow under every fourth American boy."

When I had written these words in longhand that Sunday afternoon at home, I thought little about them. But when I spoke the phrase over the network that night, I must confess it did sound somewhat harsh.

At his next press conference, FDR called it "the most untruthful, the most dastardly, unpatriotic thing that has been said in public life in my generation. Quote me on that."

A few days later, Joseph P. Kennedy, the prewar Ambassador to the Court of St. James, invited me to his suite in the Carlton Hotel. As I walked in the door, he said, "I told them [White House aides] that if the President hadn't criticized that speech of yours, there wouldn't be five thousand people who remembered it. Now five million people will remember it."

When in other speeches I got carried away and warned that we would lose our cherished liberties if we got into the war, I was also suffering from an excess of zeal for my cause.

Joe Kennedy, a friend since the early 1920s, shared my concern about our avoiding the war. He once told me that he liked Prime Minister Neville Chamberlain better than Winston Churchill because Chamberlain was interested in working out a peaceful solution. If this was so, I asked him, why did Britain let itself get involved in a war? Kennedy said it was "pressure from the United States."

Early in February, while Congress was debating the lend-lease bill, I received another visit from the Army Air Corps captain. He gave me statistics to show that the country was little better equipped with air power than it was at the time of his first conversation with me. I changed the figures around slightly to discourage suspicions that I had an informant inside the Air Corps and then issued a statement.

I called for an air force second to none as "the most effective big stick" we could have but I asserted that none of the war planes on hand as of January 1 had all three requisites necessary for combat: self-sealing tanks, armor plate, and fire power. Secretary of War Henry L. Stimson replied that my statement was "unfair," that I should have said that the materials were on hand to equip the planes with self-sealing tanks and that none would have been sent into combat without such improvements.

In a letter to Stimson, I challenged him to dispute my figures and I asked: "Don't you think, Mr. Secretary . . . that even those people who are insisting that we enter the European war now should be advised that we are not as well prepared as were England and France in September 1939?" Stimson did not answer the letter.

Congress approved the lend-lease bill early in March. The act permitted any country whose defense the President deemed vital to ours to receive arms and other equipment and supplies by sale, transfer, exchange, or lease.

Immediately afterward, I began speaking often under the auspices of the America First Committee. Today it is perhaps forgotten that the list of distinguished citizens backing the committee included a number who, like myself, were progressives on domestic issues. One was Chester Bowles, who was to become a certified liberal in the Truman and Kennedy administrations.

In the fall of 1941 my speaking tour extended to Los Angeles, San Francisco, Phoenix, Denver, Portland, and Seattle. In Seattle, we were refused the use of the city auditorium and for a time it looked as if we might have no place to meet. However, the owner of a large theater volunteered to cancel his movie for the evening in order to let me speak there.

I drew capacity crowds. Sometimes they included organized groups who came to heckle. Several times, eggs were thrown—but missed me. They didn't bother me because I had learned in my thirty years of handling rough political audiences how to make the heckling boomerang.

After Hitler broke his pact with Russia on June 22, 1941, I became the target for Communists at the America First meetings. This was a salutary development. While the pact was in effect, the Communists had supported me, as they had other non-interventionists. But it gave my enemies a chance to charge that "everyone knew" Burt Wheeler had been a Bolshevik in disguise back in his wild West days.

I also was revolted by the professional hate-groups and other crackpots who for their own unwholesome reasons supported the America First movement. I publicly condemned the Nazis' racial and religious persecutions and stated that I wanted nothing to do with organized prejudice.

The haters were as hard as maggots to shake off. For example, there was a letter from an openly anti-Semitic Kansan urging me to take out after the Jews. In my reply, which I placed in the Congressional Record, I told him I was not anti-Semitic and was trying to keep any such overtones out of our campaign.

The theme of our campaign was that, step by step, our policies were taking us right into the middle of the war and would eventually help to make the world safe for communism.

In September 1941 the United States Navy was ordered to do merchant convoy duty as far as Iceland and on October 9 the President asked Congress to modify the Neutrality Act of 1939 to permit arming of our merchantmen engaged in overseas commerce and sending them through combat zones. Six days later, the American destroyer, *Kearny*, was torpedoed and damaged by a German submarine west of Iceland.

One night in October I had a telephone call from Max Lowenthal, a well-known liberal lawyer who had headed the railroad investigating staff of the Interstate Commerce Committee and was close to the "palace guard" of the New Deal. Lowenthal said the President wanted to see me but suggested I first have a talk with Lowell Mellett, a White House aide. Mellett had been a good friend of mine ever since, as a newspaperman, he had covered my 1924 campaign when I ran as Senator Robert La Follette's running mate on the Independent Progressive ticket. I agreed to breakfast with Mellett at Lowenthal's home in Chevy Chase.

There Mellett assured me that FDR wanted to be known above all as the man who kept us out of war and that he wanted to play the key role at a peace conference.

"Woodrow Wilson had it in the palm of his hand at Versailles but he wasn't a politician and he let it slip through his fingers," Mellett explained. "But Roosevelt is a politician and he can handle these people."

"Lowell," I told him, "that's hard to believe in the light of statements made by Knox [Secretary of the Navy] and others."

"Will you believe me?" Mellett asked.

"Yes," I said, "but I doubt that you correctly interpret what's in the President's mind."

We spent five hours that morning analyzing Roosevelt's intentions. Mellett kept insisting the President wanted me to come to the White House some evening and talk the whole thing over.

"I'll be glad to go down and talk to him any time he wants," I said, "but you tell him I'm not seeking an invitation."

I never heard from the President in connection with this overture. But it galled me to think that FDR was still posing as a would-be peacemaker. It was and still is my conviction that the President felt our entry into the war was inevitable. I knew there was an emotional tug working in him. Several times in past conversations with me he had revealed himself as an unabashed Anglophile. For example, when he called me in to discuss the Court-packing bill, he commented in passing, "Well, that's what they have over in England and we ought to have it." At other times, he had sought to bolster a point on another issue by pointing out, "Well, that's what England does."

No doubt Roosevelt, both before and right after the war started in Europe, did aspire to be the great mediator at a great peace conference. But evidence has since come to light indicating that his administration's refusal to make any concessions at all to Germany's *Lebensraum* killed any chances for a peaceful settlement.

In October 1939 I had publicly urged that the President take a more positive role as a mediator "before the forces of communism have an opportunity to spread their doctrine throughout the war-torn continent." Evil as Nazi imperialism was, I suspected that Communist techniques might be even more dangerous and far-reaching.

Can anyone be certain now that the United States could have stayed out of World War II? Obviously not. What I am certain of is that FDR, from whatever motivations, never tried to keep us out of the war—while deliberately misleading the people into thinking that he was.

I believe we might have avoided an attack if the President had required Hull to negotiate seriously and realistically with the Japanese. Hull adamantly rejected and ridiculed all Japanese claims that their policies were primarily motivated by the need to contain the spread of communism in China and the Far East. The continual tightening of the screws on Japan made that government feel that negotiations were feckless, that war was inevitable, and that they would do well to hit us first. This they did at Pearl Harbor, and a few days later we were forced into war with Germany.

Once we were in the war, I never at any time favored making a deal with Hitler. But in the spring of 1944 we had reports that there was a strong movement in Germany to oust Hitler. If FDR had followed the example of Woodrow Wilson and told the German people what the allies wanted instead of insisting on unconditional surrender, the German people might have overthrown their dictator. That might have saved the lives of tens of thousands of American boys and avoided tragic political consequences. Our leaders trusted and followed "good old Joe" Stalin, so today we are reaping the global whirlwind.

Today our enemies of 1941–45 are our friends and our Russian and Chinese friends of that era are our enemies. War simply does not settle anything. I felt that it was World War I that brought about the collapse of the Czarist Russian government and alienated the Russian people from the West thereafter. We fought the first war to make the world safe for democracy—and the world got dictators and less freedom.

During the so-called "short of war" period in 1941, I shared the sentiments of Hanson Baldwin when he wrote in *United We Stand:* "To fight or not to fight should be the decision of the American people.

"We must have done with machinations behind Washington's political stage . . . we must not be edged into war without understanding what we are doing," Baldwin warned.

I was more concerned than less-informed Americans who shared my philosophy because I knew something about the machinations behind the political stage. I had had several more visits from the worried Army captain. In September 1941 he told me that the armed forces, at the direction of the President himself, had drawn up a master plan for a gigantic American Expeditionary Force. After Lowell Mellett tried to convince me FDR was sincere about the role of a peacemaker, I was eager to see how far the President was actually going in facing both ways at the same time.

I asked the captain if I could see the plan. On December 3, he brought to my house a document as thick as an average novel, wrapped in brown paper and labeled the "Victory Program." I asked him if he was afraid of delivering the most closely-guarded secret in Washington to a senator.

"Congress is a branch of the government," he replied. "I think it has a right to know what's really going on in the executive branch when it concerns human lives."

The captain left the document with me. As I scanned its contents, my blood pressure rose. I felt strongly that this was something the people as well as a senator should know about. It would awaken the public to what was in store for them if we entered the war—and the fact that we probably would. The document undercut the repeated statements of Roosevelt and his followers that repeal of the neutrality acts, lend-lease, the destroyer deal, and similar measures, would keep us out of the European conflict. From the fact that there were only five copies of the document in existence—and all were numbered and registered—it seemed probable to me that some top-ranking officer or official must have ordered or authorized the disclosure.

I was also satisfied that disclosure of the document involved no violation of existing law, and indeed no one ever suggested that the captain was guilty of an illegal act. The plan would not aid the Axis powers because it was not an operational war plan and I would not have considered exposing it if it had been. Rather it was a prospectus—a set of estimates of the manpower and production requirements we would need to win the war. And it was based on the conclusion that the *United States* would soon have to wage a global war if Germany and Japan were to be defeated.

I could have taken the document to the Senate Foreign Relations Committee, but I was sure that in view of its record of subservience to the administration the committee would bury it. So I showed it to Chesly Manly, a Washington correspondent for the Chicago *Tribune*. I liked Manly and knew his paper would give the plan the kind of attention it deserved.

Manly was as startled and fascinated as I was by the report. I arranged for him to come to my home that evening to make extracts. There for several hours we selected the most important sections and had them copied in shorthand by one of my secretaries. The document had to be back in the hands of the Army officer by early morning so it could be returned to its niche in the War Department.

The next morning the capital read Manly's account of the document in the Washington *Times-Herald,* a sister paper of the Chicago *Tribune*. Under a big banner headline, the story began:

"A confidential report prepared by the joint Army and Navy high command by direction of President Roosevelt calls for an American Expeditionary Force aggregating five million men for a final land offensive against Germany and her satellites. It contemplates total armed forces of 10,045,658 men. It is a blueprint for total war on a scale unprecedented in at least two oceans and three continents, Europe, Africa, and Asia.

"The report expresses the considered opinion of the Army and Navy strategists," the story continued, "that 'Germany and her European satellites cannot be defeated by the European powers now fighting against her.' Therefore, it concludes, 'if our European enemies are to be defeated it will be necessary for the United States to enter the war, and to employ a part of its armed forces offensively in the eastern Atlantic and in Europe and Africa.' July 1, 1943, is fixed as the date for the beginning of the final supreme effort by American land forces to defeat the mighty German army in Europe."

In the meantime, Manly wrote, the plan proposed to step up participation by the United States in the war through the "gradual encirclement of Germany by the establishment of military bases, an American air offensive against Germany from bases in the British Isles and in the Near East, and possible action by American expeditionary forces in Africa and the Near East."

The story continued with facts and statistics from the report for several more columns. They vindicated an exclusive article Manly had written after FDR and Churchill had held their Atlantic Charter meeting aboard warships off Newfoundland in August. After the President had filled in his congressional leaders back in Washington, Manly wrote that the Roosevelt-Churchill agreement called for an ultimate land invasion of the continent of Europe as the only possible method of defeating Germany, and that such an invasion would depend upon the assistance of a vast American expeditionary force. Senate Democratic leader Alben W. Barkley had done his duty for the White House by denouncing the Manly story on the Senate floor as a "deliberate falsehood."

The December 4, 1941, issue of the *Times-Herald* was a sell-out shortly after it hit the newsstands. Mass reading of the Manly story brought work to a standstill in many government departments and agencies and in the House of Representatives after it convened. The administration was too stunned to make any official comment for twenty-four hours. However, Secretary of the Navy Frank Knox, upon leaving a conference with the President, told newsmen that "all departments are investigating how they got that report." (Meanwhile, Colonel Robert R. McCormick, publisher of the Chicago *Tribune*, called it "perhaps the greatest scoop in the history of journalism" in his congratulatory wire to Arthur Sears Henning, chief of the *Tribune's* Washington bureau.)

Interventionist senators and congressmen sought to minimize the importance of the document, insisting it was merely a high command plan, not a high level commitment. But no one knew its significance better than the officer who drew up the Army part of the report—Major Albert C. Wedemeyer, who is now a retired general.

Wedemeyer has since written in his book, *Wedemeyer Reports,* published in 1958, that he was frankly appalled when he picked up the *Times-Herald* and saw his top-secret handiwork spread out in cold type. He called it "political dynamite."

"Here was irrefutable evidence," Wedemeyer wrote, "that American intervention in the war was planned and imminent, and that President Roosevelt's promises to keep us out of the war were only campaign oratory."

The brilliant Wedemeyer, then in the Army War Plans division, had been assigned to carry out a July 9, 1941, directive from the President to the armed forces secretaries to draw up an estimate of "the over-all production requirements required to defeat our potential enemies." He supervised the gathering of facts and conclusions from Army and Air Force chiefs for what became known as the Victory Program. The over-all report was approved by the joint Army and Navy board and delivered to FDR in September.

At his press conference on December 5 the President silenced questions from reporters by saying he had nothing to say about the Manly story—it would all be said by Stimson. The Secretary of War called a special press conference and read a prepared statement—no questions were permitted—denouncing those responsible for the article as guilty of a lack of "loyalty and patriotism."

Stimson called the report a set of staff studies which "have never been constituted and authorized as a program of the government. While the publication will doubtless be of gratification to our potential enemies . . . the chief evil of their publication is the revelation that there should be among us any group of persons . . . willing to take and publish such papers."

Stimson apparently did not realize that existence of the report already had been leaked to the press more than a month before. In the October 20, 1941, issue of *The Wall Street Journal,* Eugene S. Duffield had disclosed that a vast "Victory Program" was being drawn up to "beat Hitler" and that "an attacking army is contemplated." Duffield presumably had not seen the report itself and I myself did not learn of his article until years later.

Stephen T. Early, the White House press secretary, did not join in Stimson's condemnation of publication of the report. He noted that American newspapers were "operating as a free press" and said that "the right to print the news is unchallenged."

I repeat—we would not have exposed the contents of the report if we had believed it would give information of value to the axis powers. It was not an operational war plan, but it bore out my charges against Roosevelt. Significantly, the United States government overseas radio blared Manly's story for this reason. There were those in Washington who speculated that FDR himself might have leaked the report—as a morale booster to the allies who were anxious for reassurance that "the Yanks are coming" once again.

The FBI immediately began an examination of how the security breakdown had occurred. Wedemeyer was grilled and for three days Manly was called into the Justice Department for lengthy interrogations. He maintained that as a newspaper reporter he could not disclose his source. He admitted knowing me, along with many other senators. So far as I know, I was never investigated in connection with the leak. But Senator David I. Walsh of Massachusetts, then chairman of the Naval Affairs Committee, told me he was tailed for several days.

The hullaballoo over the document died as suddenly as it erupted. Three days after the story appeared, the Japanese attacked Pearl Harbor. When I heard the tragic news over the radio, I gave this statement to the press: "Let's lick hell out of them."

Chapter Two

YANKEE, GO WEST

While I was usually branded as a two-fisted Westerner, and sometimes as a natural product of Montana's brass-knuckle era, I was born and raised as a New England Yankee. To my mind there is nothing illogical in the fact that a symbol of the independent political tradition of the Northwest sprang originally from the hard-shelled heritage of the Northeast. The settlers of Massachusetts had to be tough-spirited in more ways than one. My people were accustomed to plain living, plain speaking, and uncompromising principle—an inheritance which stood me in good stead when I hit the last frontier.

Both sides of my family landed in the colonies well over three centuries ago. My great-great-great-great-great paternal grandfather was Obadiah Wheeler, a Quaker who fled from Odell, England, in 1635 to escape religious persecution. Obadiah and a good many other Wheelers—it was one of the most common surnames in America prior to 1650—founded the town of Concord, Massachusetts. He had six children by his first wife and, after her death, two sons by a second wife. These were Josiah, who was killed by Indians, and Obadiah, my progenitor.

In 1672 Obadiah married Elizabeth White, whose grandfather, William White, had been a passenger on the *Mayflower*. They inherited old Obadiah's house and extensive lands and had nine children. Their fifth son, Jonathan, was the great-great-grandfather of Asa Leonard Wheeler, who was my father.

Father married Mary Elizabeth Tyler, a descendant of the Puritan Tylers who arrived in the Bay Colony in 1631. The Tyler family included a Lieutenant Dudley Tyler, who served as an Army chaplain in the Revolutionary War. (As far as I know, this is as close as any of my forbears came to distinguishing themselves as warriors; apparently, they hated war as much as I always have.) My maternal grandmother was a Kendall, another well-known family in Massachusetts history and one to which I owe my middle name.

The turmoil and turbulence which whirled around me after I went West as a young man were missing from my early years, which were passed in a pleasant if somewhat austere atmosphere. I was born on February 27, 1882, at Hudson, Massachusetts, whence the Wheelers had long since moved. Hudson, twenty-three miles west of Boston, was then an industrial town of five or six thousand people and a typical New England town in the best sense of the word. My memories of it could be etched in a whole gallery of Currier & Ives prints. There were all the landmarks of the classic late Victorian setting—red brick town hall; prim white frame churches; sprawling white frame gingerbread houses; many with barns attached; rich green lawns; and spreading elm, maple, and fruit trees.

Hudson's principal industry was shoe manufacturing and my father, Asa, was a cobbler by trade. I was the youngest of ten children but by the time I was growing up all had left home except my brother, Ernest, six years older, and my sister, Maude, three years older. Father seldom earned more than $15 a week but we were self-sufficient and never lacked for necessities. We lived in an eight-room frame house, unmortgaged, about a mile out from town. We kept a horse and cow and raised pigs and chickens.

In true Quaker tradition, father was a peaceable man, notably quiet and unassuming. Self-educated beyond grade school, he had a natural talent for mathematics and developed a love of reading. I recall him reading aloud to us about the Civil War—and mispronouncing the word "Shenandoah" (he accented the second syllable). He even read widely of the works of Robert G. Ingersoll, whose attacks on the Bible were not well favored in our town. Father seldom got into arguments but one thing that did agitate him was intolerance. When I was a young boy, there was some activity by the notoriously anti-Catholic American Protective Association in Massachusetts. Father recalled that the Quakers had been oppressed in England and pointed out that persecution could happen here too, not only to Catholics but to any minority.

The Catholics in Hudson were the Irish immigrants and a cluster of French Canadians—who were not popular because they undercut our wage scale. Incidentally, my close association with Irish Catholics started early and continued at every turn right through my life. I always got along with these colorful people first rate, politically and every other way, and I trust our relations have been mutually satisfactory.

Altogether, my father was easygoing, not what you would call a disciplinarian. Mother was the boss. She was short and stout, with black hair worn in curls. Her complexion was darker than the blond Wheelers, whom I took after. Mother never gossiped (nor did I ever hear Father say an ill word about anybody). In fact, she held herself somewhat aloof and never became intimate with the neighbors—she would not even borrow a cup of sugar from them, though she was always friendly enough.

Mother was a Methodist and had had the strictest kind of upbringing. As a girl, she was obliged to stay indoors on Sunday and do absolutely nothing. She recalled that during thunderstorms the family had to sit perfectly still because Grandmother Kendall knew that "the people on this earth are very wicked and God has to speak to them in angry terms."

Well, Mother was not that strict with us but she exacted

obedience and set the highest moral standards. Nothing bothered her more than a lie.

"I'd rather have you steal than lie to me," she told us. "A liar can't be believed even when he's telling the truth. And if you tell one lie, you have to tell ten more."

Mother kept handy a little rawhide whip. The end of it was about as thick as my finger is now. Maude insists Mother never used it on me. Maude and Ernest thought she favored me, partly because I was considered scholarly and partly because very early I was afflicted with asthma. I was very thin. When I grew to six feet in my teens, I was shaped like a stringbean.

I seem to have inherited more characteristics from Mother's side of the family. The Tylers were willing to take a chance and risk a great deal. Mother was aggressive. If anything went wrong, she fought for us. For instance, J. C. Mackin, our elementary school principal, once decided that I was the cause of some horseplay (for once, I wasn't) while we were in line marching into school. He grabbed me by the collar so hard that he tore my shirt. This so infuriated Mother that she took me to Mackin's home that evening and really "laid him out," as the saying goes, for ripping my shirt.

Mother loved to go driving in our buggy and usually took me along. As we rattled over the gravel roads, she would sing "Carry Me Back to Old Virginny" or some other favorite. She loved to sing and she sang a great deal. I felt very close to her.

As far back as I can remember, Mother wanted me to aim for the study of law, a profession which until then included none of our relatives. Probably even more of an influence on me was my grandfather Tyler. "Old Abe Tyler" was one of the shining ornaments of our region. Like most of the other Tylers and Wheelers, he was a farmer. But people often sought him out to consult on points of law, although what he knew on the subject he had picked up by himself.

Abe Tyler was a very handsome man, with a well-built physique, sideburns, and a mustache. He was a powerful speaker. He would have scorned a microphone. His organ-like tones needed no amplifying. Nothing suited him better than the pure democracy of our town hall meetings. He would take any side of any subject. Once, when he was seventy years old and hard of hearing, a delegation came to him during a meeting and asked him to speak for them. Soon Grandfather was at the rostrum, making the rafters ring. When he sat down, the applause was explosive from everyone except those who had asked him to speak. They looked stunned. Their spokesman slipped over to Grandfather and said, "My God, Abe, you talked on the wrong side!"

Unperturbed, Grandfather shot his cuffs and replied with a twinkle, "Well, wait awhile and I'll make another speech." A little later, he again mounted the platform and this time stirringly answered his first argument. Again he brought the house down.

Abe Tyler had the kind of wit that made the Irish in Hudson kid him about having some Irish blood in his veins. On politics, he was regarded as a local sage, though he never ran for office. He discussed history and politics with the ease of a savant. Some of his ideas he undoubtedly absorbed from his close contact with Ben Butler, the famous Civil War general, lawyer, and, for five terms, congressman from Lowell, Massachusetts. Like most everyone we knew, Butler had started out as a Republican. But he didn't stay hitched. In 1882 he was elected Governor of Massachusetts on the combined Democratic and National (Greenback) tickets. In 1884 he was a candidate for President on the Greenback and Anti-Monopoly tickets.

Father and Grandfather similarly developed their own thinking on politics. Father used to take me to the Republicans' torchlight parades in Hudson but I know that deep down he was as unorthodox about politics as he was about most things. As for Abe Tyler, he once attended a national convention of the Populist Party.

Thus I had no compunctions when I found myself being carried away by the radical economic gospel of William Jennings Bryan (though I never heard him speak until I was in college). In fact, I agreed to uphold Bryan's free silver policy in a high school debate with a preacher's son. It was my first public argument.

When I became outspoken in espousing Bryan's low tariff

policies too, my brothers were disgusted. They pointed out how Massachusetts industries would suffer under free trade. All my brothers were hopelessly Republican.

Persuaded by Mother and Grandfather Tyler that I should become a lawyer, I worked at anything I could find to save something for my education. I picked blueberries and huckleberries on our place and peddled them through town, at ten cents a quart. Grandfather paid me two cents a box to pick strawberries on his farm.

We raised apples and potatoes and in addition I had my own pigs and chickens. I also had a lamb, which gave birth to twins annually. I raised the little lambs and then sold them to the local woolen mill. I had fun with those lambs—but I can't say the same for our cow. Pasture was a mile away and this meant I had to escort her along the streetcar tracks running past our house to the nearby town of Marlboro. En route, I ran the gauntlet of catcalls from the town smart-alecks who liked to sit on the fence and poke fun at the country hick with the cow.

Sometimes I earned forty cents for a whole afternoon of selling peanuts, popcorn, and lemonade at the trotting track which was hard by our back yard. I was fascinated by these races. I may be a born gambler, as some observers have concluded after close study of my career, but it was not the betting that attracted me. I was excited by the dashing panoply of the track—the beautiful horses, the trainers, the jockeys, the sulkies. I chatted with the "swipes," as those who took care of the horses were called, and I believe that at one time I knew the record of every trotting horse in the country.

Secretly, I pretended I was part of the track. In our barn I began to curry and "train" our horse as if he were a professional trotter, which he in no way resembled. I bathed his legs, soaked his feet, rubbed him down and talked to him encouragingly. When the trainers learned this, they persuaded me to hitch our nag to a sulky and drive him at his own cautious pace around the half-mile racing grounds—while they sat on the rails and shouted us on.

I was about eight years old at the time and Mother was not

amused. She worried some about my swimming in the Assabet River in summer and ice-skating there in winter. The Assabet ran right through the town and had been the scene of some bad accidents. We also fished in its waters for perch and pickerel.

Most of our excitement we created ourselves. But occasionally there was a rousing local event, like the outdoor band concerts for which the whole town turned out. For me the climax of the year was the series of sham battles re-creating the early days of the Revolutionary War on the Fourth of July. They started in Lexington and went on through Concord and other towns. My friends and I followed along, yelling, as the costumed rebels and redcoats deployed and fired their blanks realistically. No colonist in 1775 ever cheered louder than I did when a redcoat bit the dust. We had been steeped in the lore of the Revolution and I still bore a grudge against John Bull.

Another New England "game" which fascinated me was the ubiquitous horse-trading as practiced by those shrewd Yankees. Inasmuch as I loved horses and enjoyed any battle of sharp wits, I got my father to take me to the horse marts as often as possible. Gypsies came through Boston, Bolton, and Worcester with horses to trade. The farmers tried to outsmart them. I liked to watch a farmer go over a horse inch by inch, trying to find out whether he had spasms, whether he kicked, how long his teeth were, and so forth.

Once, my uncle Fred Tyler took me into Hudson with him to trade a horse. When the deal was about to be closed, I realized there was a vital piece of information which my uncle had not seen fit to broach. I couldn't resist supplying it. I pointed at Uncle Fred's horse.

"He kicks," I blurted.

The other man laughed and the trade was off. It was a long time before Uncle Fred took me with him again.

Several years later, I felt confident enough to invest some of my hard-earned savings in my knowledge of horseflesh. At an auction in Boston, I put in a successful bid of $25 on a splendid horse. The auctioneer told me to come back in a few days and take delivery. When I returned, I got a shock. The horse they presented to me was the same color as the one I had bid on—gray—but there the resemblance ended. This animal was sway-backed and looked old and tired enough to have pulled a chariot for Ben-Hur. I had been tricked but there was nothing I could do to prove it legally. I went home wiser but minus $25 and minus a horse.

Our family unit was strong and it centered around the home. There was no high or loose living. Mother, of course, opposed smoking and drinking out of her religious convictions. Father would take an occasional glass of wine, but if someone gave him a bottle of whisky it was likely to stand on the closet shelf for years. He never played cards and he never swore. The strongest term he ever used when he was really upset was "Godfrey!" Nor did he indulge in smoking—which, of course, was forbidden to me. Once, a chum, Joe Hanion, and I found a cigar and sneaked around behind the barn to try it. I smoked it enough to get sick, and Mother demanded to know the cause of my illness. I told her I had been rolling down a big hill which was near our house. But Ernest, overhearing this, told Mother he was certain I had been smoking. When I stuck to my falsehood—and Ernest stuck to his accusation—Mother took her rawhide whip and gave Ernest a hiding. The outcome of this incident so upset me I never lied to her again.

We attended the Baptist Sunday school because most of the neighborhood boys and girls drove there and gave us a ride. On Saturday nights we often went to dances at Hudson High School or at nearby Boone Lake. I recall with pleasure that there were some really nice girls and some really pretty ones in our crowd. Outside our immediate crowd there were a couple of Irish girls I was interested in, but their families were nothing less than appalled at them for smiling at a Protestant.

One girl was Minnie McCarthy, a striking blonde. We tried to meet at her aunt's house because her stepmother pretended to faint every time she heard Minnie was planning to see me. Minnie had a sense of humor and she was resourceful. Once, when she had a date with me in midwinter and her stepmother went into her swoon on schedule, the girl took a bucket of snow and dumped it on the prostrate woman to revive her. The poor stepmother never "fainted" again but I was still unwelcome.

Mamie Cunningham, who sat in front of me at school, also was a charmer. Calling at her house became downright hazardous. She lived on High Street, in an Irish enclave near the Catholic church. The second time I accompanied her home from school I was spotted as an alien. Rocks were thrown and I beat an ignominious retreat.

I played football and baseball with sandlot teams. Once, our football team went to Maynard, six miles from Hudson, and took on a team representing the woolen mill there. Those factory hands played rough. One big tackle simply picked me up —I was a lightweight end—and then hurled me to the ground, where I landed on my back. After that game, I lost interest in football.

While I had no talent for languages, I inherited my father's gift for mathematics and altogether I did well in high school without trying too hard. I had a tendency to cut up in class and several times the principal notified my father about it, although there were never any major charges preferred against me. The principal was a large, inept fellow from Maine whose name I have conveniently forgotten. He was a crackpot on bees. One question about bees would divert him from the subject at hand for the rest of the class period. We tried to make a fool of him in some ways. He suspected that I, at least, was succeeding.

Once, he took me into the basement of the school, locked the door and said he was going to give me a "thrashing." He outweighed me by about sixty pounds and I was sure he could do it. I summoned up all my forensic powers and managed to talk him out of it.

Another time, the principal summoned me to his office and thundered that once again I had been guilty of upsetting class decorum.

"Why pick on me?" I asked in a tone that millions of aggrieved students have used before and since.

"Your voice was heard distinctly," he said.

I made the point that I was often the scapegoat simply because my voice carried—almost as strongly as Grandfather Tyler's.

"The trouble with you, Wheeler," he replied, with a sad shake of his head, "is that you have no respect for your superiors."

Much the same sort of accusation was leveled at me in later years whenever I bucked entrenched authority. The charge is true to the extent that I have always pointedly avoided kowtowing to people of wealth, social position, or power.

Fortunately, the beekeeper was succeeded during my high school years by a principal who was as good as his predecessor had been bad. This was Charles Williams, then a young man. Williams was so interesting as a teacher that he had no problems about discipline.

Shortly before graduation, Williams told me he and the other teachers had been talking over what each of the graduates ought to do. They all agreed that I was fitted for the law. I explained that I had always intended to study law but that there was no money to send me to college. Besides, Mother had died two years before and it had seemed like the end of the world. My ambition had gone to the grave with her. I had given up Latin, among other subjects, which was a necessary credit for the regular high school diploma. Now I would not be eligible for college.

A few days later Williams took me aside again and made me a generous proposition. He had found out that I had done more work than anyone else in the class and that I had *almost* earned the regular diploma. He asked me whether, if the school awarded me one, I would give my word to study law. I told him I would. So on graduation night I became, as far as I know, the only Hudson High School graduate in history to walk off with two diplomas, one from the business course and one from the general course.

But first I had to go to work. Through an employment agency I got a stenographer's job with Chandler and Farquhar, a wholesale hardware firm in Boston. My salary was $6 a week and it cost me $2 a week to commute from Hudson. When I jumped to the firm's competitor for $10 a week three months later, Farquhar shook his head. "A rolling stone gathers no moss," he reminded me with a dreadfully straight face.

I rolled from one job to another in swift succession, gathering no moss but a few dollars more per week with each shift. In May 1902 I was working for the American Optical Company at Southbridge for $13 a week but switched unhesitatingly to the Draper Manufacturing Company at Hopedale for two dollars more. In September, I asked for a raise to $18 and was told I could have it in January. Many men were supporting families on $15 a week at the time and my terms must have sounded presumptuous. As a matter of fact, the highest paid man in the Draper office force was drawing $20 a week and there were other employees who had been there for twenty years making less than that. Nonetheless, I said I would have to have the three-dollar wage boost right away.

My bosses countered with a guarantee to pay me as much as I could earn in Boston or Worcester. I replied that my next stop would be neither of those places; I intended to study law. They reminded me that the state was full of young lawyers starving to death, whereas if I remained with Draper as a stenographer and bookkeeper I could look forward to financial security. This appeared to be a bleak future indeed for a young fellow who was not looking for security, financial or otherwise.

When they finally refused the raise, I quit the Draper firm and headed for the University of Michigan Law School at Ann Arbor, Michigan. The school had an excellent reputation nationally and in addition I had a report on it firsthand from a cousin, Walter Wheeler, who had been out there for a year. Walter, who was a Tufts College graduate, was the first law student I knew of in our Wheeler clan. He wrote me that he was sure I could work my way through the school.

My savings at that point amounted to $750 but I was facing a three-year course and was determined to hang on to as much of it as I could. So I got two jobs on the Ann Arbor campus. During my first and second years I earned $15 a month working in the office of Dean Harry B. Hutchins, the eminent head of the Michigan Law School and later president of the university. I did stenography and kept track of his files and other matters.

Meanwhile, I waited on tables at a students' boardinghouse three times a day. For this I got no pay but free board, which was worth $2.25 a week.

Although I could eat all I could hold in this job, my six-foot frame still packed only 130 pounds. I felt so unhealthy by spring that I sought out one of the best doctors in Ann Arbor.

"So you work in the dean's office!" he exploded. "Well, the dean has killed one man already and he's got you well on the way. If you don't get outside and get some exercise and sunshine, you'll wind up in North Carolina or Colorado."

Obviously he considered me a ripe prospect for tuberculosis. Despite his warning, I stuck to my all-work-and-no-play routine throughout the semester. Then I accepted an offer from a medical student, Alexander Sanders De Witt, whom I had met at the boardinghouse. De Witt said he made $300 the previous summer peddling aluminum ware from door to door in Illinois. This summer he had a deal to sell books and he wanted me as his partner.

The job appealed to me because it would keep me out of doors, it would reveal the corn belt to a provincial Easterner, and it would let me try my hand at selling. The book to be disposed of was a remarkable all-purpose volume, *Dr. Chase's Receipt Book*, published by the F. B. Dickerson Company of Detroit. The preface explained that it contained "the Favorite Medical Receipts of Over One Hundred of the Best Physicians and Nurses of this and Foreign Countries. It also contains the Original, Genuine, Last and Complete Collection of Medical and Cooking Receipts and the Very Choicest Medical Receipts of the World Renowned Dr. A. W. Chase."

Dr. Chase, a resident of Ann Arbor, supplied advice for facing the everyday hazards of farm life, including "Suffocation from Hanging." Also listed were 500 cooking recipes, treatments for every known disease of humans and livestock, and 23 pages on "Midwifery–Nursing." Although it seemed the book met every conceivable emergency, one of the first farm women I approached flabbergasted me by asking if it told what to do in case of "falling of the womb." I admitted I didn't know—and I still don't.

The prescriptions included some amazing homemade tonics. The most formidable was Mrs. Chase's Magic Tonic for Weak and Debilitated Females. This brew was concocted of two quarts each of whisky and cider mixed with cloves and a few ounces each of four kinds of rare bark. You shook the jug daily for ten days, removed the dregs and helped yourself to a wine-glass of the stuff after every meal.

I am happy to report that Mrs. Wheeler never felt the need of so drastic a remedy but both Chases apparently valued it as a bracer.

"I have made this for my wife several times and I did not fail to help her dispose of it occasionally myself," Dr. Chase wrote in a sly testimonial. "Her remark has often been, 'Oh! What an appetite it gives me,' etc. It is—very pleasant to take."

Thus with some justification the publisher claimed that "the old Doctor had a plain, simple and home-like style of writing never before or since attained by any other writer on similar subjects."

The book, which is said to have sold several million copies in the United States and foreign countries over a long period of years, was offered in German and Norwegian editions as well as English. The leather-bound volume sold for $3.50 and the cloth-bound for $2.50. The salesman made a 50 per cent commission on every sale. Ours was positively the "third and last edition," or so we were authorized to say, but it was hard to sell to someone who thought he had already purchased everything there was to know in the first or second edition.

Fortunately, we didn't have to tote the heavy book. We carried brochures and order forms in a schoolbag but the customer didn't have to sign anything. All he had to do was agree orally to pay cash on delivery. It was up to us to make deliveries and collect the cash in another round of calls later on.

Our first stop was at Union Grove, a railroad depot a few miles from Morrison, Illinois. It was a blistering day in June and the corn fields were shimmering. We headed for a two-story brick farmhouse a few hundred yards away and rapped on the door. It was opened by a woman with a heavy German accent. We asked her for lodgings. She said she and her husband—the name was Smaltz—never took in boarders. De Witt explained to her in his smattering of German that he was of German descent and that we were working our way through college. Apparently this kind of ambition was new to Whiteside County, for she immediately said we could stay.

For the rest of the summer this was our routine for wangling board and room at little cost in an area where there were no hotels anyway. My only complaint was that we usually wound up in an overstuffed feather bed, which set off my asthma. I spent many a night sitting up trying to catch my breath.

We stayed at the Smaltzes for a week, working the territory for miles around during the day. We split up and proceeded alone on foot from one farm to another. I don't recall ever being as tired as I was after tramping the dusty Illinois roads and fields that first day. I was so fatigued that when I got back to the fence bordering the Smaltzes' farm I lay down on the ground and rolled under it instead of climbing over.

Most of the farm families were polite to me but some were hostile. Once, I tracked down an unusually dour-looking man who was in his field harvesting. He told me unequivocally he would not even listen to my sales pitch. Undaunted, I paused in the yard behind the farmhouse as I left and tried my arguments on his wife. While I was still talking, the farmer returned from the fields and saw us. Instantly, he sicked the dog on me. I was afraid of dogs and this one was a mean-looking German shepherd. I lit out for the picket fence bordering the road, stimulated by the sound of hungry panting behind, and hurdled the fence at full speed—how I don't know.

If this does not seem like a relaxing way to spend one's summer vacation, I can only say it proved invaluable to me. Selling books door-to-door is regarded in the trade as the hardest kind of selling. I had to develop an aggressive approach toward strangers under distinctly unfavorable circumstances—and to retain my poise despite their reactions. If someone slammed a door in my face, I'd go on down the road laughing to myself and thinking, Well, you're mad at me but I'm not mad at you.

The day we hit our next way station turned out to be one of the luckiest of my life. We fanned out from Garden Plains, a whistlestop in the central part of the state not far from the Mississippi River. Close to noon, I kept an eye out for a place that might yield a meal as well as a sale. I knocked at a neat-looking house and the door was thrown open by a slender teen-age girl with dark brown hair and lively dark gray eyes. While I can't honestly report that it was love at first sight, it was clearly the loveliest sight Illinois had displayed thus far. My impulse was to hold this maiden's attention as long as possible.

But all I could do was to doff my straw hat and ask—with what I hoped was Eastern charm—if she were "the lady of the house." She shook her head with a little smile, asked me to wait, and vanished. A minute later, her mother appeared, introduced herself as Mrs. White and invited me inside. I soon discovered there would be no sale. Mrs. White owned a second edition volume of Dr. Chase, on which she was standing pat. But I stalled long enough to get an invitation to dinner, the regular noon-hour meal.

During dinner the family impressed me as being industrious and educated. Mrs. White had a strong, sprightly personality and her husband, John, a quiet, wiry man, obviously was farming his 120 acres intelligently. As for their daughter, Lulu, well . . .

We got along so well I finally asked the Whites if they could put up De Witt and myself for a few nights. Mrs. White said they never took boarders and pointed out that this would be a bad time to do so. They had no hired girl just then and Lulu was about to go away for a week to a Methodist camp meeting.

On Sunday, three days later, De Witt and I attended church at Garden Plains. As we left the church, I was pleasantly surprised to see Mrs. White and her daughter driving right past us in their snappy, two-horse phaeton. I stopped them to say hello.

"I thought you were going to a camp meeting," I said reprovingly to Lulu.

"Well, the other girl couldn't go at the last minute," she explained. "And so I didn't go."

I introduced them to De Witt and renewed my request for lodgings.

Mrs. White hesitated briefly, then smiled and said, "Well, since you're working your way through college, you can come for a few days." It was sweet music to my ears.

We stayed with the Whites a week. They turned out to have a heritage much like the Wheelers. John White's father had left England about 1840 because of discrimination by the established church. Mrs. White was an Adams whose forbears had come to this country long before that. They were devout Methodists who said grace before every meal.

At dinner the first night Mrs. White asked De Witt to say grace. I knew my grace was rusty and that night I lay awake worrying whether she would ask me to do the honors at breakfast. About four o'clock in the morning I woke up De Witt and asked him to coach me in grace-saying—which he did, as we lay there in bed. But at breakfast De Witt again got the nod, as he did at every meal from then on. Now my feelings went to the other extreme. I felt slighted.

"Why doesn't your mother ever ask me to say grace?" I demanded of Lulu one night after dinner. She explained that De Witt had told the Whites he was a talented lay preacher. De Witt was not noted for his modesty, but he did have quite a fund of knowledge that covered medicine, electricity, and languages. And I knew for a fact that he had once been paid $10 for taking an absent preacher's place and delivering a sermon (which, by the way, his brother, a clergyman, had written for him). This greatly impressed the Whites, who boasted of several lay preachers in their own families.

De Witt loved to talk and he spent almost every evening spellbinding Mrs. White. This was all right with me because I was "making time," as they say nowadays, with Lulu. He may have felt out of the running the first night. The three of us had been sitting on the front porch when Lulu said, "Let's go for a walk." De Witt must have assumed the invitation was directed at me alone, for he went right on rocking while we strolled down the road in the twilight.

Suddenly, a buggy rumbled past carrying a man and a woman. The man was smoking a big cigar and trailing smoke.

"My husband's never going to smoke a cigar like that!" Lulu

remarked. It didn't bother me at the time because marriage was not on my mind. But the observation seems the height of irony in view of the fact that an ever-present cigar became a trade-mark of my political career.

Lulu and I hit it off so well we talked incessantly, as if we had known each other for years. We would slip out of the house right after the evening meal and run down the hill to the bridge over the creek on their place.

We discussed my education and hers. Lulu's mind was keenly alive. She had attended Northern Illinois College at Fulton, Illinois, and planned to go on to Oberlin College in Ohio that fall. (Her education has continued to this day—she still takes piano lessons at seventy-eight years of age. As the mother of six children, she took college courses in languages and political sciences in Butte, Montana, and Washington, D.C.—where she was a classmate of our son, John.)

Lulu was competent in the domestic arts too. She darned my socks and shirts that week. My washing was taken care of by her mother—who refused to take a cent from De Witt and me for all this hospitality.

John White had little to say but he eloquently raised his eyebrows when I disclosed that I was a Democrat. "Then you must be Irish," he said quite seriously.

Prolonging our stay at the Whites, De Witt and I later in the week extended our forays far into neighboring Rock Island County. When I found myself in a large Swedish settlement, I worked hard at peddling our Norwegian edition because I knew Swedes could understand and speak Norwegian to some extent. I did it so convincingly that one woman told me it was being rumored around that a "Swedish book agent" was abroad in the area.

I sold quite a few Norwegian editions to those Swedes. Unfortunately, it never occurred to me—or apparently to the Swedes either—that being able to understand spoken Norwegian did not necessarily mean they could read it. When I heard later about their fuming efforts to decipher Dr. Chase's recipes, I could easily imagine the uncomplimentary names they called the "Swedish book agent."

After we had left the Whites', De Witt said, "Lulu's mother will never let you marry her." I wrote to Lulu and told her what De Witt had said. She wrote back and denied her mother had ever said such a thing. (Later, I found out that, in some of his rambling conversations with Mrs. White, De Witt had taken pains, for reasons of his own, to paint me as something short of the ideal son-in-law.) I had never said a word to him about my intentions toward Lulu and now I told him truthfully that marriage was farthest from my mind.

Ironically, De Witt's premature attempt to discourage me got me thinking more seriously about Lulu. When I returned to Illinois in September to deliver the books to my customers, I hired a horse and buggy and took her with me on my rounds.

Back on the Michigan campus in my second year, I was plunged into practical politics for the first time. Two students sought me out and argued that it was time to break the fraternities' iron grip on all student offices. They asked me to run for class president against the fraternity candidate. I told them I was too busy. But next a large group of non-fraternity colleagues called on me and persuaded me to make the race.

They may have selected me because I was well known through contact with most of the students at the dean's office. My opponents promptly circulated the false report that I was the "dean's candidate," the most damaging charge that could be made in a student election. The only thing Dean Hutchins had to do with my candidacy was the fact that he had publicly backed my position that all students should be allowed to vote regardless of whether they had paid up their class dues. The fraternities wanted to deny the ballot to non-paid-up class members, figuring it would help their own chances.

We set up a committee and assigned each committee member to interview certain members of the second-year class. Then, shortly before Election Day, each committee member rechecked the persons on his list to find out who was wavering and who was standing firm.

As the campaign heated up, J. H. McClintock, my well-to-do roommate from Iowa, told me the fraternity crowd was offering some heavy bets against me—as high as $500—and that he was anxious to take some. The contest looked like a photofinish to me and I advised him against betting. I was right. I won by seventeen votes out of some three hundred cast. But McClintock never let me forget that he "would have won $500 from those so-and-so's if you'd have let me."

Emboldened, we went on to elect non-fraternity slates to run the Webster and Jefferson political societies on the campus. When we found evidence of mismanagement of funds by the fraternity representative in the Student Lecture Association, which extended into all branches of the university, we elected our own officers there too.

As class president, I automatically became a steward of the students' boardinghouse and thereafter got my meals free. So I no longer had to wait table. But I decided not to run for president in my third, or senior, year, so I helped to elect my non-fraternity friend, W. S. Nash.

Much later an article in *Life* magazine* suggested that my career in championing the underdog had its genesis when I set out to overthrow the power of the fraternities.

"Campus society at Michigan did not welcome the threadbare young Yankee," the article said. "Through the four [*sic*] years it took him to get his law degree, he remained an outcast 'barbarian' (non-fraternity member). . . ."

This is nonsense. The fact is that the social advantages of fraternities never enchanted me and I could not have afforded them if they did. And I certainly have no recollection of feeling like an embittered "outcast." I sensed no stigma because I was working my way through school; indeed, it was a badge of honor.

As a matter of fact I believe I struck some classmates as having possibly the reverse of an inferiority complex. Much later, William L. Fitzgerald, then a successful lawyer in Kalamazoo, Michigan, amusingly described in a letter his first reaction to me on the campus.

He remembered me as "a slim, flaxen-haired chap who very early disclosed he was from the East, and while I do not say that

* May 19, 1941, issue.

he announced so at the time he gave at least the impression that he could have gone to Harvard but preferred to come West and take his chances in life in this 'wild and woolly' region. I also recall that he seemed quite sure of himself; could operate a typewriter, so he said, and in his experience to date at home had encountered some intellectuals—from which experience he should have no difficulty in his dealings with the brains of the faculty."

What I did gain from my fling at campus politics was the lesson that successful campaigns are based on intelligent organization and hard work. In fact, the strategy we used to check and recheck every student was the same technique I used in 1937 when I led the Senate fight that defeated Franklin D. Roosevelt's Court-packing bill.

But in law school I never thought of politics as a career; I was too preoccupied even to pay much attention to the 1904 presidential campaign between Theodore Roosevelt and Alton B. Parker. What I was interested in was the study of law. What excited me most was the verbal cut and thrust in the arena of the courtroom. Courses in "agency" and "contracts" carried a lot less appeal but they were easy because of my experience in writing business letters for those firms back in Massachusetts. I made fairly high grades all three years but the members of our graduating class were not ranked as they are at many law schools.

No member of my family was present for my graduation in June 1905, but Lulu was seated in a front row. She had detoured to Ann Arbor on her way home from Oberlin. We were now engaged to be married. For two years we had written to each other almost daily. I had spent the last two Christmas vacations with the Whites and had seen Lulu often during my second summer of hawking Dr. Chase's remedies and recipes in Illinois (this time on a bicycle). It tickled me that the publisher's want-ad for salesmen for the next season pointed out that one of its book agents in a single summer had netted $300 and a wife!

Lulu and I went directly from the commencement exercise to her home to discuss our plans with her parents. My savings weren't much more than $500 because I had suffered a $300 casualty. I had invested that sum in the Moline (Illinois) Building & Loan Association, which was headed by a University of Michigan graduate, but it had gone into receivership. We decided to postpone the wedding until I was able to hang out my shingle. But where? Dean Hutchins had advised me to go East, on the theory that "if you want to practice law the place to go is where the money is." He said he could get me into one of the big New York law firms.

But returning East seemed stultifying. I was anxious to go anywhere that was wide open with opportunity. Back in Illinois, the Whites mentioned that Lulu once visited an uncle living in Telluride, Colorado, and it proved to be an exhilarating little gold-mining town in the mountains. I said that ever since I was a child I had dreamed of going West. In Hudson there had been a great deal of uninformed talk about the "wild West." Most of the notions about the Great Plains came from dime novels—which I was forbidden to read for the simple reason that they would send me straight to hell. But once I did smuggle in a paperback account of *Jesse James Out West.* I even read it to Mother. The funny thing was she didn't object—I think she was as fascinated as I was.

Soon I was to discover that Jesse James's fictional adventures were not so preposterous after all.

Chapter Three

A FRIENDLY GAME OF POKER

On Sunday morning October 15, 1905, I stepped off a train at the Northern Pacific depot in Butte, Montana, and shivered. A sudden snowstorm had whipped out of the mountains and in my light summer suit and straw hat the air was bitter cold. All the rest of my worldly goods were carried in a small handgrip. Turning up my collar, I put my head into the wind and made for the downtown section of the city. There I settled in a rooming house on West Broadway and began to compile a list of the lawyers in Butte.

My shivering may well have been due more to my bleak prospects than to the falling barometer. For three months I had been crisscrossing the Great Plains on a job hunt. When I kissed Lulu goodbye on the banks of the Mississippi, I had blithely set out to answer the advertisement of an elderly lawyer in Eureka, California, who wanted to turn his practice over to a young man. But in San Francisco, I had found that the only way to get to Eureka was by boat, and it no longer seemed worth the trouble.

So I trekked from town to town, seeking out established lawyers who might need a young associate. I invaded law offices in Los Angeles; Portland, Oregon; Tucson, Arizona; Telluride, Montrose, Ouray, Pueblo, and Denver, Colorado; Salt Lake City and Ogden, Utah; and Pocatello, Idaho, my last stop before entering Butte. True, I had seen more of the West than Lewis and Clark but unfortunately no one had snatched me up as a fledgling Clarence Darrow.

Only two lawyers were willing to give me a chance—in Ouray and Montrose. After staying long enough to look both places over, I decided that neither one offered much opportunity. Almost everywhere I was greatly in demand as a stenographer, and I worked as one for a while in Telluride to help finance my vagabond itinerary. My original savings of $500 was steadily melting, although I never slept in a Pullman or ate in a diner. Most of my meals consisted of apples and railroad lunch-counter doughnuts.

One trouble was that I had to approach lawyers as a stranger. I had no letter of recommendation and no introduction. I simply walked in off the street, displayed my Michigan law degree and explained who I was. Maybe I was too late in heeding Horace Greeley's advice but I hated to give up on this fabled land.

When I sniffed the atmosphere in Butte, I found it refreshing. It was a mining town in boom time, friendly and gay—what could be better for a young lawyer? Optimistically, I set out to interview every successful lawyer in the city. It took me the better part of a week and yielded exactly one offer. That came from John A. Shelton, who had a two-room office in the old Hirbour Building. But Shelton would pay me only $50 a month and he was reputedly a difficult man to work for. I turned him down.

Depressed again, I decided to try Spokane, Washington, for the simple reason that I had never been there. I checked out of my rooming house and started down Oregon Avenue to catch the four o'clock train. At the corner of Nevada Avenue and Front Street, there was a little yellow saloon. Standing in front of it were two men, respectably dressed and oozing with geniality. As the taller man beamed, the smaller one spoke to me.

"Is the train always this late?" he asked.

I said I didn't know it was late. He said he had just learned it wouldn't come through for two hours. He added that they were from Indiana and on their way to the Lewis & Clark Centennial Exposition in Portland, Oregon. He invited me to join them in a drink while we killed the time. When I said I didn't drink, he suggested we sit down and have a cigar. I accepted the cigar and followed them into the saloon.

They headed directly to a table opposite the bar. Two men were sitting there as if waiting for someone. One had jet black hair with streaks of gray that made him distinguished looking. The other was a big, sloppy fellow who looked more like he belonged in the place. They addressed the man who had spoken to me outside as "Gladney."

"How about a friendly game of cards?" Gladney asked me as we sat down.

A lawyer in Denver had advised me as a newcomer to the West never to play cards with strangers. But everything about Gladney was so normal, ordinary, and average that you would never have suspected him of anything but stuffiness, while his companion was the kind of open-faced man you would have trusted with your last will and testament. I said I wouldn't mind a game of auction pitch, which I had played at a penny a point back in Massachusetts commuting between Hudson and Boston.

"Oh, no, let's play poker," Gladney said. The big, sloppy fellow shuffled a deck of cards and the two began to play while the rest of us watched. When they had played two hands of stud, Gladney said it was a shame their guest had to be a spectator. I then confessed I knew something about the game, having played it occasionally in college. Gladney asked his partner if he could stake me to some chips so I could get into the game. The big fellow nodded and Gladney gave me nine dollars' worth of chips.

I drew two jacks. One was face down. Since my face-up jack was high, it was up to me to open. I bet $5. The big fellow dealt the third hand, giving none of us much of anything. So I bet $10. The dealer promptly raised me $25. Gladney immediately dropped out, but as he did so he leaned over and whispered that if I lost he would pay all my losses while if I won we would split. Then he gave me a quick look at what purported to be a certified check for $2000 on a bank in Indiana. With a "what-can-I-lose?" feeling, I stayed in the game.

But I was out of chips and when Gladney tried to push some more of his toward me, the big fellow said sharply, "You can't do that!"

"Well, I can bet my own money," I said. I felt good about those two jacks—he had nothing on the board to alarm me—and since I am by nature a plunger I decided to go for broke. I had $65 in cash on me and on the fourth round, when the big fellow once again dealt himself nothing good, I bet $25. Again he raised me, this time $50. This nettled me some but I always prided myself on never falling for a bluff. I called the raise.

On the fifth hand the dealer gave me a deuce and himself a trey. He already had one trey face up and now I began to worry a little. But I bet $50 and he raised me the same amount. By this time I was owing the pot and was obliged to write out a check on my bank account in Montrose, Colorado, for $150—all the money I had left in the world.

Sure enough, as we turned up our hole cards, the dealer produced still a third trey. Three treys beat my pair of jacks. He raked in the pot and I sat there dumfounded. Gladney made a show of tearing up a check—presumably mine—while the other two men simply puffed their cigars and stared at the table, as stony-faced as pallbearers.

Gladney handed me $11—enough to cover my ticket to Spokane. Without a word, he and his companion rose and started in the direction of the depot. I followed, speechless and miserable. As we reached the end of the block, Gladney muttered that he had promised to meet his wife at the drugstore and abruptly disappeared. This sounded fishy, inasmuch as they had stressed that they were traveling alone. All at once it dawned on me that the whole incident had been prearranged and that the poker game had not been on the up-and-up. Although I heard the whistle of the train as it steamed into the station, I angrily did an about-face and hurried back to the saloon.

If I had known then what I know now about those unscrupulous characters, I never would have gone back into that place. But I was swept along by the outrage of a young man who felt he had been tricked. I banged open the door of the saloon and walked in just in time to catch Gladney and the other two men dividing up my money.

"Here's three dollars for you," the black-haired man said swiftly as soon as he saw me. Nodding toward Gladney, he said, "He was just claiming it."

Well, of course, this was absurd on the face of it. I pocketed the three dollars and said brusquely, "All right, now come across with the rest of it."

"If you'd won, wouldn't you have kept the money?" the black-haired man countered.

"Yes, but I'd have won it squarely and you people didn't," I said, my blood pressure at the boiling point. They didn't deny my accusation. Instead they stalled, asking me who I was. I told them I was a lawyer and warned that I would get my friend, Jimmy Healy, the local prosecutor, on their trail. This overconfident threat had an effect. They grudgingly handed me $30 and I figured I had gonc about as far as I could go. I walked out and headed back toward the depot only to discover the train for Spokane had left.

I was now in an acute state of frustration. I went to dinner at a nearby restaurant and turned my dilemma over in my mind. I concluded that since I couldn't do much more traveling on my shrunken resources I might as well give Butte a try. I sought out John A. Shelton that evening and told him I'd accept his job offer after all. He told me I could share his apartment until I got my feet on the ground.

Shelton was a short, heavy-set bachelor in his mid-fifties, with balding gray hair. He was a good lawyer but part of his income was due to his business of making collections for eastern firms from people in Butte who owed them money. These onerous non-legal chores fell to me.

A few weeks later, Ed Lamb, the assistant district attorney for Butte, said that if I was in court the following Saturday he would get Judge Michael Donlan to appoint me to represent an impoverished defendant. The fee would be $50. I was eager to take advantage of both the money and the experience.

On Saturday, Donlan assigned me to defend "Montana Slim" —I never knew his real name—against a charge of blowing up a safe in an Arizona Street saloon. An alleged confederate, Joe Spreich, was to be tried on the same charge and was being represented by another young lawyer.

When I visited the jail to talk with my client, the jailer, Billy Hagerty, said, "Oh, you're the light-haired lad Gladney held up down at the Northern Pacific depot!" He told me Gladney was occupying a cell there at the moment and that I could see him.

When Gladney was brought out at my request, I stared at him disgustedly.

"I just wanted to see how you looked behind bars, you S.O.B.," I said.

"Well, they never cashed that check, did they?" he asked. This raised my eyebrows.

"I thought you tore it up," I said accusingly.

"No, they promised they wouldn't cash it," he replied. I said I didn't know whether they had cashed it or not. Actually, I had been worried about whether that $150 check really had been torn up by Gladney. As it turned out, they never did cash it, probably for fear I'd have them prosecuted.

The police were holding Gladney in the hope he might have some leads on a holdup at Hennessy's store in Centreville. Hagerty told me that whenever Gladney decided to work a new town he went first to the chief of police and unabashedly asked if he could be given a free hand in playing cards in return for supplying the chief with tips about the activities of local crooks. I gradually learned that I had had the dubious distinction of being taken by one of the most fabulous confidence men then practicing in the West. ("Gladney" was apparently not his real name but it was the only one I heard him called.)

One source of information about him was Mike Daly, a big, cold-blooded saloonkeeper. I met Daly when he was being defended in 1910 by Matt Canning, then my law partner, after Daly had shot and killed one of his customers, a "Cousin Jack," the nickname for all immigrants from Cornwall. Daly told me that in laying poker traps Gladney had caught much bigger suckers than Burt Wheeler. Once, he reputedly had relieved two newly arrived Scots of their entire grubstake of $10,000 in a single all-night session of poker.

After Daly had served an eighteen-month murder sentence, he stopped me on the street and said he had just run into "your friend, Gladney."

"I said he ought to retain you because you'd become the best lawyer around," Daly continued with a chuckle. "But Gladney said, 'No, I'm afraid he'd send me to the pen for keeping him in this damn town!' "

Long before that, I would have thanked Gladney for stranding me in Butte. I liked it. Butte for a half century now has been variously described by literary visitors as a Rabelaisian, unreal, and always pictorial town. It squats amid the Rockies and on top of what was called "the richest copper hill in the world." It is safe to say that no one who has ever been there has forgotten it.

By the time I arrived, people had come to Butte from everywhere, and quite a few had made enormous fortunes. Butte department stores sent buyers to Paris for gowns and in the snooty Silver Bow Club millions of dollars' worth of jewels glittered at every dance.

Butte miners were then receiving $3.50 to $4 a day, which beat the prevailing wage scales of the eastern factories. There was a large proportion of single men in its population of 45,000 and the downtown area shrieked with vitality. It boasted the "longest bar in the world" (a whole block long and manned by fifteen bartenders). In "Venus Alley," its three-block red-light district, more than seven hundred girls of all sizes, colors, and nationalities offered themselves. The concentrated bawdiness was said by aficionados to compare favorably with that of the Barbary Coast in San Francisco.

Butte was a good theater town, a regular stop for touring road companies of Broadway shows. Its citizens also supported an assortment of lusty sports, including horse racing and dog fighting.

Butte is not a pretty town. It is a honeycombed hill throwing up a network of trestles, railroad tracks, bunkers, transmission lines, etc. The fiery smelters which shoot glowing abstractions into the big Montana sky also sometimes cover the entire city in winter with a soot that prevents you from seeing across the street. The arsenic smoke long ago killed all grass and trees in Butte.

Yet there was something inspiring to me in the sight of the miners' neat one-story houses. Many of them did their own painting and plumbing and I was amazed at how clean and well furnished the houses were and how well dressed the wives and children were.

Above all, it was a generous, democratic community. It didn't make any difference who you were, where you came from, or how much money you had. How you fared depended entirely on yourself. If people liked you, they liked you. If they didn't, well, they didn't, and it was just too bad.

In 1930, when my family was in Washington and I was on a trip to Butte, I wrote to Mrs. Wheeler: "Butte looks rough, tough, and dirty, but I love the old place." Later on, back in Washington, my five-year-old daughter, Marion Montana Wheeler, greeted me with, "That's Daddy—rough, tough, and dirty." I asked her where she had heard such language and she told me that Mrs. Wheeler had read my letter to the family.

Getting back to my first client, "Montana Slim," his case was dismissed without explanation before I got a chance to defend him. So I helped the other young attorney appointed by the court to represent his co-defendant, Spreich, a local youth. It was my first courtroom case, and Spreich was convicted largely because of the testimony of two city detectives. "Slim" later told me the detectives had lied.

"If we'd used as much nitroglycerin as they said we had, we

would have blown up the whole damn town," he said. As a "pro," he evidently hated to see a conviction based on inexpert testimony.

My first real client turned up in the person of a grocer I called on in my capacity as collection agent for Shelton. He asked me to represent him against his deceased wife's relatives, who were charging him with misusing the funds of her estate. Between $30,000 and $40,000 was at stake and I finally managed to get the suit thrown out of court. When the estate was settled a year later, I collected a fee of $2000.

But I had trouble making ends meet that first year because I had quit Shelton after three months, having had a hard time collecting my $50 a month. T. M. Clowes, a well-to-do Butte resident and the father of Tim Clowes, a former law schoolmate of mine at Ann Arbor, said he would go good on the furniture if I would set up a law office with Tim. With a desk, two chairs, and a set of the Montana statutes, we opened for business on the second floor of the Lizzie Block at Park and Main streets.

Business suffered because Tim was a day and night playboy, preferring the pool hall to the office. The problem was solved when he soon decided to go to Alaska. Dr. W. E. Dodd, an optometrist who had the next office, told me he would take over payment of the furniture if I would continue the practice on my own.

The Lizzie Block (as a building was known in Butte) had stores on the first floor, offices on the second and a rooming house on the third. To reduce overhead, I rented another office which amounted to a room and a half. The main room was partitioned in two. One half of it became my office and the other half of the "suite" became my living quarters. I bought an old iron cot and the landlady on the third floor loaned me some bedding. I leased space in my office to a real estate man and the desk to a traveling salesman of calendars. Thus the net cost of the place was shaved to four dollars a month.

Soon I was able to do a return favor for Dr. Dodd. As an optometrist, he advertised that he could correct cross-eyes and cure certain diseases. The late United States Senator James E.

Murray, then county attorney, charged him with practicing medicine without a license. The case was tried before a justice of the peace. I represented Dodd and won. The trouble was that the practice of optometry was not permitted in Montana. In 1911, Dodd and some other optometrists engaged me to lobby with the legislature in favor of an optometry bill. It was my first crack at lobbying and I was successful—the bill became law.

Needing a steady income to fall back on that first year on my own, I made the rounds of Butte merchants, asking if I could handle their collections. Credit was easy in bustling Butte at that time but the merchants prudently retained lawyers to collect the payments. The lawyers were allowed to keep 25 per cent of what they collected. One merchant grumbled to me that he had more trouble collecting his share from the lawyers than he did from the customers. I assured him I would subtract my 25 per cent after each collection and turn in the rest immediately—which I did.

I took my first clients where I could find them, and I found most of them in police and juvenile court. Once, I was surprised to find camped on my office doorstep the proprietor of one of the fancier "parlor houses" in Butte. This prosperous madam wanted me to represent her in some litigation involving real estate. I pointed out that I had never patronized her place —or indeed any other in the red-light district—and asked why she didn't retain one of the lawyers who were her steady customers.

"When I want to play, that's one thing," she explained. "When I want someone to look after my business, that's something else."

I took her case, which was entirely paperwork, and felt I had learned this lesson: when a person needs a lawyer, he wants the best one he can find. I have on occasion advised a young lawyer not to pass his time sitting around playing cards during the day with potential clients. No matter how friendly they are at the time, they will look for a lawyer who tends to his practice when they need legal help.

In my second year on my own, my practice improved to the

point where I could make a down payment on a $4000 four-room brick house on Second Street near the heart of the town. It was one of the more substantially built houses in that area and, with additions made as our family grew, it was to prove large enough for the Wheeler family all the years we lived in Butte.

The neighborhood was made up of railroad men, small merchants, and workers with modest incomes; I was the only professional among them. My choice of living there after I could afford an expensive residential section undoubtedly was worth extra votes every time I ran for office. But in truth this was not my motive in refusing to move. I simply enjoyed associating with these hard-working, fun-loving Irish, Welsh, and Cornish families. There was no pretension and there was plenty of merriment.

When I purchased the house I had no furniture and no plans for occupying it until I could bring Lulu there as my bride. Meanwhile, I began enjoying Butte. My asthma had not bothered me since my arrival and the dry climate as a whole charmed me. Three days of cold weather—or one of those Butte-type sudden snowstorms—would be followed by a quick thaw. Even when the temperature dropped to 15 or 20 degrees below zero, I never felt the chill like I did during higher readings in Boston and Chicago.

The Montana summers were perfect—the nights always cool enough to require a blanket—and the trout fishing in the mountain streams became one of my favorite pastimes.

My original disaster with poker in Butte left no trauma. I played the game every weekend with other young lawyers and doctors. We rented a hotel room and the games went on all night. It was not unusual for someone to lose $2500 or $3000 by the time the sun came up, though luckily it never happened to me.

I shared a room in a private home with another lawyer, Irving H. Whitehouse. When Lulu and I set Saturday, September 7, 1907, as our wedding date, Whitehouse agreed to be my best man. Early in September, we took the train to Clinton, Iowa, which is on the Mississippi, and there caught a river boat for the short distance to Albany, Illinois, which was a mile and a half from the White farm.

There were nearly a score of other passengers on the boat. I asked the pilot if he carried that many every morning. He said no.

"What's going on?" I asked.

"John White's daughter is getting married," he told me.

I asked him who was the fortunate bridegroom.

"Oh, some damn book agent that was around here a few years ago," he answered, obviously unimpressed. I decided not to introduce myself.

Lulu and I were married at the Methodist Church in Albany. On our honeymoon we observed the fashion of the time by inspecting Niagara Falls, then went on to Massachusetts to visit my folks. We also toured Lexington, Concord, and other historic places, and bought some furniture for our home. In Marlboro, we went to the theater to see a play with a wild West theme. In one scene, a fierce-looking fellow strode out on the stage, fired off a gun, and announced that he was from Butte, Montana. I was already concerned whether Lulu might be apprehensive about settling in so notorious a spot. But she told me she had read a book, *The Perch of the Devil* (meaning Butte), and was prepared to accommodate herself to perhaps the toughest town in the West. But she had always prided herself on being a tomboy on the farm, so she would not allow herself to be intimidated. Even so, the adjustment was something of a shock, and not an easy one to make. Some years later, she told one of the children that at first she felt as if she was living in hell but, like me, had come to like the place.

The day after we set up housekeeping in Butte I was stopped on the street by the clerk in Judge Donlan's court. He congratulated me and I thanked him, agreeing that "I've got a nice little wife."

"Oh, I'm not congratulating you on your lovely bride," he replied. "I'm congratulating you on your partnership."

I said I didn't know what he was talking about. He told me that Matt Canning was going to offer me a full partnership. I was flattered. Canning was a brilliant criminal lawyer, a tall, black-haired man whose complexion was so dark he was called "the Nig." It was said he had studied for the priesthood in his native County Mayo, Ireland, but had run away to America and studied law. I had tried a few cases against him but I hardly knew him personally. I was well aware that he had a successful practice.

When Canning sent for me, he explained that I was to look after the law while he looked after "the politics." This was agreeable to me because I had never taken much interest in politics and was inclined to dismiss it as a "dirty business." I accepted his proposition.

Soon after joining Canning I had my first case in federal court. The employees of the telephone company had struck for higher wages and the company had won an injunction to keep the strikers from picketing. When the company brought in strikebreakers, the union chased them out of town. As a result, Joseph Shannon, state president of the Western Federation of Miners; William Cutts, president of the carpenters union; and a few other union officials were cited for contempt for allegedly driving the two non-union men out of Butte. The Miners union retained Canning and me to defend Shannon. I tried the case, which was before Judge William Hunt in Helena.

Echoing the philosophy of the time, the judge lectured the defendants: "If this sort of thing is permitted to go on, it will only be a short time before a Mason may say to a Catholic, or a Catholic to a Mason, or a Christian to a Jew, 'You cannot work on this building,' or 'You cannot work in this place.'" Then he found Shannon and two other defendants guilty. Shannon was over six feet tall and powerfully built. When the marshal took him by the arm to lead him off to jail, he pulled a full quart of whisky from his coat pocket and drained the contents without a stop. I was impressed.

During the trial, the telephone company used a witness whom I suspected might be a labor spy. I took a chance in my cross-examination and asked him whether he was a detective. Somewhat to my surprise, he replied that he was.

Several years later I was in Spokane trying a personal injury case against the Bunker Hill Mining Company with the help of another Butte lawyer, H. Lowndes Maury. This same detective came to our hotel room and informed us he was to be a witness in a personal injury case I was soon to try in Butte against the streetcar company. He claimed that he was reluctant to testify against my client, a milkman who had been hit by a streetcar, because he was a "nice old fellow." However, he said he would be forced to testify by the company unless we gave him some money to get out of the country and go to Canada. I refused.

When he left, I said to Maury, "That man is a detective." Maury scoffed but I was sure. I was not sure, though, that he had recognized me. When we got back to Butte, there was a letter from him saying: "I know that you recognized me and that's the reason I'm writing you. I was the detective that testified in the case before Judge Hunt in Helena." He again stated he would not testify if I would help him in some way. I ignored the second overture.

The night before the case against the streetcar company was to be tried, Peter Breen, a counsel for the company, telephoned me a proposal to settle for $5000. I said I would not settle for less than $7500. He called back and agreed to $7500.

Later, when the check was being turned over to me in the company's office, I remarked to the president, J. R. Wharton, who was a Sunday school teacher: "I want you to know that if it hadn't been for the fact that you sent a detective to me as a witness to try to get me to bribe him, I would have settled for $5000." Wharton remained glumly silent in the face of my accusation.

I rode down on the elevator with George Shelton, chief counsel for the company and a lawyer of high integrity. He asked me if my charge against Wharton was true and I assured him it was. "It sounds just like the old hypocrite," Shelton commented.

My first criminal case involved, in true Western tradition, a train robbery. Two young men about twenty years old had gone to the top of a mountain outside Butte and blockaded and held up the Northern Pacific's crack train, the *North Coast*

Limited. They bungled the job and killed the fireman and the engineer.

John Towers, one of those charged with the murders, sent for me while he was lodged in the Butte jail and asked me to defend him. I never sought criminal cases because I found I was inclined to get too emotionally involved with the defendants. I told Towers I was reluctant to take his case.

But the next thing I knew Towers had been transferred for trial to the town of Boulder, about twenty-five miles away, and had informed Judge Lew Calloway there that I was his lawyer. This made me even more reluctant. The court would pay me $100 to defend Towers because he was penniless, but the expenses connected with a trip to Boulder would exceed that amount. When I stalled, Calloway sent word that if I didn't come to Boulder in a hurry he would send a sheriff to bring me there. I went.

The prosecutor was the county district attorney, Dan Kelly, later Montana state attorney general. Kelly started off by introducing evidence which I considered irrelevant and improper. But every time I objected Calloway peremptorily overruled me. The judge seemed determined that Towers should be found guilty. After I had objected a score or more of times, he called me into his chambers during a recess and warned me that a young lawyer ought not to invite trouble with the judges around the state. When I continued to object to Kelly's maneuvers, the judge went so far as to threaten me with contempt!

Towers figured he had a perfect alibi. He said he had registered into a cheap boardinghouse in Butte about the time the crime was committed many miles outside of town. I produced the registration ledger of the boardinghouse and its proprietor swore to its accuracy on the witness stand.

The morning after all the evidence was in for both sides, Towers rose in court—without any advance consultation with me—and changed his plea to guilty. I was astounded and angry because he had always protested his innocence to me. Judge Calloway sentenced him to life imprisonment.

Later that day Towers disclosed to me what had happened. Calloway and Kelly apparently had become concerned that

Calloway had handled me so unfairly that a higher court might reverse a conviction. So on the night before the case was due to go to the jury Kelly and a Northern Pacific detective had spirited the defendant out of his cell and had taken him to the judge in a hotel room. Towers was told that if he pleaded guilty he would get off with life whereas if he persisted in pleading innocent he would be hanged.

The trial was like an electric shock to a young fellow just out of law school. Judge Calloway's conduct was the most outrageously high-handed I have ever seen. I can only conclude that he was carried away by the sentiment in Boulder demanding a conviction of the man involved in the murder of the two trainmen. Judge Calloway made up for it later. He became a highly respected member of the Montana State Supreme Court and was always friendly to me.

In any event, I did not let this episode form my opinion of the bench as a whole. The judges in the state then were generally good—and colorful. My favorites were the aforementioned Judge Donlan and Judge Jeremiah J. Lynch. Donlan's whimsical commentaries were legendary.

In uninhibited Butte the defendants were often more than a match for him. Once, the authorities asked him to commit Timothy ("Google-Eye") Harrington, a Democratic precinct worker and noted alcoholic, to the state insane asylum because there were no facilities for alcoholics.

"Tell me, Tim," inquired Donlan, peering over the bench, his eyes quizzical under his close-cropped gray hair, "are you really crazy?"

"Well, I must be," Harrington shot back disgustedly, "if I've been stealin' elections for the likes of you for the past ten years."

Another time, Donlan had an Irishman before him charged with stealing sheep. He lathered the culprit in his rich brogue, winding up with the declaration that if the defendant were being tried for sheep stealing in "the old country" he would be hanged.

"Yes," the defendant acknowledged, "and if you were in the old country you'd be in the dock with me."

Donlan's droll dicta eventually undid him. A Finnish woman asked for a divorce on grounds that her husband had beaten her up. He granted the divorce but couldn't resist a dry observation.

"Next time, marry one of those 'harps' up in the Gulch and see how gently they treat you," he said.

The Dublin Gulch, an Irish settlement in Butte, was insulted by this public slur on the quality of its manhood. When the judge came up for re-election, the Gulch voters marched to the polls against him virtually en masse and Donlan was defeated.

I enjoyed trial work. But in my case defending Spreich, the safe-blower, I was so nervous about being on my feet for the first time in District Court that when I finished my summation everything went blank. I hardly remembered where I was and could not have repeated one word I had said. I thought I had flopped. But the District Attorney, I. G. Denny, a native-born Southerner who was famous for his hearts-and-flowers style of oratory, walked over during the recess, put his arm around me and said, "Young man, if I had you in training for a while, I could make an orator out of you." I thought: What an awful liar you are!

After his career as D.A., Denny taught oratory and law to students. I never took his course, nor did I ever care to become an "orator" as such. It seemed to me that many criminal lawyers wasted emotional flamboyance on a jury. What I strove for was a repetition of the basic facts in various ways because I discovered that many jurors did not get the facts or the law the first time around. I always looked the jurors directly in the eyes and even addressed some of them individually if I knew their names.

I never got over being nervous when I set out to argue a case. I once confessed this to an old-time lawyer but he smiled and reassured me.

"The lawyer who isn't nervous when he's about to face a jury will never make a good lawyer," he said.

Canning and I each made an income of $5000 during our first year as partners—good money for those days. But while I enjoyed the law I could no more have avoided politics in Butte than I could have avoided people. It used to be said that "in Butte politics comes next to copper, and more than once the election of 'honest, stalwart men' had taken priority over the red metal." In the city the Republican Party did not amount to much but the fights within the Democratic Party kept us all busy.

Despite Canning's promise to handle all the politics himself, he asked me in the fall of 1908 to help out Johnny Doran, who was the boss of the seventh ward, where I lived. Canning himself was running for the nomination as county prosecutor against Tom Walker, brother of Frank C. Walker, who was to serve under Franklin D. Roosevelt as Postmaster General and Democratic National Chairman. Doran, running as a delegate to the county convention, was "in trouble," as the saying goes, and I called on my neighbors, Democratic and Republican alike, to vote for me and Doran's slate in the primary. Unlike primaries today, anyone registered in his precinct could vote in either party primary. You just wrote out your ballot and dropped it through a hole in an old hatbox.

Walker defeated Canning by six votes. At almost the same time, my political career began. Doran, the ward boss, placed my name on the slate of delegates to the forthcoming Democratic county convention and I attended a convention for the first time. The convention authorized a committee to pick the ticket for the legislature. The committee, meeting in the offices of a wholesale liquor company nearby, sent for me and asked me to become a candidate on the slate. I turned it down, on the advice of Canning. He denounced it as the "Company ticket" and blamed the "Company" for engineering his defeat.

The Company, as it was cryptically known to everyone in Montana, was both ruthless and resourceful. I was to do battle with it for many years. Here I had better explain briefly what it was and how it had been gobbling up large and small enemies long before I arrived on the scene. The massively corrupt story of the Company begins with Copper King No. 1, Marcus Daly, a native of Ireland, a man of wit and charm, and a shrewd prospector and businessman. In the 1880s, Daly, a mining engineer, purchased the Anaconda, a Butte silver mine, for $30,000 on the hunch it contained copper. What it contained was the world's richest vein of copper.

In 1898 Daly negotiated with the Standard Oil Company and formed one of the largest trusts in financial history, the Amalgamated Copper Company. It controlled 75 per cent of the stock of the original Anaconda company as well as that of other companies. But it faced a worthy rival in another copper king, Frederick Augustus ("Fritz") Heinze, a gay, handsome German-Jewish-Irish mining engineer who was acknowledged to be one of the most ingenious industrial pirates of his time. Heinze had come to Montana in 1889 and made friends and money rapidly. Heinze fought Amalgamated with the corporation's own money, claiming that the ore in Amalgamated's richest mines "apexed"—reached their surface peaks—in his small plots of adjoining ground. By buying up certain judges, he was able to tie the hands of the giant—while he feverishly worked at mining copper from its mines.

Heinze at the same time enlisted the support of the people of Butte by preaching against "the dangers of foreign combines and monopolies" and by raising wages and shortening hours in his mines. This ate into Daly's long-time popularity with the miners and forced Amalgamated to liberalize their wages and hours.

Amalgamated's strategy was directed from its headquarters at 25 Broadway, New York City. Heinze fought it with one hundred lawsuits brought by his staff of thirty-seven lawyers. Simultaneously, he waged what was literally underground warfare; when his men occasionally broke through the Amalgamated diggings, the miners from the rival companies battled one another with steam and hot water, dynamite and slaked lime, causing at least two deaths.

Brought to a standstill by Heinze's nagging litigation, the Amalgamated on October 22, 1903, struck back with all its economic and political power. It closed down every one of its operations in Montana—mines, smelters, copper refineries, lumber mills, coal mines, company stores, railroads, etc. Twenty thousand men were thrown out of work. Amalgamated delivered this ultimatum: (1) Heinze must sell certain stocks that provided the grounds for most of his lawsuits, and (2) the governor must call a special session of the legislature to pass a law allowing a party to a lawsuit to take its case to another jurisdiction if it considered the judge corrupt or prejudiced. The second demand of course was designed to permit Amalgamated to shop around for a judge who had not been bribed by Heinze.

Governor Joseph K. Toole, a Democrat, was anti-Amalgamated but with the state in economic paralysis he had little choice. He called the legislature into session and it dutifully approved the bill demanded by the Company. A year later Heinze sold out to Amalgamated for the "nuisance value" sum of $10,000,000.

Thus a few years before I arrived the lesson for Butte was clear: no matter how clever, unscrupulous, or spendthrift the opponent, you couldn't lick the Amalgamated. The Supreme Court's anti-trust decision in 1911 forced a paper reorganization and Amalgamated, the holding company, subsequently dissolved itself into the Anaconda Copper Mining Company. (Interestingly, an anaconda is a man-killing python.) Regardless of its shifting corporate entity, it was always referred to during my time in Montana as "the Company," a simple yet awe-inspiring term. Eventually, it was selling one-third of all the copper output in the United States and one-fourth of the world supply.

In the background of the Daly-Heinze struggle for power was a fascinating political feud between Daly and William Andrews Clark, a dour Scotch-Irish Presbyterian who had made millions in Montana in banking, real estate, smelting, refining, and silver and copper mining. Legend has it that Clark sneered at Daly and Daly sneered back. In any case, Clark had a passion to enter the United States Senate when Montana achieved statehood in 1889. Daly was determined that this would happen only over his dead body. And this was almost literally the way it happened.

The fight lasted until the turn of the century and saw the theft of ballots, the murder of an election judge, and bribery on a mass scale. In his book, *The Devil Learns to Vote—the Story of Montana*, Christopher P. Connolly reports that Daly spent an estimated $2,500,000 of his profits from Amalgamated to try to keep Clark out of the "most exclusive club in the world." Clark's failure to make the club for twelve years may be explained by the fact that he spent somewhat less than that, and spent it clumsily.

United States senators were then elected by the state legislature instead of by popular vote. In 1899, Clark bought up members of the Montana legislature singly and in groups. Clark's two sons were quoted in the statehouse as quipping: "We'll either send the old man to the Senate or the poorhouse." While Clark was more or less secretly buying up GOP legislators, Daly, also a Democrat, was openly teamed up with the Republicans.

Clark was declared elected in the 1899 session after eighteen tense days of balloting and after he had reportedly bought up all but fifteen Republican votes. However, twenty-seven Montana legislators petitioned Congress to bar him at the door, on grounds of corruption. Daly demanded, and got, an investigation of the charges by the Senate Committee on Privileges and Elections.

Never was there a clearer case of the pot calling the kettle black. Both the Daly and Clark forces testified during the hearings and the three thick volumes embracing the testimony reveals a sordid picture. Clark was accused of having spent $431,000 to purchase forty-seven legislators' votes; he admitted spending $272,800 to get elected. The committee found him guilty beyond all reasonable doubt and voted to declare title to his seat void. But before the committee report could be filed on the Senate floor, Clark resigned. He had another trick up his sleeve.

The Clark forces lured pro-Daly Governor Robert B. Smith out of Montana on a pretext and swiftly handed Clark's resignation to pro-Clark Lieutenant Governor A. E. Spriggs. As acting governor, Spriggs accepted the resignation and immediately appointed Clark to the seat from which he had just been barred. Smith rushed back into the state and declared the appointment invalid because it was "tainted with fraud and collusion." The seat remained vacant until 1911, when Clark and Heinze joined forces, Daly died, and Clark at long last got himself elected to the Senate without leaving a smell in his wake.

When I got into Butte politics, I could sense the bitterness over the Clark-Daly feud lingering in Silver Bow County, in which the city was located. The county delegation had played an unlovely role in the scandal and was still considered by many to be a salable commodity. It was of course dominated by "the Company." The saying was that if you wanted to run for office in the county you had to go hat in hand to the Company's suite on the sixth floor of the Hennessy Building and say, "Please, sir, may I run for anything from dog catcher to sheriff?"

The Company had a powerful ally in its so-called "twin," the Montana Power Company, and in its satellites among the other big interests of the state, such as the railroads and the banks. The Company kept in close touch with Democratic Party politics down to the lowest levels. Most of its officials not only made substantial contributions but were active as delegates to city, county, and state conventions; and they ran for the legislature.

In March 1909 I was elected to represent my seventh ward in the Democratic city convention. At the convention, Cornelius Kelley, then head of the Company's legal department and later the president and chairman of the board of the Company, nominated Phil Gillis, a loyal friend of the Company, for chairman. A motion was made to close the nomination when Paddy Duffy, ex-president of the Miners union, suggested that someone else be given a chance. He nominated me. Joe Griffin, a young lawyer friend of mine, slipped over and warned me not to let my name be put up against the Company candidate—I'd be "murdered" in the balloting.

"Listen," I replied. "I didn't have anything to do with this and didn't even know anything about it, so let it go. I don't care."

The fact is I was so surprised I didn't know what to do. I heard the roll called and could hardly believe my ears when it was announced that Wheeler had defeated Gillis, 30 to 24. Stunned, I didn't make the customary acceptance speech after ascending the rostrum. I simply went about my business as chairman—which was mainly to make sure the votes were counted honestly.

The contest was for the Democratic nomination for mayor. It was between Charley Nevin, the Company candidate, and Phil Goodwin, who was tied up with the old Clark henchmen. Nevin won the nomination and got elected.

The principal contest at the county conventions was over the county officers. The jobs paid about as well as the state jobs and the Democratic nomination in Silver Bow County was tantamount to election, with little time or expense required. To win the Democratic nomination, it was best to claim nativity in County Cork and second best to claim birth in some county in Ireland with slightly lesser prestige in Montana.

Butte was then predominantly Irish, though the Irish did not have a majority in the Miners union. An Immigration Commission study in 1912 revealed that the English made up the largest single group among Butte's miners, with the Irish a close second and the French, Canadians, Finns, Germans, and Scandinavians trailing in that order. The newer arrivals were southern and eastern Europeans. The mixture of Irish, Welsh, and Cornish miners was said to have been the deliberate policy of Marcus Daly. It usually led to riots on the Fourth of July, when the Irish celebrated by baiting the English. The story is that some young Irish miners once complained to Daly, "Marcus, we don't understand you. You go over to Ireland and bring us here and then you go to Cornwall and bring those 'Cousin Jacks' in and we don't get along with them." Daly is reported to have answered: "When you Irish are fighting with the 'Cousin Jacks,' you are laying off Marcus Daly."

In selecting a twelve-man county slate for the legislature, the Company felt that an all-Catholic ticket was undesirable, even though every Irishman in Butte was an aspiring politician. Being neither Irish nor Catholic I had two points in my favor. At the Democratic county convention in 1910, the nominating committee asked me to stand for a seat in the legislature. One committee member mumbled vaguely to me afterward that I would be expected to do "a few little things" for the Company but in my utter naïveté I thought nothing of it.

A fight was made against our slate on the convention floor. W. W. McDowell, a mining promoter who was on the slate but was not too popular, got worried about having his nomination ratified. He told me that if he were nominated and elected he expected to be re-elected Speaker of the House. If I would help ensure his nomination, he pledged he would appoint me chairman of the House Judiciary Committee after he became Speaker. I did what I could for McDowell and the convention nominated him.

The party assigned me to campaign for election with John K. O'Rourke, the picturesque sheriff who flaunted gorgeous cravats said to cost five dollars each. The prescription for a successful campaign was simplicity itself: you planted a foot on the bar rail and bought "drinks for the house" in every saloon and casino in Silver Bow County and as often as possible. Since there was no paper money in Montana then, you tossed out a fistful of silver or, better yet, a five, ten, or twenty-dollar goldpiece. And if you expected change you could have stood there until doomsday without getting any.

Every self-respecting drinker in Butte took his whisky straight, with a beer chaser. Debonaire "Jawn" O'Rourke never spent less than $40 in a saloon and often as much as $100. This was not extravagant, considering that the job of sheriff in wide-open Silver Bow County was reputed to be worth $40,000 to $60,000 a year on the side.

With a wife, a mortgaged house, and a moderate income, I had to try to get by as O'Rourke's frugal companion. At Democratic headquarters shortly before Election Day, "Cuinane" Sullivan, a sometime saloonkeeper, asked me when I was coming up to his place in the Gulch. I realized what the trip would cost me. I also knew that Sullivan was one of those who got a keg of beer and some cases of whisky and opened a bar thirty days before the election, just to reap the windfall from the candidates.

"I don't believe I'll be able to make it," I told him.

"Well, if you don't get up there, you'll be badly beaten," Sullivan warned.

Sullivan was wrong. I carried the Gulch. In fact, I got only one less vote there than Paddy Duffy, former president of the Miners union, and a Gulch resident. I placed fourth highest on our county ticket, getting only thirty-five votes less than the top man. Our twelve-man slate was elected save for John McGinnis, who was a one-time lieutenant of Heinze.

It proved that you could be elected without a rain of gold across the bar. I had insisted on making a few speeches and discussing issues, and I didn't spend more than $20 altogether. A fourth of that was invested in Walkerville, an old mining town north of Butte. I had bided my time until all but ten persons had left the bar, then casually tossed a five-dollar goldpiece on the counter. The bartender blandly rang it up, and I had to borrow a nickel to get a streetcar back to Butte.

Chapter Four

"YOU CAN'T LICK THE COMPANY"

It sounds incredible now but when I went to Helena for the opening of the legislature in January 1911 I was naïve enough to believe I would be allowed to act as a free agent. True, I had been on the Company slate and I knew its interests and its influence. But I assumed—maybe out of my inherited idealism—that the corruption so rampant in the city council would not reach the state level—or me. And while I had heard of the competitive vote-buying by Clark, Heinze and Daly I was optimistic enough to think that such contempt for the democratic process belonged to the past.

Several decades later, I ran into Cornelius Kelley in a New York club. He was then chairman of the board of Anaconda and I was a United States senator.

"You know, you educated me," I joshed him.

"Well, we didn't do a very good job of it," he replied with a laugh.

Helena (once called "Last Chance Gulch") is a beautiful capital, shimmering in pure air with snow-capped Rockies rearing as a dramatic backdrop in all directions. In 1911 Helena reflected the prosperity of the "Treasure State," which was rich in gold and silver mining, cattle, sheep, and timber. The enormous stone capitol was one of the finest in the Northwest and the town was ornamented with elaborate mansions built by the stockmen and the mining barons.

The life of the capital looked less admirable from the inside. It is not unusual for a state legislature to be dominated by big interests but I believe that in Helena at that time the lobbying was bolder and the big interests were fewer and bigger. The legislature met every two years and was paid $10 a day for sixty days. But the hospitality was unlimited and ceaseless in the suites kept by the Company in the Old Grandon and Helena hotels. Nor was there any scarcity of entertainment for the lawmakers. Shortly after I arrived, I was invited to join a party of my colleagues going down to Boulder Springs, where there was a resort hotel owned by James A. Murray, an old-time Butte gambler whose nephew had been prosecutor in the optometry case. Girls as well as transportation were supplied for that long lost weekend and I'm quite sure Anaconda picked up the check, though I can't prove it because I didn't go.

In the 1911–12 legislature the Democrats controlled the House, the Republicans controlled the Senate, and the Company controlled the leaders of both. I was surprised to find myself immediately chosen to be secretary of the House Democratic caucus. After all, I was a novice in politics and the youngest member of the House (just turning twenty-nine). In addition, McDowell, as soon as he was elected Speaker, fulfilled his personal pledge by naming me chairman of the Judiciary Committee. To put me in this powerful post, he had to bypass some veteran legislators and some prominent older lawyers.

The primary task of that legislature was to fill one of Montana's two seats in the United States Senate, since the term of the incumbent, Republican Thomas H. Carter, was expiring. The Democrats were confident of replacing him with one of their own party because they outnumbered Republicans by 56 to 45 in the legislature as a whole.

The Company split the Democrats, however, by backing W. G. Conrad, a Great Falls banker and long-time Democratic wheelhorse. The favorite of the Democrats was Thomas J. Walsh, a brilliant Helena lawyer. The Company hated Walsh because he had tried and won mining and personal injury suits against it; some went so far as to call him an "ambulance chaser," simply because he had clients who had been injured by the railroads. He also had defended labor leaders, another unforgivable sin in the eyes of the Company.

The Company dominated the Silver Bow delegation but I felt impelled to support Walsh as much the better man, though I had met him only once. When I was working for Shelton, he had happened into the office late one night, found me working, and smilingly warned that this was a sure way to acquire gray hairs.

Only two other members of our delegation refused to go along with the Company. One was Joseph Binnard, a young lawyer who also admired Walsh. The other was Paddy Moore, who was holding out—with his tongue in his cheek—for Tom McTague, an ex-owner of the state penitentiary.

Once, when I spotted Moore in the bar at the Grandon, I said, "Paddy, why don't you get in line and vote for Walsh?"

"Don't be a damned fool all your life," he replied with a wink. "W. A. Clark is coming out for the Senate next week and we'll all be able to make a piece of money."

Clark had no intention of taking on another fight for the Senate. He owned the Butte *Miner* and was stringing along with his old enemies at Anaconda on almost everything.

Moore, a member of the bartenders union, later shifted to Walsh. When he returned to Butte one weekend, some of his union cronies had stood him up against the wall and threatened him with bodily harm if he didn't get behind the candidate who had defended union leaders.

But Walsh was opposed by virtually all the newspapers and by the interests who always truckled to the Company. I was so incensed at my anti-Walsh colleagues on our delegation that at one meeting I lectured them that they should get behind this popular Irishman because he had campaigned to help put them into the legislature. This appeal got nowhere. Paddy Duffy got up and said he had been elected because he had been president of the Miners union. Jim McNally insisted that he had been elected because he had carried a union card for thirty years. All this dismayed Paddy Moore, a short, heavy-set man who sounded as if he were a member of the Abbey Theatre company in Dublin.

"You're all damn fools," he told us. "None of you would be here if I hadn't sung 'Where the River Shannon Flows' all during the campaign."

Moore couldn't make a speech to save his life. His vote appeal rested on a much sounder foundation: he could render a sentimental Irish ballad in a way that made tears flow like the Shannon itself in every barroom in Butte, or at a public gathering.

When the legislature took its first ballot, Walsh got only 28 votes out of 102 cast. Eighteen went to Conrad and 31 to Carter. The other 25 votes were scattered. And 51 were necessary to elect.

The next vote was taken a month later. It showed: Carter, 40; Walsh, 24; and Conrad, 24. The balloting dragged on in this inconclusive fashion from day to day, with the Republicans concentrating on Carter and the Democrats hopelessly split. I was told that the Company forces were supporting Conrad in an effort to deadlock the legislature and then select a dark-horse candidate of their own choosing in the last-minute back-room dickering.

Binnard and I kept stubbornly with Walsh. One day I was buttonholed by John McGinnis, the lone loser in our county delegation in the election. He asked if Binnard and I would represent a Frenchman who was anxious to block Mayor Nevin's proposal to move Butte's red-light district from the center of town to the outlying "Flats." McGinnis said we could earn a fee of $2000 each. When I pointed out that nothing could be done in court because the bawdy houses were operating in violation of the law, he said, "All you have to do is ask John Moroney to call the mayor and tell him to do nothing about it." Moroney was president of the Daly Bank and Trust Company and top lobbyist for the Company at Helena.

I asked McGinnis what Moroney would want in return for this favor. He replied: "Nothing. Moroney likes you."

"I've never met him," I said. "Won't he want me to switch my vote from Walsh to Conrad?"

McGinnis assured me I wouldn't have to be in any hurry about it—I could switch later on.

"What you're really asking me to do is sell my vote for $2000," I said.

"What have you got in the back of your mind?" McGinnis exploded. "What do you really want? You can't lick the Company. You might as well join them."

Next, Harry Gallwey, majority leader of the state senate and president of the Butte, Anaconda, and Pacific Railway, demanded to know when I would swing over to the Company's choice. I liked Gallwey—he was a charming and decent fellow ordinarily—but I tried to convince him I was for Walsh all the way.

"We'll *make* you vote for Conrad," he said quietly.

"You'll *what?*" I yelled. "Listen: you can take me out and string me up on a telephone pole but, by God, you can't make me vote for someone I don't want to vote for!"

By now I was recognized as the leader of the diehard Walsh forces and the price on my vote was going up. A well-known Helena gambler approached my room and said he could get me $5000 if I would vote for Conrad. Despite my refusal, he returned several times, apparently assuming I was playing hard to get. Finally he said he would pay as high as $9000 if I would desert Walsh. When I again smilingly shook my head, he gave up, remarking that "you're the damnedest politician I ever met."

With the senatorial election still up in the air, Moroney himself sent for me at his sumptuous private suite in the Helena Hotel. The long-time head of the Anaconda political machine, he was small and redheaded, with a pointed nose, a thin face and an exceptionally sharp mind.

"What's the matter—why can't we get together?" Moroney asked me immediately. I told him I didn't know whether he took me for a fool or a thief but that I was neither. He then told me that Walsh could not be elected. He asked me to suggest a compromise possibility. I named several, including Walsh's law partner, the respected Colonel C. B. Nolan, who was a noted orator, but Moroney objected to all of them.

Moroney said he liked Nolan and would walk barefooted from Butte to Helena for him but that Nolan couldn't be elected. He added that I knew very well he could get enough Democratic votes to elect Carter but that John D. Ryan, board chairman of the Company, and Carter wanted to avoid another scandal.

Montana was anxious to avoid a repetition of the 1893 fiasco, when the legislature's inability to agree on a candidate for the Senate left the seat vacant for two years. Finally, after the 79th ballot, there was a movement from both sides toward Judge Henry L. Myers of the Fourth Judicial District. Walsh assured me that Myers would make an honest, independent senator. (As a member of the 1893 legislature, Myers had accepted a large sum of money from W. A. Clark—but only to use it as evidence to expose Clark.) So I went along in supporting Myers and he was elected on the 80th ballot.

The second major issue of the session was adoption of a direct primary law—to which both parties had committed themselves in the last campaign. Early in the session, we in the Democratic House put through a bill patterned on the philosophy of the wide-open Wisconsin law. The Republican-controlled Senate passed a bill restricting participation by the people and giving more control of primary machinery to the political parties.

In a Senate-House conference, both bills were scrapped in favor of a compromise which provided for the nomination of United States senators by straight party convention. I was one of the nine House members who fought the compromise on the grounds it was "not the bill the people want."

This measure was enacted, but in the subsequent general election of 1912 the people took matters into their own hands and overwhelmingly adopted an initiative measure based on the Wisconsin law. Under this system, the primary voter receives the ballots of all parties, votes the ballot of his choice, and discards the unused ballots in a box provided for the blanks.

Most of the bills I sponsored concerned proposals long sought by the labor unions. Butte then had the reputation of being "the strongest union town on earth." Every job in town was organized. There was even a chimney sweeps union composed of two chimney sweeps. The Butte Miners union was already thirty years old, a member of the Western Federation of Miners which in turn was affiliated with the American Federation of Labor. It had won the eight-hour day in 1900, when Heinze set that pattern in his mines and forced Amalgamated to follow suit. Wages were higher than in any mining camp, although the cost of living in Butte was higher too.

While the Company allowed the union to do all the hiring, it otherwise did not permit anything like the independence exerted today by big unions protected by across-the-board contracts and federal law. The miners had been used as pawns in the Heinze-Amalgamated struggle and the Company had played politics with the internal affairs of the union ever since.

My No. 1 bill was based on a model measure drafted for the AFL by Judge Alton B. Parker, the Democratic nominee for President in 1904, to assist workmen in their personal injury suits. In those days, unless a lawyer represented the Anaconda interests or their affiliates, his most lucrative practice was in representing people with lawsuits against them. By now I had had enough direct experience in representing miners and railroad workers in personal injury cases to realize the crying need for a radical change in the legal concepts covering employee accident claims.

It was taken for granted at that time that an employee assumed the normal risks of the industry in which he was employed. Also controlling was the ancient principle that the responsibility of a "fellow servant" for an accident relieved the employer of any damages. My bill abrogated the "fellow servant" doctrine completely. It also eliminated the assumption-of-risk defense by an employer. And it provided that contributory negligence did not bar a recovery but limited the liability of an employer in proportion to the extent of contributory negligence.

The measure caused an immediate uproar when it was reported to the House floor for debate. The Helena *Independent* in its issue of January 27, 1911, noted that it was the subject of "determined attack" and that the bill's opponents were aiming at its "emasculation." Although it marched toward passage on a Friday, the Company marshaled its forces over the weekend. On Monday it was referred back to the Judiciary Committee, where, according to the *Independent* two committee members "agreed that the bill was altogether too radical and sweeping." They promised to come up with a compromise which covered only the most hazardous jobs. But even this milk-and-water substitute failed to pass the Senate.

However, I did see through to enactment my loan shark bill. It regulated assignment of wages as security for loans and fixed a rate of interest for such loans at 12 per cent. This may seem like little enough regulation, but it was an improvement. As a collection agent, I had seen far too many miners go deeply into debt over assignment of their wages.

I also pushed hard for my bill requiring coal dealers to weigh coal on public scales. It slid through the House but was blocked by Chairman John Edwards of the Senate Judiciary Committee. One day Edwards, who was the Republican boss of eastern Montana, had the gall to put his arm around me and ask me to get my committee to approve his railroad bill. I told him I would not only have his bill reported unfavorably but I would give the same treatment to all his other bills—until he had my coal bill passed by the Senate and signed by the governor. It did not take Edwards long to do precisely that, and my coal bill became law.

I also used my power as chairman to block any bill that was obnoxious to me, simply by neglecting to call a committee meeting to consider it or by postponing consideration until it was too late in the session to have it passed. For this reason some of my colleagues called me a "dictator," as they did later when I was chairman of the Interstate Commerce Committee of the United States Senate.

In February I had a little fun with the Constitutional Amendment to enfranchise women. Representative Jeannette Rankin of Montana, the first female in the United States to be elected to Congress, pleaded with the legislature to ratify the measure. I voted for it but I could not resist some prearranged byplay with Dan O'Hern, who was presiding. I proposed amending the Amendment so as to limit the right to vote to women with six children. O'Hern, with a straight face, ruled my proposal out of order. That night, after the bill had passed the House, O'Hern and I were having dinner at the Grandon. A couple of suffragettes who must have thought we were taking their crusade lightly said in loud tones: "Look at those two crooks over there!"

As a matter of fact, I strongly believe women should not only vote but also run for public office. None of the women who have been elected to the Senate or the House have shown up badly. The ones I have known were forthright and honest, and some showed tremendous courage. Take Jeannette Rankin, who stood up and voted against our entry into World War I in the face of contrary public sentiment and appeals from her family and friends. The late Representative Edith Nourse Rogers, a Republican from my old district in Massachusetts, was another outstanding member of Congress.

In the legislature, I was successful in pushing through the bill backed by the labor unions to ban the sale of prison-made goods. But I turned down the union leaders when they asked me to sponsor a bill to prohibit the use of prisoners on road gangs. I felt this was the only way Montana would get any highways built in that era.

As a whole, the conduct of the labor leaders in Helena surprised me. I expected them to line up one hundred per cent with the progressive legislators but they played along with the Company on all bills except those which affected labor directly. I thought one labor leader went to extremes of subservience when I saw him obsequiously holding the coat of a company official in a hotel lobby.

On the other hand, I was pleasantly surprised by my colleagues in the legal profession. Although lawyers are probably more criticized than any other class of men, it was a group of young lawyers in the Montana legislature who courageously fought for liberal legislation, for Walsh's election, and against corporate control.

Two of the most likeable lobbyists I became acquainted with in the capital were Frank Conley and Tom McTague. Conley and McTague were in the penitentiary business—that is, they had built a prison, leased it to the state, and ran it themselves. The situation was, of course, ripe for abuse. It used to be said —without proof—that any big interests that wanted to get rid of someone who was a thorn in its side could get him shipped to the penitentiary without a court sentence.

A previous legislature had purchased the state prison from Conley and McTague, paying a price set by a commission of outstanding citizens after a careful appraisal. Now, in 1911, came a bill to pay an additional $69,000 for property which Conley and McTague contended they had not been properly compensated for in the sale. When their case was presented to the Committee on Institutions, of which I was a member, it didn't impress me at all. A poll of other committee members made it obvious that a majority opposed the measure.

After the committee meeting, Gus English, a Republican member and a Company man, buttonholed me and said, "Look, I can get you $50 for this if you'll switch. Conley and McTague are fine fellows, I've done business with them before."

"You get all the money you want, I'm out of it," I told him.

"Well, if you don't take it, I can't get it," English complained.

"Well, then, as far as I'm concerned," I answered, "you're not going to get it."

At the very next meeting of the committee there was a miraculous change of sentiment and the bill was reported out favorably. Ironically, one member who switched was Eddie O'Flynn, a lawyer from Butte who had boasted to me on the way to Helena about how he was going to stand up against the Company. He afterward got a retainer from one of the Company's affiliates. The skillful lobbying by Conley and McTague had paid off, in the literal sense of the word. I got a taste of it myself. Conley told me in the House lobby he had a lawsuit against him in Deer Lodge, where the prison was located. He wanted to retain me as one of his attorneys for $500.

I told him bluntly that I was against his bill and that he was making a mistake if he thought I might change my vote.

"I'm running the penitentiary and don't want to be in it," Conley quipped, shrugging and walking away. I heard nothing more about it until I was back in Butte later on. Conley left word at my office he wanted to see me in the Butte Hotel. When I arrived, he pulled out a roll of bills and said, "Here's the five hundred. The case has been settled and I want to pay you."

I told him he didn't owe me a thing because I had done no work in the suit and had voted against his bill. Conley looked amazed.

"I have been going to the legislature for twenty years or more," he said, leaning back in his chair. "You're the second man I've offered money to who wouldn't take it. The other was Albert Galen."

(Galen was a former attorney general of Montana. As we shall see later, I was to have a run-in with him which demonstrated that Galen either lost, or temporarily misplaced, the integrity he displayed to Conley.)

Conley sent for a fifth of champagne after I declined his $500 and we had a friendly drink, presumably to celebrate my resistance to money.

The Company lobbied loyally for all its friends, regardless of what they were pushing in the legislature. For example, Moroney once sought me out in the House lobby and mentioned that Dr. Joseph Scanlan, whose family owned the insane asylum then being leased to the state, was anxious for passage of the bill to buy the asylum for $750,000. I had opposed it because I thought the price should be set by a commission of reputable private citizens, as had been done in purchasing the prison. Moroney explained that Dr. Scanlan wanted to retain me to make a speech for his bill on the floor of the House.

"If they're right on the proposition, they don't need me," I told Moroney. "And if they're wrong, there's not enough money to buy my vote."

The asylum bill failed during that session.

A state employee finally gave me a friendly tip that unless

I began lining up with the Company I couldn't expect to go back to Silver Bow County safely. There was a hint that I literally would not be permitted to *live* in the county. But the main point was that the Company never forgets or forgives its enemies. I told the employee that if I had to leave Butte I would at least be leaving with more money than I came with.

Was I utterly disillusioned by the corruption in the capital? I was dismayed, of course, but not disheartened. I never claimed to be more honest than most people but bribery offended my conscience. Aside from that, I had sense enough to know that once you took their money you had to do as they said. You lost not only your integrity and self-respect but your independence in action if not in thought.

Some of the bribe-takers used to say, "No one is going to know but the bribe-giver." But I will never forget the time L. O. Evans, a Company lawyer, said to me: "You think your friend, Joe Kirschwing, is honest. Well, I have the list and I can show you he was paid." It astounded me that this friend, a stalwart, forthright liberal was supposed to be on the secret payroll—and also that the information was being passed on. I was learning that the people who can buy you and thereafter have you in their pocket have no respect for you.

Still, I did not look down my nose at my colleagues for doing what came naturally to them. We used to say that anyone who was a Company stooge was "wearing the copper collar." I was fond of most of these fellows and I enjoyed needling them about the chores they had to perform for the Company. This was to be my lasting attitude in a long career of political fights: I never carried the bitterness around in my soul because I knew it would not hurt the other fellow, only me.

I want to make it absolutely clear that I did not feel the intolerance for my opponents that many supposedly tolerant "liberals" display today toward those who disagree with them. I did not assume that *every* member of the legislature who disagreed with me or Walsh was crooked or in any way dishonest. There were many who honestly believed that because the Company employed more people and developed the state it *should* dominate the economy and political life of the state.

They also seemed convinced that those of us who disagreed with their philosophy were not only liberals but wild-eyed radicals!

I also felt the Company had a right to employ lobbyists to protect their legitimate interests before the legislature. Unfortunately, so much money had been thrown around dishonestly during the fights between Heinze, Clark, and the Company that all Montana had been corrupted and some politicians looked upon public office as a legitimate way of making fairly big money.

All in all, I had a taste of politics and I liked it. I had started a fight against the Company and I intended to finish it. I have always relished a fight but in this one I knew I could look for little outside help, for I had by now confirmed my suspicion that I could trust few politicians.

Why was I fighting the Company? It was definitely not because I considered myself any kind of "flaming liberal." I had not at this point worked out a philosophy of Progressivism—even though 1911 saw the beginnings of Progressivism in the state. (Between 1911 and 1920, a total of 66 laws were passed which benefitted farmers and ranchers in Montana; 40 other laws passed by the legislature favored laborers.) What I was working and voting for was simple justice for the workingman—who needed a great deal of legal help to get his rights in dealing with management.

There were other more emotional motivations. I had been outraged by the way the Company had undermined Walsh, a man of the highest ability and integrity. And I deeply resented being told what I *had* to do. I would not be pushed around.

Back in Butte, I reopened my law office. Canning and I had dissolved our partnership after one year for personal reasons which in no way impaired our friendship and respect for each other. I had no trouble finding clients. My record of standing up to the Company brought me a steady flow of people who were suing the Company or one of the railroads.

The year 1911 was a particularly bad one for mine accidents. One of the worst had involved "the nippers"—school-age boys who before the restraint of the child labor laws were hired to carry tools from place to place in the workings far below ground. On this occasion, the drilling steel which the boys loaded in the elevator cage with them got loose from its moorings and ripped into the shaft's timbers on ascent. The eight "nippers" were literally ground to pieces.

My working day extended far into the evening because nearly all my clients were workingmen and this was the only time they could visit my office. The Anaconda attorneys began to complain that they paid me more money than any attorney in town. I added insult to injury by blandly using the excellent law library in the Company's offices in the Hennessy Building to look up my cases.

I also sought advice from the outstanding lawyers in Butte who were handling the same kinds of cases. Alec Mackel, of the firm of Mackel and Meyer, advised me never to leave an Englishman on a jury in suing a company for damages because the English were notoriously conservative. On the other hand, Mackel said, the Irish were the most desirable jurors on such cases because they were always very free with other people's money. He went on to warn me further never to leave an Irishman on a jury if you were prosecuting a case for the government because "the Irish are always against the government." Mackel's rule of thumb turned out to be reliable.

Chapter Five

MR. DISTRICT ATTORNEY

Even before I returned home from the legislature new political avenues were opening up. On March 7, 1911, I picked up the Anaconda *Standard* and to my surprise read this speculation about the situation in Butte:

"Down in the seventh ward they are talking of having B. K. Wheeler, representative in the legislature, get into the race for the Democratic nomination for mayor. The young attorney is well-liked down in his section and that section has been shy on mayors until Charley Nevin moved into the annexed district. In all his doings, BK has received credit for being actuated by the best of motives. He has some good hard will of his own and should he get into the race and win out it will be found that Butte has a mayor who knows things and can do things the way that strikes him as the right way . . . he has not been consulted about the matter of placing him in the long list of candidates but some of his friends say he might be induced to get in the going and carry the banner of Democracy to victory."

That was a flattering notice from a Company-owned paper.

For some reason the Company allowed a modest amount of editorial independence to be exercised by the *Standard,* which was printed in the little town of Anaconda but circulated all over Butte, twenty-six miles away, because of its excellence. The Company controlled directly or indirectly most weekly and daily newspapers in the state except the Great Falls *Tribune,* the strongly Republican Miles City *Star,* and a daily paper in Kalispell.

The day after I read the story in the *Standard* some friends did prevail on me to let my name go up at the city convention. However, I ran a poor third and on the third ballot, along with the rest of the trailing candidates, I withdrew in favor of John Quinn, a former sheriff of Silver Bow County and long-time Democratic politician.

A few weeks later, the Reverend Lewis J. Duncan, a Unitarian minister and Socialist Party secretary, was elected mayor by a landslide, winning more votes than his Democratic and Republican opponents combined. Quinn grumbled that he himself bought more votes than he got. In many areas, Quinn's organization paid from two to three dollars for votes. Apparently, many of the persons presumably "bought" had gone blithely ahead and voted the Socialist ticket.

(Pressing money on voters was not the only way the Butte Democrats tried to keep control of elections. They had a habit of casting ballots for absent voters—meaning voters who had not shown up at the polls by a certain hour. I always made it a point to vote early rather than run the risk of finding I already had been voted when I arrived at the polling place.)

The Socialists elected every one of their candidates for city office plus five of their nine candidates for aldermen. Financial scandals had played a big role in ending the Democrats' long tenure at city hall. For example, the outgoing city treasurer was said to be owing the city $12,000 which he had allegedly pocketed, and an audit of the books showed many shortages and a total debt of $1,500,000 built up for the city over a period of ten years.

Duncan was inaugurated with an announcement that he would close all dance halls in the red-light district, ban the sale of liquor in "any place where there is traffic between the sexes," and provide a regular system of physical examination for the women in the red-light district. He also established a substation in the district where men could check their valuables before patronizing the bawdy houses. But he eliminated the $10 license heretofore required from the prostitutes because he considered it a source of graft for the police.

Other reforms announced by Duncan was a city purchasing department to check extravagance and to keep a close audit of city accounts.

Duncan came to my office shortly after the election and offered me the post of city attorney. I told him I would think it over.

"Think it over but don't talk it over," he said. He didn't want the word to get around that he was considering me. I was surprised that he was, inasmuch as I had never had anything to do with the Socialist Party. But I never heard any more about the offer from the new mayor. The job went to H. Lowndes Maury, later a law partner of mine, reportedly because the Socialists had insisted on the job going to a party man. In my opinion, Duncan made the best mayor Butte has ever had, as far as honesty was concerned. It was generally admitted there was no graft or corruption during his term.

In 1911 the only place the Socialists elected an alderman was in my own seventh ward. I was accused of being responsible for his election because I had refused to keep a Democratic candidate out of the race. There was a feeling the Republican candidate might have beaten the Socialist if the Democrat had not entered the race and split the anti-Socialist vote.

This may have been one reason why I was defeated in the subsequent primary as a delegate to the county convention. It was my first defeat at the polls. I later learned that the Company had passed the word that anyone could go to the convention but me. The Company brought in a lot of people outside my ward to vote for my opponent, Billy Bawden, and I wasn't there to challenge them. I had expected that my election would be routine and was fishing, seventy miles away, on Election Day. Bawden was a friend and neighbor of mine and was a partner in an iron works which did most of its business with the Company.

The county convention elected delegates to the state convention. The state convention held in the spring of 1912 in Butte was to select the delegates to the Democratic National Convention to be held that summer in Baltimore. Walsh wanted to be a delegate-at-large to the national convention and the Silver Bow delegates led the drive for him at the state convention. He was one of the eight Montana delegates who were selected to go to Baltimore with instructions to support Representative Champ Clark of Missouri, then Speaker of the House, for the presidential nomination. Of course, that marathon convention finally chose Woodrow Wilson.

After he was selected as a delegate, Walsh asked me to help him out in a suit he was handling against the Company. I went to see Con Kelley, its chief counsel, to serve some papers and I couldn't resist needling him.

"Well, it looks like you fellows can't beat Walsh now," I said.

"If it wasn't for you and your friends, Walsh never would have been heard of this year," Kelley complained. We left the building together and he seemed friendly enough. But later Tom Norton, a pro-Company member of the legislature, said Kelley told him that he, Kelley, should have "taken Wheeler by the seat of the pants and thrown him out of the office."

Walsh had suggested earlier that I run for the nomination for state attorney general. I wasn't interested. But when the Company beat me as a delegate to the county convention, I changed my mind. I wrote to my friends around the state, telling them I would let my name go up for attorney general in the coming state convention at Great Falls, where the state ticket would be nominated. But I warned them that if they supported me they could expect an uphill fight, inasmuch as I was not even a delegate to the convention.

At Great Falls, the convention chose Walsh as the Democratic Party nominee for the Senate by acclamation. Then the fireworks began. I had three opponents for the nomination. Among them was Dan Kelly, the prosecutor in the Towers case.

The Great Falls *Tribune* reported: "The big fight of the convention proved to be the contest over the nomination for attorney general, which started in a four-cornered contest, resulting in two withdrawals and a finish between the two leaders that, in a horse race, would be referred to as of the eye-lash variety . . . after McConnell of Helena made the nomination of Mr. Kelly there came one of the best things at the convention. It was Colonel Nolan's [Walsh's law partner] nomination of BK Wheeler of Butte. He referred to the fact that Wheeler had been denied a place on the delegation from Silver Bow County and that the candidate was a political orphan thereby, but the colonel bespoke fair consideration for him and declared that he was clean, capable and fearless. He said that it was true that he came from Silver Bow and that he was not one who believed it impossible to find a good man in Silver Bow County. He told of Wheeler's work in the legislature and the fact that he had made foes there because he was fearless. The colonel was at his best and his audience was with him when he spoke."

The first ballot showed: Wheeler, 147; Kelly, 109; Wilson, 106; Verge, 88. I maintained a comfortable lead but on the fifth ballot Verge withdrew and on the seventh ballot Wilson withdrew and asked his supporters to vote for Kelly. This shot Kelly slightly ahead of me–226½ votes to 223½ votes–and gave him the nomination.

The Anaconda *Standard* referred to my "remarkable fight" and noted that "Silver Bow did not support him except with two votes that clung tenaciously from start to finish." Several delegates from Silver Bow insisted they had voted for me but that their votes were not counted. I had no evidence of skulduggery but I had not been overjoyed that the votes were counted by D. Gay Stivers, a lawyer who reputedly headed up the Company's goon squad. Kelly was elected in the Democratic victory that fall. Significantly, he resigned as attorney general in mid-term and joined the Company as a counsel.

Back in Butte, the Democratic ticket for the legislature was again hand-picked by a committee dominated by the Company and as far as I knew I received no consideration at all for renomination. So within a brief time a quick one-two punch showed me what I was up against in fighting this octopus.

During the hectic national election campaign that year, Montana received its usual lively working-over by major political figures. Theodore Roosevelt, the Bull Moose candidate, made a number of stops in his trip across the state. Clarence Darrow spoke in Butte for the Socialist candidates. William Jennings Bryan pulled large crowds in stumping the state for Woodrow Wilson.

The Democrats needed all the speakers they could recruit for eastern Montana. Sentiment was strong for Roosevelt, who had lived on a ranch there and called Montana his second home. I was asked to go over there because they needed someone who wasn't identified with the Company to speak for the whole Democratic ticket. It was the first time I had ever spoken outside Butte. I traveled around with Judge John Hurley who had only one arm. Judge Hurley was a rough-hewn, tobacco-chewing character and a great storyteller. Many of his stories were risqué. At the meetings, the farmers would call out to Hurley and ask if he had any new stories.

I recall speaking in Terry, a little town in Prairie County. The small hall in which I spoke had a stove near the entrance. There were no more than a dozen in the audience. Part way through my speech, a dog trotted up on the platform, sat down and watched me. I finally got a reaction from that cold audience by remarking that the dog was obviously the most intelligent one in the room because he was the only one listening.

Hurley taught me a lot about campaigning in small towns. When we arrived in one, he would make the rounds of the saloons to drum up an audience for the meeting that night. I got acquainted with quite a few people who were very friendly to me when I ran for office later on. Thus this was an invaluable experience, even though the campaign was largely at my own expense.

During the campaign, I heard Walsh speak for the first time. He asked me what I thought about it later. I told him it was a good speech for a bar association meeting but that he was speaking over the heads of the farmers. I suggested to Walsh that he tell a few stories but he said he didn't know how. That was one of the reasons Walsh was always a complete enigma to his fellow Irishmen who dominated Montana political life.

Unlike almost every other Irish politician of that time in Montana, Walsh was no back-slapper. He neither smoked nor drank, and his humor was very dry and rarely expressed. He was of medium height and always dignified, with black hair and a magnificent black mustache which curled at the ends. He impressed the public with his sheer ability, integrity, and industry.

I wound up the campaign by appearing at several rallies in Butte. Both Republicans and Democrats there were concentrating their fire on the Socialist ticket for county offices. Typically, a Republican advertisement warned that the "big mining companies of this district would be compelled to close up their properties for an indefinite period in consequence of the declared policy of Maury and other Socialists." Also typically, a Socialist official charged in an article in the *Miners Magazine* that "Jerry Egan and Roy Alley, leader of the Amalgamated politics in Butte, led the mob of drunken Democratic hoodlums in an attack upon the city hall with threats to 'lynch and murder every damned Socialist in Butte.'"

Wilson carried the state handily over Teddy Roosevelt, with President Taft running a poor third. The Democrats rode into state offices. Outside of South Butte township, where the Socialists elected two justices of the peace and two constables, the Democrats made a clean sweep in the county, although in several places their margin was slim.

The legislature convening in January 1913, acknowledged the unanimous endorsement of Walsh at the state Democratic convention in Great Falls by electing him to the United States Senate overwhelmingly. (Four months later came adoption of the Seventeenth Amendment, providing for direct election of Senators by the people.) The legislature also adopted an amendment to the state constitution providing for woman suffrage, but workmen's compensation legislation again failed to pass.

After his election Walsh told me he would have me named as United States District Attorney when Wilson took office in March. I happened to be in Washington in March for the purpose of being admitted to practice before the Supreme Court. Walsh then told me that the term of James Freeman, then the District Attorney for Montana, had not expired and he offered me the position of solicitor in the Treasury Department. I had no idea what kind of position it was and told Walsh I would not take it unless I could have the D.A. job when Freeman was out. He told me he could not very well do that. So I said I had no desire to move to Washington and would wait for the vacancy as D.A.

It was not until October 1913 that Freeman resigned. The newspapers in Montana then announced that my appointment by Wilson as D.A. was satisfactory to the state's two senators and its two congressmen, Tom Stout and John M. Evans. The Anaconda *Standard* noted that "in the position of U.S.D.A., Mr. Wheeler will be in close touch with the administration and in a position to wield a wide influence politically in Butte and throughout Montana."

The position paid $4000 a year plus expenses. The only way the government could expect to get a competent lawyer to take the D.A. post at that salary was to allow him to continue an outside practice. Thus I was able to continue my own thriving law business in Butte—providing I was willing to keep long hours. I usually returned to my office after dinner and remained there until 10 or 11 o'clock. This schedule, together with my traveling around the state as D.A., left little time for family life. Mrs. Wheeler had to umpire and mediate the usual intra-family squabbles, and she managed to find time also to run the choir in the local Methodist Church and stay active in the Ladies' Aid Society.

Sam Ford, a Republican who had been assistant to Freeman, stayed on at my request for almost a year until I became familiar with the administrative work required in the D.A.'s office. Some Democrats complained about my keeping a Republican on for so long but I wanted all the help I could get. At thirty-one, I was the youngest federal D.A. in the country and anxious to prove myself.

As my assistants I appointed three men who were older than I and who were good lawyers. They were Frank Woody of

Missoula, who had served in the legislature with me; Homer Murphy of Helena, a protégé of Walsh; and James Baldwin of Butte.

The job in Montana required a great deal of travel because federal court was held twice a year in five different places in the state—Butte, Great Falls, Helena, Missoula, and Billings. Billings in the eastern part of the state is about four hundred miles from Missoula in the western part. In addition to the ten regular terms of court, there were often special terms required by a heavy load of cases.

When I took the job, I made up my mind to present all the cases to the grand jury myself and to personally try, or at least assist in trying, every one of my cases in court. I wanted to make the most of this opportunity to become a good trial lawyer. The experience turned out to be as good as I had hoped. For example, I learned early to present my strongest cases first in order to obtain the grand jurors' confidence. Once I had their confidence, I could get an indictment on any case I presented. Indeed, in the average case the grand jury would ask me whether an indictment should be returned. Care was required to prevent an indictment where the case was weak.

This was particularly true in the case of Indians, who were wards of the government. Anti-Indian prejudice was strong in Montana then. The Western sentiment that "the only good Indian is a dead Indian" was still widespread. A federal law at that time made it illegal to sell liquor to an Indian. I immediately discovered, to my disgust, that the government's Indian agents were using decoys to enforce the law.

Here's the way it worked: the Indian agent would send a half-breed—who couldn't be recognized as an Indian—into a saloon and have him buy a drink. The saloonkeeper immediately would be arrested. There was a time when all the saloonkeepers in Helena were under indictment simultaneously, all through the use of decoys.

My first step was to call together all the saloonkeepers in each community and tell them I would not permit evidence to be gathered in this way because it was abhorrent. But I made it clear I would prosecute them to the limit if I caught them breaking the law. At the same time, I dismissed a number of cases in which the violations had been brought about by decoys.

One Indian agent angrily told me he would report all this to Washington. I told him I would appreciate that because I had been trying to think of a way to call this despicable practice to the attention of my superiors. I never heard anything more about that threat. The situation in my opinion stemmed from the fact that the Commissioner of Indian Affairs, Cato Sells, a Texan, was a fanatical prohibitionist. His main conception of his duties as "protector" of the Indians was to see to it that they did not come into contact with firewater.

In trying these bootlegging cases, I found out how to tell when a full-blooded Indian was lying on the witness stand. If he talked with an expressive use of his hands, in the traditional fashion, he was sure to be telling the truth; if he held his hands in his lap and failed to get enthusiastic about what he was saying, I could make up my mind that he was telling a lie.

There was a good deal less federal regulation of commerce and industry then than there is today and bootlegging among Indians was one of only five categories of cases that commonly turned up. The others involved counterfeiting, white slavery, postal violations, and land fraud cases. Since I had practiced law by myself most of the time up to then, I was accustomed to rely on my own judgment in trial work. I was not used to seeking advice or accepting advice, much less dictation, from anyone. Now, when I went into court as D.A., I frequently found that witnesses had disappeared or died. I would inform the judge of this fact and he would dismiss the case. One agent sent out from Washington by the Justice Department told me I would get into trouble if I did not first get clearance in writing from the Attorney General before moving a dismissal after an indictment had been obtained. I explained there was actually no time for such communication back and forth and that I was willing to take the responsibility for all the dismissals in my district. That was the last I ever heard of that.

At the same time, I managed to clean up a backlog of cases which had been gathering dust in the D.A.'s office. One of the most interesting involved Ben Phillips, a prominent Montana Republican charged with land fraud. Phillips had been indicted at least eight years previously but under two successive national Republican administrations there had been no urge to prosecute him.

Phillips, like a good many others in the early days of the West, would employ people to move to unoccupied land, set up a shack (which was on wheels and could easily be removed), and supposedly do enough work to qualify for 160 acres under the Homestead Act. After this employee had obtained his patent to the land, he would deed it over to his employer (Phillips), who paid all his expenses and let him keep a small piece of the tract.

In this way, Phillips had obtained thousands of acres—so many indeed that a county in northeastern Montana was named after him. (It was so large it later had to be subdivided into several counties.) Phillips was charged with defrauding the government but when I suggested prosecuting the case Attorney General Thomas W. Gregory asked me whether it would be worthwhile, since it was weak in evidence and weak in law. I pointed out that "here is a man who stole a whole county" and said I wanted to give it a try. I went ahead and Phillips pleaded guilty. He was fined $500 by Judge George M. Bourquin, the federal judge for the district of Montana. I was not satisfied, but there was nothing I could do. Judge Bourquin never conferred with me about the sentences he would impose.

Bourquin was handsome and distinguished looking, with an austere glint in his eye, and was one of the few men in Montana who carried a cane—a gold-headed one. He had served as chairman of the Republican state convention in 1912 and had sat for one term as state district judge in Butte. I had supported his Democratic opponent, Jimmy Healy, when he ran for that office and so we were not very friendly when we began our relationship.

Judge Bourquin was a model of judicial integrity. He would never permit anyone to talk with him about a case. Rather than risk an offhand conversation with anyone on his travels around the state, he went out of his way to keep strangers at more than arm's length. When he sat down to dinner in a hotel dining room, he would insist that the other chairs at the table be turned up, to discourage anyone who might be tempted to join him. Immediately after dinner, he would retire to his room for the evening. He never allowed anyone to sit next to him on the train. He was a naturally very nervous and irritable person and had a reputation for dealing harshly with anyone who sought to influence him in the slightest. I never went near him but Homer Murphy used to go into his chambers and tell him risqué stories which made the judge laugh.

The judge was conscientious and extremely hard working. As soon as my staff and I finished presenting a case, he would call for the next one without a recess, and we might have four or five cases tried in a single day. This kept us up late nearly every night preparing for the following day.

In the summer of 1915 I enjoyed my first real vacation. With Lulu and the children—there were now three—I camped out at the foot of Lake McDonald in Glacier National Park for several weeks. Up to then, I had had only a few days of fishing at a time down on the Madison River in southern Montana. Our vacation was virtually a court order from Bourquin. Near the end of a sixty-day session at Great Falls, in June 1915, he said to me: "When this term of court is over, you get out and go up in the mountains. You're getting nervous and irritable and the court is getting irritable and we might have a blow up and it won't do either of us any good to go on this way. I'm going away to the mountains for a rest and you should certainly do the same."

Judge Bourquin was always very lenient with a defendant. Sam Ford, my Republican holdover assistant, used to take a fellow who had pled guilty and dress him down roughly in court to try to impress the judge with the severity of the crime. When I objected to this, Ford told me I was "chicken-hearted." But I told Ford that his trouble was that he had never been on the other side defending anyone. I said he had been on the public payroll prosecuting people ever since he left college.

I discovered that I got better results in dealing with Judge

Bourquin by relying on simple presentation of the facts rather than adopting the role of the relentless prosecutor. In October 1914 I brought suit against the Great Northern Railway and the Winston Brothers for $250,000 for starting forest fires along their roadbeds in the Flathead and Lewis and Clark National Forests. William Wallace, then assistant United States Attorney General, told me he didn't think I could win any case against the Great Northern, which had already carved out a tremendous empire along the northwestern part of the country. I told him I thought I could get a conviction and I did.

However, the judgment awarded was a mere $50,000 and I suspected the companies had gotten to someone on the jury. They were represented by Tom Walker of Butte and a well-known corporation lawyer from Minneapolis. The out-of-state lawyer kept filling the record with a variety of extraneous matters. Murphy, my assistant, kept after me to object but I told him to be quiet. I was biding my time. I watched Judge Bourquin get more and more restless. Finally, he could stand it no longer.

"If the District Attorney won't object to these questions, I will," he said irritably. His objection to the defense's tactics was much more effective with the jury than my objections would have been.

I was similarly suspicious of jury tampering in a bankruptcy case I tried against Bill O'Leary of Great Falls, one of the ablest criminal lawyers in Montana. Murphy tried it the first time and got a hung jury and so I tried it again. I managed to get a conviction. When I accused O'Leary informally of having had a man on the first jury, he told me he had never fixed a jury in his life.

But he admitted to this practice: every time there was a wedding in town, he would send flowers or a little present. Whenever a baby was born in Great Falls, the parents would get a congratulatory note from O'Leary. When there was a funeral, he sent a wreath. So, O'Leary told me, he was always sure of having someone on a jury who remembered him gratefully.

As D.A., I too used my knowledge of human nature in the

selection of a jury. For example, I always excused Charley Russell, the famous painter of Montana cowboys and Indians, when he turned up on a panel of veniremen. Russell was the kind of person who would never vote to convict.

My political future in Montana was at stake when I prosecuted the Northwestern Trustee Company case. This was a corporation organized, according to their literature, to engage in large-scale building of houses and apartment houses throughout Montana and to lend money to farmers at six and eight per cent through a land bank to be established. A number of prominent men in business and politics were involved. The company had been organized by William Rae, Democratic state treasurer; A. M. Alderson, Democratic secretary of state; D. G. Bertoglio, an important Democratic businessman in Butte; J. W. Spear, ex-mayor of Great Falls and a prominent attorney; and several Republican bankers.

The picture of Democratic Governor Sam Stewart was printed on one of the fancy brochures and he was described as one of the leading stockholders, although he had not actually bought any stock in the company. Stock was issued at par value of $10 a share. Two fiscal agents and real promoters, Robert M. Sidebothan, and J. G. Wilmont, sold a lot of the stock to farmers for a fee of 25 per cent on all sales. They optioned off the balance of the stock to the directors at five dollars and $7.50 a share on loans on property and then proceeded to raise the stock to $20 and $30 a share without rhyme or reason.

The case was first brought to my attention by the postal inspector, who charged the directors with using the mails to defraud. The inspector said he thought I might not want to prosecute the case because there were so many prominent Democratic politicians involved. I told him if he had the evidence I would prosecute. Rae, who was a good friend of mine, came to me to find out if there wasn't some way he could be left out. I told him there was no way. He asked me if I would object if he took the matter to Washington. I told him not at all. I said if the Attorney General told me to drop the case I would do so.

Rae took up the case with Attorney General Gregory, who

refused to interfere. I told Rae I had to either go ahead with the case or resign.

Assistant Attorney General Wallace, who was a former attorney for the Northern Pacific Railway, told me later that if I had not gone ahead with the case he would have thought I was as guilty as the defendants were. Both Rae and Alderson had voted for my nomination for state attorney general at the 1912 convention.

Nonetheless, I got them all indicted in July 1916 for using the mails to defraud by falsely alleging that the concern was profitable and capable of paying a dividend of six per cent from the time of organization. I requested an early trial but it was put off until after the election that fall. The Democrats faced a hard fight to stay in the top offices of the state.

Needless to say, the Democratic politicians were furious at me. I did issue a statement just before the election absolving Governor Stewart of official connection with the scheme. Certain Republican speakers had been insinuating that the governor was involved. At the same time, I recommended that the legislature pass a law forbidding all state officials from permitting their names to be used in connection with any corporation selling stock to the public and making them ineligible to serve as directors or officers of any private corporation.

Rae and Alderson were defeated in their races for re-election as state treasurer and secretary of state, respectively. Stewart was re-elected governor but by only 9000 votes; Wilson carried the state by 35,000.

The case finally came to trial in January 1917, in Helena, while the legislature was in session there. The Helena *Independent* reported that the "cream of legal talent of the state was involved." Colonel Nolan, Walsh's law partner, was one of the defense attorneys. Rae and Alderson were represented by Albert Galen, former Republican state attorney and brother-in-law of former U. S. Senator Thomas H. Carter; and by Dan Kelly, former Democratic state attorney general and now a Company lawyer. Sidebothan was represented by Henry C. Smith, a former judge of the Supreme Court of Montana, and James Hawley, a former governor of Idaho.

The principal charge was that the Northwestern Trustee Company had sold stock on the representation that the proceeds would go into the company's treasury when actually over 30 per cent was used for promotional expenses. Most of the prosecution witnesses were farmers who testified that they bought stock because of the promise of big dividends which never materialized and because of the prominence of the names of the directors and officers. Kelly, inevitably, charged in his argument to the jury that the case had been instigated by me for the "political assassination of Rae and Alderson."

During the trial I asked Judge Bourquin to lock up the jury because the defendants were prominent politicians who spent a lot of time around the hotel lobbies and in bars in Helena. I told the judge I had seen Kelly buying a drink for one of the jurors and talking to several of them in a hotel lobby. At the end of the session that day, Judge Bourquin noted my request about locking up the jurors. But he announced he would allow them to go their ways—with the extra precaution of reminding them to do their duty as a jury.

The trial lasted ten days and the judge then virtually instructed the jury to bring in a verdict of guilty for all the defendants. The jury found only Sidebothan and Wilmont guilty, and on only one count. Judge Bourquin called me in and was very upset because the jury had ignored his instruction.

"You told me about those attorneys buying drinks for the jurors," he snapped. "I think you should cite them for contempt of court."

I then told him that additionally one of the government agents from Washington had seen Galen and Kelly making signs to one of the jurors through a window in the jury room while the jury was deliberating. However, I reminded him I had asked to have the jury locked up during the trial and since he had refused it would now look like I was a poor loser and wanted to get even with these two attorneys by citing them for contempt.

"The fact that you've got a building in Butte that you haven't paid for shouldn't deter you from doing your duty," Judge Bourquin replied sternly. This was a reference to a hotel I had recently built in Butte. The judge was throwing out the ridiculous hint that I was afraid my mortgage would be foreclosed through the Company's influence if I cited Galen and Kelly.

When I continued to do nothing about the contempt charges despite his prompting, Judge Bourquin asked my assistant, Homer Murphy, to get me to file them. That didn't work either so he finally sent for me and made out a court order directing me to file the charges.

When they were tried, Kelly denied under oath he had bought a drink for a juror. Sitting in the audience was J. Wellington Rankin, a prominent Republican lawyer and brother of Representative Jeannette Rankin of Montana. Rankin had been with me and several others when we had all spotted Kelly in earnest conversation with the juror in the hotel lobby. We had watched them repair to the bar, where Kelly had stood the juror to at least one shot. Much to his amazement, I called Rankin to the stand, and he testified to the above facts.

The juror who got the drink was a railway employee from Deer Lodge, Montana. He admitted on the stand that he had approached Galen and Kelly during the trial but only to discuss a piece of legislation in the legislature. He denied talking to them about the case. The aforementioned special agent from Washington testified that he had seen both Galen and Kelly signaling to a juror at the window while the verdict was being reached. Joe Kirschwing, a former colleague of mine in the legislature, also testified against the two attorneys on this charge.

Judge Bourquin fined Galen and Kelly $500 each for their misconduct. Galen and Kelly appealed their convictions to the Circuit Court of Appeals, which upheld the fines. Galen then applied for certiorari to the United States Supreme Court for a hearing but was turned down.

The newspapers reported that Galen beat up Kirschwing for testifying. Afterward, every time Galen got drunk, which was quite often, he went up and down the streets of Helena cursing "BK" (as I always was known in my Montana days). Kelly also nursed a grudge against me for the contempt conviction.

As for the Montana newspapers, my prosecution of the defense attorneys in the case and its aftermath only made them step up their already bitter attacks on me.

I didn't forget these ugly events either. In 1929 President Herbert Hoover decided to appoint Galen to the Interstate Commerce Commission. When notification of this came to me as a Montana senator, I went to Hoover and told him I would oppose confirmation of Galen because he had tampered with a jury. The President told me he was aware of the incident but pointed out that Galen had since distinguished himself as a major in the Army in World War I and had been elected to the Montana State Supreme Court.

I told Hoover I was familiar with Galen's entire record—including the fact that he had voted on the side of the railroads in every railroad case that came before him on the Supreme Court. I reiterated that I would fight the nomination.

President Charles Donnelly of the Northern Pacific Railroad, a former Montana lawyer and friend of Galen, vainly tried to make me withdraw my opposition to Galen. So did Frank Kerr, president of the Montana Power Company. President Hoover finally nominated William E. Lee, from Idaho, a local attorney for the Northern Pacific, to the vacancy on the ICC. Galen later campaigned unsuccessfully for the Senate in 1930 against Walsh. He died afterward when he fell out of a boat and was drowned.

Chapter Six

LIBEL, MAYHEM, AND MURDER

During the years immediately preceding our entry into the First World War I took some interesting cases which were unconnected with my role as District Attorney. One resulted in my being challenged to a duel and another made me the unsympathetic prosecutor in a bizarre murder case. This period further alienated me from the Company because it dramatized my sympathies for the rights of organized labor during a series of violent events in Butte.

In June 1914 open rebellion broke out in the Miners union against its leadership on the ground that it was too conservative, despite the fact that some of its officers were Socialists and the Company felt its leaders were becoming too radical.

An angry faction marched on the union's own hall on North Main Street in Butte, urged on by many mischief-minded strangers in the city. The demonstrators dissolved into a mob which gutted the hall, destroying furniture and records. A few of them carried off the burglarproof safe containing $1600. A new union was quickly organized. It claimed 4000 enrolled members immediately and refused to affiliate with the Western Federation of Miners. Its leaders, I subsequently learned, were members of the IWW and detectives hired by the Company to infiltrate the union and foment trouble. It was part of the Company's plan to break the strong Miners union.

When President Charles Moyer of the WFM held a membership meeting in what was left of the union hall, a crowd of unhappy miners and the curious gathered outside. A union member entering the building to attend the meeting was shot in the head, apparently from the inside of the hall. Guns blazed immediately from the windows and in the street, killing one passer-by and wounding several others. After the hall was emptied, a group of men went to a nearby mine, stole a large quantity of dynamite, and proceeded to blow up the hall. It was completely leveled.

The June week tensions became even worse in the later summer when the Company shut down seven of its Butte mines and laid off 2000 miners.

There was a brief quiet period during which the new union claimed it had enrolled 8200 members, despite the Company's use of the layoff to weed out militant workers who it said were responsible for the mass repudiation of the old union. Then, in late August, violence erupted again. At midnight, an office maintained by the Company at one of its mines was dynamited. It was the office which issued "rustling cards," or permits without which a miner could not seek employment—and which the miners considered an effective system for "black-listing" the dissidents.

The union charged that the Company had blown up its own office to throw suspicion on the new union. It was noted earlier that day forty leading citizens of Butte had secured permits to carry guns and had organized a new-style vigilante group to protect "the business and homes of Butte."

In early September, Governor Stewart was prevailed on to call out the state militia. Butte was suddenly under martial law. In charge of the National Guard was Major D. J. Donohue and Major Jesse B. Roote. Roote had served with me in the legislature and we used to kid him because he carried a gun during the sessions; now he was judge of the summary court. Leaders of the new union were arrested and charged with inciting a riot by making speeches against military rule. Others were held in jail without bond on charges of carrying concealed weapons.

Once martial law was in force, the Company reopened its mines. It then announced it had reached an agreement with the other mine owners not to recognize either the new or the old union. Thus was abolished the closed shop which had prevailed for several score years in Butte. It was not until 1934 that the Company again recognized any union of its miners.

Next Socialist Mayor Duncan and Democratic Sheriff Tim Driscoll were impeached "for refusing and neglecting to perform their official duties" in connection with the disturbances. Among those supporting the proceedings was my old rival, Dan Kelly, now the state attorney general and soon to be a lawyer for the Company. Judge Roy Ayers of Lewistown was called in to preside over the impeachment. Ayers heard the testimony and on October 6 removed Duncan and Driscoll from office. The city council elected its president, Clarence Smith, another Socialist, to succeed Duncan and the county commissioners appointed John Berkin, a foreman at a Company mine, to succeed Driscoll.

Duncan said: "I have not been ousted because I neglected to do my duty but because I had the courage to act by a higher human principle than is approved by the capitalist class. I have regarded human life as of greater moment and value than property . . . I did not issue an order which, if obeyed by the police of the city, would have cost hundreds of lives and would have settled nothing." Driscoll stated tersely: "If I had to kill a thousand men to hold the job, I don't want the job."

The militia took its work seriously. Commandant Donohue warned H. Lowndes Maury, a Socialist and soon to be my law partner, to cease agitating or go to jail. As a member of the school board, Maury had introduced a resolution protesting the occupation of the school by the militia. Two weeks later Maury was barred from trying cases in military court "because of inflammatory utterances."

However, the state Supreme Court on October 8, 1914, ruled out the use of military courts and ordered that all prosecutions be turned over to civil authorities in civil courts. It held that the writ of habeas corpus may not be abolished. The high court upheld the right of the governor to send troops but for all practical purposes the decision took the heart out of military rule and it ended a month later.

Meanwhile, the Anaconda *Standard* was seeking to alarm the public with rumors of a coming invasion by the IWW. The story, fantastic as it sounds, was that a marauding band of IWW's, apparently 3000 strong and more bloodthirsty than any war party of Blackfeet Indians, was heading toward Butte out of northeast Montana. Nothing turned up to support the scare headlines.

I was not in Butte when the violence began in June but along with many others in Butte I suspected the Company was responsible for it. It was common knowledge that the Company had brought in a good many Pinkerton and Thiele detectives who became leading members of the IWW and agitated in the new union after the leadership of the old one had been discredited. Indeed, Major Donohue told me some time after he directed the military rule in Butte that from his personal knowledge a big majority of the alleged labor leaders during the riots were detectives.

In any event, the net result of the violence to the Company was achievement of two objectives—to rid it of any contractual relationship with a union and to terminate the administration of Socialist Duncan. I went to the Company myself to try to set up a meeting with the union leaders looking toward a new relationship, but L. O. Evans, chief counsel for the Company, dismissed my efforts with the statement that I was obviously prejudiced in favor of the workingmen.

Soon I became involved in an interesting case which came as an aftermath of military rule. Clarence Smith, who had succeeded Duncan as Socialist mayor of Butte, was arrested on a charge of criminal libel for an article in the Butte *Socialist* in which one Otto Pufahl was described as an "alcoholic degenerate" in a story of a barroom incident. Pufahl had bought two of the occupation soldiers a drink and a bystander had struck him, remarking, "Take that, you soldier-loving S.O.B." Pufahl had the fellow arrested by the two soldiers. He later was released on the plea of his sweetheart after he had agreed to kiss the American flag.

Alec Mackel, who was city attorney and one of the older lawyers defending the Socialists and union leaders, asked me to look over the information in the case. I decided it was defective and convinced Mackel that it was. Mackel then asked me to argue the demurrer over in Bozeman, a farming community where the case had been transferred. I ended up arguing the whole case for the defense, with the assistance of a Republican judge, E. K. Cheadle, and a local attorney. I was severely criticized in the newpapers for defending a man in the state courts while I was federal D.A. There was of course nothing improper or unethical in doing this at the time.

Smith's defense against the libel charge was that it was true. A number of witnesses from Butte testified that Pufahl was frequently drunk in public. Pufahl insisted that a periodic jag did not constitute degeneracy, and he won admission from some of the defense witnesses that they had observed other men in Butte just as drunk.

I argued with Judge Benjamin Law over what constituted criminal libel. He contended that truth of the statement was not a valid defense to a criminal libel action. "Suppose a man maliciously publishes something that is true?" he asked. I maintained that libel is malicious defamation and that in order to defame one must make a false statement.

We insisted that the arrest of Smith was simply political persecution. Cheadle asked the jury of ranchers: "Who believes that the defendant would be here if he were not mayor of Butte and he were not a Socialist?"

Closing the argument for the defense, I said: "I came here not to defend Clarence Smith as a Socialist but to see justice. If the county attorney can send a man to jail because he is a Socialist, he can send you there because you are a Democrat or a Republican." I insisted the evidence showed that Pufahl had degraded himself. Referring to Pufahl's complaint that after publication of the article, the schoolteachers in Butte would not speak to him, I said publication of the article was a blessing to the schoolteachers of Butte.

"I think the fair girls of Silver Bow County deserve to be saved from the likes of that man," I told the jury. "If the statements in that article were not true, why did not Pufahl go back to the stand and deny them?"

As for the testimony regarding Pufahl's unsavory reputation, I said that if this testimony were not true the county attorney should prosecute the witnesses for perjury.

The county prosecutor, Joseph McCaffery, told the jury that in deciding the case "you will say to the newspapers, 'You shall not libel our citizens.'"

To McCaffery's obvious amazement, the jury acquitted Smith. Judge Law told me later that if the jury had not acquitted him, he would have had to throw the case out on the ground that the information was defectively drawn, as I had originally found.

McCaffery by this time had been defeated for re-election by my former law partner, Matt Canning. When Canning took office in January, he immediately dismissed the libel case against the assistant editor of the Butte *Socialist* arising out of the same story about Pufahl. Canning's chief deputy, A. B. Melzner, also dismissed cases against a number of miners charged with destroying jail property during their detention. And thus the slate was wiped clean of the arrests made during the two months of military rule in Butte.

In the spring of 1915 Charles Lane, a Democrat, was elected mayor of Butte along with nine Democratic candidates for aldermen. The Socialists were knocked out of all municipal offices and the four-year reign of the Socialists in Butte was ended.

During 1915–16 I undertook two other important cases which had nothing to do with my job as D.A. In one I defended some labor leaders and in the other I prosecuted a murder case.

In April 1915 the Empire Theatre in Butte dispensed with its union musicians and the musicians union promptly threw a picket line around not only the theater but also the property of every merchant who crossed the picket line to go to the theater. The theater went into court and got a temporary injunction against the union and the Silver Bow Trades and Labor Council, restraining them from continuing the picketing.

The unions asked me to serve as chief defense counsel during the show-cause hearing. The hearing turned into a massive battle of witnesses and lasted seventeen days. The employers of Butte were out to attack the secondary boycott as a weapon of organized labor; it had been upheld as a constitutional exercise of free speech by the Montana State Supreme Court. A total of eighty-eight businessmen paraded to the stand to tell the dire consequences of the boycott. They were directed by attorney Jesse B. Roote, who had been judge of the summary courts during the period of martial law. I countered with seventy-eight witnesses who testified that they had not been threatened in any manner by the union representatives who carried the "unfair" banner in front of the theater.

The Anaconda *Standard* reported one incident during the trial which reflected the bitterness that still existed over the stormy destruction of the Miners union and its closed shop.

"During the examination of Charles Copenharve, city editor of the *Standard*," the article related, "inharmony broke loose. Attorney Roote had been trying to introduce some testimony as to what took place during the 'reign of terror' in Butte last summer. The court did not think it advisable to go into the matter but attorney Wheeler said he would have no objection if it were meant to go into the 'reign of terror of the military courts' of which Major Roote has been a part.

"Later attorney Roote, in seeking the same kind of information asked the witness if any committee called on him 'at the time when Muckie McDonald and other anarchists were trying to run the town with the assistance of the United States District Attorney.'

"Attorney Wheeler, who holds the position of District Attorney, was up on his feet in a minute. 'I suggest that Major Roote go on the stand!' he exclaimed.

"'If you want me to go on the stand, I'll do it,' Roote replied, 'and tell how he sent a telegram to Senator Walsh he was ashamed to sign. I would not have referred to this but he insulted me when he made his reference to the military courts.'

"'I know you are very touchy on the subject,' began Wheeler. 'We cannot try this matter out here,' exclaimed Judge Clements."

Roote was so furious at me that after the altercation in court he actually challenged me to a duel. He was a hot-headed Southerner and so I forgot about his silly challenge and he never mentioned it again. As for the wire he was referring to, I have no idea what he had in mind, inasmuch as I never sent any wire to Walsh during the military occupation or at any other time.

Roote refrained from speaking to me throughout the trial, presumably considering it beneath his dignity. He did deign to speak with Jimmy Healy, who was assisting me in trying the case. Originally, he suggested to Healy that I name three judges for the hearing and he would select one of the three. I named the aforementioned John Hurley, with whom I had stumped during the 1912 campaign; Benjamin Law, who had presided over the Smith libel trial; and James M. Clements. Judge Clements was considered very close to the Company but he was also friendly to me because I had once done him a favor. Healy, not knowing this, had warned me not to name Clements because Roote would surely seize on that name.

Roote did pick Clements and felt so good about his choice he acted extremely cocky throughout the trial, even to the extent of leaning cozily on the judge's bench while presenting his case. He dragged in every conceivable piece of evidence which he thought might prejudice the judge. Healy and I objected but Judge Clements overruled us and it began to look as if he were on the side of the plaintiff.

In my summation argument, I stressed the importance of the case in the eyes of organized labor in Butte. The *Standard* reported my argument as follows:

"Attorney Wheeler followed for the defense. He said the defendants were called on to defend an action not only of the Empire Theatre but every one of the charges the detectives of the employers' association could find after raking the city with a fine-tooth comb. Much of the testimony, he said, was hearsay . . . he claimed he was not defending the Empire suit but one instituted and instigated by the so-called employers' association.

"'The two greatest weapons in the hands of labor are the strike and the boycott. There is no question but the strike is legal. Notwithstanding persons may be injured in their business, courts have held so and public opinion has recognized this principle.

". . . 'It is necessary to have labor organizations in the community,' he concluded. 'The plaintiff is merely a tool of capital to dominate the labor organizations which have done so much to build up this community. There is an effort to show the best citizens are trying to break up organized labor not only in this county but the state.' He described the testimony of some of the witnesses for the plaintiff as 'vilifying evidence' by men who had been opposed to organized labor for years. 'The Supreme Court has held that if a man were clothed with a right he did not lose that right when he did the same thing in combination with others . . . in the present case the purpose was to get the public not to patronize the Empire.'"

Two weeks later Judge Clements denied the injunction in the Empire case. He scathingly denounced the unions for resorting to such a weapon—calling it "repugnant to my personal sense of justice"—but held that under the law he could make no other ruling. He had struck a notable blow for that kind of boycott at the time. The decision was appealed by the theater on up to the state Supreme Court, where the denial of the injunction was affirmed.

My most exciting criminal case was offered to me by Wade Parks, the prosecutor in Sanders County at the extreme western end of the state. I knew Parks personally and had marveled at the wild-eyed proposals he had made at state Democratic conventions. He was a good talker but was an old Socialist who was more interested in philosophy than he was in the law. He was inexperienced in trial work and now he was faced with a murder case which was too much for him. He asked me to come in and handle it as a special prosecutor.

The murder had occurred on September 28, 1916, in broad daylight on a main street of the picturesque little town of Thompson Falls, which is the county seat and close to the Idaho boundary. Miss Edith Colby, a newspaper reporter, had shot A. C. Thomas, owner of a rival paper and chairman of the Republican central committee of Sanders County. Miss Colby explained that Thomas had called her a whore. The incident had grown out of some bitter political warfare.

Until recently, Miss Colby for six years had resided in Spokane, Washington. She was to be defended by John I. Mulligan, a prominent Republican in Spokane and well-known as a clever criminal lawyer. Parks was scared to death of tangling with Mulligan, who had written a book on his profession. Parks also was well aware that sympathy in Thompson Falls was almost 100 per cent on the side of Miss Colby. After all, she had been subjected to the ultimate insult for a woman. I decided to take the case because it would be a supreme test in courtroom tactics. No woman had ever been convicted in Montana of more than manslaughter.

The case came to trial early in December in the little Thompson Falls courthouse. The room was jammed to the doorknobs with the press and public. The case had attracted headlines all over the country and the trial was being covered by special correspondents from the Hearst syndicate and the major press associations. Once again, Judge Clements was presiding.

The defense was insanity. Miss Colby was forty-three years old, a comely woman, tall, well dressed, and intelligent, exuding the respectability of a clubwoman. Mulligan put her on the stand early. She explained quietly that she had been interested in politics in Spokane. She had served as assistant city labor agent and had been an unsuccessful candidate for city commissioner in 1915. Parks and I had learned that she also had been a detective for a time in Spokane, working with the Pinkerton and Thiele agencies, but we didn't know the nature of her work.

Miss Colby testified to having had some treatment for mental illness. During one stay in a sanitarium, she said, she had become engaged to be married to the doctor who was in charge of the institution, but nothing had come of this. Ever since, she said she had had attacks of nervousness and had been troubled with insomnia.

She related she had come to Thompson Falls during the summer of 1916 to work as a reporter on the *Independent Enterprise,* which was hotly opposed to Thomas' leadership of the Republican party there. While working on an assignment she had criticized Thomas to his face. He had replied by telling her she ought to be "down on 'the line'" (in the red-light district) along with the other prostitutes. (Thomas obviously had used the term figuratively rather than literally; no one would ever mistake Miss Colby for a Jezebel.)

Infuriated, the defendant testified, she had borrowed a .32-calibre revolver and, at ten-thirty the next morning, had accosted Thomas on the sidewalk as he was leaving a hotel. She demanded an apology.

"He sneered at me and doubled up his fist like he was going to strike me," she continued. So she promptly opened fire. There were four shots. Two missed Thomas altogether but one struck him in the abdomen and the other in the right arm. He died some hours later.

When I began my cross-examination, I ran into trouble as soon as I brought up the shooting. Miss Colby abruptly rose from the witness chair and ran to the open window, where she gulped some fresh air. Then she suddenly fell in a heap beside the jury box as if in a faint. She was quickly revived and I decided to postpone further questioning about the murder incident. I started asking her questions about Worcester, Massachusetts, where she had been raised.

Worcester is near my home town of Hudson and I had been there many times. I drew Miss Colby out about her home town and her early life. She responded fully and keenly. Mulligan got worried because her interest in my questions revealed Miss Colby to be quite alert and normal.

"I object!" he finally called out to Judge Clements.

"Well, what is the purpose of these questions?" the judge said, turning to me.

"It ought to be very apparent to the Court why I am asking these questions, in view of the plea of insanity," I replied. The objection was overruled.

I continued to ask Miss Colby about Worcester and she finally commented with a smile, "Apparently you know as much about Worcester as I do." She was now perfectly relaxed and I thought it was safe to return to the circumstances of the murder. I brought out that after she had been insulted by Thomas she had consulted a local attorney. This fellow had blandly suggested that she had three alternatives. She could slap Thomas' face, get a whip and horsewhip him, or get a gun and shoot him. This was about the most incredible advice I have ever heard of a lawyer giving a client. Miss Colby had forthwith acted on Alternative No. 3. (Previously the defense had put on the stand Justice of the Peace W. E. Nippert, who testified that Miss Colby had consulted him after the insult and he had said he would applaud her—not fine her—if she slapped Thomas' face.)

My next questions went as follows:

WHEELER: When you talked to your lawyer and he told you to go and buy a gun, you intended to go and buy that gun?

MISS COLBY: Yes.

WHEELER: You went out with the intention of meeting Thomas, didn't you?

MISS COLBY: Yes.

WHEELER: When you met him you intended to ask him to apologize, didn't you?

MISS COLBY: Yes.

WHEELER: And when he wouldn't apologize you pulled out your gun and aimed at him—and you intended to aim at him, didn't you?

MISS COLBY: Yes.

WHEELER: And when you pulled the trigger you intended to pull it, didn't you?

MISS COLBY: Yes.

Now I had established premeditation. Winding up my cross-examination, I startled the witness and the courtroom audience by suddenly pointing my finger at a woman in the audience dressed in a black veil and deep mourning. She was Thomas' widow.

"Did you know Mrs. Thomas?" I cried. "Did you know her when you fatally fired the shots?"

Miss Colby's frame shook with sobs as she replied: "At that time, I did not even know there *was* a Mrs. Thomas."

Mulligan interjected pompously: "This is the meanest trick I ever saw done in a courtroom."

A key witness for the defense was to be Dr. E. L. Kimball of Spokane, a specialist in mental illness, or an "alienist," as they were called in those days. Dr. Kimball was to testify on Monday. To be ready to tackle him, I called to Thompson Falls on Friday the former superintendent of the Montana State Hospital for the Insane, Dr. A. C. Knight. Over the weekend Dr. Knight and I strolled around the town while he drilled me in the various types of mental illness, their symptoms and effects.

On the witness stand, Dr. Kimball testified that Miss Colby was too ill at the time of the murder to be responsible for her act. He said she was suffering from "emotional melancholy." When I began the cross-examination, I was worried, as I had been all weekend, that I would be unable to keep straight in my mind all the ramifications of insanity on which I had been briefed by Dr. Knight. But luckily it all came back to me with crystal clearness. As I began to question the alienist, I placed before me on the table a 500-page volume whose title the witness could not see. It was a law book having nothing to do with the mind, but I kept referring to it as if it were the latest treatise on psychiatry. I bluffed my way through a long and involved discussion of the various types of mental disorders.

The cross-examination lasted nearly three hours. The purpose was to draw Dr. Kimball into such a detailed explanation of insanity that the jury—and possibly the doctor himself—would become confused. After the session, Dr. Kimball approached me mopping his brow.

"I've been on the witness stand a hundred times but that was the most grueling cross-examination I've ever had," he said. "What school did you graduate from?"

"Michigan," I said.

"I knew it," he said, grinning. "I'm from Michigan. I graduated from Michigan."

The next day I summoned Dr. Knight, my weekend tutor, to the stand. In part, this dialogue took place:

WHEELER: Would you say Miss Colby is insane medically or is she criminally insane?

DR. KNIGHT: I would say in my opinion she is not criminally insane, is not medically insane in the light of the definitions I have given. . . .

WHEELER: Is hysteria insanity?

DR. KNIGHT: No.

WHEELER: How do you come to the conclusion Miss Colby is not insane?

DR. KNIGHT: From the education she received, her nervous attacks, her ability to hold various positions, her explanation of many of her acts . . . she went and secured a gun and had it in her possession, that being a criminal act . . .

WHEELER: Does she come under any of the different classes of insanity considered?

DR. KNIGHT: No.

Under cross-examination by Mulligan, Dr. Knight said that disappointment in love, change of life, and other conditions could cause insanity.

MULLIGAN: This girl not being able to sleep except with chloroform for a year after that second love affair, failing in business affairs, coming to Montana, having a man tell her she was a "red-light woman" and he would put her in the red-light district, you think all these conditions would not produce insanity?

DR. KNIGHT: Yes.

MULLIGAN: You think these conditions *could* produce insanity?

DR. KNIGHT: Yes.

Parks, who assisted me during the trial, turned out to be none too stable himself. He had an obsession about being spied on. He had been a detective himself at one time, working for the Western Federation of Miners and Clarence Darrow back in 1907 when Darrow defended "Big Bill" Haywood of the WFM in Boise, Idaho. One aspect of that case had amused me. Parks said they had brought in a pretty woman to get next to William E. Borah, who was prosecuting the union officials for the state, but that she had fallen in love with Borah and the union never could get a word of information out of her. I later became a great friend and admirer of Borah during our years of association in the Senate.

Parks was upset when we discovered the defense had imported a number of detectives from Spokane to try to find out what we were doing. One night we were out for a walk and heard what sounded like a gunshot. Parks jumped a couple of feet and said, "My God, they're shooting at us!" When he calmed down, he reminded me again of how careless it was for me to leave the door of my hotel room unlocked. I told him there was nothing the detectives could find in my room except some dirty shirts. Parks was so nervous that when we discussed the case in his county attorney's office he would keep his hand on top of the little wood-burning stove there. He was afraid it had been wired electronically to eavesdrop on us and he claimed he could jam the results in this fashion.

Parks gave our opening summation of the case. He made a reference to testimony by Miss Colby's mother, who dramatically sat beside her throughout the trial, frequently sobbing and wringing her hands. She had come from Worcester for the trial.

"You know from the words of her aged mother that Miss Colby was a detective in Spokane," Parks said to the jury of farmers and ranchers. He had hardly uttered these words when the defendant sprang from her seat, peeled the cloak from her shoulders and seized a chair as if to attack Parks. At the top of her voice, she shouted: "This is all a lie! I will not stand for this!"

It took Mulligan, a stocky man, and two courtroom attendants to remove Miss Colby forcibly to an anteroom. Her shrieks could be heard for several minutes through the door before they calmed her down.

In his summation, Mulligan said that "this man, Wheeler, wants to send Edith Colby to be hung by the neck." He tried to pose a stark choice for the jury by demanding either acquittal or hanging. He said that the United States District Attorney had come all the way to Thompson Falls, like Shylock, to get his "pound of flesh."

"Wheeler wants the scalp of Edith Colby to take home, as the Indians did in the days of old," Mulligan cried, as he paced in front of the jury box. "God knows what bull sack is open over here. But I do know it is necessary to protect the citizens against the politicians and I do know that mental prostitution will turn heaven and earth to accomplish its ends . . . and I say the man who defends these stories against her is a cur unfit to live, and worthy to die. When Thomas hurled that insult, he drove into her heart the arrow that took away her reason! It was her duty to seek vindication . . . I say to you, return her to the arms of her aged mother!"

Rising for my summation, I decided to pick up Mulligan on that last heartrending phrase and turn it against him. Sitting next to Miss Colby—with his arm all but around her—was a secretary of the Spokane pressmen's union, one Al J. Germain. Germain had visited Miss Colby in her cell, testified to her character, and in general acted solicitous throughout the trial. He was pale, with a sallow complexion, and a poor specimen from any angle.

I began by stressing that I didn't want to see Edith Colby hanged.

"I just want to see her convicted and put in jail so she will not go out and shoot someone else," I told the jury. The feeling in Thompson Falls was running so high against the prosecution that the tension in the court was crackling as I continued:

"I wish I could ask you to acquit her. I feel sorry for Edith Colby, for her poor old mother, for anyone so foolish as to commit a crime. I was born sixteen miles from her old home, in the old state of Massachusetts. But when women violate the laws, they place themselves in the same position as men who violate the laws.

"If you were to agree with Mulligan, gentlemen of the jury," I went on, my voice rising, "you would return to anarchy. Yet they ask you to place her in the bosom of her mother! If she were my daughter, I would rather have her go to jail than return to the arms of Al Germain!"

Instantly, I heard a commotion and scream. My back was to the defendant's table and as I whirled I saw Miss Colby topple to the bench beside her and lie there frothing at the mouth.

Turning back to the jury, I remarked quickly: "This scene being enacted on the stage now was enacted this forenoon. And who but Mulligan is directing the acting?"

"I presume she should die to satisfy you!" Mulligan shouted at me above the pandemonium that was erupting. The judge called a recess while they escorted the defendant out to calm her. As I pushed my way through the hostile audience, I brushed past a friend.

"What do you think of it?" I asked him nervously.

"What do I think of it?" he snapped. "I think *you* ought to be hung!"

I escaped from the muttering crowd to a nearby saloon where I could settle down. When the court resumed three hours later at seven o'clock, I leaned over the bench and told Judge Clements privately that I was worried about the temper of the crowd and the temperament of the defendant. He told me there was nothing I could do but continue. I tried to continue my summation as if nothing had happened, proceeding more carefully.

"You have heard the denunciation of the county attorney and myself," I said. "As for myself, I care not, having heard talk from other Mulligans. I say to you, Mulligan, it was the most cowardly, nasty trick on your part I've ever heard of. Why does he, Mulligan, appeal to your passions and not to the facts? . . . I have been paid by the county commissioners and no one else. What he wants to make you believe is that he is here to defend the down-trodden. If he is, where did he get his detectives? . . . Remember that man out there on the hill, his face toward the sky, you citizens, because of four bullets fired by Edith Colby. She showed you how she opened the gun so skillfully and fired it as a cowboy would."

At this point, I snapped the revolver four times and waved my hand in the direction of the defendant. A few minutes later my summation was concluded.

The jury began to deliberate at eight o'clock. At four o'clock in the morning, after taking forty ballots, it found Miss Colby guilty of murder in the second degree—an unprecedented conviction in Montana for a woman. Judge Clements sentenced her to ten to twelve years. The jurors later said they gave no weight to Miss Colby's histrionics in the courtroom.

Miss Colby's face remained deadpan as the verdict was given. Before I left the courtroom, she came over and asked, "Mr. Wheeler, would you have tried as hard to acquit me as you did to convict me?"

"If I had taken your case, I would have," I replied. This seemed to cheer her. Later, the sheriff told me that when she returned to her cell she had kicked up her heels and said, "Well, Mr. Wheeler said that if he was defending me he would have tried just as hard to defend me."

Dr. Kimball confided to me that he had advised Mulligan not to put Miss Colby on the witness stand because she might appear too normal. Mulligan had been confident about it but he admitted ruefully to me after the trial that when she had played into my hands during the questioning about her home town he had whispered to her: "My God, what are you doing—falling in love with this fellow? Don't you know he's trying to hang you?"

In exchanging post-mortem professional opinions about the trial, Mulligan and I discovered we had both sought advice from the same person—Ed Donlan, a Montana state senator and local Republican leader. All the persons Donlan had advised each of us to leave on the jury panel in our own interest were identical!

Actually, I felt sorry for Miss Colby. Although she obviously knew what she was doing when she committed murder, she was an emotionally disturbed woman and her outbursts in court might well have been genuine. Long before she had served ten years, I recommended a pardon and she got it.

The very first night I was back in Butte after the Colby trial, Lewis Duncan, the mayor, asked if he could come to my office with a person he wanted me to talk to. He brought Mrs. Jack Adams, widow of a brilliant mining engineer for the Company. She hated the Company and although her husband had died of natural causes she frequently charged in public that Con Kelley, then chief counsel for the Company, and John D. Ryan, chairman of the board, had somehow caused his death because they were jealous of his knowledge of mining operations. She told me a fantastic story and I was satisfied that she was mentally upset. She wanted to sue Kelley and Ryan and I convinced her she had no case.

Afterward, she wanted me to collect about $40,000 she had on deposit with Heilbronner's, a brokerage firm in Butte. I collected it, with some difficulty—after telling Heilbronner that Mrs. Adams might do something violent to him if he failed to pay her promptly. He paid the money and shortly thereafter committed suicide. A number of Company officials lost money in the ensuing bankruptcy. Soon another broker also committed suicide, when a shortage of funds was uncovered. These brokers had been engaged in little more than a bucket-shop operation.

Mrs. Adams went to Santa Barbara, California, and stayed at the palatial Mission Inn. One day I received a telephone call from her informing me that she was arrested and charged with insanity. It seems that when the hotel had asked her to pay her huge bill she had whipped out a gun and refused to pay it. There was no doubt she was not in complete control of her faculties. I went to California and was confronted by the proprietor of the Mission Inn and some high-powered corporation lawyers. They told me she had been talking around the hotel about how some agents of the Company had been shadowing her and trying to frame her arrest. They wanted me to agree to have her jailed for insanity.

I told them I would demand a jury trial and they would have a hard time getting a jury to convict so fine-looking a woman. Mrs. Adams was middle-aged, handsome, well dressed, aristocratic in bearing, and intelligent—except for the obsession that her husband had met with foul play. The corporation lawyers tried to laugh off the idea that a jury trial could be obtained on an insanity charge. But I knew I was right, because the Montana statute code was patterned closely after California law. The result was that the case against her was dismissed.

However, I was afraid Mrs. Adams might get into some serious trouble and I tried to persuade her family to have her committed to an institution. This effort was unsuccessful. Later, I heard that she had gone to a bank where she had an account and demanded that all her money be turned over to her—at gun-point.

After dealing with Edith Colby, Wade Parks, and Mrs. Adams in quick succession, I went home to Mrs. Wheeler and pointed out that all of them had been a little abnormal in their conduct. I said I was beginning to wonder whether it was I who was off the beam—or everyone else.

Chapter Seven

THE D.A. IN TROUBLE

Immediately after the United States declared war on Germany in April 1917, I was confronted with mass hysteria over alleged spies and saboteurs, and it still saddens and angers me when I think about it. Up to then, Butte had been divided sharply between the interventionists and those who hated the English. The Irish miners, always the most vocal in the community, naturally had no sympathy for the British, the oppressors of their homeland. Many other nationalities, such as the Finns, had strong Socialist leanings and opposed the war on ideological grounds. They maintained it would further enrich the capitalists at the expense of the working people of the world.

The Anaconda Company officials and those dependent upon the Company generally supported all-out war. I myself had always been pro-ally. I used to have frequent arguments with some of my friends who were pro-German. Whenever we bogged down into disputes about English history, I called upon Charles Cooper, an English-born court reporter who was a real scholar on the subject. Cooper, a non-practicing lawyer, was eventually elected to the Supreme Court of Montana. He was to become better known as the father of Gary Cooper, the late Hollywood star.

My opponents in those "debates" kidded me about bringing in the "expert," Cooper, to settle points at issue. But, as sympathetic as I was to the cause of England and France, I never favored our getting into the war and have always regarded it as a tragic mistake. On the other hand, Federal Judge George Bourquin, who was of French descent, frequently urged U.S. intervention and criticized President Wilson for delaying aid to the Allies.

"I hope to see the day when Berlin will be a cowpath and the Allied flag will be flying over the Krupp factory," the judge would say.

After Congress declared war on April 6, my office became the busiest place in Butte. Montana was going crazy with reports of slackers and rumors of spies. As if this were not enough, Butte's Irish—organized as the Pearse-Connelly club—staged a large anti-war parade and rally a week after the declaration of war.

It was my duty as D.A. to enforce the first military conscription law, which provided for registration of all male citizens from twenty-one years of age to thirty, and their possible subsequent draft into the armed forces. U. S. Attorney General Thomas W. Gregory ordered the federal district attorneys and marshals to do everything possible to arrest and prosecute all persons responsible for anti-draft agitation.

The same day I issued this statement: "The office of the District Attorney will be active in gathering evidence in such cases of [draft] evasion, and registrars are duty bound to report any that come under their observation. There will be no possibility of anyone being favored by this office."

Shortly thereafter, I added this: "Complaints will be solicited. Any man within the draft age who is heard making the remark that he will not register will be warned during the day by the Attorney's force. If he has not registered by nine P.M., he will be taken promptly to jail."

Soon James Trainor, secretary of the Pearse-Connelly club,

was arrested for distributing an anti-draft pamphlet and held under $20,000 bond on orders of myself and Edward J. Byrne, a Department of Justice investigator sent to Montana by Bruce Bielaski, then head of an organization which later became known as the FBI.

On draft registration day, the papers reported that "Butte was on the verge of a serious riot for a moment" when many Finns, led to believe that registration meant immediate shipment to the front lines, marched uptown shouting protests. Twenty men and one woman were arrested for leading the sign-carrying demonstration which, of course, numbered many Irish in its ranks. Nonetheless, 11,603 persons were registered for the draft in Silver Bow County that day.

The draft riots were forgotten three days later when fire broke out in the shaft of the Speculator Mine and in the Granite Mountain Mine. One hundred seventy-five miners lost their lives in the explosion. The fire had started when an assistant foreman accidentally brought the flame of his carbide lamp in contact with an exposed inflammable cable between the 2400- and 2800-foot level in the mine. Because the foreman had a German name it was widely believed this was an act of sabotage directed by the Kaiser.

The dead miners were found piled up against bulkheads of solid cement, although the state law required that all bulkheads in the mines must have an iron door which can be opened. Almost immediately a new union was organized to demand improved safety regulations, better working conditions, a six-dollar-a-day wage irrespective of the price of copper, and abolition of the "rustling card" system (without this card issued to you by the Company you could not obtain employment in the mines). Governor Sam Stewart ordered troops of the National Guard, two hundred strong, rushed to Butte. They remained there throughout the war.

The mine operators refused the new union demands, blaming the mine disaster on the influx of the IWW, a name which became synonymous with "pro-German" in the area. The miners' strike, called on June 15, was denounced by management as an enemy plot.

When the federal court term was ended in mid-July, seventy informations had been filed for refusing or failing to register for the draft. Judge Bourquin sentenced thirty-six draft-evaders to jail for one day and the rest were given 30–60 day sentences. Military recruiting officers grumbled about Bourquin's leniency. The judge declined to be swayed by the hysteria. For example, John Korpi, a leader of the Finnish anti-draft riots, was indicted by a grand jury for conspiring and confederating with others in overt acts. Several weeks later, Judge Bourquin found the defendant not guilty on a directed verdict of acquittal.

Similarly, the same month he dismissed the conspiracy case against the Irish leaders in the Pearse-Connelly club. He found that the evidence was "not sufficient to prove the offense and hence the case should not be sent to the jury." He said in his opinion "rights must be protected by the courts at all times but more zealously at a time like this . . . when passions are more or less aroused." I heartily concurred with this view, although I did feel that the judge was wrong in finding that there was not sufficient evidence to submit the case to the jury.

When the first draft cases were presented in court, I was taking a short vacation at Lake McDonald—a fact duly noted by the newspapers. In September, the newspapers began to register their dissatisfaction with the treatment of the alleged draft-dodgers. One headline in the Helena *Independent* read: *WHEELER TOLD TO GO AFTER SLACKERS IN BUTTE.* The story said I had been instructed by Attorney General Gregory to make every effort to apprehend missing men and take all precautions against the escape of men called up for induction.

Judge Bourquin issued the first decision of a federal court on the question of the draftability of aliens, and it had wide repercussions. He found in the case of a man held for trial by a military court for evading the draft that aliens were not subject to the draft under the Selective Service Act. He granted a writ of habeas corpus to the defendant, holding that he could not be held for trial in a military court since he was not in the military service. Draft authorities were prepared for protests. After all, one-fourth of the men accepted for service in Butte were aliens and many of them were already in military training at a distant Army camp.

By his scrupulous attention to the law and refusal to be swayed by the hysteria, Judge Bourquin rendered ineffective efforts of the State Council of Defense to enforce its so-called "work-or-fight" orders issued later during the war. The Council was a semi-official body of private citizens appointed by Governor Stewart to give what they regarded as a super-patriotic lift to the war effort.

Investigation of draft cases took a great deal of time in the D.A.'s office and the *Independent* began calling Butte a "slacker's paradise." This was a canard. Actually, Montana gave a larger percentage of its sons to fight in the First World War than any other state in the union. A report of the Adjutant General said in November 1917 that since war was declared, a total of 3049 Montanans were serving in the Regular Army—though the state's quota was only 752. When the first draft contingent left for training at Camp Lewis, Washington, Butte staged a farewell demonstration described as the greatest in history.

But events had meanwhile taken some ugly turns. In July, the militant Frank H. Little, an IWW agitator, told a rally in the ball park that soldiers sent to Ludlow, Colorado, in the coal strike there were "uniformed scabs" and "simply thugs in U.S. uniforms." In another speech, Little was reported to have attacked President Wilson, advising the miners that it would do no good to send resolutions to the President protesting the deportations of their fellow copper miners in Arizona. Another Little remark quoted by the Anaconda *Standard* and vigorously denounced by the newspapers was that "The IWW do not object to the war but the way they want to fight it is to put the capitalists in the front trenches and if the Germans don't get them the IWW will. Then the IWW will clean the Germans."

Immediately after Little's inflammatory speech in the ball park I was besieged with demands to prosecute him. I went to see L. O. Evans, chief counsel of the Company, with a copy of the espionage act. I asked him to point out under what section I could prosecute Little. Evans' only reply was that district attorneys everywhere else in the country seemed to be able to find ample grounds for prosecution—but he could not point to any provision of the law under which Little could be prosecuted.

The next day, August 1, 1917, Little was dragged from his room by six men and was hanged, in his underwear, from a railroad trestle on the outskirts of Butte. As soon as I got the news, I issued this statement:

"The lynching of Frank H. Little, said to be an international officer of the IWW, is a damnable outrage, a blot on the state and county. There is no excuse for this murder. The murderers should be apprehended and given the severest penalty of the law. My office and every special agent in my jurisdiction will assist the state and county authorities to catch the men who committed the awful crime. Every good citizen should condemn this mob spirit as unpatriotic, lawless, and inhuman. Nothing worse could have happened at this time to handicap the government in its effort to raise an army by the draft. It is the worst thing that could have occurred to prevent a settlement of the labor troubles here. Drastic action should be taken to bring the guilty to justice . . .

"Personally I think any man who talks against the government and the soldiers who will go to France should be condemned and he should not be attacked by a mob. If there is no law to bring him into courts to answer for his statements—and there is no law—no violence of any kind should be administered to him. The espionage law does not apply to the statements made by Little. The people should ask Congress to pass a law that will bring men to justice who preach against the government but the law should take its course.

"If there had been a law to prosecute Little my office would have done so. My department made a thorough investigation of the case and we could not by any stretch of the imagination have indicted Little."

But my views on mob violence were not generally supported in the Montana press. For example, the *Independent,* in an editorial on the lynching, on August 2, 1917, said: "There was but one comment in Helena, 'Good work: Let them continue to hang every IWW in the state.' That seems strong language and a strong public opinion for as conservative a city as Helena. It might seem too strong under different circumstances . . . the *Independent* is convinced that unless the courts and military authorities take a hand and end the IWW in the West there will be more night visits, more tugs at the rope and more IWW tongues will wag for the last time when the noose tightens about the traitors' throats."

This attitude sickened me but unfortunately it represented the sentiment among Butte businessmen and merchants as well. A coded Vigilante leaflet had been pinned on Little's body warning of other lynchings to come, after the practice of the Vigilantes during the Montana gold rush days—and the letter "W" was among the letters separated by dashes. Thus: "L–C–D–C–S–S–W–T. 3–7–77." The numbers presumably referred to dimensions of a grave in the cryptic slogan so familiar to Montanans. A number of my friends told me the letter "W" could stand only for Wheeler. Other initials were presumed to refer to union strike leaders.

The Butte miners did not share the bloodthirsty philosophy of the *Independent*. Some 3500 of them, according to an estimate by the Anaconda *Standard*, followed Little's body on the three-mile march to the cemetery, while another 10,000 or so crowded the streets to watch in silence.

As might be expected, a coroner's jury rendered a verdict that Little was killed by unknown persons. Later that year it was reported that Vice President Thomas R. Marshall remarked on a return from a speaking trip out West that "they hung an IWW leader in Butte and it had a very salutary effect. The Governor of Montana had been too busy to issue the announcement of a statutory reward for the apprehension of the men who did the hanging."

United States Senator Thomas J. Walsh condemned the lynching and several times called for legislation "to curb the violence of agitators who oppose the constituted government of the country" and to "suppress agitators who in the name of labor, are treasonably trying to tie up industries of the country."

I heard a novel theory of the reason for the lynching when

I conferred on business at the Justice Department in Washington several months later. Assistant Attorney General William C. Fitts asked me who had hung Little. I said I didn't know. Fitts advised me that *he* knew. He said Bill Haywood, general secretary of the IWW, had arranged for the hanging because Little was getting too powerful in the IWW and Haywood wanted him out of the way.

"You may know more about it than I do but in my humble opinion he was hung by agents of some of the companies," I told Fitts. Fitts' attitude may be partly explained by the fact that he had conducted the nation-wide raid on IWW headquarters by U.S. marshals in September 1917.

John Lord O'Brian, then a special assistant to the Attorney General in charge of war work, told me not to pay any attention to Fitts because the Department did not consider him an expert on the IWW.

But to me the most bizarre element of the war hysteria was the spy fever, which made many people completely lose their sense of justice. All labor leaders, miners, and discontented farmers were regarded by these super-patriots as pacifists—and ipso facto agents of the Kaiser. There were increasing reports of enemy airplanes operating out of mountain hideaways south of Missoula in the Bitterroot Valley. Just how and why the German High Command expected to launch an invasion of the United States through western Montana, 6000 miles from Berlin, never made the slightest bit of sense to me, but the reports generated by this kind of emotion could not always be brushed aside.

The fears of a bombing attack became so persistent that I tried to scotch them by sending Special Agent Byrne to investigate. Byrne went to Missoula and returned with a negative report. I wired Washington that there was nothing to the story, though our newspapers were full of "evidence" of enemy operations. Here is a typical example from the Helena *Independent* of October 17, 1917:

"After the war started there were persistent stories in the Flathead reserve that airships were seen crossing the country and were always going south. A newspaperman put the story on the wire that the Germans had a haven in the wilds west of Missoula. Three months ago, two reputable women residing near Missoula said that they saw a burning airship fall into the forest near Hamilton. The sheriff of Ravalli County investigated and came back looking very mysterious. What he learned he probably told the secret service only . . ."

Later in October the *Independent* reported that another newspaper, the *Missoulian,* had unearthed evidence that Germans had a wireless plant in the mountains and thought it was supplied by hostile aircraft. The evidence amounted to this: an old logger noticed the lights of a cabin on a mountain. He investigated and "found a tree had been trimmed, some pieces of copper wire and some other stuff that showed that someone had lived there." The logger instantly concluded that "this was the place where those fellows had been sending messages but they certainly did cover up their tracks when they left." He buttressed this tale with the fact that he had seen two strangers around that summer too.

Because reports were coming in from very reliable people, the Department of Justice insisted that I continue the investigation of possible infiltration by the Huns. I sent a federal marshal to Missoula and he came back with nothing at all to report. When the Department still demanded to know if there was an iota of truth behind the alarm, I went into the Bitterroot Valley myself.

There I talked to an old railroad man who found a sensible explanation for the dreaded aircraft. He pointed out that if you looked overhead as you drove through a winding pass in the Bitterroots, the North Star appeared first on the right hand and then on the left hand. Since it appeared to be moving, it was taken for the taillight of a German bomber. Once the nervous patriots were convinced they could see the plane, it wasn't long before they also imagined they could hear the roar of its engines.

It must be remembered that the airplane was an excitingly new and mysterious machine in the West. While Americans living on the coastal areas feared submarine attack, inland Westerners had no trouble at all worrying about invasion from the air. As I have already indicated, the Montana newspapers at times even encouraged the panic. For example, the state capital at Helena once got into a serious alarm over fast-spreading rumors. The Helena *Independent* of October 18, 1917, offered a $100 reward in a front-page banner headline to anyone who could find the airplane that was said to be flying over the city.

"Are the Germans about to bomb the capital of Montana?" the editorial asked. "Have they spies in the mountain fastnesses equipped with wireless station and aeroplanes? Do our enemies fly around over our high mountains where formerly only the shadow of the eagle swept?"

This state of mind got utterly out of control two weeks later. The *Independent* reported seriously and proudly that Helena citizens—unnamed—had fired the first shots discharged in America at an airplane.

"Incensed by recent visits," this incredible story continued, "citizens fired shots at it. . . . Governor Stewart, informed of the attack, promises to follow it the next time in his auto and intimated that he would take an expert rifleman with him."

The *Independent* reported that over in Butte people were not only sighting airships. "Mysterious autos began to skim about at night," this reporter noted darkly. "Several people declared that these autos carried small wireless apparatus."

Literally hundreds of stories were brought to me about individuals who were alleged to be German spies. The trace of a German accent was almost enough to make one suspect in some areas. However, most of the reports were based on feuds among neighbors who seized on the spy scare to try to settle old scores. For example, one woman told me a neighbor was very pro-German and made no secret of his sympathies. I said I would have the Bureau of Investigation, as the FBI was originally called, look into it. Whereupon she commented: "I told that old German I'd get even with him."

A man named Knute Simmons in Centerville reported that a group of men were drilling with guns in the basement of the Catholic Church there. I asked Byrne to check up on it. Byrne found the men had no guns, that it was just an athletic program sponsored by a fraternal order. However, Simmons persisted in his demand that I do something to prevent the training program in the Catholic Church. Finally, I asked Simmons if his wife was German and he said she was. I told him that several people had called me about some statements that she had made. I pointed out that if I prosecuted on the basis of every story brought to me I'd have to prosecute Mrs. Simmons. Simmons left me alone after that.

One of the most fantastic spy stories involved some of Montana's leading citizens. It broke first in the October 18, 1917, edition of the Butte *Post*, under the headline: *FEDERAL OFFICIALS HINT AT SECRET GERMAN ACTIVITY IN BUTTE INTENDED TO INTERFERE WITH COPPER PRODUCTION*. The implication was that the government had at last found evidence of German influence among the striking miners and the IWW in particular. If the reader carefully read through all of the story, he could learn factually only that the District Attorney had arrested an alleged German spy and had ordered him interned under a presidential warrant providing for internment of enemy aliens.

The alien, Carl von Pohl, was working in the IWW but as an undercover employee of Oscar Rohn, president of the South Butte Mining Company and president of the Employers Association in Butte. Rohn eventually told the full story of his employment of von Pohl at a hearing before the State Council of Defense in June 1918.

Rohn said von Pohl had come to him right after the war started with reports of IWW activities and volunteered the information that the IWW was planning to move into Butte to start trouble. Rohn decided to hire von Pohl, an alien, to go into German communities and "make the Germans loyal or neutral." Rohn knew that Thomas Marlow, president of the National Bank of Montana in Helena and a director of the Anaconda Company bank in Butte, was employing another German for the same purpose.

Von Pohl agreed to the plan, according to Rohn, but on condition that the dangerous characters he put the finger on would be allowed to get out of town. Men who are betrayed, von

Pohl was quoted as explaining, always "got the betrayer and I do not want to be found dead and called a suicide."

Rohn testified that his stool pigeon fed him sensational information. One bit concerned a woman night-club entertainer. She and some Butte citizens were said to have been in the pay of the German government and were transferring intelligence via a wireless plant in Spokane, Washington, to Mexico and Uruguay, and from there to Germany. Rohn was so convinced of the authenticity of this plot that he obtained morphine for von Pohl to administer to the woman spy in order to give von Pohl an opportunity to search her trunk. Von Pohl later had to admit he found nothing to prove her connection with the enemy. And ultimately, with no evidence at all produced, he claimed that the spies he was trailing had escaped from Butte.

Rohn went on to tell the Council he had paid von Pohl a total of $5085 for his expenses and those of his agents who operated out of a fake real estate office maintained by the East Butte Mining Company. Rohn insisted he had no reason to suspect von Pohl's loyalty, despite the mass of activity he was furnishing about German activities because he was "doing good work weeding out undesirables from the mine workers." Von Pohl had kept an index card of Rohn's employees and reported that "ninety were ticketed as dangerous agitators out of the 2000 miners."

Rohn's examiners on the Council were puzzled as to "why a man such as von Pohl with pro-German sympathies would fight the IWW?" Rohn held that von Pohl was too intelligent to aid the IWW and, besides, he had a wife and four children to think of. Rohn went on to explain that he had employed another half score of persons to spy on his stool pigeon.

"Spotters put on the lower level of the Pittsmount Mine by von Pohl were spotted by other spotters and were reported 'right,'" Rohn said.

Roy Alley, who directed the Anaconda detective force, told the Council that reports of von Pohl and his men concerning the IWW corresponded substantially with those he received from his detectives "planted" in the same meetings. But he said that his own "large and more or less competent force of detectives had failed to set eyes on the couple that von Pohl was trailing as German spies."

L. O. Evans, general counsel for Anaconda, told the Council that he had advised Rohn against hiring von Pohl in his "makeup of a comic opera German spy"—von Pohl sported a Vandyke beard and foreign-looking greenish-gray suits—but that he gave Rohn credit for directing attention to the labor trouble that later developed.

After the news broke that von Pohl was arrested because of his pro-German utterances, I received numerous complaints about the alleged pro-German sympathies of Rohn. The State Council of Defense, trying to untangle this curious situation, asked me if the rumors and reports inimical to Rohn had not come from the IWW. "On the contrary," I replied, "they emanated from friends of Rohn, prominent men at Butte and these had expressed doubts of Rohn's innocence."

Actually, these reports were coming from friends of W. A. Clark, Jr., the famous multimillionaire's son, who was jealous of Rohn because he was corresponding with Clark's former wife, who had divorced him. One day the Butte postmaster, who was opening Rohn's mail, brought me one of Rohn's letters and said it must be a code letter. I took one look at it and said it was no "code" at all—just the letter of a man writing to his sweetheart.

I told those people who were demanding prosecution of Rohn that I would act only if they brought me some legitimate evidence of his pro-German loyalty. Rohn himself came to me and asked me to issue some kind of statement clearing him of disloyalty insinuations. I said my job was to prosecute, if I uncovered violations of the law, and that clearances were beyond my job. Rohn then demanded the hearing by the Council. It finally decided that while Rohn had been "indiscreet" there was no evidence that he was disloyal.

Other Montanans suspected of disloyalty did not fare so well at the hands of busybody citizens. In the fall of 1917 so-called "Liberty Committees" were organized in most of the small towns of the state to deal directly with anyone accused of being pro-German or who refused to buy the number of Liberty bonds that these communities would assess against an individual as his "quota."

According to the Anaconda *Standard,* a so-called "third-degree committee" in Billings rounded up "pro-Germans and financial slackers" there in November 1917. A city council member was forced to resign his job and carry an American flag through the streets. The owner of a meat market who had torn up his Liberty loan subscription blank was forced to kiss the flag. In Red Lodge, a coal mining center, the Helena *Independent* reported that "two Finnish IWW leaders were beaten and strung up by members of the Liberty Committee . . . the Finns in Red Lodge have prepared themselves for just what they got."

Mickey McGlynn, an organizer of the radical Non-Partisan League, objected to a story circulated in Miles City that a trainload of Belgian children whose arms had been cut off by the Germans were to cross the state. McGlynn was charged with saying: "The Germans never done that; it was done in the factories in Chicago. They were sent through the country to create feeling against the German nation." A mob took McGlynn to the basement of the Elks Club, beat him up severely, and drove him out of town. Prominent businessmen and lawyers were involved in the beating.

State Attorney General Sam Ford, my former assistant, tried to initiate prosecution of the men who expelled McGlynn in a Miles City court but the Justice of the Peace refused to issue any warrants. Instead, McGlynn was arrested by local authorities for sedition and was later convicted for his remarks under the state sedition act. But the state Supreme Court reversed the decision.

I requested federal marshal Joseph Asbridge to investigate the instances of mob violence but we found that there was no federal law that could protect the victims. Asbridge, however, concluded that the mobs were becoming such a problem it might require the attention of Congress. He had found threats of lynchings against alleged disloyal persons in Livingston and said they could not be taken lightly.

Non-Partisan League organizers were "deported" from town

after town in eastern Montana when they attempted to conduct meetings. Attorney General Ford continued to try to stem the tide of hysteria. He publicly called on the State Council of Defense to take steps to prevent further interference with organizers and speakers of the NPL in the state. The Council refused to guarantee the right to free speech.

R. B. Martin, the NPL organizer, came to me when I was in Missoula and told me he would be barred from speaking at a meeting at Montana State University in Missoula even though he had a certificate from Secretary of the Treasury William G. McAdoo accrediting him as a speaker for the Liberty Loan drive. I told Martin I was going to the theater and invited him to go with me. As we approached the theater, several men stepped out of the darkness and warned Martin that if he tried to go ahead with his speech he would be tarred and feathered. I told the spokesman that Martin had a certificate from McAdoo and should be allowed to speak. I said that if necessary I would call on the Army captain stationed at Fort Missoula to protect him. When the man repeated his warning, Martin changed his mind. I urged him to go ahead and speak because it would be "good publicity for the League." Martin replied that this was all very well but he would rather be a live organizer than a "dead martyr."

A representative from Scotland Yard who had traveled around the country came to see me in Butte. He said there was much more hysteria in Montana than there was in London, where the bombs were dropping. I was impressed when he told me that in England they let pacifist speakers hold public rallies in Hyde Park in London during the war to "get it out of their system." Yet Congresswoman Jeannette Rankin of Montana, a Republican who had voted against our declaration of war on Germany, had been denied permission to make an address for the Liberty Loan in Deer Lodge "because of her IWW and NPL leanings," to use the phrase of the secretary of the local businessmen's association.

I was shocked that the American people could be so carried away and lose their sense of right and justice at so critical a time. It was a lesson I never forgot. Twenty years later, when

I led the fight against the attempt to pack the United States Supreme Court, it was not because I agreed with the Court—indeed, I disagreed with many of their decisions. It was in large measure because I recalled how the local state judges, elected to office, were carried away by the World War I hysteria in their own communities when rendering decisions. It was the federal courts—particularly the Supreme Court—which in most instances upheld the right to freedom of speech guaranteed by the Constitution of the United States.

President Franklin Roosevelt sent one of the top labor leaders, Sidney Hillman of the CIO, to urge me not to fight the Court-packing bill. I explained to Hillman how I felt.

"I went through the First World War hysteria and I wouldn't have believed the American people could so completely lose their sense of balance," I told Hillman. "Another hysteria might sweep this country and it might be against your people, or some other group, and when that time comes they will all be looking to the Supreme Court to preserve their rights and uphold the Constitution. This legislation of Roosevelt's would not reform the Court. It would destroy it."

I told Supreme Court Justice Louis D. Brandeis what I had said to Sidney Hillman and Brandeis replied, "Good for you. A lot of people need to be told that."

There was little hysteria in the Second World War, compared to the first one, except on the West Coast, where the United States confiscated Japanese property and interned American citizens just because they were of Japanese blood. This was a violation of the Constitution and violated the very principles of the Four Freedoms, for which the President said we were fighting. There was no law on the books to sanction this high-handed action.

I protested to various high-level government officials, including the late Secretary of War Robert P. Patterson. I had always had respect for Patterson as a very able lawyer, but when he defended the internment of American citizens as a necessary action under the circumstances, I was surprised and disillusioned.

So far as I know, there was no case of disloyalty ever brought against any of these people. If the federal government can get away with such treatment of citizens of Japanese descent, it can do the same to any minority. It should demonstrate to the American people that there is all too little difference between us and any other people when a war or hysteria, or both, grip the nation.

Those of us who were called upon to enforce federal wartime measures faced a severe problem. Most of the legislation passed in the first few weeks of our participation in the First World War was not well drafted and represented an entirely new body of law. It included an espionage act, the Selective Service act, and a presidential proclamation for the control of enemy aliens. The provision of the espionage act that sent other D.A.'s off on a wave of arrests read as follows:

"Whoever, when the U.S. is at war, shall wilfully make or convey false reports or false statements with intent to interfere with the operation or success of the military or naval forces of the U.S. or to promote the success of its enemies and whoever, when the U.S. is at war, shall wilfully cause or attempt to cause insubordination, disloyalty, mutiny, or refusal to duty in the military or naval forces of the U.S. or shall wilfully obstruct the recruiting or enlistment service of the U.S. to the injury of the service or of the U.S., shall be punished by a fine of not more than $10,000 or imprisonment for not more than 20 years or both."

The public assumed, without any contradiction of federal authorities, that this made criminal any expression of pacifist or pro-German opinions.

The distinguished John Lord O'Brian, in a postwar discussion, said this law was aimed solely to protect the work of raising and maintaining our Army and Navy and drew its authority solely from the provisions of the Constitution which empowered Congress to raise and maintain armies.

The presidential proclamation on the control of enemy aliens forbade the possession of firearms, prohibited approach to forts and arsenals, and provided for detention of offenders. The U. S. Attorney General issued a circular to be publicized by District Attorneys which said to such aliens in brief: "Obey the law;

keep your mouth shut." Later on, all enemy aliens were required to register with the government.

Hundreds of cases of alleged disloyal persons were brought to my office for prosecution, many of them by local police officers. Like the report of spies, I found that most of them were inspired by old grudges, malicious gossip, barroom conversations, etc. Most of the cases looked ridiculous to me and I refused to bring indictments. After several months, the newspapers began criticizing me for failure to act. But my careful study of the espionage act convinced me that there was not one word in it to make criminal the expression of pacifist or simple pro-German opinion.

In view of the newspaper campaign against me, Federal Judge Bourquin, courageous and scrupulous as usual, told me to "send some of those sedition cases up to me and I'll take care of them. I'm in a stronger position than you are."

No one could imply that stanchly Republican Bourquin was a Socialist, whereas the Helena *Independent* had gratuitously explained that "Mr. Wheeler is not a Socialist but lives in a more or less Socialist atmosphere."

The *Independent* on October 19, 1917, said that "Mr. Wheeler, we fear, is too much given to looking for laws to restrain the activity of federal officials. The *Independent* would be much better pleased if, in the von Pohl case, he had grabbed the fellow, thrown him in jail, carried his papers to the office and gone through them thoroughly instead of going to court begging for a search warrant, only to be refused."

That was the sort of statute-be-damned attitude which was second-guessing my every move. Soon the *Independent* launched a campaign demanding my resignation, with a threat to my sponsor, the esteemed United States Senator Walsh, who, like me, was a part-owner of this influential newspaper.

"When T. J. Walsh is a candidate [in 1918]," the *Independent* warned, "the one issue he is going to face is Bert [*sic*] Wheeler."

This kind of newspaper abuse had its effect. People avoided me on the street and nudged one another to point me out in hotel lobbies, muttering threats I could overhear. By now I had developed a hard protective covering and the criticism did not really bother me. Nonetheless, friends warned me that I had better be more careful, lest some terrible violence be visited on me. Laughing, I replied that I was probably the safest man in Montana because if anything happened to me people would immediately blame the Anaconda Company—which its officials well knew.

However, I was concerned about the reaction of the Department of Justice in Washington to this drumfire of newspaper criticism in my state. I knew that John Berkin, a Company man who had been appointed sheriff of Silver Bow County after the ouster of the incumbent sheriff over the Miners union violence in 1914, had been assiduously clipping all the adverse comments in the *Independent* and Butte *Miner* and sending it to my superiors, as well as to the Army and Navy Departments, in Washington. So on a trip to Washington in the winter of 1918 I made it a point to call at the Department of Justice.

Some of the officials clearly wanted a less restrained interpretation of the sedition law from me. But not so Bruce Bielaski, director of the investigative division. Bielaski said he had read my lengthy reports of the situation in Butte and agreed that widespread prosecution would cure nothing. He said he had learned in the course of his investigations that most of the labor troubles in the big cities was caused by the miserable working conditions maintained by large corporations. Bielaski also said he had never been able to uncover any trace of German influence in the IWW in Butte.

John Lord O'Brian, then special assistant to the Attorney General in charge of War Work, told me: "Our difficulty has not been with District Attorneys like you. Our troubles are caused by District Attorneys who try to prosecute everyone for treason when there is no evidence."

However, things came to a head—and exploded in nationwide repercussions—in the case against Ves Hall, a stockman in Rosebud County, and A. J. Just, an Ashland, Montana, banker. They were charged with seditious utterances said to have included statements that Germany had a right to sink the *Lusitania* as a munitions carrier whether American citizens were aboard or not, that the U.S. had no right to fight outside its boundaries, that the U.S. was fighting for "Wall Street millionaires," etc. Falkner Haynes, a Rosebud County attorney functioning as special prosecutor during my absence in Washington, called me following the arrests and demanded authority to proceed with the prosecution.

Haynes complained that while he was waiting for my answer, Just and Hall went to Butte to see me on the advice of a local judge, Charles L. Crum, who was acquainted with me. Haynes forwarded an affidavit on the case and I presented the case to a grand jury in Butte, where the two men were subsequently indicted. Judge Bourquin set the case for hearing in Helena.

I was not anxious to proceed with what I considered a weak case but there was a lot of agitation in Rosebud County for immediate trial of the men, so I consented to let Haynes go ahead with the prosecution during my absence. It was the first case of an alleged violation of the espionage law to go to trial in Montana and therefore received considerable newspaper coverage. My former law partner, Matt Canning, was defending Hall, whose case came up first. Hall claimed that most of his remarks were made in a joking manner in the course of a casual argument about the war effort. Judge Crum testified as a character witness for Hall.

After hearing the evidence, Judge Bourquin directed acquittal of Hall without referring the case to a jury. In his decision, he noted that "the declarations were made at a Montana village of some sixty people, sixty miles from the railway, and none of the armies or navies were within hundreds of miles so far as appears. The declarations were oral, some in badinage with the landlady in a hotel kitchen, some at a picnic, some on the street, some in hot and furious saloon argument." Therefore, the judge concluded, the inference that the defendant was seeking to obstruct the armed forces appeared "unjustified, absurd, and without support in evidence."

In the course of the decision, Judge Bourquin again showed his concern for my problem in trying to carry out the intent of the law. He said that "U. S. Attorneys throughout the country have been unjustly criticized because they do not prosecute where they cannot."

Few other federal judges in the country were writing such decisions in the face of public clamor for suppression of all "disloyal" speech. Even Senator Walsh joined in the unfavorable comment on Judge Bourquin's opinion when the senator argued on the Senate floor for adoption of his amendment to the sedition law which was much broader in scope than the law at that time.

After the trial of Hall, Defense Attorney Canning was attacked in the lobby of the Placer Hotel by a deputy sheriff from Hall's home county. Special Prosecutor Haynes had an altercation with Judge Crum in the library of the State Attorney General's office. Haynes claimed that Crum pulled a gun on him after Haynes called Crum pro-German.

The trial put a final nail in Crum's professional coffin. He was asked to resign by a "Committee of One Hundred of Rosebud County" for alleged disloyalty and pro-German sentiments. Formal charges calling for his impeachment were drafted by Haynes when Crum refused to resign from the bench, and sent to a special session of the legislature called by Governor Sam Stewart. Crum then resigned apparently with the understanding that the governor would accept his resignation and recommend that impeachment proceedings be quashed. His letter said his resignation was "not a confession that I have been guilty of any crime" but only because he had reached a "limit of human endurance." Crum said, "I feel that a trial of my case would simply provide an opportunity for certain people to pose before the public and the press as super-patriots."

Despite Crum's resignation, and although public sentiment was by no means unanimous against him, the legislature went ahead and impeached the judge and the Senate found him guilty without a single dissent. I considered this a tragedy, for I thought Crum was a fine and honorable man.

There was a more significant reaction to the Hall decision. Governor Stewart several days afterward called a special legislative session asking for legislation to curb sedition and disloyalty in Montana, in view of the failure of federal officials to take action. He also asked that the State Council of Defense, which he had appointed, be given legal status.

The governor's message was flatly opposed at the Great Falls convention of the American Society of Equity, which was the largest farmers' cooperative organization—numbering some 15,000 members—and a forerunner of the Non-Partisan League. I was invited to address the Equity and took advantage of the opportunity to rip into the big interests of the state and defend my record as D.A.

When the legislature met in special session, there was criticism of me for this speech and other actions which rankled the lawmakers. The newspapers also were unhappy about my Equity speech, which they reported in exaggerated fashion. They didn't dare attack Judge Bourquin for his decision in the Hall case because his reputation for dealing with any interference with the processes of his court through stiff contempt penalties was well established. Also, the mining companies had no desire to antagonize him because they had important claims cases pending before him. So the brunt of the protest about the Hall case fell on my head.

On February 24, 1918, a House resolution demanding Bourquin's resignation was tabled and a substitute resolution asking me to reinstitute proceedings against Just and all other persons who had violated the espionage act was unanimously adopted.

Two days later the House voted on a resolution asking me to resign, on the grounds I had been derelict in my duty in prosecuting cases under the espionage law. The resolution lost by a vote of 30–29 but the *Independent* insisted it had actually carried because the clerk of the House had erred in recording one member's vote. The paper noted darkly that, while I had escaped condemnation, the close vote "should tell those responsible for his appointment that there is strong feeling against the young man from Butte."

I was out of the state during consideration of the House resolution. When I returned I issued this statement:

"No deep surgery is required to determine the objectives of those who fostered and fathered this resolution. That the people may know I want to draw attention to certain facts. No one urging the resolution found it convenient to state that more than 750 arrests have been made of slackers and more than 300 tried all because of the activities of my office. . . . It may be stated that while I do not agree with Judge Bourquin in his position in the Ves Hall case I was not in a position to charge him by affidavit with personal bias and prejudice, and I will go further that while I believe his view is erroneous in this case I certainly credit him with being honest in the view taken."

Had I publicly agreed with Bourquin's construction of the sedition laws, I would have been subject to attack for counseling disrespect of the law and refusal to do my duty. As long as I was D.A., my job was to enforce the laws as enacted by Congress without question or interpretation.

The state legislature adopted without dissent a state espionage act which was later used successfully by Senator Walsh as a model for his 1918 amendments to the federal law. It provided penalties of $10,000 and imprisonment up to twenty years for anyone who uttered, printed, wrote, or published "any disloyal, profane, scurrilous, or abusive language about the form of government of the U.S. or the Constitution . . . or the military or naval forces or the flag" or the uniform or "any language intended to bring the form of government, Constitution, flag, uniform, armed forces into contempt, scorn, contumely or disrepute."

When the federal law was made to conform to the Montana statute in May 1918, John Lord O'Brian said the difficulty was that it "covered all degrees of conduct and speech, serious and trifling alike, and in the popular mind gave the dignity of treason to what were often neighborhood quarrels or barroom brawls." Attorney General Gregory issued a circular to the D.A.s asking us to administer the new law "with discretion" and not as a means of suppressing legitimate criticism of government policy.

By April the Montana newspapers were reporting that the two Montana senators were split on the question of my retention as D.A. This was not exactly news. My term had expired on November 1, 1917, after four years, and I had continued to hold office because of the failure of Thomas J. Walsh and Henry

L. Myers, both Democrats, to agree on a new appointment.

Walsh, facing re-election in November 1918, issued a long statement explaining that he had long felt he should make his decision after investigating particular cases in which it was charged I had been derelict in my duty and not be influenced in the decision by the general denunciation of me.

"I have interrogated the Attorney General concerning Wheeler's record," the Walsh statement continued, "and am advised that it is good and that he is uninformed concerning any case in which Mr. Wheeler should have prosecuted when he did not prosecute or otherwise fail in discharge of his duties.

"One newspaper charged him with responsibility for the lynching of Little at Butte because it asserted he had not caused the arrest of that troublesome agitator before he fell victim to the violence of the mob. I asked the Attorney General to inquire particularly into that accusation and am advised by him that no blameworthiness attached to Wheeler in connection with the incident. Some criticism has been directed against Wheeler because he had not taken appeal in the Ves Hall case but the Department of Justice advises me that no appeal or writ of error lies in that case."

Walsh went on to note that the people of Montana were "intensely patriotic" but that unfortunately the law "was not broad enough to include the case of many who, by their unpatriotic comment, aroused resentment and were subjected to arrest by local authorities . . . many well-intentioned people readily listened to general accusations made against Mr. Wheeler and assumed him to be in some way derelict."

The senator concluded that refusal to reappoint me as D.A. under such circumstances would only further subject me to charges of disloyalty or sympathy with disloyalty.

The Helena *Independent* insisted editorially that the only way to determine who was responsible for the failure of the prosecutions was to "let Wheeler go. The blame *may* be his . . . There are many patriotic lawyers in Montana ready and willing to take his place and if the blame is on the Judge it can be shown."

Soon Senator Myers, apparently to force the issue, recommended the appointment of Stephen J. Crowley of Great Falls to succeed me.

"I have no word of disrespect for BKW but I don't believe that the majority of people of Montana want Mr. Wheeler reappointed and I feel sure a majority of the Democrats of Montana do not."

However, after conferring with Attorney General Gregory in Washington, Myers for some reason withdrew Crowley's name and recommended E. C. Day for the position instead. The press promptly interpreted this to mean that the Department of Justice was disposed to get rid of me.

When there were no developments at the White House on the Myers' recommendation, I was subpoenaed to testify before the State Council of Defense. But before I had an opportunity to be heard, the state and county Councils of Defense in joint meeting adopted a resolution protesting to President Wilson and the U. S. Senate against my reappointment as "inimical and injurious to the best interests of this state and the peace of its people." During the noon recess, the Councils apparently decided this was premature damnation of a man who was under subpoena to testify before them in a few days and so the resolution was rescinded at the afternoon meeting.

The first day of the hearing was held behind closed doors but the Council quickly decided it would be the better part of valor to open the hearings to the public. Among the witnesses against me were prominent Butte mine officials and Secret Service agents.

W. A. Campbell, editor of the *Independent* whom I had once prosecuted for contempt of court, questioned me about why I had not participated in war activities in Butte. I replied that I had recently addressed the Masons on the Red Cross drive but that I had made no public addresses because I had not been advised to do so. My refusal to appeal the Hall acquittal was dwelt on at some length and I again described the legal difficulties involved and pointed out that I could not have charged Judge Bourquin with bias or prejudice. After several charges that I was friendly with NPL leaders, I was dismissed and the Council turned its attention to Oscar Rohn and his fantastic employment of von Pohl.

When my inquisition was concluded, the Council reaffirmed its earlier resolution against me and added: "The Council does not desire to impugn either the integrity or the professional ability of Mr. Wheeler but the Council is of the opinion that at this critical time in our nation's history . . . all federal and state officials must not only possess honesty and ability but must be vigorous and enthusiastic in the suppression of internal disorders."

The controversy over my public record even got into the churches. After my hearing before the Council of Defense, a resolution was introduced at a meeting of the Council of Federated Churches of Butte in support of me. It provoked a lively debate. One objection to the resolution was that it would drag the Federated Churches into party politics. One speaker insisted that the Council "had not defamed Mr. Wheeler's character." An amendment was offered expressing the Federated Churches' confidence in my integrity and character but expressing the belief that the matter was not properly before that body. However, the entire topic was finally laid on the table with only two negative votes.

I was particularly upset by this mixing of church with state because Lulu, my wife, had long been a tireless worker in the Methodist Church. Whenever she was not caring for our five children she was engaged in fund-raising campaigns for the church, assisting the choir and even, when necessary, scrubbing the church floor.

Lulu's refusal to sign a pledge to participate in the "sugarless and wheatless days" conservation program, however, had caused widespread gossip in Butte. Always a strong-minded individual, she had informed those who solicited her signature that she would eliminate sugar and wheat from her table when grain was no longer being made into whisky and beer.

In September 1918 the Miners union and the local of the IWW went on strike again after their demands for a six-dollar-a-day wage were refused by the Company. Con Kelley, now vice president of the Company, publicly stated it would never deal with the union. Butte police then staged a series of raids at the request of the county Council of Defense. The police were aided by troops commanded by Major Omar N. Bradley, who was to become one of the outstanding generals of World War II. The targets included the IWW headquarters, the Miners union hall, and the offices of the Butte *Bulletin.*

The entire staff of the *Bulletin* was arrested and hauled before the county Council of Defense and charged by the county attorney with sedition under the state law for urging curtailment of the production of copper.

"There was no disorder save by the raiders," Judge Bourquin commented on the raids later, in connection with the deportation case before him. "These armed [raiders] perpetrated an orgy of terror, violence, and crime against citizens and aliens in public assemblage, whose only offense seems to have been peaceable insistence upon an exercise of a clear legal right."

I returned from a court term in Great Falls to find the mines shut down. I consulted with the union leaders and told them if they would go back to work I would try to obtain immediate consideration of the dispute by the War Labor Board. I told them the government needed copper. The union leaders agreed to go back and I made a public statement urging the miners to end the strike and submit their grievance to the board. The union wanted to use a ball park on Second Street for a meeting to call off the strike but Roy Alley, a Company official, refused to let the miners use it.

Disgusted, I called Alley and told him the Company would look ridiculous if the public found out it wouldn't make the park available for a meeting which might end the strike. The Company quickly agreed, and a mass meeting of the miners took place at the park.

At the meeting, "Big Bill" Dunn, editor of the Butte *Bulletin,* a labor sheet, urged the men to go back to the mines, as did my assistant, James H. Baldwin.

"The office of the United States District Attorney wants to meet you halfway," Baldwin said.

But two men claiming to represent the IWW told the miners

that this was an IWW strike, not an AFL affair, and not to pay any attention to Dunn.

I got both these representatives into my office, one at a time, and accused them of being detectives. One admitted it and the other denied it. Subsequently the second fellow was confidentially described to me by the District Attorney in Spokane as "a Pinkerton man." At a second mass meeting of strikers, Dunn denounced the two phony IWW men as labor spies and the strikers, after some commotion, voted to return to work on the promise of getting their case considered by the War Labor Board.

Meanwhile, I became embroiled in a bitter exchange of letters with my old rival, Dan Kelly, now a Company attorney, over a speech he made to the Rotary Club charging that federal government officials appointed to guard men and property "are counseling every day with the men back of the movement to curtail production." I replied that the IWW was encouraged to call the miners strike by "paid agents" for the Company who were planted high in the IWW union.

My letter to Kelly and his windy reply—in which he accused me of just about every wrong under the sun—were printed in full in the Anaconda *Standard* of October 3, 1918. Colonel C. B. Nolan, Walsh's law partner, telephoned me in some anxiety the next day and asked if I planned to issue any more statements like that. I said that as long as the Company kept up its attack on me I would hit back with all the ammunition I had.

"Such statements won't help man, God, or devil," Nolan lamented.

Nolan persuaded me to accompany him and Hugh Wells, Democratic state chairman, to Washington to take a new federal position.

It was apparent that Wells and Colonel Nolan wanted to kick me upstairs. They warned Walsh that unless he got rid of me he would be defeated. Finally, Walsh came to see me alone at the Raleigh Hotel in Washington. The senator, whose wife had recently died, was sick, tired, and worried.

"Well, I guess they will beat me for re-election if you continue as D.A.," he said. I replied that every enemy I had made in Montana had been made because of my original fight for his election by the legislature. Tears sprang to Walsh's eyes. I tried to explain that the corporate interests who were attacking me were also opposed to him. But I told him that if he felt my remaining would hurt him politically, I would resign. I said I had seen a letter written by Charles Kelly, president of the Daly Bank, to the effect that they thought they could beat Walsh except for the fact that President Wilson wanted him re-elected.

Attorney General Gregory assured me I did not have to resign as far as the Department of Justice was concerned—seven of his men had been sent to Montana to investigate me and couldn't find a thing. He offered me a federal judgeship in Panama.

"If you're going to deport me, you'd better make it Siberia," I told Gregory. "I understand people don't live very long down in Panama."

Nolan and Wells were determined to get me a job so as not to antagonize my friends against Walsh. I was offered the rank of colonel if I would go to work in the office of the Judge Advocate General, who at that time was Major General Enoch H. Crowder. I pointed out that if I wasn't patriotic enough for the District Attorney's office I certainly ought not to be patriotic enough for the Army. I added that I didn't intend to accept a position to save face for them.

"You tried to talk Walsh into asking for my resignation and I owe you absolutely nothing," I said. Wells became equally frank.

"If McAdoo resigned, I think they'd make you Secretary of the Treasury just to get rid of you," he said.

Walsh urged me to issue a statement saying I was resigning for the good of the Democratic Party. I refused. I finally issued a simple statement that I wished to withdraw from the office of D.A. "in order to satisfy the friends of T. J. Walsh who believed my retention in office would mean his defeat as a candidate to succeed himself in the Senate."

Walsh announced his intention of recommending E. C. Day as my successor, adding that "I feel impelled to say in justice to Mr. Wheeler that he sought no other place in the public service and declined an offer made by the Attorney General whose confidence, despite anything that has transpired, he continued to hold."

I felt sorry for Walsh because I knew how distasteful to him this episode was. The Montana press, of course, was jubilant over my resignation. The *Independent* said that only those elements "which have had immunity for the last two years" would protest the passing of Wheeler from public office.

My enemies really did assume my public career was ended.

Chapter Eight

"BOXCAR BURT"

When I resigned as District Attorney on Walsh's suggestion that my remaining in that office might defeat him, I vowed to do everything possible to wrest control of the Democratic Party from the Company. Within a year I was accused of "stealing" the party and in so doing I became the focal point in one of the bitterest and roughest political campaigns in American history. More than once, in fact, I was very nearly lynched.

But my first concern after resigning was to devote myself to my law practice. Fortunately, I was busier than ever. All the hullaballoo over my record as D.A. and my fight against the Company swelled my prestige with small farmers, workers, and businessmen. I took in as my new partner James Baldwin, my former assistant as D.A., after dissolving my partnership of several years with H. Lowndes Maury, one-time city attorney on appointment of Butte's Socialist Mayor Lewis Duncan. Maury was a brilliant, colorful, and witty little man from an old Virginia family. He had opinions on all subjects and loved to discourse on them at length. Maury was an indefatigable letter writer, mailing off his thoughts almost daily to President Wilson, Governor Stewart of Montana, and newspaper editors. Perhaps fittingly, a son, Reuben Maury, has been chief editorial writer for the New York *Daily News* since 1926 and won the 1941 Pulitzer Prize for editorial writing.

My law cases during this period were never dull. One was an outgrowth of the war hysteria. J. E. Keeton, a railway shop machinist in Livingston, brought suit for damages of $100,000 against six prominent local residents for "violating his liberty and bringing him shame and disgrace" in forcing him to kneel in the public square and kiss the American flag.

The defendants—all leading citizens—included John A. Lovelace, a wholesale groceryman, and two ranchers. They were represented by James F. O'Connor, Speaker of the Montana House. The defense claimed that Keeton had refused to sign a food pledge card when first approached and later signed under pressure, declaring: "You can make me sign but you can't make me eat the damn stuff."

When the Keeton case came up for trial in February 1920, I defended him without a fee. He had a wife and a son who was about to go to war when the incident occurred. He was helping his wife with the washing one morning when he was called to the door by several women whom he mistook for saleswomen. He told them he didn't want anything and shut the door. Only later, he learned they were working for the Loyalty League, seeking his pledge to abide by sugarless, meatless, and wheatless days. Shortly afterward, Keeton was dragged into the street by a mob, along with two German saloonkeepers. The mob forced him to kneel and kiss the Stars and Stripes.

The local judge disqualified himself because of the prominence of the defendants and Judge Roy E. Ayers, who later became a congressman from Montana and then its governor, was called in to preside. To stir up feeling in the community, the Livingston *Enterprise* carried this headline every day in large type in a box on the front page: *DUNN, DEBS, AND WHEELER*. William ("Big Bill") Dunn was the brilliant and caustic editor of a radical labor paper, the Butte *Bulletin*, and a backer of mine. Debs was Eugene V. Debs, the pioneering leader of organized labor in the United States. Both were anathema to the big interests and the press in the state.

In his address to the jury, O'Connor violently attacked my patriotism in the war and raked up all the old charges about my allegedly being soft on seditionists. O'Connor also charged that Keeton had referred to the soldiers as "sons of bitches," emphasizing the slur on the good mothers of Livingston.

In my reply I said to the jury: "The language that flowed from this man's mouth would indicate he is accustomed to associate with people from the underworld."

The courtroom was jam-packed. I believe people had come to count on me to create some fireworks. During the recess, three women stepped up and asked how I had found out about O'Connor's unsavory reputation with the town's seamier set—female as well as male. I assured them it was an open secret.

As the trial neared its climax, I persuaded Judge Ayers to agree to instruct the jury to bring in a favorable verdict for Keeton. The defendants had no defense and, while the judge was a friend of theirs, the case was so clear-cut he really had no choice. The court recessed for an evening session in which we were to make our final summations.

Immediately after we recessed, Lovelace amazed me by inviting me to dinner. Lovelace was a prominent Democrat whom I had reason to think liked me. So I reluctantly accepted—after warning Lovelace that the dinner would not sway my plan to attack him unmercifully in my final argument.

There was nothing but small talk from Lovelace during the meal and I suddenly had a premonition that he was diverting me for some reason. I excused myself as quickly as I could and hurried to the courthouse, where I found Judge Ayers half drunk. I asked him where the instructions to the jury were and he said they were all right. When I looked on his desk, I discovered that the instructions directing the jury to bring in a verdict for the plaintiff were missing. Apparently the defendants or friends of theirs had stolen the instructions while plying the judge with liquor.

I soon found a copy of the missing instructions in the wastebasket. Fortunately the judge was just sober enough to read them to the jury. The jury then awarded token damages of one dollar to Keeton—about what I expected. It was a moral victory and Lovelace wept openly in the courtroom.

The principal hotel in Livingston, the Park, was owned by old Jim Murray, the uncle of the late United States Senator James E. Murray. Since all the defendants were staying there I preferred to stay at a "hotel"—little more than a two-story wooden shack—on the outskirts of town. As I was packing to leave the night after the trial ended, one of the defendants, a rancher named Kenniston, came to my room. He told me he had been with the other defendants and that they were drinking and threatening to beat me up before I got out of town.

Kenniston said he felt ashamed of his role in the Keeton affair, explaining that he had come into town the day of the incident and, after drinking too much, had joined the mob which manhandled Keeton. To clear his conscience, he escorted me to the train and made sure nothing untoward happened.

In another case before Judge Ayers, in Lewistown, the opposing counsel was Colonel C. B. Nolan, law partner of Senator Walsh. I was still annoyed at Nolan for urging my resignation as District Attorney. He was a formidable opponent. He had a reputation as a great orator and an accomplished storyteller, both in and out of court. After Nolan concluded his stemwinding argument, I knew I had to do something to destroy it.

"You think you have heard a masterful argument," I told the jury. "You may think this is one of the colonel's great orations. Well, I have heard him on a great number of occasions and I can assure you this was a very poor example of Nolan's art. You know why? He cannot make an argument here because his heart isn't in this case. He knows his client is in the wrong."

Nolan was furious and demanded that the judge stop this line of attack, but Ayers would not interfere. The result was that the jury brought in a verdict for my client.

The next day, when I was about to take the train to Butte, two men approached me and asked how I liked the verdict. I said I was delighted with it. They then reminded me that they had served on the jury and said they had voted for my client because "we wanted to show the Butte *Miner* and the Helena *Independent* and that whole crowd what we thought of them for forcing you out as district attorney."

I handled a number of lawsuits brought against "Horse Thief" Kelly, a well-to-do moneylender in Plentywood, in northeastern Montana near the Canadian border. Kelly was cordially hated in his community and would have had no chance with a jury. I succeeded in proving there was not sufficient legal evidence of crookedness to warrant Kelly's cases being submitted to a jury and got them dismissed.

As often as I could I continued to make speeches all around the state. After I handed in my resignation as D.A., Joseph Asbridge, the U. S. Marshal, told me he had good news.

"The newspapers are going to lay off you," Asbridge said.

"My God, you don't call that good news, do you?" I exclaimed. "I'm going to make them keep after me."

I knew that if the papers suddenly stopped denouncing me the people might forget me, or—what was worse—assume I had gone over to the Company. So I devoted a major portion of every speech to attacking the majority of the Montana press. In Missoula, I pointed out that both papers, the *Missoulian* and the *Sentinel*, were owned by the Company. The morning paper would flay the Democrats and the evening sheet would rip into the Republicans. There was no difference in the quality of the writing because all the editorials on both papers were written by the same man. The next morning the *Missoulian* had only a squib saying I spoke there—but a two column editorial denouncing me. The head waitress handed me the paper as I went in to breakfast, saying, "Us girls do not agree with the *Missoulian*." The rest of the Company papers then did what I had hoped for; they all carried editorials attacking me.

What bothered the Company officials was this: while they had blocked me from becoming Attorney General of Montana and had gotten me ousted as United States District Attorney, they were unable to keep me from capitalizing on these defeats by conducting a prosperous law practice and carrying on my fight against them through every available channel.

It seemed to me the best instrument for taking control of

the Democratic Party in Montana away from the Company was the Non-Partisan League. The League had been organized in 1915 by ex-Socialist Arthur C. Townley in North Dakota. By 1918 the League was reported to have had some 50,000 members in Minnesota, 40,000 in North Dakota, 25,000 in South Dakota, 21,000 in Montana, 30,000 in Wisconsin, and some 56,-000 more scattered through nine other states. The League, almost completely composed of farmers, was working for a comprehensive reform of social and economic conditions. The farmers had been more or less at the mercy of the local banks, absentee railroad owners, and grain operators.

In North Dakota, the NPL had carried its entire slate into office by winning the Republican Party primary in 1918. In Montana, two NPL candidates were elected to the state senate on the GOP ticket. The NPL in 1919 claimed thirteen members of both parties in the House. Four eastern Montana counties were considered so strongly NPL that the Helena *Independent* suggested they ought to secede and join the state of North Dakota. An important NPL victory was the election of court reporter Charles Cooper, a friend of mine, as associate justice of the state Supreme Court on the Republican ticket.

So great was the fear that the NPL would capture the Democratic and Republican primary machinery that both parties got the 1919 legislature to abolish the direct primary system in the state. Montana's six-year-old law, adopted by initiative, provided that a voter was given the ballots of all parties on entering the polling place. Of these he selected the ballot of the party he wished to vote for and discarded the others in a box provided for the blank ballots.

Wisconsin was the only other state at that time which had so wide-open a primary. The Montana legislature junked this and returned to the old convention system.

But the new primary law had to be submitted to the voters. Its sponsors wanted a special referendum election in September 1919 so the party convention could select the candidates for the 1920 election. The NPL was violently opposed to a special election in September, pointing out that the harvest period would permit only a small turnout of farmers and play into the hands of the politicians. I enthusiastically joined the NPL campaign to invoke the referendum provisions of the state constitution and hold up the proposed law until the general election of 1920. I spoke in virtually every county of the state in the spring and summer of 1919, denouncing the amendment to steal the direct primary from the people.

At the end of June 1919, I helped set up a permanent organization to fight the amendment. We issued a statement urging every citizen to meet this attack on popular government. I was a member of the organization's executive committee, which numbered both Republicans and Democrats. The group was set up independently of the NPL because the League was being stigmatized in the press as "red socialist."

However, it was the NPL which went out and rounded up 27,500 signatures on petition—enough to force postponement of the referendum on the new primary law until the regular election in November 1920. This was a remarkable undertaking in the short space of a few months, considering that the total population of Montana was approximately 500,000, widely scattered over a tremendous area.

Following this success, the NPL had jubilant hopes of nominating the gubernatorial candidate in both major parties. Their plan was to nominate me in the Democratic primary and Sam Ford, my former assistant and now state attorney general, in the Republican primary. But the labor people in Butte argued that such an ambitious plan would only serve to split the opposition to the Company by dividing the political forces of farmers and workers.

When the NPL held its convention in Great Falls in June 1920, I was in Butte packing to go to Helena to argue a case before the Supreme Court. When the telephone rang, I was not surprised to hear the voice of Larry Duggan, sheriff of Silver Bow County. Duggan was at the convention and asked me if I would run for governor with NPL endorsement on the Republican ticket. I said no and hung up.

I had anticipated something of this sort. After I had delivered my rousing speech to the Equity convention (thickly populated with NPL supporters) in 1918, I was approached by Townley, the League founder.

Townley told me the NPL probably would want to run me for governor in 1920 and asked for my reaction.

"No," I told him. "I understand you're really the governor of North Dakota, that you go in and pound the table and tell the governor what to do. You couldn't do that to me. If you did, one of us would be thrown out of the office and I don't know which one it would be."

"I don't want to be governor of Montana, I want *you* to be governor," Townley replied. He added this amusing explanation:

"Don't tell me about these 'honest farmers.' I elected the governor and the state officers and the members of the state legislature in North Dakota. But big interests came here with their whisky and their women and took them away from me like Grant took Richmond. I had to build a corral around them to keep the booze and whores away from those fellows. Some of them acted as if they'd never been off the farm before."

What he was saying was that, on the basis of my Equity speech, he realized I knew the score and would not be taken over by the Company. He preferred me as a candidate to a naïve farmer.

Thus, when the NPL convention was getting underway in Great Falls, I told Mrs. Wheeler I would probably be asked to run for governor on the Republican, Democratic, or an independent ticket. I asked her what she thought I should do. She replied that I ought to run. She was still sizzling over the way the Company had mistreated me and wanted me to strike back.

Duggan called me a second time the same day and asked if I would run with NPL endorsement on an independent ticket. He called me back a third time and suggested the Democratic ticket. This time I said I was willing to run for governor in my own party.

It is true I had dashed off a letter to Walsh after my disillusioning departure from the D.A.'s office that I hoped to be "endowed with good judgment enough to remain out of politics in the future." But later I determined I would get back at the

Company if it was the last thing I ever did. So here was my chance to win back control of the Democratic Party for the people.

The NPL convention at Great Falls endorsed me as the gubernatorial candidate overwhelmingly, the five other candidates receiving only a few scattered votes. In my acceptance speech, I warned that a political defeat would destroy the NPL. I also urged adoption of an appropriate party label. The next day the convention selected the Democratic label.

I had warned Mrs. Wheeler that if I got into it, the gubernatorial race would be a "mean, dirty campaign."

"If you can stand it, I can," was her only comment.

The press immediately went after me in full cry as I began my campaign for the Democratic nomination. The Butte *Miner* started referring to me derisively as "Butte's leading farmer" and said there was "no apparent obligation upon the part of a lawyer to study farming or know anything about that useful occupation in order to become the standard-bearer of those Townley tillers of the soil."

My first campaign stop after the NPL convention was Dillon, in the center of the ranching country south of Butte. I was scheduled to address a rally but the Dillon city council hastily passed an ordinance which prohibited speeches in the city hall without permission from the local Democratic or Republican county chairmen. Knowing full well the violent feelings of both chairmen against the League, I didn't even bother to ask permission. Instead, I said I would speak on a street corner, but the chief of police warned me that if I did he would have to arrest me.

We adjourned to a ranch about a half mile from the city limits. F. A. Buzell, a farmer from Conrad, used a Ford truck as a platform to try to get the meeting underway. Immediately, a phalanx of men, apparently white-collared professional fellows, marched on the scene. They began catcalling and heckling Buzell, shouting, "When did you ever run a farm?"

They were under the impression that Buzell, who was speaking, was me. I was out in the crowd, so I walked over to the hecklers and asked them to let Buzell speak. When they figured out who I was, some of them said: "This isn't the man we want —it's Wheeler we're after!" Quickly there were cries of "Get a rope!" and I began to feel uncomfortable. A group made a rush for me and would have dragged me off to God-knows-what fate when a local barber who was not even connected with the NPL pulled out a penknife and stabbed one of the ringleaders. This threw the crowd into confusion and in the melee I managed to slip away.

As we escaped from the ranch in an auto, my local NPL friends warned me that if I went back to Dillon to spend the night I would surely be assaulted. Instead, a farm hand drove me to the nearby small town of Bond, where I would be able to catch a train for Butte that night. The railroad station turned out to be a boxcar parked on a siding, since the station served only as a loading point for cattle. There was no town within driving distance and only one farmhouse nearby.

The ranch hand, an overseas veteran of the World War, left Buzell and me to wait for the train which was to come through late that night. But soon he came back armed with a rifle. He said several automobiles full of men had come to the ranch looking for me. He stationed himself near the door. When the posse drove up and started to open the door of the boxcar, our protector cocked his gun.

"I'll shoot anyone full of lead who opens that door!" he called out.

There was no doubt he meant what he said and efforts to open the door halted. But quite a few of the mob hung around until the train pulled in around midnight, so Buzell and I didn't dare risk capture by trying to hop aboard. We spent the night in the "station" and in the morning Sheriff Duggan of Silver Bow County arrived and drove us back to Butte.

I was dismayed when one of our escorts told Mrs. Wheeler that the enemies of the NPL would surely kill me before Election Day. I pooh-poohed this warning and told her I was not worried. She took my word for it and made no objection. If I had been married to a nervous or timorous woman, I would never have been able to conduct that campaign or many others later on.

After our rescue by the sheriff, Buzell told me he had been sure he was going to die in the boxcar because his mouth was so dry from fear he couldn't swallow the strychnine pill he took for his heart condition. I admit I wasn't very relaxed that night myself.

The barber who saved my life with a penknife was indicted for assault. I went back to Dillon to testify for him. Every time I was asked a question on the witness stand, I seized the opportunity to make a speech to the jury about how our meeting was broken up. I kept this up in the face of angry and repeated admonitions from the judge, who happened to be Democratic county chairman. The jury finally acquitted the barber.

The Butte *Bulletin,* the state's only labor paper, charged that the mob action had been organized by "interests connected with the First National Bank of Dillon." The Butte *Miner* countered with a half column of statements from individuals who were quoted as holding that mob action was justified if that was what it took to silence Wheeler.

And the Helena *Independent* commented: "The people of Dillon may have dealt wrongly with their problem but the fact that Wheeler has reached down to levels so low that any number of people . . . could be prevailed on to run him out of town like a cheap mountebank and dangerous citizen shows what people all over the state think of Wheeler."

The episode prompted the opposition press to start referring to me as "Boxcar Burt." More violence was threatened when I addressed a crowd in the county courthouse in Choteau, in north central Montana. A half dozen or more ferociously anti-NPL Republicans moved up out of the audience onto the stage shouting that I deserved to be hanged. Dr. Harry McGregor, a Great Falls physician and a stanch backer of mine, got up from his seat on the platform and barred the way. The doctor stood only five feet, six inches, but was a scrappy 170-pounder who had learned to box during his student days at the University of Iowa.

"If any one of you touch this man, I'll knock hell out of you!" McGregor cried out. The little doctor's pugnacity sent the pack of would-be lynchers back into the audience muttering to themselves. Near the end of the meeting they moved toward the auditorium exits, obviously waiting for me to try to leave the hall. Dr. McGregor immediately stationed himself at one of the doors and successfully stood guard long enough for me to depart.

Press reports of the kind of crowds I was drawing panicked the anti-Wheeler Democrats. They called a meeting to select a single slate of Democrats for endorsement by the Democratic Central Committee, so that I would have to face one opponent rather than four or five and thus presumably stand a better chance of taking a licking. All the other candidates were persuaded to step aside and make way for the committee's so-called "solid front" slate to "preserve the integrity of the party." W. W. McDowell, the lieutenant governor and my former friend and colleague in the Montana legislature, was picked to oppose me for the gubernatorial nomination.

In my campaign I never mentioned McDowell's name. But I was worried about the potent Irish vote in Butte. James E. Murray—later U. S. Senator—was carrying on a campaign in Montana for the freedom of Ireland and held large rallies in Butte in which McDowell was always a principal speaker. When Eamon de Valera of Ireland came to Butte, he was given a big breakfast at the Silver Bow Club and the elite of Butte flocked to hear him. McDowell, introducing the distinguished visitor, concluded his remarks by saying that as lieutenant governor he was turning over the key to Montana to de Valera. The Irishman was given a standing ovation.

Soon a delegation called on me to ask my view on the freedom of Ireland. I told them frankly that I didn't know enough about the question to issue a statement. I pointed out that the Irish themselves seemed to be badly split on the various proposals. And I added that I was sure I was as well informed as my opponent on that score.

All the Democratic press supported McDowell. The Montana Development Association, a group of self-appointed superpatriots similar in nature to the wartime Council of Defense, issued a bulletin describing the primary race as "a straight fight between the reds and the Americans." The Butte *Miner* told its readers that "no man can sit quietly by and see his state virtually made an annex to Bolshevik Russia." "Bolshevik Burt" became the way much of the Montana press liked to refer to me.

For two weeks before the primary the Butte *Bulletin*, the only newspaper supporting me, carried a banner headline quoting my pledge: *"IF ELECTED I WILL NOT PUT THE ACM OUT OF BUSINESS BUT I WILL PUT IT OUT OF POLITICS."* The ACM was of course the Anaconda Copper Mining Company. The slogan of the NPL candidates was: "We are opposed to private ownership of public officials." The Anaconda *Standard* countered with the threat that an NPL victory might convince the Company that it should transfer its operations from Montana to Arizona, Mexico, or South America—localities where it already had begun operations.

I wound up my campaign speaking from the balcony of the Butte Hotel (also referred to as Liberty Hall), promising that if the citizens voted the straight labor ticket the lynchings, murders, and crimes against the workers would be stopped. The *Bulletin* reported that "never since the old Heinze days has so large an assemblage gathered to hear campaign issues discussed." The crowd numbered some 5000.

I won the nomination of August 26, 1920, with a majority of 14,000 over McDowell out of the 50,000 total vote, carrying Butte with a majority of 2000. The NPL carried every post on the ballot and won most of the county positions. Nominated with me on the Democratic ticket were Roland C. Arnold, a well-to-do farmer, running for lieutenant governor; Louis S. Irvin, a suave, handsome lawyer who was a half-breed Indian and married to a Blackfoot Indian, for attorney general; and Richard Haste, brilliant publisher of a farm paper, for secretary of state.

After taking a two-week rest at my cabin on Lake McDonald in Glacier National Park, I returned in time to greet James M. Cox, the Ohio governor who was the Democratic presidential candidate, when he arrived in Great Falls. I rode with him to Helena as part of a reception committee that included prominent Democratic officials who were some of my bitterest enemies in the Company. I was pleased when Cox, upon his departure, issued this statement to the Montana Democrats: "You have in this man Wheeler a splendid and courageous man."

Senator Walsh also endorsed me, declaring that no Democrat could justify a refusal to support me because I had won the nomination "by perfectly lawful means" and "by a most decisive vote."

I selected as the new Democratic state chairman Judge John E. Erickson, one of the few state district judges who had withstood the war hysteria with me when I was D.A.

The Democratic State Central Committee met in Helena on September 10 and a group of old-line party regulars introduced a resolution repudiating all the men who had won in the primary with NPL support, and appointing new candidates. As soon as I could get the floor, I rose and said:

"Gentlemen, we stand only to place humanity above the dollar. I challenge anyone to point out one act of mine that does not square with Jeffersonian principles . . . I'm going to be elected, gentlemen, without the assistance of the big interests or the profiteers' league."

I went on to pledge unequivocal support for the national ticket of James M. Cox and Franklin D. Roosevelt for President and Vice President, explaining:

"After I talked over the situation in North Dakota and what led to the NPL movement there, Governor Cox told me he would have been for a state-owned elevator and a state-owned flour mill . . . the Montana Development Association says they are the only Americans—they are the profiteers' league and they captured the Republican ticket, and if you will have it that way, the NPL captured the Democratic ticket. Which do you prefer?"

The convention adopted a platform incorporating many of the NPL's demands, including equal taxation, state hail insurance, grain inspection and grading to give farmers full value for their produce, exemption of homestead improvements from taxation, and support for cooperative marketing. In addition, the convention pledged to reclaim the vast arid lands and oppose a monopoly control of natural resources. Of more concern to the labor unions were pledges to outlaw blacklisting, guarantee free speech, and increase workmen's benefits. Today these proposals hardly seem wild-eyed and radical but in 1920 they alarmed the well-entrenched reactionaries.

The GOP convention adopted a platform which denounced state socialism and appealed for support by the Democrats to preserve the American way of life. It nominated Joseph M. Dixon, a former United States senator and the manager of Teddy Roosevelt's 1912 "Bull Moose" campaign, to oppose me. Dixon was about as liberal as I was and the Company ultimately and reluctantly decided to back him as the lesser of two evils.

For a time the Democratic (Company-controlled) papers didn't know what to do. The Butte *Miner*, referring to the fact that Dixon had sought NPL endorsement, stated that "there is [no] lesser evil offered in this case."

I started right off with a slam-bang campaign, speaking three or four times a day in town after town across the big state of Montana, which is more than 600 miles by auto lengthwise. I insisted that the real issue was whether the farmers and laborers were going to get a square deal against the profiteers.

"Public ownership of grain elevators and flour mills is no more socialistic than public ownership of the public schools," I told my audiences. I would describe the miserable housing conditions in the Dublin Gulch section of Butte and ask if there was anything wrong with aiding home construction with the loan of state moneys.

I often pointed out that I had been "born in the shadow of Bunker Hill and know no other form of government than the American system—and want to know no other."

By the end of October, the old Democratic bosses with few exceptions had re-formed their political lines to support the national ticket—and oppose our state ticket. They called their organization the Montana Democratic Club. Senator Henry L. Myers came out from Washington to lead the fight, complete with brass bands and torchlight parades. He asked for repudiation of "this theft of our party name . . . by a coterie of hybrids, Bolsheviks, and radicals."

I in turn denounced Myers as a tool of the copper interests, banks, and profiteers. Thereafter there was no more hesitation by the Democratic press. All but two of the newspapers in the state took up the cry against Wheeler as "red socialist" and tried to connect my campaign somehow with stories of Russian labor camps, nationalization of children and the bomb plots that were an aftermath of the Communist revolution. Not a line was carried about the large crowds I attracted, or the content of my speeches. Posters were splashed all across billboards showing a huge red hand dripping blood.

Senator Myers predicted "riots, insurrections, and murders in every industrial community of the state" if I were elected.

Indeed, there was nothing—literally nothing—we were not accused of. Some of the papers began charging that the NPL was anxious to try to popularize "free love" in America. The sole basis for this—and of course no basis at all—was the fact that some books discussing free love had been found in the state libraries of North Dakota. Since the NPL was in power in the state, the alarmists charged that it had planted them there.

In Billings, I decided to have some fun with the "free love" rumor. I brought up the name of Charles Bair, a Republican, a wealthy sheepman, and part owner of the Billings *Gazette*.

"You all know Charley Bair," I said to the crowd. "Now let me ask you something: If there was free love in North Dakota, do you think Charley Bair would still be in Montana?"

My jab at Bair got a laugh because it was well founded. When I was District Attorney, some of the citizens of Billings had got me to indict Bair under the white slave act. It was no secret that he had taken a woman to Washington, D.C., and other cities outside Montana without the marriage sanction. When I brought the case before the grand jury, the woman refused to testify, obviously because Bair must have made a settlement with her. So I tried to indict both of them for conspiracy but the grand jury balked. It was easy enough for a prominent citizen in a small town to intimidate a grand jury in those days and I am sure Bair took care of this one.

Bair was just as carefree as he sounds and he enjoyed my public crack at his penchant for illicit amour. However, I provoked a more sensitive reaction when I singled out Richard Kilroy, editor of the Anaconda *Standard*, for similar effect on Election Eve. Addressing a crowd massed in the streets before the Butte Hotel, I said:

"You all know Dick Kilroy. You know the kind of life he has led. If there was free love in North Dakota, do you think he'd still be in Butte?"

The day after the election, Kilroy cussed me out when he was being shaved by Harry Thompson, a Butte barber. Thompson told me he replied to Kilroy:

"Well, you told lies about Wheeler [in the *Standard*] and he told the truth about you."

Thompson related that Kilroy, who had watched my Election Eve speech from a nearby building, looked aggrieved and said, "But I had my *daughter* with me!"

The campaign was so nasty that even the religious issue was raised against me—from both ends. A story was circulated among the Lutherans that I was a Catholic and another rumor was planted among the Catholics that I was a member of the violently anti-Catholic American Protective Association. Neither charge contained a shred of truth.

However, I like to get off a good quip whenever possible. So when a persistent heckler at one of my meetings insisted that I state my religion, hoping the answer would alienate some of my supporters, I replied, "My mother was a Methodist, my father was a Quaker, I attended the Baptist Sunday school as a child, I am married to a Methodist and like most of you men most of my religion is in my wife's name." After that statement, some of the preachers in Montana began praying for the salvation of my soul.

Soon B. K. Wheeler loomed as the biggest bogeyman in Montana—to hear my opponents tell it. The well-to-do women of Butte organized themselves into the "Home Guards" to defend their homes and their churches from the sinister influence of the NPL-Democratic leader. They warned other women that if I were elected their children would be taken away from them and raised in institutions in Russia.

The super-patriots who made up the Montana Development Association circulated a letter among employees of their members urging them to "vote against the so-called Democratic state ticket nominated by the NPL at Great Falls, not for your employer's sake but for your own sake." The Butte *Miner* carried this editorial, unsigned, in big black type: *DON'T LET THE RED HAND STRANGLE BUTTE. VOTE THE REPUBLICAN TICKET*. It was accompanied by a picture of a large hairy fist.

Senator Walsh returned near the end of the campaign to speak for our ticket but fell ill and couldn't carry out his schedule. However, on Election Eve he told a rally in his home town of Helena that "I am not half-hearted in my support of Mr. Wheeler. He has been tried by fire. He risked his future, politically and professionally, rather than compromise with wrong and injustice when he was a member of the legislature ten years ago and he has been hounded ever since with an impossible fury and rancor that knew no bounds."

As for fears of an NPL administration in Montana, the senator said: "I haven't become alarmed lest a movement with which Governor Frazier and Dr. Ladd have identified themselves is going to culminate in the nationalization of women or the confiscation of private property . . . [or] is the deluded victim of Bolshevists or anarchists."

Four days before the election I was badly injured when an automobile in which I was riding ran across an embankment and overturned near Philipsburg. I suffered three broken ribs but managed to deliver my speech on schedule at Anaconda that night. Because there were rumors that the Company had done this to me, I assured my listeners that "it was an accident pure and simple and nobody was responsible."

In my Election Eve appeal from the balcony of the Butte Hotel, I admitted stealing the Democratic Party but asserted I stole it from "the Standard Oil Company and intend giving it back to the people." (Standard Oil Company organized and controlled Amalgamated Copper Company which in turn controlled Anaconda for many years.)

But the fear campaign had its effect. Montana voters apparently were afraid my election would end the prosperity the state had been enjoying. They were swept by the same yearning for "normalcy" expressed by the American people as a whole when they put Warren G. Harding in the White House by a landslide. Also, I believe the Democratic plea for participation in the League of Nations found little appeal in Montana.

Harding and Dixon, the Republican candidate for governor, received almost exactly the same number of votes, 109,430 to 111,113, respectively. Though I led Cox, the Democratic candidate for President, 74,875 to 57,330, my vote nevertheless made me the worst-defeated gubernatorial candidate in Montana history. Several other NPL candidates and I did manage to carry Silver Bow County by the slim majority of 138 votes despite the threat of a ghost town. But I carried only one other industrial town—the railroad center of Three Forks—and two counties, Sanders and Mineral. My analysis convinced me that if the labor vote had stayed with me in Butte, Great Falls, and Helena, I might have won in the face of the nation-wide Republican sweep. But of course I had no basic political "machine" to fall back on, and the labor vote was subject to the same influences as other elements.

Naturally, the Montana press was almost unanimously exultant. Once again, my political obituary was in print. The Anaconda *Standard* crowed about the "eclipse of Wheeler" and drew the lesson that "a candidate cannot be expected to climb into power in this city by attacking one of its leading industries. Mr. Wheeler, an accident in politics, chewing the cud of bitter reflection today, has found this lesson an expensive one . . . Butte spat him out of her mouth with all the noisome crew of reds and wobblies who followed him." The election headline in the *Standard* editorialized even more than its editorial. It screamed: *BUTTE KICKS OUT THE RED AND ELECTS AMERICANS TO OFFICE.*

A rough election post-mortem was yet to come. One day in December, as I was standing on a street corner in Butte talking to ex-Governor A. E. Spriggs, I noticed out of the corner of my eye that D. Gay Stivers, head of the Company's goon squad, was approaching. I had a hunch Stivers was looking for trouble and told Spriggs I was going to move on. Before I took more than one step, Stivers was alongside me and had clouted me on the left temple, blacking my eye and knocking me to the ground. I was sensible enough not to rush back at Stivers, for I knew he was a gunman and that something worse might happen. Passers-by were outraged and summoned a policeman to arrest Stivers. He collared both of us and hauled us into police court.

When the Stivers case came up, he defended his action, saying I was a "liar and character assassin" in some of my remarks at the outdoor Election Eve rally. Stivers cited my rhetorical question to the crowd: "'Who hanged Little?' Ask Colonel Stivers—he knows."

(Frank Little, an IWW organizer, had been yanked out of his bed by a mob and hanged from a railroad trestle during the recent war because of his open contempt for the war effort.)

The judge dismissed the case against Stivers with the remark that "any man with red blood in his veins would have done the same thing."

When I protested this highly unjudicial opinion, the judge retorted: "It is not necessary for me to offer any excuse to you . . . I said to him [Stivers] that his actions were justified under the circumstances and I do not care to hear any criticism from you."

There was tremendous resentment over the judge's comments and the incident only served to increase the general hatred for the Company.

Chapter Nine

A PLACE IN THE SUN

The winter of 1920–21 turned into a classic example of political irony: the economic disaster which my opponents said would result from a Wheeler victory in the 1920 gubernatorial race followed swiftly after my smashing defeat.

The Anaconda Copper Mining Company closed down three mines just twelve days after the election, reducing operations to 50 per cent of normal. By mid-December, a wage cut of one dollar a day was announced to "avert a complete shutdown," according to the Helena *Independent*. Despite the cut, the Company suspended all its mining operations on April 1, 1921, because of the depression in the metals market, where copper was down to eleven and a half cents a pound. Some 4500 employees were directly affected in Butte, 1300 in Anaconda, 200 in Great Falls, and more than 2000 were laid off in the Company's auxiliary industries—coal mining, lumber, railroading, and so forth.

Immediately after the election, I took a trip to Massachusetts to visit my relatives. By the time I returned to Montana the economic collapse had reached panic proportions. Attending a Masonic banquet in Butte, I was asked to say a few words. I told the audience I must be in the wrong place.

"When I read in the papers that the mines are closed, farm prices are falling and farms foreclosed," I continued, "I said to myself, 'I am sure I must have been elected governor and that I should be living in Helena.'"

In my campaign for the Senate in 1922 I developed this into a story which quickly circulated all over the state. It went like this: A young man was applying for United States citizenship. He was asked by the examining judge to name the governor of the state. The applicant replied without hesitation—"Wheeler." When he was corrected, he said, "All I know is that all the papers, the bankers and the politicians said that if Wheeler was elected all the mines would close, the banks would foreclose the mortgages on the farms and everybody and everything would go broke. Now, Judge, the mines have closed, the farmers are losing their farms and it looks as if everybody is going broke—so I think Wheeler must be governor."

Even before the collapse helped ease my feeling of defeat I had accepted it without bitterness or rancor. I told people truthfully that I didn't think of it as a disaster because I had never really expected to be elected. Nor had the position of governor, with its executive and administrative duties, very much appeal for me. I felt I was more naturally suited to the role of legislator.

In Governor Dixon's message to the legislature in January 1921 he dwelt on the state's serious financial situation and asked for a tax on the state's new oil industry, a license tax on all metal production and an income and inheritance tax to meet the large government deficit. The mine operators accepted the challenge and called a meeting at the state capitol to fight any tax on mines. The press followed up with a plea to let business alone and cut state expenditures rather than increase income. The legislature adjourned without enacting one of Dixon's tax proposals.

Undismayed, the governor called the lawmakers back into special session and repeated his request for increased revenues and a tax commission to study revision of the entire tax burden of the state, declaring that the people's desire for equitable taxes had been thwarted by a vicious lobby.

In the special session, Dixon was finally able to win a small tax on oil production and an additional license tax of 1.5 per cent on the "net proceeds" of the mines along with a "bachelor" inheritance tax. However the "net proceeds" license tax meant little because in addition to permitting deduction of all overhead and improvements costs, the mines could show that they had no "net proceeds" in the year of 1921. Farmers and ranchers had no "net proceeds" either but they paid their property taxes on full valuation, good season or bad.

I missed no opportunities to jibe at the Company officials about "their governor"—and what a shame it was he had stolen my alleged "Bolshevik" program of 1920—and even went to Helena and spoke before the legislature and urged the members to vote for much of Dixon's program. When Governor Dixon vetoed a loyalty oath bill for teachers on the ground it was unconstitutional and would lead to political "heresy hunting," it further angered his sponsors. Despite the veto, Professor Arthur Fisher was suspended from the law department of the University of Montana following charges preferred by the American Legion for his activities in my gubernatorial campaign and for editing a liberal newspaper, the *New Northwest*.

In January 1922 the Anaconda Copper Mining Company announced that with its purchase of the American Brass Company in Connecticut to manufacture finished copper products it would reopen the mines again. The acquisition of the world's largest brass firm, giving the Company a completely integrated operation, was portrayed in the Company papers as a magnanimous gift to the people of the state to assure continuous operation of the mines.

But while the reopening of the mines after nine months gave employment to 23,000 men in Montana, it did not alleviate the depressed price of farm products or prevent the foreclosure of mortgages.

In April 1922 the late Cordell Hull, then Democratic National Chairman, came to Montana for a meeting of the party leaders. As part of his aim to unify the state organization, he sought me out before the session. He said he had been told I could name and elect the Democratic candidate for the Senate. I denied I had that much influence but told Hull I had decided to go after the Senate seat myself. Hull said it would be better if I stepped aside so a "unity candidate" could be selected. I replied that as far as I was concerned there was a more important consideration than party unity. I said I would insist on making sure the Democratic Party was not controlled by the copper and oil interests—and was pledged to progressive ideals.

Right after my defeat for the governorship, I announced that if Democratic Senator Myers ran for re-election I would oppose him. I had voted for Myers when I was a member of the legislature in 1912 (senators were then elected by the legislatures) but notwithstanding he had come to Montana and made vicious speeches against the people supporting me.

It was not too long thereafter that he announced he would not seek re-election. However, three other candidates of some stature in the state opposed me for the nomination. They were Judge J. F. O'Connor, former Speaker of the House who had the support of a number of prominent party leaders and the Democratic press; Hugh Wells, former Democratic state chairman who had sought my removal as District Attorney; and Tom Stout, a liberal independent newspaper publisher and former congressman. Wells, a stockman and banker, was distinguished by his tour of the state in his private airplane—surely one of the first politicians to campaign in this fashion.

In the formal announcement of my candidacy on June 1, 1922, I emphasized the plight of the farmers and promised to seek safeguards "against exploitation by unscrupulous financiers." I also pledged to work for repeal of the "nefarious Esch-Cummins law which has permitted looting of the people of the nation by excessive freight rates, guaranteeing 6 per cent on billions of dollars of watered stock." The Esch-Cummins Transportation Act of 1920 provided for the return of the railroads to private control and widened the powers of the Interstate Commerce Commission to include, among others, the initiation or establishment of rates that would yield to the railroads as a whole 5½ to 6 per cent on the aggregate value of their property.

My program for labor was to "give to labor its just proportion of the products of its toil and granting its just demands concerning the right to organize, hours of labor, and working conditions." I supported a soldier's bonus to be paid from excess profits accumulated during the war and proposed that the tariff be taken out of politics and placed in the hands of a commission of expert economists. On the prohibition issue, I came out for strict enforcement of the law.

In the summer of 1921 some Non-Partisan League leaders had come to my summer camp in Glacier National Park and urged me to run for the Senate. I made no promises, since I doubted at that time I could win and I knew that many of the leaders of labor and the League had been bought off during the election in 1920.

Later on I was urged by many of my friends to enter the primaries and decided to do so. But I told the League leaders that I would only run if they did not endorse me, that while I wanted the support of the farmers I did not want the League's endorsement. I took the trouble to go to their convention at Great Falls in May 1922 and urge my friends to vote against such an endorsement.

A radical group in the League endorsed State Senator John Anderson to run in the Republican primaries for the Senate. Anderson had been one of the outstanding members of the League and had campaigned with me when I ran for governor. It was thought he would divide the League vote and hurt my chances for the Democratic nomination, particularly since most of the farmers had formerly been Republicans.

Very early in 1922 I had a lucky break. A party came to my office and wanted to bring suit for damages against Roy Alley, one-time secretary to Company president John D. Ryan and now a part of the Company's political and intelligence operation (which included the hiring of Burns and Thiele detectives). I called Alley into my office and offered him a chance to settle.

Alley so appreciated the fact that I didn't drag him into

court under what would have been embarrassing circumstances he disclosed his troubles with his employers. He related that he and some other employees had obtained a patent but were having difficulty getting the Company to compensate them adequately or make a royalty arrangement.

Seemingly relieved at the opportunity to unburden himself, Alley went on to reveal to me the names of all the daily and weekly Montana newspapers the Company controlled financially. What was more interesting, he ticked off the names of the leading individuals of the state who were manipulated like puppets by the Company. One of them was Harry Hudson of the machinists union. I had always figured Hudson as a good labor man and I was shocked when Alley told me Hudson was a Pinkerton detective in disguise. He also identified the various leading Democratic politicians of the state who were "Company men." Some of these names surprised me too.

"We've done everything we could to destroy you in a political way and in an economic way," Alley told me. "We could take the political leaders away from you, the farm leaders and the labor leaders, but we couldn't take the people away from you."

In the spring of 1922, after visiting the Company's New York office in connection with his patent problem, Alley said he had told Cornelius Kelley, then Company president, that I would be elected to the Senate.

"Kelley asked me if this was my judgment or my prejudice," Alley told me, "and I said it was my judgment."

Alley's prediction began to come true late in August when I won the primary nomination after an exhaustive speaking tour. I polled 20,914 votes, more than the combined total for my three opponents. The Republican nomination for the Senate was won by Congressman Carl W. Riddick after a close contest with J. Wellington Rankin, a successful Helena lawyer who later became United States District Attorney in Montana. Anderson, the pro-League candidate, came in fourth in the GOP primary and promptly announced he would take the stump for me because of Riddick's reactionary record in Congress.

During the primary campaign Sam Goodman of Helena

came to me and asked what I thought of my chances. I asked him if he wanted to make some money and told him to bet that I would get more votes than any two of the other candidates. He said, "You can't do that." When I went to Butte, a gambler asked the same question. I repeated what I had told Sam Goodman in Helena and then told him to post $1000 to $2000 that I would get more votes than all three. He said, "You couldn't do that." "Well," I said, "it will be my money." He posted the $1000 against $2000. I beat all three, and won the bet.

The sun was indeed beginning to shine when at the Democratic convention in Helena called after the primary ex-Governor Sam Stewart, who had previously fought me at every turn, introduced me as the hero of the lost battle of 1920.

Enjoying complete acceptance by the party for the first time in my political career I commented on the fact that the Company representatives were seated in the same room with Non-Partisan Leaguers and concluded that "the war is over." I pledged myself to support all candidates that had been nominated "whether I liked him or not."

My victory also forced my erstwhile critics, the Democratic press of the state, to do an about-face and soft-pedal opposition to me. The Company strategists realized they could not expect to openly attack me and at the same time hope to achieve the Company's goal of electing a Democratic Legislature which would defeat Governor Dixon's tax program.

James Hobbins, assistant to the president of the Company, had sought me out at the convention. I asked him what the Company was going to do about my candidacy and he replied that they planned to pursue a hands-off policy. "That's all I want," I told him. "But the first time you make a break I'm going to kick hell out of you, and I'll know when you do because I know every one of your stool pigeons around the state."

They wanted Carl Riddick, conservative Republican, elected. They brought into the state many prominent Republican speakers. Senator James E. Watson of Indiana, Republican leader in the Senate, gave out a strong statement for Riddick who had at one time in his career been a fellow Hoosier.

For a change, my speech to the convention was quoted in

full by the Helena *Independent.* Since I was running for the Senate, I devoted most of it to national and international affairs. I dwelt on the growing economic chaos and privation in country after country and attributed it to the impoverishment of peoples by their autocratic governments during the preceding one hundred years. I rejected the idea that we should let Europe alone to work out her own problems. Referring to the sacrifices made by American doughboys of World War I, I said: "They fought to make the world a better place in which to live. Can we drop the challenge now? Can we turn our back on Europe when she is sinking fast? We cannot play the part of a selfish rich man." (These lines may surprise those pundits who have classified me as an isolationist.)

I also gave considerable attention in my speech to the economic tragedy of the farmers—and the failure of the Harding Administration's temporizing schemes to offer any relief. I traced the history of the railway labor dispute over wages and vigorously attacked Harry M. Daugherty, the Attorney General in Harding's Cabinet, for seeking an "unwarranted injunction, asking that the employees not be allowed to present their side of the case to the public." I concluded by pointing out that the Democratic Party could win by fighting for the cause of the masses and "if we don't, we will lose because we ought to lose."

Senator Thomas J. Walsh paid me a gracious tribute in his address to the convention. He said I was "no political accident coming to the surface amid the troubled waters of political unrest.

"He has never had the patronage of the wealthy and powerful corporate interests that have so largely influenced public affairs," Walsh said. "On the contrary, he has encountered their stubborn and . . . their vindictive opposition. Nevertheless, he has prospered . . . and may with safety be entrusted with a part in the business affairs of this, the foremost nation on earth."

Stumping across the state, I attacked Riddick's voting record in Congress in support of the Harding program. Among other things, I castigated him for voting against an investigation of Daugherty—a project which was to become a turning point in my career a little over a year later. I repeatedly denounced the Republicans' national tax program as a "help-the-rich" device. When I largely ignored the local tax situation, one editorial writer commented that "he took us to Russia and the battlefields of Europe and Asia but had nothing of import to say about Montana."

W. W. McDowell, the Democratic campaign manager, finally telephoned me and asked why I wasn't speaking for the party candidates for the legislature. I replied that I was busy with my own campaign.

"Well, they don't like it," McDowell grumbled.

"Who do you mean by 'they'?" I demanded.

"The people across the Hill," he replied, referring in accepted terms to the Company and its so-called "richest hill on earth," a vast mound of copper in Butte.

"'They' can go to hell—and you can tell them I said so," I replied.

McDowell pleaded with me to let Lester Loble or Andy McConnell, leaders of the 1920 secession movement of the Democratic Party, tour with me to speak for the local candidates. I said I would not permit them on the same platform with me.

The editors of the Butte *Bulletin*, the radical labor sheet, warned its readers not to be confused because the "copper press is mildly supporting Wheeler." It explained: "They conjecture that they probably wanted to send him to Washington because they know he can't hurt them there." A vote for Wheeler was a vote against Hardingism, the paper added. This was a theory frequently advanced during the campaign to explain the incongruities presented between the national and state issues.

I felt I should look after myself. I saw no obligation to pull the Company's chestnuts out of the fire after the way they had elected Dixon over me in 1920. Openly in the campaign the Company was saying and doing nothing. They knew that if they hurt me they would be hurting the chances of the Democratic legislative ticket. And while they had no desire to see me get up in the world, they could think of more worrisome places for me to go than the Senate. After all, one man in 96 in Washington, D.C., couldn't do them nearly so much harm as one man disposing of their state-wide interests as governor.

Actually, the Company foresaw little chance of my being victorious in 1922 after I had taken such a bad beating only two years before. I encouraged this notion. I kept telling one of my campaign colleagues—whom I knew to be secretly reporting on me to the Company—that I didn't think I had a chance. I knew that if the Company didn't think I had a chance it wouldn't spend so much money to try to defeat me.

My opponent, Riddick, attacked me on both flanks, accusing me in one breath of having sold out to the "big interests" and in the other of being the candidate of the NPL. Citing my support by the Helena *Independent* and the Butte *Miner*, Riddick said this was proof I had made a "deal" to sell out. Shortly afterward, his organization published full-page ads entitled LEST WE FORGET, reminding the voters I had been the NPL candidate just two years before.

This advertisement also said *Montana Wants Service—Not Shame,* and reprinted the resolution presented to the state legislature in 1918 calling for my resignation or removal for failure to prosecute seditionists wholesale.

The Democratic State Central Committee publicized a letter to me from Federal Judge George Bourquin, a Republican, defending my record on sedition prosecutions as being "in furtherance of sound public policy and in vindication of your official oath . . . and duty to yourself, to the court and to society." Judge Bourquin concluded his letter by writing that "you will remember you declined a like statement by me in the fall of 1918 and I make it now with no object but simple justice to an able, diligent, and conscientious prosecutor in a most trying period of our country's history."

J. Bruce Kremer, Democratic national committeeman for Montana who had opposed me in 1920, assured audiences in the senatorial campaign that the attempt to link me with red radicalism "is without foundation in fact. His Americanism is declared to be unquestioned." The Republicans replied with full page ads picturing Wheeler, Kremer, and "Big Bill" Dunn, editor of the radical Butte *Bulletin* in bed together. The caption —naturally—was that politics makes strange bedfellows.

For the first time, Mrs. Wheeler took an active part in my campaign. She toured the state, speaking to women's clubs, emphasizing that the Democratic platform had a "bone dry plank" and discussing the Harding tariff and Daugherty injunctions.

To enliven the campaign I challenged Riddick to a debate but he had no desire to try to outtalk me. He proposed that the debate be conducted in the columns of the newspapers. I scorned a "letter-writing fray," adding in my reply to Riddick: "Some people have been unkind enough to suggest that you do not write all the letters and speeches bearing your name, and in justice to yourself the people should have an opportunity to see and hear you."

Apparently, Riddick's attack failed to stir the populace. On Election Eve, betting odds in Butte started out at even money but swung to 2–1 in my favor two hours later when all betting pools closed and gamblers refused to take any more money at any odds on me.

The returns in Butte by nine o'clock showed that I was carrying Butte by 6500. That was a large majority in those days. The aforementioned Hobbins and John Templeton, a lawyer, were walking up the street when Templeton said, "It looks like Wheeler is going to be elected." Hobbins said, "Oh no! Wait until the 'cow counties' come in." They bet $50. When the so-called "cow counties" came in, I carried most of them and was elected. I realized then that the story I had told for their benefit that I didn't have a chance had been effective.

Far from being submerged in the rural areas, I got an additional 12,000 majority outside the cities—enough to win by 88,205 votes to 69,464. In the other state-wide contest, the Republican candidate, Lew Calloway, for Chief Justice of the state Supreme Court, received almost the same vote as I did in winning. My victory was not shared by my party. The Democrats won one of the congressional districts but the Republicans won all the other positions, including a majority in the legislature. Governor Dixon also won approval for a permanent tax commission to study revision of the tax structure.

I issued a statement attributing my victory to "a repudiation of the reactionary policies of the Harding Administration. Montana people are progressive and want to join with progressives of other states in waging the battle for some constructive legislation in the interest of the average citizen." I noted the election of other progressives—Smith W. Brookhart of Iowa, Robert B. Howell of Nebraska, Clarence C. Dill of Washington, and Lynn J. Frazier of North Dakota—as indicating a national swing away from Hardingism.

Senator Robert M. La Follette, the Wisconsin Republican, was so heartened by the election that he issued a call for a meeting in Washington, D.C., in December to organize a progressive bloc in the next Congress and a national Council of Progressives to work with the bloc. The specific purpose was to defeat the ship subsidy bill, anti-strike legislation, and the proposed transfer of federal forests to the Department of Interior under Secretary Albert B. Fall.

I hurried to Washington to attend the conference along with three other Democratic senators, Henry F. Ashurst of Arizona, Robert L. Owen of Oklahoma, and Morris Sheppard of Texas. We were joined by eight Republicans, including William E. Borah and George W. Norris besides La Follette. The senators were bolstered by a delegation of 19 Republican and seven Democratic members of the House. The conference agreed to try to "drive special privilege out of control of the government and restore it to the people."

I addressed the progressive conference banquet, attended by some 800 delegates and discussed a serious problem in Montana—high freight rates and a shortage of boxcars to move the first good crop harvested in several years. I said also that I heartily approved of the conference's demand for the release of "free speech" prisoners still languishing in jail for World War I prosecutions. In this context, I called myself a true conservative, explaining that I believed in returning to the Declaration of Independence and the Constitution—"from which we have wandered in recent times."

Although I was associated with politicos generally labeled "liberal" and "progressive" throughout most of my career, I have always thought of myself as basically conservative, inasmuch as I fought for preserving what is best in our American heritage.

I was so impressed by the non-partisan unity achieved by the progressives of both parties at their convention that when I returned to Montana I predicted the "elimination of party lines in national affairs." However, I had no reason to suspect how often partisan lines would become entangled in my career after I took my seat in the Senate for the opening of the new session three months hence.

Chapter Ten

COMMUNISTS AND SENATORS

Itching to try out my toga, I departed Butte for Washington on March 1, 1923, with high hopes for legislative action. However, in the national capital I discovered that this was the last thing the Senate wanted. The opening of the new session of Congress was a mere formality. As soon as the new members were sworn in, Congress adjourned until December. The lawmakers had little to do during the Warren G. Harding era of complacency.

Many senators were planning trips to Europe during the long recess, and when I learned that fares were cheap on government-owned shipping lines, I decided to go too. I had a great curiosity about postwar Europe, though little realizing what a "liberal" education this journey would bring me.

Impulsively, I wired Mrs. Wheeler on Friday to meet me in New York on Monday.

"We're going to Europe," I explained in the other ten words of the telegram. This startled her, to say the least, but she had long since learned to enjoy taking my impulses in stride. She arranged for a neighbor in Butte to stay with the children and caught the first train for New York, arriving Friday morning, March 16. (We now had five children—John, Elizabeth, Edward, Frances, and Richard, in that order—and had decided not to move the family to Washington until the fall school term.)

We sailed away to England with no thought of anything but enjoying a vacation—our first real one—and incidentally learning what we could. After stops in Paris, Rome, and Venice, we broached the main object of our interest—that vast, somewhat sinister shadowland of Russia. We asked James Causey, a banker and head of the American Relief Association in Vienna, what our chances were of getting there. Like other Americans we met in Europe, Causey expressed concern for our personal safety. These alarms only heightened our determination to see the Soviets.

In Germany we saw heartrending instances of the struggle against galloping inflation. As in Austria, the aristocrats, untrained for work, were peddling anything they could sell to survive in a revolutionary society. In discussing the financial crisis in Germany and Austria, we heard the rumblings of anti-Semitism of a defeated people seeking a scapegoat. The plunder of art treasures flooding the market and usury in loans by the banks were always attributed to the Jews.

Altogether, my encounters with the poverty of begging children in France and Italy, the devastating inflation of Austria and Germany and the cynicism everywhere about American idealism in the writing of the peace, strengthened my conviction about the futility of war.

In Berlin we were entertained by Colonel and Mrs. Benjamin D. Foulois (he later was to be promoted to general and become head of the Army Air Corps), and Norman Hapgood, former United States Ambassador to Norway, and Mrs. Hapgood. They were waiting for visas to get into Russia and urged us to go there too. When we applied for such visas in Berlin, they were granted immediately.

We got into Russia via Lithuania and Latvia. I was impressed with the large number of British freighters doing business in the harbor at Leningrad. In Moscow, we were lodged in the Sugar Palace, home of the head of the Russian Sugar Trust before the 1917 revolution. It was a magnificent residence, taken over by the government and used by a number of Soviet officials, including Maxim Litvinov and Lenin's doctors from Germany. We were the only foreigners there. In fact, I was the first, or at least among the very first, United States Senator to visit red Russia. I was promptly besieged by newspaper reporters. I refused to comment, explaining that I was on an unofficial inspection tour.

Moscow throbbed with life. The spacious Moscow Art Gallery was crowded with visitors. We discovered that the ballet and theater were equally popular. One Sunday morning we went to the "Living Church," formerly the Church of the Savior, for a four-hour service which included a two-hour concert of sacred music. We were amazed to find that 10,000 people had paid admission to stand throughout the long service.

Litvinov, then in the Foreign Office, granted me an interview and I questioned him closely about the Soviets' rigorous censorship of the press and speech. He replied that such restraint would be necessary for perhaps 50 years of re-education and thereafter the people would accept the communist way of life without question. At the time, under Lenin's New Economic Policy, a few small business and service industries were being restored to private ownership. This retreat convinced me that capitalism eventually would be restored, with the exception of government-owned and operated manufacturing trusts, railroads, public utilities, and the farmers' co-op.

Later Mrs. Wheeler met Mrs. Litvinov and they talked mostly about their children. When Mrs. Wheeler said our children were attending public schools, Mrs. Litvinov looked astonished and exclaimed: "You *don't* send your children to public schools!"

In a conference with Foreign Minister Tchitcherin, he asked me when the United States would recognize Communist Russia. I asked: "When are you going to pay your bills?" Tchitcherin replied that his government did not assume any obligations of the Czarist regime. He said, "This is a new world." I told him it might be a new world to him but not to Americans. He asked me about Secretary of State Charles Evans Hughes. He said he had attended a conference with him during the Czar's regime and liked him. He said Hughes was in favor of Russia having a warm water port then but not now.

Tchitcherin added that Russia's debts to the United States did not amount to much and he pointed out that the United States owed Russia reparations in connection with the Siberian occupation. He suggested that a commission could study the whole situation and strike a balance between the respective claims.

Next, I told Tchitcherin that Bishop Edgar Blake of the Methodist Church, then visiting in Russia, had tried in vain to get an audience with the foreign minister to discuss the impending trial of an Orthodox bishop for treason. Tchitcherin sent for Bishop Blake at once. He explained to the bishop that they had letters written by the Orthodox bishop to the head of the Catholic Church in Poland asking to borrow money and stating that while he couldn't pay it back now he would do so as soon as the counterrevolution was successful. Bishop Blake and I argued that any such trial, regardless of the Soviet claim that it had nothing to do with religion, would only further inflame public opinion in the United States.

The trial, which had been scheduled for the following day, was postponed and the priest never was tried on the charge, although several other clergymen were executed on similar charges.

We were escorted through many industrial plants in Russia and were impressed over and over by the hunger for American machinery and factory methods expressed by everyone we talked with.

We met a number of enthusiastic American radicals in Moscow, including Max Eastman and Anna Louise Strong. I passed up an opportunity to be introduced to "Big Bill" Haywood, former secretary of the IWW whose name had been a byword in Butte. I felt that such a meeting would be misrepresented by the newspaper correspondents following me around. It was bad enough that I was always identified in the Russian press as a former counsel for Bill Dunn, editor of the radical Butte *Bulletin* and subsequently an editor of the official New York Communist organ, the *Daily Worker*. I had once defended Dunn in court.

On May Day in Leningrad, we watched a parade of 20,000 persons marching in a procession that took six hours to pass a given point. When I noticed that most of these obedient demonstrators made the sign of the cross as they passed the cathedral, I felt the Communists would have a hard time in their attempt to stamp out religion. But when I returned to Russia in 1930 with Senator Alben Barkley and Senator Bronson Cutting, I found I had been wrong.

In a newspaper interview after I returned from Russia, I proposed recognition of the Soviet regime—solely in the economic self-interest of the United States. I said I had discovered on my trip that Britain and France were buying cotton from us and reselling it to the Russians at a profit. I argued that it was silly for us not to recognize the Soviets when doing business with them might help pull us out of a growing depression.

A weekly paper in Red Lodge, Montana, said I ought to be deported for urging recognition of a Communist government. My comment was: "Where would you deport me—back to Massachusetts?"

In speeches all over Montana during the summer of 1923, I continued to denounce the economic blockade of famine-stricken Russia as "stupid and inhumane" in the face of the tremendous surpluses of wheat piled up in America. I noted that the British never let differences in political ideology stand in the way of doing business.

For that viewpoint I was harshly attacked by the National Civic Federation. My reply, as carried in *The New York Times*, was this:

"I have more faith in the wisdom and judgment of the American people than have the men who appear to make up the personnel of your organization . . . I believe this government of ours, as well as the Christian religion, is able to withstand all attacks from whatever source, because they are founded on truth, faith and justice. . . . I shall continue, therefore, to advocate the recognition of Soviet Russia by the U.S. and other nations, believing that is the only correct position for an intelligent American to take."

Over the following decade I stated this position before many forums. I also spoke on other aspects of foreign policy as seen through my European journey. I criticized the Versailles Treaty for its arbitrary division of European countries.

"I do not believe the United States should enter any alliance . . . to guarantee the provisions of any treaty made or to be made," I said. I also denounced "commercial wars [to make] . . . countries safe for selfish rulers" and pledged that I would oppose "foreign expeditions as long as I am Senator."

While I was in Butte, "Big Bill" Dunn, the editor, came to see me and asked how things were in Russia. I told him that a friend of mine had quoted Bill Haywood to the effect that he would rather live in jail in America than out of jail in the Soviet Union. Haywood had made a career of criticizing the government and felt he was in a strait-jacket in Russia.

"Bill," I said to Dunn, "what you ought to do is go to Russia for two years. When you came back, you'd get down on your knees when you passed the Statue of Liberty and thank God for this country."

"Bad as that?" Dunn asked me dubiously.

I said it was.

That summer the progressives had an opportunity to pick up another seat in the Senate in a special election by choosing a successor to Senator Knute Nelson of Minnesota, who had died. I enthusiastically accepted an invitation to speak for Magnus Johnson, a Farmer-Labor candidate, against the nominee of both the Republicans and Democrats.

When I arrived in Minneapolis, a banker whom I asked to cash a check warned that "this fellow Johnson is a wild man and a Bolshevik." I told the banker that I myself had been called worse names than that. I said I didn't know Johnson and had never heard him speak but that I was willing to help elect a man who would rouse the East about the plight of the farmer before the banks went under with him.

During the final weeks of the campaign, I stumped with

Senator Henrik Shipstead of Minnesota and Senator Lynn J. Frazier of North Dakota. The Washington *Post* called the special election a "choice between the policies of Harding and the policies of La Follette." The Minnesota press tried to conjure up the spectre of a revolution following Johnson's election —just as the Montana press had done to me in 1920. Even so, Johnson won by over 90,000 votes. Three years earlier, Harding had carried the state by 360,000.

When he arrived in Washington, Johnson walked into the trap that awaited all those "insurgents" who had the temerity to invade the gentlemen's club that is the Senate. Looking for feature angles, the press was ever-ready to picture the Western progressives as a bunch of horny-handed rubes who were attempting to wrest control of Congress from the sophisticated "Old Guard" in both major parties. Johnson was persuaded to pose for photographs milking a cow, while his wife swept the sidewalks of the capital in a calico dress. A United States senator's constituents never like to see him act the buffoon; Johnson was defeated two years later. Senator Smith W. Brookhart of Iowa fell into the same snare when he obligingly assumed the role of a country bumpkin dedicated to cleaning up the "wicked" city of Washington by campaigning against "wild parties."

Due to the long recess that followed after the convening of Congress in March, I never served during the administration of President Harding, who died in San Francisco on August 2, 1923, although I had been elected nine months before his death. When I came to Washington that fall, I was surprised to receive a telephone call from a stranger who said he was a newspaperman and asked if I would like to see President Calvin Coolidge. He said he would make the appointment. I suspected he was a staff member of the White House trying to find out if I would accept before issuing an invitation. I said I would accept.

When I sat down in the White House with Coolidge, he opened the conversation by saying he understood I had been to "Roosia," as he pronounced the word. He added at once that he understood the Russians had no religion. I assured him the

Russian people were very religious, despite the Communists' efforts to wipe out their beliefs, and I cited some religious demonstrations I had witnessed.

"But they don't pay their bills," Coolidge grumbled. I then told him of my conversation on that subject with Tchitcherin. He was noncommittal and shifted over to the farm problem. I told him the plight of the farmer in the Northwest was serious.

"When a man can't make any money in a business, what does he do?" Coolidge asked.

"Like you, Mr. President, I was born and raised in Massachusetts," I replied. "When the cotton and woolen manufacturers can't make any money because of the competition from England and Japan, they come to Congress asking for a tariff."

Coolidge again abruptly changed the subject, noting that Senator Francis E. Warren of Wyoming had come from Massachusetts and a number of other Easterners had gone West and become successful in politics and business.

Thereafter I took every occasion to condemn the Coolidge nostrum to the farmers to "diversify your crops, work hard and don't expect any help from Washington." In an article in *The New York Times,* I wrote:

"When the manufacturing interests . . . come here to Washington and inform Congress that they can no longer make a profit in manufacturing of boots and shoes or cotton and woolen goods because of economic conditions in the world, they are not told to go back and start diversified manufacturing. When they ask Congress to stabilize the price of products and compel the American public to pay exorbitant prices for the articles they manufacture, they are not told that it is economically unsound to place a tariff on their products. Nor are they told that they should shut up their factories and go into some other business . . . that they are Bolshevists and even Socialists."

I argued that the government must assume some responsibility for the farmers' plight. The wheat farmers had gone into debt in answer to the government demand to expand their acreage during the war to provide grain for the allies. Then, plagued by several years of drought, they had to borrow money to keep their farms. Now they were forced by deflationary policies of the Federal Reserve Board to pay off debts incurred during a period of inflation with money obtained during a government-created deflation. As a result, the farmer was forced to sell two bushels of wheat to pay back the price of one bushel he had borrowed.

I proposed that the government assume the role of middleman, to purchase wheat and sell it "with regard to the requirements of both the producer and the consumer . . . there are today millions of men, women and children throughout central Europe and even England, who would gladly consume our surplus wheat if they were able to buy it."

While I denounced Republican indifference, I recognized that the Democrats had no solution. I announced I would not be bound by any action of the Democratic caucus or follow the advice of its Senate leadership. The Democrats, I said, were "sitting back . . . and hoping to be elected not by their own methods but by reason of someone else's mistakes."

This attitude, plainly expressed, was enough to mark me off as an atypical new senator. In addition, my behavior immediately after the Senate reconvened in December 1923 broke a rule and a tradition. The rule was broken inadvertently. On the very first day, I strolled onto the Senate floor with a cigar characteristically clamped in my mouth. I took a puff or two—and was instantly called to order by the President pro tempore, Senator Albert B. Cummins of Iowa. He tartly called out that no smoking was permitted. I hadn't even thought about it, since smoking had been permitted during sessions of the Montana legislature.

The United States Senate welcomes newcomers—but doesn't care to hear a peep out of them for a long time afterward. A freshman is expected to take his seat in the last row, silently learn proper senatorial decorum from the veterans, and in time perhaps come to be accepted as a member of the "club" within the club that is the heart of the Senate. My bright greenness, coupled with my natural lack of caution, caused me to violate this tradition almost at once. In my anxiety to take the progressive bloc's aims in deadly earnest, I stalled the Senate machinery for over four weeks.

The 1923–24 session of the Senate was made up of 51 Republicans, 43 Democrats, and two Farmer-Laborites. But because there were eight progressives among them the Republicans were not sure of re-electing Cummins as President pro tem, the Senate officer who presides in the Vice President's absence, which is usually frequent. But Cummins was out of favor with the progressives and he was due by seniority to be the next chairman of the important Interstate and Foreign Commerce Committee. The progressives announced they would support Cummins for presiding officer only if he would forego the chairmanship. La Follette, the leader of the progressives, was the Republican next in line for the chairmanship.

Recognizing that Cummins was vulnerable in seeking to hold on to both posts, Senate majority leader Henry Cabot Lodge and other GOP leaders tried to persuade him to give up the Senate presidency in favor of running the committee. Cummins refused. The Republicans then struck a bargain with the Democratic leaders by offering them increased representation on important committees in exchange for supporting Cummins for both positions.

Meanwhile, I had learned that my major committee assignment was Agriculture. I went immediately to Senator Walsh, a member of the Democratic group which controlled committee assignments. I pointed out that my primary goal was to launch a campaign for lower freight rates for the West and that I needed to be on Interstate Commerce. If I wasn't appointed to that committee, I said I wanted to be left off all committees. The ultimatum worked. I got my preference.

Customarily, the majority party names the committees and their chairmen and the Senate confirms them by "unanimous consent." This means tacit approval—no vote is taken. On December 10, 1923, Lodge went through the routine motion of offering the resolutions on committees and asking for unanimous consent. The resolution on the committee chairmen had to be considered separately from that naming the committee members. Realizing that Cummins was likely to be approved as chairman of Interstate Commerce by default, so to speak, I felt in no way bound by the "deal" the Democratic leadership had made. I whispered to Clarence Dill, of the state of Washington, sitting at the next desk, that I wanted to fight the Cummins nomination. Dill said all I had to do was object to Lodge's request for unanimous consent.

"I object!" I called out, startling myself as well as everyone else. I was immediately aware of the breach of etiquette I had committed when senatorial heads swiveled toward my desk in the last row. Now I was looking into a mass of raised, tufted eyebrows. With two words I had shattered a hardy tradition. Down in the well of the Senate, several senators began talking at once in an effort to clarify the situation. The confusion caused by my brashness is evident from the following excerpt from the Congressional Record:

MR. BRANDEGEE: Who objected?

THE PRESIDENT: The senator from Arkansas.

MR. ROBINSON: I have not objected. I merely stated that any senator has the right to object.

THE PRESIDENT: The junior senator from Montana objected.

MR. BRANDEGEE: Did the senator from Montana object to the resolution?

MR. WHEELER: I objected.

MR. BRANDEGEE: Very well.

Joseph T. Robinson of Arkansas, the Democratic leader, thereupon suggested a separate roll call on Cummins and a little later the roll was called. My theory was that the progressive Republicans could never vote for Cummins and that the Democrats would be obliged to vote for their senior member on the Interstate Commerce Committee, the colorful Ellison D. ("Cotton Ed") Smith of South Carolina. I made it clear that this was not a personal fight against Cummins but an ideological one.

"The people of my state and other states in the West made the issue of freight rates and the Esch-Cummins law an important issue in the election," I explained. "Those who championed the law were defeated . . . the people do not want the man who championed the cause of the railroads as chairman of the committee which regulates them . . ."

Smith had opposed the Esch-Cummins law, which among other things guaranteed the railroads six per cent despite the fact that La Follette and the progressives had claimed there was a tremendous amount of watered stock in the railroads and had demanded an investigation of their capital structure.

On the first ballot, Cummins got 41 votes, Smith 39, and La Follette got seven. (Progressive Republicans William E. Borah and James Couzens supported La Follette. Dill, a progressive Democratic, and I voted for Smith.) Since a majority of the number of senators voting was required, Cummins was not elected chairman.

The leaders of my party clustered around, urging me to withdraw my objection and allow the Senate to proceed as it always had.

"You got the committee you wanted, so what are you fighting for?" demanded Senator Claude A. Swanson of Virginia. "Why don't you follow the leadership?"

I laughed and asked him, "Who's leading?"

There were rumors that enough Democrats might absent themselves to make a possible majority for Cummins. I served notice that if any such maneuver was tried I would take the floor and brand the absentees as "allies of the Old Guard."

"That would simply prove that there is no real difference between a reactionary Republican and a reactionary Democrat—except that some of them live in one section of the country and the others in another section," I said to some of my colleagues.

Word got around that Joe Robinson, the Democratic leader, had told the GOP leadership that he deeply regretted the deadlock which might end in the election of "Cotton Ed" Smith. At one point the deadlock came within one vote of being ended when five progressives switched from La Follette to Smith—enough to elect him. However, a Democrat, William C. Bruce of Maryland, then switched his vote from Smith to Cummins to prevent an election which, he argued, "would have been tantamount to a victory for La Follette." Bruce denounced me for refusing to abide by the Democratic agreement. I retorted that any Democrat who voted for Cummins was "a traitor to the farmers and thousands of other men and women who had in 1922 voted against the Esch-Cummins law."

With the Senate still deadlocked near the end of December, Senator James A. Reed, the articulate Democrat from Missouri, took the floor and argued that the chairmanship was an honorary position carrying no special authority. The time had come, he told the Senate, to quit the "boy's play" over the issue.

I replied that in my limited experience in the Montana legislature I had learned the hard way what powers a chairman could wield. After all, I had been a committee chairman myself.

"If the chairmanship doesn't amount to anything," I continued, "why do the Republicans object to Senator La Follette, who should rightfully be the chairman?"

The issue, I stressed, was whether the spokesman for the railroads should hold the reins of this particular committee. It could scarcely be dismissed as "child's play."

The chamber began to fill up with senators looking forward to watching the upstart from Montana slapped down by Reed, who was famous for his vitriol. The Missourian disappointed his audience. He simply took out a cigar, angrily bit it in two, and stalked from the chamber. Later, as I left the floor, Reed came up to me and said, "Where are you going, boy?" We took a walk together, talked most of the evening, and struck up a lasting friendship.

Midway through the long series of inconclusive roll calls, Senator La Follette issued from his sickbed a statement that the election of Smith would be a "clear-cut victory" for the progressives, as long as the Old Guard refused to support either James Couzens of Michigan or Robert B. Howell of Nebraska, both liberal Republican members of Interstate Commerce. But the Republican leadership preferred to see a Democrat elected rather than vote for a progressive. It turned down name after name from the ranks of the insurgents.

On January 9, 1924—thirty days after I had sounded off—the stalemate ended. La Follette, back in the Senate, persuaded five other progressives to vote for Smith on the thirty-fifth ballot. This elected a Democratic committee chairman in a Republican-controlled Senate, an extraordinary occurrence. The railroad brotherhoods rejoiced at the defeat of their arch-enemy, Cummins. La Follette wrote in their paper *Labor* that Cummins' defeat was a substantial victory for the people, adding: "Senator Wheeler, who objected to the election . . . when confirmation was sought without a record vote . . . deserves a large share of credit for the successful issue of the Progressive fight."

There were flattering notices in other quarters. William Jennings Bryan, the veteran leader of the agrarian Democrats, said, "It is inspiring to know that men like Senator Wheeler have the courage and ability to challenge the aristocracy of money in the legislative halls." Clinton W. Gilbert, Washington correspondent of the Philadelphia *Evening Public Ledger,* wrote that "if I were to pick the best fighter in the U. S. Senate, I should lay my money on Burt Wheeler, the new Senator from Montana."

From then on I had many graphic examples at hand to use in speeches to Eastern audiences to prove my contention that party labels are meaningless—a truism in Midwestern and Western politics. For example, I told an audience at Ford Hall Forum in Boston that it was becoming "more and more difficult to distinguish a Republican from a Democrat by what he advocates." I saw Congress as divided between reactionaries and progressives, with the division cutting across party lines. I hit back in this speech at the charge of Senator Irvine L. Lenroot, a Wisconsin Republican, that "the tendency toward blocs was a tendency toward the Sovietism of Russia." There were always blocs in Congress, I explained, pointing to the "financial bloc" and the "railroad bloc" as two that were never idle.

When I first came to Washington, I thought I had all the answers on how to settle the economic ills of the country. I was eager to help the farmer and the laborer and couldn't wait to get started. Gradually I had to change my ideas on some specific remedies. For example, I had thought government ownership of the railroads would help reduce the freight rates. But when I saw the clumsy and wasteful manner in which many departments and agencies administered their programs, I changed my mind about government ownership.

As for the Senate itself, I was no more awed or intimidated than my tradition-busting debut suggests. One of the first bits of advice I got was realistic. The courtly and acidly eloquent Senator Henry F. Ashurst, whom I had known on the campus of the University of Michigan, told me: "This is the most selfish body of men in the world. Don't do anything for anybody here and expect him to do something for you in return. They won't take that attitude toward you."

Senator Walsh, a scholarly man, took a different view. When I complained to him that the Senate wasn't providing me with the action I was accustomed to in Montana, he counseled patience. He said the Senate was "like a great university—if you pay attention you can learn a great deal." In time I was to discover that Walsh was right. I found that there were some very able men on both sides of the aisle and I learned much from them.

But my first glimpse of the Senate as it operated from the inside was not inspiring. Not long after I took my seat, a friend asked me my opinion of the "greatest deliberative body in the world."

"It reminds me of the city council in Butte," I said facetiously.

This quip got back to the Senate Democratic leadership and didn't do me any good.

Chapter Eleven

ROXY AND THE "OHIO GANG"

On February 20, 1924—while still a brand new freshman—I rose nervously in the Senate to deliver what proved to be the most important speech of my career.

I had introduced a resolution to create a select committee to investigate Harry M. Daugherty, the Attorney General of the United States and the former number one crony of the late President Harding. The resolution directed an inquiry into the "alleged neglect and failure" of Daugherty to prosecute those accused in the newly exposed Teapot Dome scandal as well as "many others for violation of other federal statutes."

My speech reviewed Daugherty's many questionable associations and the fact that a cloud of rumored corruption had hung over the Justice Department since Harding had been inaugurated.

"Here the Congress of the United States had appropriated one million dollars for the detection and prosecution of crime," I told my colleagues, "and . . . we find the Department of Justice, instead of trying to detect the greatest crooks and those guilty of the greatest crimes against the nation that have ever been perpetrated, we find the Department of Justice protecting them all during this time; we find them protecting them tonight, because I am reliably informed that only last Sunday night the Attorney General of the United States held a conference with Ed McLean." (Edward B. McLean, multimillionaire publisher of the Washington *Post* and playboy member of the Harding coterie, was involved in the Teapot Dome conspiracy.)

"Mr. President," I continued, "the evidence in this case, if it be true, would warrant one in thinking that the Attorney General of the United States, now occupying the highest legal position in the government, is guilty of many crimes."

Senator Frank B. Willis, an Ohio Republican who was filling Harding's old seat in the Senate, jumped to his feet protesting that "if one-tenth of the charges that have been made here by the Senator from Montana are true, then instead of there being an investigation the Attorney General of the United States ought to be impeached, removed from office, disqualified to hold office, and be subjected to criminal proceedings besides."

I noted that there had been a move in the House to impeach Daugherty more than a year before but that, instead of investigating the Attorney General, the House leadership "tried the Representative who had the temerity to stand up and file those charges."

(Representative Oscar E. Keller, an Independent Republican from Minnesota, had moved the impeachment of Daugherty, but the House Judiciary Committee had allowed the Attorney General to submit his defense in writing and thus avoid questioning. The committee promptly absolved him of guilt—in handling war fraud cases and of bias against labor—and then sought to smear Keller.)

The New York Times called my indictment of Daugherty "the most sensational speech of the present Congress." The late Paul Y. Anderson of the St. Louis *Post-Dispatch* described it as "an attack so savage that even the Senate flinched." The United States Senate was not accustomed to hearing a cabinet officer so bluntly arraigned. Nothing at that point had been nailed down about Daugherty's reported malfeasance and it was apparent that many senators wondered if I had blundered far out on a shaky limb.

My speech had put Daugherty's fat in the Senate fire—and placed a question mark over my future in that body. Vaguely I sensed that this step would make me or break me—one of us would win. But I had been in bare-knuckle fights before; I assumed there was nothing the opposition could do to me that hadn't been tried in Montana. I was mistaken. I did not anticipate the fantastic tactics and personalities that would cross my path. Harry Daugherty was a defiant and vengeful man who was ready to strike back with all the considerable resources of the Department of Justice.

If the Republican leaders were skeptical of some of my charges, they took no chances. After my speech, Senator Henry Cabot Lodge, the venerable GOP leader, led a group of senators to the White House and advised President Coolidge to get rid of his holdover Attorney General. Coolidge refused.

According to William Allen White, the famous Kansas editor, the President later explained to a friend: "I ask you if there were any man in the Cabinet for whom . . . if they were still living . . . President Harding would more surely demand his day in court, would more surely *not* dismiss because of popular clamor than the man who was his closest personal and political friend?"

The original resolution I had drawn up earlier in February had called upon Coolidge to request Daugherty's resignation. Pending in the Senate at the time was a resolution calling for the ouster of Secretary of the Navy Edwin Denby for having turned over the Navy's oil reserves to the Department of the Interior—where they were soon leased secretly to the oil companies.

I agreed to line up the progressive Republicans for the Denby resolution in return for the promise of Senate Democratic leader Joe Robinson to have the Democrats support mine. Robinson a little later persuaded me to rewrite my resolution so as to call for an investigation of Daugherty, instead of his resignation, because the Attorney General was loudly demanding his "day in court."

My revised resolution also called for creation of a select investigating committee, since Senator Frank B. Brandegee, the Old Guard Connecticut Republican who was chairman of the Judiciary Committee, had no desire to handle this hot potato. Bolstered by the company of Senator Robert La Follette, the distinguished Republican progressive leader, I next called on the Senate's presiding officer, Senator Albert B. Cummins. We asked if he would follow our recommendations in naming the members of the special committee. Cummins stalled, pleading he would first have to check with Willis and Lodge. This annoyed La Follette. He pounded the table and surprised me by saying somewhat roughly to Cummins: "Albert, we'll *make* you do it!"

When we heard nothing further from Cummins, I incorporated into the resolution the names of the committee members. Besides myself, they were: Republicans Smith W. Brookhart, of Iowa; George H. Moses, of New Hampshire; and Wesley L. Jones, of Washington; and Democrat Henry F. Ashurst, of Arizona. I picked Brookhart as chairman because he was a liberal and because I found in a talk with him that he shared my desire for an objective but thorough investigation.

Thus, though the Senate was GOP-controlled, I felt I had a committee that would lean 3–2 in my favor. When the resolution came up for action on the floor, there was a good deal of grumbling by Republicans over the fact that I had the effrontery to name the members of the committee I was proposing. Lodge called this an "insult" to Cummins, since the presiding officer traditionally has the prerogative of selecting the members of a select panel. However, the Senate finally approved my resolution on a roll call vote of 66–1. Then the members of the new committee elected me to present the case against Daugherty.

For the Republicans, the new probe was adding weal on woe. My Montana colleague, Senator Thomas J. Walsh, was already giving them fits by pressing his investigation of the smelly Teapot Dome affair through the Interior Committee.

I had also played a role in the origins of his probe—which was to continue, with historic results, for five years.

En route to Washington, D.C., after my election to the Senate in November 1922, I had paused at Billings, Montana, and run into an old friend, Tom Arthur. Arthur was the representative in Montana of the Texas Company and was one of the leading Democrats in the state. He brought up the subject of Teapot Dome, which was still in the rumor stage. He told me he knew it was a "crooked deal" and deserved a complete public airing.

In Washington I attended a conference of progressives called by Senator La Follette, who had introduced a resolution for a Teapot Dome investigation in the previous session but had gotten nowhere. La Follette broached the subject to me and said there was only one member of the Interior Committee capable of handling it—the patient, scholarly, upright Walsh. He asked me to get Walsh to take over the job.

I mentioned the request to Walsh and he replied, "Well, I can't do everything."

"Senator," I said, "I don't know anything about this except that when I passed through Billings, Tom Arthur said he thought Teapot Dome was a scandal and ought to be exposed."

"Did Tom Arthur say that?" Walsh asked. He was impressed that a man who represented an oil company thought the Teapot Dome deal reeked. This bore out information he had received from Democratic Senator John B. Kendrick of Wyoming, where the Teapot Dome reserve was located.

Meanwhile, I began hearing reports about Daugherty. A member of the Federal Trade Commission told me the Attorney General had not prosecuted numerous cases recommended by the FTC. There were also much more sensational rumors floating about. But my first interest was to find out if he really was ignoring the trusts and other big combinations that were in restraint of trade. As soon as I announced I would introduce a resolution, tips came to me in bunches that Daugherty was up to his neck in massive graft.

The Senate Republicans' anxiety about my proposed investigation did not stem from any love of Daugherty. Much as I disagreed on issues with Lodge and the other conservative Republicans, I respected them as dignified, able, and honest senators. Daugherty was not their type but, more than that, they had a distaste for crooks in high office. They had looked upon Harding as a good fellow but a weak President who had surrounded himself with an inferior and unsavory clique of politicians. Now the "Ohio Gang"—as it soon came to be known during our hearings—was posthumously ruining the dead President's reputation and the senior GOP senators hoped to make the developing scandal as light a burden as possible for Coolidge in the 1924 presidential election.

The hard-boiled Daugherty himself was not panicked. Shortly after my resolution was passed, he confidently informed a group of worried Republican senators that he would take care of "this upstart from the sagebrush" in his own fashion. It was said that no one, not even a President of the United States, could intimidate Harry Mijacah Daugherty. He was a poor boy from Washington Court House, a small town in Fayette County in southern Ohio, who had worked his way to a law degree at the University of Michigan, my alma mater, in 1881, the year before I was born. He soon discovered that he was far more successful at running a political machine than he was at running for office. In the summer of 1920 he hit the jackpot; in the now famous "smoke-filled room" in Chicago, Daugherty manipulated the dark-horse nomination of Warren G. Harding to be President of the United States and his meal ticket.

As Attorney General, Daugherty looked the part of a prosperous Scotch-Irish politician of his day; gregarious and self-assured, sporting a derby, a high stiff collar and a diamond stickpin, he was obviously and always for his friends all the way.

Taking on this Midwestern Mikado, our special committee was treated like a poor relation by the Senate. Our hearings had to be held not in the spacious marble-walled caucus room—scene of so many major investigations—but around a large table in Room 410 of the Senate Office Building. This virtually put us in one another's laps and restricted the size of the public audience. For my work space, I was assigned a small outer office of Room 410 and eventually I was "evicted" even from those cramped quarters.

For an investigator I had only a young Montana lawyer, Arthur B. Melzner, to start with, plus a couple of staff members from my own office. But soon I was offered auxiliary help from an unexpected source. Charley Michelson, then a reporter for the New York *World* and later the astute publicity director of the Democratic National Committee during the New Deal, introduced me to Frank A. Vanderlip, a prominent retired president of the National City Bank in New York and a Republican. Vanderlip somewhat earlier had charged that Harding had sold his Ohio newspaper, the Marion *Star*, for more than twice what it was worth. As retribution, Vanderlip had been forced to resign from the many institutions of which he was a director. Now he wanted to expose the Harding Administration. He put at my disposal all the investigators and resources of the Citizens Federal Research Bureau, which he had set up and financed to "ferret out corruption in Washington." Vanderlip and his private bureau proved to be invaluable to the Daugherty investigating committee.

Now some of the people who had sent me tips of the Attorney General's venality refused to come forward and testify. But a steady flow of new allegations arrived in the mail. Several letters urged me to contact a Miss Roxy Stinson, divorced wife of Jess Smith, Daugherty's close friend who had committed suicide in 1923. Before I had time to look into this tip, two men from Buffalo, New York, showed up in the committee office. One was Henry Stern, a lawyer, and the other was one A. L. Fink. When I came upon them, they had just about talked Brookhart into issuing a subpoena which they promised to deliver to Miss Stinson in Columbus, Ohio.

"You mustn't do that—do you know these people?" I asked the chairman, who was inclined to be too trusting. Brookhart explained that the two strangers had been sent by Senator James W. Wadsworth of New York, and Colonel William ("Wild Bill") Donovan, then a United States District Attorney in upstate New York. Wadsworth and Donovan were Republicans and I suspected this was a sly attempt by the GOP to find out how much Miss Stinson knew before we could get to her. I told Brookhart I would take the subpoena and deliver it myself. A few hours later I boarded a train for Columbus. I allowed Stern and Fink to tag along. They had kept insisting they only wanted to do a public service and, besides, Fink said he knew Miss Stinson.

Fink introduced me to her in the living room of her home in Columbus. Roxy Stinson was then approximately forty years old, a statuesque redhead, with the figure of a showgirl. When I told her the committee needed her testimony, she balked. I promised her national publicity but she said that was one thing she wanted to avoid. I then promised we would keep her from getting publicity. When she still demurred, I flashed the Senate subpoena calling for her appearance "forthwith." I said she had to come with us immediately. She gave in, but asked if she could call someone first. I said no.

Miss Stinson packed a bag and soon the four of us were headed back to Washington. On the train, I got Roxy alone for a short time and questioned her about what she knew in a very general way. It was enough to convince me she could blow the case against the Attorney General wide open. Also, she agreed to tell everything she knew—and *only* what she knew. I realized it was urgent to get her on the stand before Daugherty's friends could scare her into silence.

When we arrived in the capital, Miss Stinson begged me to let her telephone Ned McLean, the Washington *Post* publisher and Harding crony who was a friend of hers. I said it was out of the question. I put her up in the Washington Hotel under the "protection" of my sister, Mrs. Maude Mitchell, who was my secretary. Maude took all the phone calls and kept Roxy in the room—and all the would-be visitors out.

I hastily set the opening hearing for two o'clock the following afternoon, twenty-four hours earlier than I had scheduled. Then, on March 12, 1924, I sprang my glamorous surprise witness. I could hardly have found anyone more ideal to get the hearings rolling full tilt. The press—which was scribbling furiously from the opening gavel—noted that Miss Stinson was fashionably dressed and attractive. Sitting with a sealskin coat draped over her shoulders, she talked in a low voice. Though she was obviously under tension, I believe she came through as an utterly credible witness. She told of a curious relationship with Jess Smith, and how it made her privy to high-level intrigue.

Miss Stinson testified that she had married Smith, who was twelve years her senior, when both were living in Washington Court House, Ohio, in 1908. There was an amicable divorce eighteen months later. Since then, she explained, Smith had danced attendance on her regularly, become her confidant, and generously shared with her the fruits of his profitable deals with Daugherty. She indignantly denied that she and Smith had lived as man and wife after their divorce. She obviously had a sisterly affection for her ex-husband. He, a weak character, must have depended on her for emotional support.

Smith was an oddball in the gaggle of amoral opportunists who joyously trailed Harding from Ohio to the White House. Miss Stinson described him as Daugherty's "bumper," which in her lexicon meant "intimate friend."

A foppish small-town merchant who yearned to mingle with Very Important People, Smith had attached himself to Daugherty like a faithful puppy. Daugherty rewarded this fealty with companionship and power. They shared Daugherty's apartment in the Wardman Park Hotel in Washington and Smith was assigned his own office in the Justice Department. Though never on the government payroll, Smith traveled free on a Department pass and was widely accepted as the unofficial "deputy Attorney General." He accompanied Harding, who also counted him a friend, on presidential junkets and he roistered with Daugherty and his fellows at the notorious "Little Green House on K Street," the nerve center for their shady transactions.

When the high-flying "drugstore sport" blew his brains out early one morning in the Wardman Park suite, all Washington was shocked—and not a little curious. Daugherty was quoted to the effect that coincidently with Smith's death all their records somehow had gotten burned. There were demands for an investigation to determine whether Smith was murdered.

Miss Stinson said on the witness stand that she got acquainted with Harding during the presidential campaign. The following questioning ensued:

SEN. WHEELER: Did you afterward visit at his home?
MISS STINSON: Yes, sir.
SEN. WHEELER: Whereabouts was that?
MISS STINSON: At Marion, Ohio.
SEN. WHEELER: And who with?
MISS STINSON: Mr. Jess Smith.
SEN. WHEELER: And what have you to say about whether you subsequently met the President; and if so, where?
MISS STINSON: We called at their home, and went from their home to dinner at Dr. Sawyer's sanitarium, where Mr. Harding had me as a dinner partner. He sat by my side—and he was very attentive.

Just prior to his coming to Harding's inauguration, Miss Stinson testified Smith was worth "between $150,000 and $175,000." When he died, she said, his estate was appraised at "approximately $250,000." But for six months before his death Smith had been excitable and jumpy.

"He was in constant fear," Miss Stinson continued. "He asked me to bolster him up, to cheer him up . . . he was home for two weeks prior to his passing away. The last evening he spent cautioning me what not to tell, what not to do, and what to destroy, and I said finally, 'Well, I will either tell or I won't, so let's don't talk about it any longer.'"

"I haven't told anyone," she added. "I have been approached many times in the last seven months from angles, all angles, but I am here to defend him . . . Jess Smith gave his life for Harry Daugherty; he absolutely adored him."

Miss Stinson said "tortures of pressure" were brought on Smith from sources she did not know "to try to betray Harry Daugherty, which he would not do." She quoted Smith as saying to her in desperation, "I am not made for this. This intrigue is driving me crazy. If I could just come home, but I am in now and I have to stand by Harry." Roxy charged that Daugherty

1, 2, 3. Yankee Boyhood. Burton K. Wheeler, youngest of ten children, grew to early manhood in Hudson, Massachusetts.

4. Midwest Wedding. Armed with a law degree from the University of Michigan, Wheeler was married to Lulu M. White in September 1907, in Albany, Illinois.

5. Western Lawmaker. Wheeler launched his career of political independence by taking a seat in the Montana House of Representatives at the age of twenty-eight.

6. Lawyer for the Underdog. Wheeler won his reputation defending labor leaders and, as Montana's District Attorney (1913–18), keeping a cool head amid war hysteria.

7. Crusading Senator. As a brash freshman, Wheeler became nationally controversial in 1924 by ousting Attorney General Harry M. Daugherty. Shown here are members of the select investigating committee: (l. to r.) Senators Wheeler, George H. Moses, Smith W. Brookhart, Wesley L. Jones, Henry F. Ashurst.

Underwood & Underwood

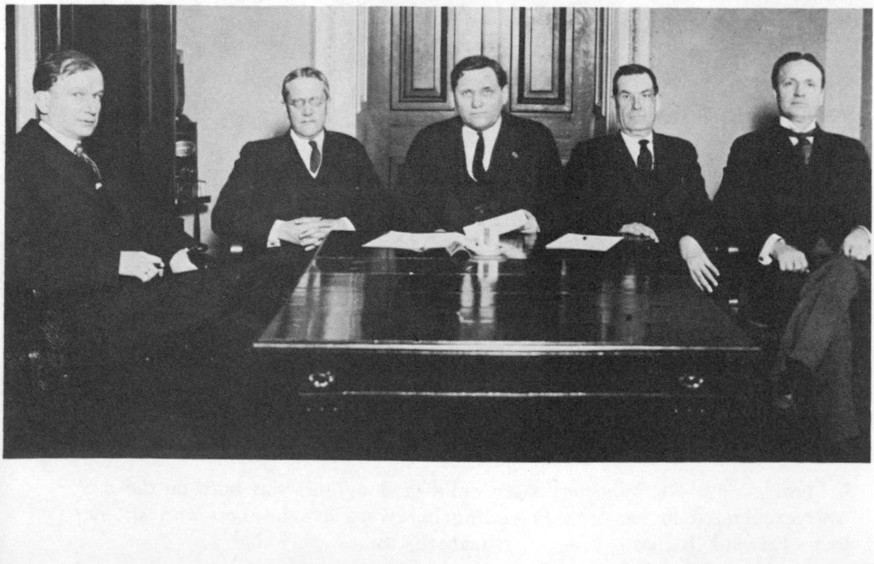

John M. Baer

8. Vindicated. This cartoon in the weekly newspaper, *Labor*, followed the 1925 trial in which Wheeler was acquitted of a "frame-up" charge of conflict-of-interest.

Underwood & Underwood

9. Family Man. The Wheelers' sixth child (a daughter) was born on the day he was exonerated in his trial. Preceding her were five brothers and sisters: (l. to r.) Edward, Richard, Frances, Elizabeth, John.

10. Maverick. Frequently cartooned, the Senator was portrayed this way by R. G. List for the book *Sons of the Wild Jackass* by Ray Tucker.

Harris & Ewing

11. Party Bolter. Wheeler temporarily deserted the Democratic party in 1924 to run as Vice President on the national Independent Progressive ticket headed by Senator Robert M. La Follette (left). They drew the biggest third-party popular presidential vote in history.

12. Triumphant Lawmaker. Wheeler played the key role in passage of Roosevelt's controversial Public Utilities Holding Company Act of 1935. Here he watches FDR present one of the signing pens to Thomas G. ("Tommy the Cork") Corcoran, the President's legislative aide. Shown (l. to r.) are Senator Alben Barkley; Senator Wheeler; Senator Fred H. Brown; Dozier A. DeVane, Federal Power Commission solicitor; Representative Sam Rayburn.

13. Two "Cowboys." The Senator, with daughter Marion and son Edward (second from right), calls on Gary Cooper on Hollywood movie lot. Montana-born Cooper was the son of a close friend of Wheeler's. At far right is movie "czar" Will Hays.

Berryman, Washington Evening Star

14. The Third Term. The entry of Roosevelt's name in the Illinois primary of 1940 was considered bad news to three leading possibilities for the presidential nomination —Wheeler, Farley, and McNutt.

Rockford Register-Republic

15. Horsemanship. The Wheelers raised all their children to ride. Here they set out on a morning canter with daughter Elizabeth.

Time, Inc.

16. Man of the Week. *Time* magazine carried this portrait of Wheeler on the cover of its April 15, 1940, issue over the caption: "The Democratic party has a great future."

Acme

17. Non-interventionist. The Senator joined Charles A. Lindbergh at an America First rally before 20,000 persons in Madison Square Garden on October 30, 1941.

Parrish, The Chicago Tribune

18. FDR's No. 1 Antagonist. Wheeler, an original backer of Roosevelt, angered the President by defeating him on his court-packing bill in 1937 and by opposing his interventionist war policies in 1940–41.

19. Crony of Cactus Jack. Vice-President John N. Garner once saluted Wheeler as having the most important senatorial attribute—guts.

20. Wheeler on Wheels. The Father of many transportation laws launched the first run of the B&O *National Limited* with decorative assistance.

21, 22. Mountain Man. Now a prominent Washington lawyer, Wheeler spends his summers at his lodge on Lake McDonald in Glacier National Park. Here he exhibits trout catch with son Dick and Filipino houseman Simeon Arboleda and (below) plays cards with Mrs. Wheeler (striped dress), Arboleda, and Mr. and Mrs. Gene Sullivan.

23. Life with Father. Having reared a family as independent-minded as themselves, the Wheelers have learned to take a ribbing from their sons and daughters: (l. to r.) Edward, his father's law partner; Elizabeth (Mrs. Edwin A. Colman), Milwaukee, Wis.; Richard, a Denver radio executive; Marion (Mrs. Robert Scott), Bethesda, Md.; John, a corporation vice president of Pasadena, Calif.

was "morally responsible" for the death of his closest friend.

The witness said her ex-husband kept telling her about the "deals" he and the Attorney General were making. Smith himself expected to clean up about $180,000 through the nationwide exhibition of a film of the 1921 championship fight between Jack Dempsey and Georges Carpentier. Interstate shipment of the fight film was illegal but the imaginative Daugherty clique found a loophole.

Since the movie's interstate shipment—but not its showing—was banned, a "scapegoat" would be found in each state who would pay the relatively small fine that would be levied for the violation. The film could then be shown as often as the exhibitor wished in that particular state.

To keep the scapegoat from being jailed as well as fined, however, the case had to be steered to a judge who could be fixed. Jess Smith claimed that he and Daugherty were able to fix federal judges in twenty states. The scheme had been hatched in the cunning brain of "Jap" Muma, who was general manager of Ned McLean's newspapers. (Despite his queer name, Muma was no more Oriental than any of his fellow Ohioans.)

Daugherty was directly implicated in the fight film conspiracy through the testimony of two former secret agents of the Justice Department. They said they were told the details by Muma.

On occasion, Miss Stinson testified, her suddenly influential ex-husband brought back to Washington Court House "grips full of whisky." The witness said "he drank a part of it" and divided the rest with her and Mal Daugherty, Harry Daugherty's brother. Sometimes he would bring a "great weekend case" of liquor which she said was as large as a table in the committee room.

Smith apparently had ready access to whisky during Prohibition. Miss Stinson explained: ". . . he would make reference to permits that would let people get liquor. That was when they were first in office, you understand. But that did not last very long because they were afraid of it."

(Subsequently the butler at the "Little Green House on K Street" testified that twice he saw a Wells Fargo wagon deliver twenty cases of liquor there. He said each load was "guarded" by a man he assumed to be a revenue agent because he was armed and wore a badge.)

She and Smith spent a week in New York City at the time of the Dempsey-Carpentier fight, Miss Stinson related. They saw a good deal of Joe Weber, of the famous theatrical team of Weber & Fields. Weber took them to dress rehearsals and got them theater tickets. All Weber wanted was a parole for his wife's brother who was in the penitentiary.

"It was Mr. Daugherty that was the one to get the parole, or see that it was gotten," Miss Stinson recalled from overhearing the conversations between Weber and Smith. Later, she said, Smith complained to her of Weber that, "I don't know whether we are going to bother with him or not. He is awful cheap and wants something for nothing."

Smith shared with Miss Stinson the stock that he and the Attorney General had mysteriously acquired. She couldn't recall how many shares she got, but she said they were in the White Motors and Pure Oil Companies.

Alert as they were, even Daugherty and Smith apparently could miss a good thing during the Washington gold rush under Harding. Miss Stinson testified that her ex-husband once told her that five friends of theirs had cleaned up no less than $33,000,000 in a Sinclair oil deal in just five days. She continued: "I said . . . 'Were you and Harry in on it?' He said, 'No, that is what we are sore about.'"

Miss Stinson charged that Daugherty was back of many attempts to "intimidate" her into keeping her mouth shut. Only a month previously, she related, the aforementioned A. L. Fink, whom she had known for some time, persuaded her to meet with him at the Hotel Hollenden in Cleveland on the pretext of explaining a business deal. She occupied a separate room that night, she explained, but discovered too late that Fink, who had taken care of the reservations and registration, had listed them as man and wife. Miss Stinson asserted that this "frame-up" was an attempt to compromise her in connection with Fink's demand that she withhold her story from the committee. Her voice broke in describing this incident and several times she seemed on the verge of hysterical tears.

Miss Stinson was in the witness chair for five days. Her testimony of course drew overflow audiences. A reporter for the Washington *Times* wrote that these sessions "had all the atmosphere of a murder trial, combined with the bated breath excitement of the opening of King Tut's tomb—the King Tut in this instance being poor Jess Smith."

Daugherty countered with a violent attack on the character of our witness. He sneered at Miss Stinson as a "disappointed woman," an "angry woman," and a "malicious woman." Along with many newspaper editorialists, he tried to dismiss her testimony as "hearsay." But in a conspiracy, which is what I was charging, evidence is admissible which might otherwise be deemed hearsay, to establish the terms and conditions under which the conspirators acted.

Significantly, virtually all the important statements made by Miss Stinson under oath were subsequently corroborated by other witnesses. We invited Daugherty's two defense counsel—former Senator George E. Chamberlain and former Congressman L. Paul Howland—to cross-examine her but they abandoned the questioning after only five minutes.

My second witness was one of the most incredible figures in the annals of cloak-and-dagger work in this country—Gaston B. Means. Means had been a German government agent in 1916 and also a close associate of William J. Burns in Burns' famous detective agency. He followed Burns into the government when the latter was made head of the Bureau of Investigation—later the FBI—by Daugherty.

Means was then fiftyish, a powerful-looking, heavy-set man with a large head and a legendary reputation as a confidence man. When a newspaper correspondent brought us together, he was under suspension by Daugherty, but I was suspicious. My suspicion was well founded, for it turned out later that he was still a paid informant for Burns, and apparently sent to us to find out what we had on Daugherty.

At this time Means told me he was a friend of Burns but would give me all the information he could to hang Daugherty.

He assured me he could throw some light on an aircraft case that was puzzling us and so I put him on the stand. He made sensational headlines by testifying that, in February 1922, he had received one hundred $1000 bills from a Japanese representative of Mitsui and Company and, on instruction, turned the bills over to Jess Smith.

The Mitsuis controlled the Standard Aircraft Company, which in 1921–22 was under investigation for wartime fraud by the United States government. One of the charges brought against Daugherty in the House was that he had failed to press the case against the company.

We were unable to produce direct corroboration for Means' story but we concluded that some sizable payoff must have been made after we heard the testimony of Captain H. L. Scaife, a bearded former Justice Department investigator. Scaife's study of the records showed that Standard Aircraft had overcharged the government by $2,267,342 on its war contracts (while failing to deliver a single fighting plane to France). Oddly, Scaife testified, his report and all its copies had gotten "lost" and then the whole case was "blocked" on a higher level. Scaife quit the Department in disgust.

Another possible corroboration of the reported $100,000 payoff was testimony by Miss Stinson that Jess Smith once returned from Washington proudly wearing a money belt stuffed with seventy-five $1000 bills.

Means turned over to the committee ten little black books which he claimed were "minute-by-minute diaries" filled with damaging evidence of his spying for Smith, Burns, and Daugherty. However, when I asked the committee staff for the books later on to examine them I was told they had been turned back to Means. He had presented a committee employee with an order for the books purportedly signed by Brookhart. I found that the signature was a forgery and I never again saw the little black books.

The rascally Means was more trouble to us than he was worth. During the hearings, he turned up frequently at my home in the evening and warned Mrs. Wheeler that my life was in danger. This psychological warfare included advising her against buying candy peddled in the neighborhood, for fear my enemies would try to poison the children. He also explained that assassins might try to kill me by forcing my car off the road. The idea that my enemies would try to harm me was as silly as it had been in my Montana days; from a public reaction standpoint, it would be the worst thing they could do.

However, Mrs. Wheeler and I knew there were men hiding behind our own shrubbery day and night watching to see who came and went. As a precaution, Vanderlip had his chauffeur drive me to Capitol Hill every morning and bring me back in the evening.

At one point, when our hearings were temporarily off the front pages, Means offered to blow up our sun porch to get me publicity as the victim of a bomb plot. He also told me fantastic stories—entirely uncorroborated—about how he had collected money for crooked officials in the Harding Administration; sometimes, he said, he buried it in the ground. He also told me he had been hired by Mrs. Harding to spy on the President's girl friend, Nan Britton.

Means had a brilliant mind and could have distinguished himself if he had used it in constructive channels. But you never knew when he was lying.

The Justice Department eventually used an old charge to get Means sent to the Federal Penitentiary in Atlanta. He died in 1937 in another prison after being convicted of providing fake clues in the Lindbergh kidnaping.

Domestic spying offered almost unlimited job opportunities in Washington in the spring of 1924. *The New York Times* reported that the city was a "detectives' paradise," estimating that some five hundred sleuths were playing "hide and seek" in the capital. The government's operatives joined in the game. Members of Congress who had complained of surveillance by the Bureau of Investigation had their suspicions confirmed by our investigation. We took testimony that Department of Justice agents had ransacked the offices of senators Thaddeus H. Caraway and Robert M. La Follette and Representative Roy O. Woodruff, a progressive Michigan Republican.

My own office was rifled during the hearings on several

occasions. Government-hired detectives hung around the committee's offices constantly. (Thanks to my experience in Montana, I had long since learned to spot a detective at fifty paces.) Some of our witnesses were approached to find out what testimony they would give. Others were shadowed. J. Edgar Hoover, then assistant chief of the Bureau of Investigation, sat next to Daugherty's defense counsels throughout the hearings.

John S. Glenn, a certified public accountant, testified about a direct approach made to him to try to pin something on me. Glenn had known me when I was District Attorney in Montana and he served there as a special agent for the Department of the Interior. He related that on March 6, six days before the hearings opened, he was contacted in Nashville, Tennessee, where he was then living, by one C. F. Hateley, an agent for Bureau of Investigation chief Burns.

Glenn said he met the agent in a hotel and that "Mr. Hateley stated to me that he was there on a strictly personal mission, and he asked me if I knew Senator Burton K. Wheeler . . . he further asked me what kind of fellow Wheeler was, to which statement I replied that Wheeler was as square a man as anyone I ever met. He asked me about Senator Wheeler's morals, to which I stated to him that Senator Wheeler's morals were beyond reproach . . .

"He stated to me that he wanted me to try to pull Wheeler off Daugherty," Glenn testified. He said Hateley offered to pay his expenses if he would come to Washington. Glenn said it was impossible for him to go then and that anyway "I didn't think it was possible to do anything."

Senator Ashurst, a member of our committee, finally exploded verbally on the Senate floor. "Illegal plots, counterplots, espionage, decoys, dictographs, thousand-dollar bills, and the exploring of senators' offices come and go in the pages of this testimony," Ashurst told the Senate. "And these devices, these plots, counterplots, spies, thousand-dollar bills and ubiquitous detectives were not employed . . . to detect and prosecute crime, but were frequently employed to shield profiteers, bribetakers, and favorites. The spying upon senators, the attempt to intimidate them . . . are disclosed by this Record."

Parading to our witness chair were bootleggers, promoters, and influence peddlers who had swarmed to Washington in the wake of the "Ohio Gang." (As far as I know, I was the first to use this phrase. In a statement on April 23, 1924, I referred to the "Ohio Gang, known as 'Us Boys' and numbering about a dozen high officials in the Justice Department.") We filled the record with evidence of the illegal sale of liquor permits and paroles to bootleggers, and of Daugherty's participation in stock market pools as well as the illegal distribution of the Dempsey-Carpentier film.

Less colorful witnesses charged Daugherty with failure to prosecute the numerous war fraud cases exposed in House committee investigations. Federal Trade Commission officials complained that Daugherty had ignored their requests for prosecution of tobacco and lumber companies, the International Harvester and General Electric corporations as illegal monopolies. Several lawyers told of his manipulation of court decrees in monopoly cases against the Boston & Maine Railroad and the New York, New Haven & Hartford. Still others accused Daugherty of defrauding Indians in Oklahoma, and of failure to prosecute several nation-wide lotteries.

Small wonder that the Department of Justice was nicknamed the "Department of Easy Virtue." However, ours was by no means the only congressional inquiry then rattling the skeletons in Washington closets. Walsh's Teapot Dome hearings were running simultaneously and there were five other investigations in full swing—looking into the Internal Revenue Bureau, the Shipping Board, the aircraft trust, alleged land frauds, and evidence that members of Congress had "sold their influence" in liquor and pardon deals. The stock greeting between government officials, according to the current wisecrack, was: "Good morning, have you been subpoenaed yet?"

Two weeks of our hearings were enough for President Coolidge. He asked for Daugherty's resignation. While the President did not say he asked for his resignation because of Daugherty's refusal to turn over certain files requested by the committee, the ouster of Daugherty followed immediately after his refusal. It would have been "treason to do so" was Daugherty's defense of his rejection of our committee's demand.

"The files I refused to deliver," he cried, "were demanded by Brookhart and Wheeler, two United States senators who spent last summer in Russia with their Soviet friends."

"Daugherty has taken refuge behind the last resort of modern knaves," I retorted, "striving desperately to divert the public mind from their own corruption. When all else fails, they trot out the old 'red peril' bugaboo."

Daugherty felt that my trip to Russia was his best weapon against me, and my image as a Bolshevik grew in his mind with time. When he wrote a book in his own defense some years later, he said the man "who came to the Senate with the determination to drive me from the office of the Attorney General [was] the communist leader of the Senate . . . Wheeler is no more a Democrat than Stalin, his comrade in Moscow . . ." Daugherty pictured himself a martyr, no less than "the first public official that was thrown to the wolves by orders of the red borers of America."

Daugherty's resignation was followed a month later by that of Bureau of Investigation chief Burns. Burns quit immediately after Harlan Fiske Stone, the newly appointed Attorney General, requested information on his predecessor. It was said that Burns sacrificed himself rather than become an informer on Daugherty and the operations of the Justice Department.

Stone, who was destined to become Chief Justice of the United States, ordered the files of the Department turned over to the committee but they appeared to have been already emasculated. Stone promised that the system of espionage and the use of the Bureau of Investigation for political and personal ends would cease. Hoover, who became acting chief of the bureau, gave similar assurances.

Meanwhile, we were checking up on the assertion by Daugherty's friends that whatever grafting may have been done by the Attorney General's cronies he himself had not profited personally. Vanderlip urged us to examine the records of the Midland National Bank of Washington Court House, owned by Daugherty's brother, Mal. I dispatched to the Midland Bank,

John L. Phelon, formerly a bank examiner for the Second Federal Reserve District.

Phelon shrewdly went straight to the certificates of deposit and discovered $74,000 in deposit slips bearing the signature of H. M. Daugherty. Daugherty's tax returns showed that he had listed $27,000 in debts for 1920 (against assets of $10,000) but no debts at all for 1921. His salary as Attorney General in 1921 was $12,000.

Phelon pored over the deposit slips until the bank closed that afternoon but when he returned to finish the job the next morning he was barred at the door by Mal Daugherty. (During the trial of the American Metals Company in an alien property case in 1925, it was disclosed that Harry Daugherty had gone to his brother's bank after Phelon's visit and burned the ledger sheets covering his own account, his brother's, and another account known as "Jess Smith extra."

On April 11 Brookhart and I held a public hearing in Washington Court House to put Phelon's findings on the record and question Mal Daugherty. After checking into a hotel there the previous evening, I was approached by Philip Kinsley, a Washington correspondent for the Chicago *Tribune* who was covering our hearings. Like most of the Republican newspapers, the *Tribune* had attacked the investigation of the Attorney General but Kinsley must have liked me. He tipped me off that there would be an attempt to plant a woman in my hotel room for blackmail purposes that very night.

Only an hour later I was standing in the lobby when a good-looking bleached blonde warmly introduced herself and struck up a conversation. She said she was a beauty parlor operator who was thinking of opening a shop in Washington, D.C. She wanted to know if I thought this was a good idea—and if I might be of assistance. I told her beauty shops were out of my field. When this didn't discourage her ploy, I made an excuse and walked away.

At our hearings the next day Phelon testified that the Midland Bank had some amazingly large deposits for a bank capitalized at only $100,000. The deposit slips he had a chance to examine before being barred from the bank totaled $274,027.86, including the $74,000 deposited in the name of H. M. Daugherty. Some of the other large deposit slips turned out to bear fictitious signatures when we checked out the names.

We had subpoenaed Mal Daugherty to appear at this hearing with his bank records but he sent word that the committee had neither the power nor the jurisdiction to make him do so. At our request, the Senate quickly cited him for contempt. He applied for an injunction against the committee and in June his legal position was upheld by Federal Judge A. N. J. Cochran, sitting in southern Ohio.

His brother's "out" was all the excuse Harry Daugherty needed. For his repeated claim that he was eager to testify he now substituted the assertion that the whole proceeding was illegal and that it would be improper for him to appear.

Daugherty was attacked on the Senate floor for seizing on a technicality to avoid questioning, and the angry Senate voted to take the highly unusual step of itself employing counsel to appeal the decision to the Supreme Court. The Court did not act on the appeal until January 1927, two and a half years later, but *The New York Times* noted that its decision was "one of the most sweeping ever handed down by the tribunal."

The decision reversed the lower court ruling, holding that our investigation was ordered by Congress for a legitimate object and that the bank records were pertinent to our inquiry. "The power of inquiry—with the process to enforce it—is an essential and appropriate auxiliary to the legislative function," the Supreme Court explained in part. (A Supreme Court decision in 1880 in *Kilbourn v. Thompson* had left this enforcement power in doubt for forty-seven years.)

Our investigation by this time had long since ended and the Daugherty bank records had been destroyed. But the decision affected immediately a number of the other investigations still underway. And it has supplied firm legal underpinnings for every congressional investigation since then.

One of the most important scandals we brought out was the handling of funds by the Alien Property Custodian. The APC is charged with seizing and operating the holdings of enemy aliens in this country during wartime. The holdings amounted to hundreds of millions of dollars after both world wars and the former owners maneuvered through the courts and Congress to try to get them back. Some 49 per cent of the internationally owned American Metals Company had been taken over by the APC in World War I on the ground that it belonged to the Germans. In 1921 an agent of the company presented a claim of $7,000,000 to the United States government on behalf of the Swiss owners.

The $7,000,000 claim was approved by Daugherty two days later, after the agent paid $441,000 in Liberty bonds to John T. King, Republican national committeeman from Connecticut, for "services"—which consisted of introducing the agent to the Alien Property Custodian, Thomas W. Miller, a close friend of Daugherty, and Jess Smith. It was brought out during the trial which followed the hearings that at least $200,000 of this sum was paid over to Jess Smith "for expediting the claim in Washington," that Mal Daugherty sold at least $40,000 worth of these bonds and deposited the cash in his brother's account, and that Miller himself received $50,000. Miller was convicted in 1927 and sentenced to eighteen months in prison. Smith and King died before standing trial.

Harry Daugherty, however, escaped conviction when two juries were unable to agree after listening to his attorney plead that Daugherty would risk martyrdom to protect the name of his friend, the late President Harding.

Unfortunately, the evidence of corruption and malfeasance unfolded by the Daugherty and Teapot Dome investigations were a little too rich for the blood of the Republican newspaper publishers. Their papers largely ignored the detailed testimony of the economic questions involved in anti-trust cases and the testimony of a Daugherty assistant on his inability to secure action on war fraud cases.

The New York *Herald Tribune* called Walsh and Wheeler "the Montana scandalmongers" and the Cincinnati *Times Star* said my committee was an example of "Bolshevik justice."

The principal criticism of our committee was that the testimony came largely from "ex-convicts, divorcées, discharged government employees, and men under indictment."

"Daugherty did not associate with preachers," I replied to this charge. "The witnesses were not friends of the committee. They were called because they had dealings with Daugherty and his close associates. The character of the witnesses in a hearing of this kind is determined largely by the character of the central figure."

Felix Frankfurter, then a professor of law at Harvard and later a Supreme Court Justice, wrote in the May 21, 1924, issue of *The Nation:*

"It is safe to say that never in the history of this country have congressional investigators [Walsh and Wheeler] had to contend with such powerful odds, never have they so quickly revealed wrongdoing, incompetence, and low public standards on such a wide scale and never have such investigations resulted so effectively in compelling correction through the dismissal of derelict officials. . . . There is no substantial basis for criticism of the investigations of Senators Walsh and Wheeler."

As for the charge that I used the "dragnet method" of spreading on the record a mass of undigested testimony, the fact is I was swamped with so many reports of wrongdoing it would have taken years to sift them. Knowing how Daugherty had dodged scrutiny in the abortive House investigation, I felt I had to strike quickly before the inquiry could be undermined.

Even so, we were thwarted by our inability to obtain many of the witnesses we needed. As in the Teapot Dome probe, many of them fled the country or simply disappeared. Some witnesses who cooperated with the committee were notified that their employment with the government was terminated.

Of the minority of newspapers which gave full coverage to our hearings, one of the most generous with space was the chain owned by William Randolph Hearst. The Hearst editorials sometimes took a dim view of our charges but the hearings were played heavily on the front page. Therefore, I was surprised and puzzled when a Hearst reporter I knew well came to me and said, "Hearst isn't going along with you any more on the publicity." I asked why not.

"Burns has gotten after Hearst and is threatening him with something," he replied.

After some prodding, the correspondent explained: "Well, they have a case against Hearst for taking Marion Davies across the state line. They've told him they'll prosecute unless he lays off your investigation."

I surmised he was telling me this to find out whether I would continue the hearings if my chief source of publicity was cut off. I assured the reporter that I would go ahead even if there was a total blackout of news coverage. The Hearst man said this was what he expected I would say.

Whether Hearst was ever swayed by this alleged blackmail attempt—or if it was ever seriously threatened—I don't know. News stories in the Hearst press did decline to some extent after that but it could have been due to a tapering off of sensational testimony rather than to any outside pressures. But the report if true indicated how far the Justice Department would stoop to try to curtail publicity about the hearings.

The major reprisal against the investigation occurred less than four weeks after the hearings began. On April 8, I was indicted by a federal grand jury in Great Falls, Montana, on the charge that I had unlawfully accepted a retainer from Gordon Campbell, an oil man, to use my influence in obtaining oil and gas permits from the Secretary of the Interior.

The action did not come as a complete surprise. Vanderlip had gotten a tip from one of his friends on the Republican National Committee that there would be an indictment, and I had heard that government agents were out in Montana combing my past.

Nonetheless, I was upset. Even though I knew the charge to be false, it was the first time in my life that I had been accused of doing something illegal. Luckily, I was bucked up at that point from an inspiring source—Supreme Court Justice Louis D. Brandeis. The Justice was a new and valued friend. After my election to the Senate in November 1922 he had written me suggesting that we get acquainted when I came to Washington. I was flattered that I had attracted the attention of the eminent liberal jurist.

On the night after my indictment, Justice and Mrs. Brandeis invited Mrs. Wheeler and me to dinner at their apartment.

After the dinner, Brandeis took me into another room and asked, "Are you worried?" I confessed that I was a little shaken because I had never before been called a crook, not even by my bitterest enemies in Montana.

"They're trying to stop you," Brandeis said. "Don't let them stop you, because that's all they're trying to do!"

Nothing could have boosted my morale more than this encouragement from a Supreme Court Justice whose dissenting opinions were making legal history. The next day I took the Senate floor and made an emotional speech in which I denounced the indictment as a "political frame-up."

"I am going on with this investigation and I am not going to be stopped by threats," I told my colleagues.

The Senate on a unanimous vote appointed a special committee of three Republicans and two Democrats to investigate the charges against me. Senator William E. Borah was chairman. The other members were Republicans Charles L. McNary of Oregon and Thomas Sterling of South Dakota. The Democrats were Claude A. Swanson of Virginia and Thaddeus H. Caraway of Arkansas.

After holding extensive hearings, this special committee issued a report which "wholly exonerated" me from "any and all violations" charged in the indictment.

"The committee further states," the report said, "that in its opinion Senator Wheeler was careful to have it known and understood from the beginning that his services as an attorney for Gordon Campbell, or his interests, were to be confined exclusively to matters of litigation in the state courts of Montana, and that he observed at all times not only the letter but the spirit of the law."

The only dissenter was Sterling, who contended that the committee had no business delving into a case which was before another branch of the government.

Having been familiar with the law when I was United States District Attorney in Montana, I had been careful to avoid falling into a conflict-of-interest situation. This is what happened: After I was elected to the Senate, Campbell, a geologist, asked my law firm to represent him in the state courts of Montana in eighteen cases brought for and against his companies. The most important was a receivership case against his company involving properties worth several millions of dollars. I agreed to defend him in the receivership case, as a lawyer, but I warned that under no circumstances could I, as a Senator, represent him for compensation in any matters pending before the federal government.

I tried and won the receivership case before I left for Washington, while the other cases were tried by my partner, James H. Baldwin, who later became a federal judge. A few months later on March 14, 1923, Campbell sent me a telegram in the Senate Office Building asking me to arrange a meeting with the solicitor of the Interior Department. When the wire arrived, I was out of the office preparing to go to Europe. My secretary, Richard A. Haste, made the appointment for Campbell to meet the solicitor, Edwin S. Booth. (The meeting occurred while I was abroad.) This is what he knew I would do routinely for any constituent.

However, Justice Department operatives on my trail entered Campbell's office in Great Falls without a search warrant and seized all his letters, telegrams, and files. They used the telegrams to make it appear that I had interceded at the Interior Department for Campbell in return for a fee of $2000. Campbell had paid me a $2000 fee in January—solely for handling his litigation.

As Campbell testified before the Borah committee, there was no relation between the fee and his visit to the Interior Department. Also, Booth told the committee that I had never appeared at the Department in connection with Campbell.

Our committee brought out through the testimony of Bureau of Investigation chief Burns that even before our hearings began Daugherty had sent three agents to Montana with instructions to dig up some dirt on me. A. A. Grorud, a Republican former assistant attorney general in Montana, testified that he was buttonholed by still a fourth investigator, one Blair Coan, who was unabashedly in the employ of the Republican National Committee. Coan had come to Montana with twin targets—Walsh and Wheeler.

". . . he wanted something on Walsh so that he could smear him, because he wanted to stop him in the oil investigations here in Washington," Grorud testified. ". . . he had already smeared Wheeler in such a shape that he had him sewed up, he said."

I learned that the grand jury proceedings had been odd. No minutes were kept in my case, although they were kept in another case heard by the same grand jury. And the grand jury balloted seven or eight times before they voted to indict me.

The Senate adopted the majority report of the Borah committee by 56–5. Senators Borah, Norris, Walsh, and Reed, the articulate Democrat from Missouri, immediately offered to defend me when the case came to trial.

I wanted an immediate trial but it was set for hearing on September 1. By that time I was campaigning for Vice President on the Independent Progressive ticket and so I requested a delay. The trial was put over until April 15, 1925, a full year after the indictment had been returned.

Before that—in January 1925—I learned the Justice Department had a new indictment in store for me. This one was sought before a grand jury in Washington, D.C., and alleged conspiracy in connection with the transaction alleged in the other indictment.

At this time Attorney General Stone's nomination to the Supreme Court was pending before the Senate. It was immediately sent back to the Judiciary Committee for questioning about the new indictment of me. Stone explained that testimony could not be taken about the oil transaction without indicating that I was in some way involved in it. He said, "I therefore came to the conclusion that in fairness to him . . . an opportunity should be given him to explain his connection with the transaction to the grand jury."

Stone was then confirmed by the Senate, but only after a number of senators condemned him for seeking a second Wheeler indictment. Walsh insisted that this indictment, like the first, was a plain case of political reprisal. He maintained that Stone, contrary to popular opinion, had kept all the Daugherty appointees in the Justice Department. Senator

Walsh also argued that the second indictment was brought because the government was afraid of losing the long-delayed first case.

The Washington grand jury heard numerous witnesses but failed to return an indictment. It was then recessed for four weeks. Meantime, a so-called "mystery witness" was brought in all the way from Cuba, and this time the grand jury indicted me.

When the first trial opened in Great Falls, Montana, it looked like a Justice Department convention. My friends counted some 25–30 agents on the main streets.

I discovered I had many loyal friends in Great Falls. One night I received a telephone call in my hotel room from a stranger asking me if I would be interested in reports of the nightly telephone conversations between the Justice Department in Washington and the special prosecutor in the case. Naturally, I was. The caller said that if I was in the room at a certain time every night he would give me a fill-in. The long-distance telephone calls turned out to be fairly routine progress reports to J. Edgar Hoover; they proved only that the Bureau chief was keeping close tabs on the trial.

I also had friends at the Western Union office. They offered to let me read the telegrams passing between Washington and the Department of Justice men assigned to the case.

The high point in the trial came when the government sprang another "mystery witness." This one turned out to be George B. Hayes, a New York lawyer. Hayes testified that between the hours of five and seven o'clock in the evening on March 16, 1923, he had met me at Peacock Alley in the old Waldorf-Astoria in New York, the meeting having been arranged by phone by Edwin Booth, the solicitor of the Interior Department. He said I proposed that he represent me in connection with some oil leases in which I could not appear in person because I was a senator. According to Hayes, I told him the fee would run into at least a million dollars and would be split 50–50.

When Hayes was sworn in, I did not recognize him. However, A. B. Melzner, who had been secretary to our investigating committee, happened to hear the news while he was driving West. He hurried to Great Falls and testified that he had introduced Hayes to me in the committee's office a year after the alleged meeting in the Waldorf. Melzner said Hayes had told him he had never met Senator Wheeler previously.

Now I did recall Hayes. A witness appearing before us in connection with Hayes' involvement in a bootlegging case had said that Hayes "would kill his own mother for five cents."

I testified in the trial that I had never seen Hayes except during the hearings. Further, I informed the jury that on the day of the alleged Waldorf conference, Mrs. Wheeler and I had been busy until late in the afternoon shopping for clothes; we were due to sail for Europe the next morning. Then we rushed back to the hotel to dress for dinner and attend a performance at the Metropolitan Opera House with the famous Colonel E. W. House, who had been President Wilson's right-hand man, Mrs. J. Borden Harriman, and a party of their friends.

In New York, the newspaper revealed that Hayes had four judgments against him totaling over $300,000 for federal income tax violations at the time the Justice Department asked him to testify against me. They also uncovered three complaints in the hands of the District Attorney in New York charging him with withholding funds from clients.

Senator Thomas J. Walsh, my chief defense counsel, told the jury in his closing argument: "There is nothing whatever in this evidence on which you would hang a dog." William O'Leary, an outstanding criminal lawyer in Montana who had also volunteered his services, was equally contemptuous.

"I wonder what they in the East think we are made of," O'Leary said to the jury. "I wonder if they really expect to bring a witness from New York to Montana with a tale like that and expect a sane jury to believe it."

H. L. Mencken went even further in his column in the Baltimore *Sun*.

"After filling the newspapers with fulminations for weeks on end," Mencken wrote, "all the Daugherty gang could produce at Great Falls was a lot of testimony so palpably nonsensical and perjured that the jury laughed at it. Hayes was the star witness. He lied boldly, but to no effect. The others either lied in the same way, or lost their courage and gave evidence for Wheeler."

The jury took two votes. The first was to go to dinner at the expense of the government. The second was to acquit me. At the very moment the verdict was being announced, I was handed another bit of good news. Mrs. Wheeler had just given birth to our sixth child in Washington, D.C.

I mused wryly that while the government's case had fallen apart its attempt to time the trial with the human gestation period had been almost perfect. Seven months previously, the late Eleanor ("Cissie") Patterson, a leading Washington hostess, had tipped me off that Colonel Donovan, then an assistant Attorney General, knew Mrs. Wheeler was pregnant and scheduled the trial so as to coincide with the expected date of the birth. She said the idea was that I would probably ask for a continuance and the government could then drag the case out. But I didn't do so.

We named the baby Marion Montana Wheeler, in honor of a great progressive, Robert Marion La Follette, and the great state where I had just been acquitted.

A *New York Times* reporter wrote that "no trial . . . has created so much interest or engendered so much bitter feeling." He was right. Immediately afterward, I was approached by Harry Thompson, a one-time Butte butcher and an old friend who had come all the way from Seattle to watch every minute of the trial.

"I've got someone who'll throw Hayes into the Missouri River and no one will ever know about it," Thompson said. I hesitated a moment and then said, "No."

"Well, you find out what his haunts are in New York and I'll have someone take care of him there," Thompson urged. I again shook my head.

On my return to Washington, I went to see La Follette and found him seriously ill. Earlier, sick as he was, he had offered to go to Great Falls and defend me in the trial, "shout from the housetops, or do anything else you want me to do." Now, as he lay in bed, I told him about Thompson's offer to have Hayes murdered and I confessed that I had hesitated before turning down the temptation to vengeance.

To my surprise, La Follette, never a man of violence, commented harshly, "Why did you hesitate? It's the only kind of language men like Hayes understand." Two weeks later, on June 18, 1925, the progressive leader died.

I had one more trial to face. Already a Wheeler Defense Committee had been formed to help defray my mounting legal expenses. The committee was headed by Norman Hapgood, editor and columnist, and included, among others, Charles W. Eliot, president emeritus of Harvard; Felix Frankfurter, of Harvard Law School; Josephus Daniels, former Secretary of the Navy; and William Allen White, the distinguished Kansas editor. Some 1900 persons contributed a total of $15,000 to the fund.

The Washington, D.C., indictment charged that Gordon Campbell, Senator Wheeler, and others had conspired to secure more permits to prospect for oil in Montana than any or all of us could lawfully hold. My attorneys—Walsh, Charles A. Douglas of Washington, and Arthur Garfield Hays of New York—filed objections that the double jeopardy protection of the Constitution had been violated because I had been acquitted on similar charges in Montana. Further, they said the indictment showed no violation of any federal law.

Justice Bailey of the Supreme Court of the District of Columbia heard the arguments and quashed the indictment. He found that we had been indicted for a crime which did not exist, since there was no limit on the number of permits for prospecting intended by Congress. The Justice Department did not appeal the decision.

Senator Walsh however refused to let the matter drop. In a resolution adopted by the Senate, he demanded an accounting of the expenses incurred by the Department in the Wheeler cases—plus an explanation of its failure to proceed against Hayes for perjury. (The Treasury Department had quietly disbarred Hayes on charges growing out of his tax frauds.) The Justice Department admitted that my trial had cost over $61,-

000 but John G. Sargent, the new Attorney General, upheld his assistant, Donovan, in refusing any data on the status of Hayes.

That was the final official action resulting from my speech against Harry Daugherty on February 20, 1924, but echoes of our investigation were heard for years. In January 1929 the press reported that Donovan was heading the list for appointment as Attorney General in the Hoover Cabinet. Senator Borah told me he went to President-elect Hoover and warned that he and Walsh would fight a Donovan nomination because of his prominent role in the Wheeler prosecution. Borah told me that Supreme Court Justice Stone also went to Hoover and strenuously objected to Donovan as Attorney General. Donovan was then passed over and William D. Mitchell was nominated for the post.

Why had Stone, a man of the highest character, allowed the first indictment to proceed against me after he became Attorney General? Shortly after he took over, I heard through a mutual friend that Stone wanted to see me. When I called on him, he made it clear that the indictment would never have been initiated if he had been in charge at the time. The reason he proceeded with the case was clearer to me later on when Senator Kendrick informed me he had asked Stone point-blank why he had done so. "They lied to me," Stone said to Kendrick. I took this to mean that he was referring to Donovan. Stone and I became very good friends but I never had anything to do with Donovan, who went on to fame as chief of the super-secret Office of Strategic Services in World War II.

In another sequel, some Democrats suggested after Franklin D. Roosevelt was elected in 1932 that if I objected to J. Edgar Hoover he would be replaced as director of the Bureau of Investigation because of his role at the Justice Department in 1924–25. Hoover got wind of this talk and came to see me. He insisted he played no part in the reprisals against me. I had no desire to ask for Hoover's head on a platter—and I'm glad I didn't.

Our investigation of the Attorney General was one of the shortest and least expensive in history. The hearings lasted slightly more than three months and cost approximately $13,-000. (No self-respecting congressional probe committee today would get less than $200,000 to operate.)

Yet we questioned 115 witnesses whose testimony and exhibits covered 3338 printed pages. The consequences were far-flung. Driven from office, as noted, were Harry M. Daugherty and William J. Burns. Daugherty was indicted and escaped conviction, as explained, but his friend, Alien Property Custodian Miller, went to jail, and so did a Daugherty partner in a scandalous pardon case.

Mal Daugherty was indicted on five counts and convicted for the free and easy way he ran his bank. The verdict was reversed on appeal, but the bank crashed, owing $2,600,000 and causing tragedy to many innocent Ohioans. There were many other personal tragedies resulting from exposure of the Daugherty ring.

However, the final echo of the case that I personally heard was a happy one. In 1954 I received a telephone call from Roxy Stinson. She told me she had been married after the hearings and had been living happily in Oklahoma with her husband ever since.

Had it not been for the inquiries into the Justice Department and the Teapot Dome deal, the American people might not yet have known that the Harding Administration was responsible for the most cynical gang of looters that ever descended on the national capital. Since then, numerous other congressional committees have acted as "watchdogs" over our ever-growing bureaucracy. I consider them to be absolutely essential to our system of checks and balances—and in the best tradition of a truly democratic republic. Federal office holders today wield vast power and allocate millions, even billions of dollars; all of them are as human as the rest of us, and inevitably a percentage of them are inefficient or crooked. Only surveillance by experts in another branch of the government can keep crookedness and laxity to a minimum.

We continually hear about the menace of communism—and it *is* a real menace—but there is no greater menace to free government than corrupt officials and those who would corrupt them. Corruption in government destroys the faith of the people in a republican form of government to such an extent that it is eventually overthrown by a Fascist or Communist dictator—and freedom is at an end. There are countless examples of this.

True, investigating committees are susceptible to abuse. They must lay down and observe rules of fairness—as most of them have. The Brookhart-Wheeler committee went further than the average committee does even today because we permitted Daugherty's pair of defense counsels to sit with us at the committee table and cross-examine witnesses. This is a rule that should be adopted by every investigating committee, in my judgment. Yet, possibly because we were breaking new ground in delving sweepingly into the actions of executive departments, Walsh and I were accused of being "scandalmongers." I know of no one whose name was despoiled unjustly during our hearings.

No doubt the most important effect of the Daugherty investigating committee was that it set in motion the Supreme Court decision in the Mal Daugherty case which has given the necessary authority and scope to successor committees. In retrospect, maybe the brothers Daugherty made a contribution to their country after all.

Chapter Twelve

"PROSECUTING" SILENT CAL

An immediate effect of our well-publicized investigation of Attorney General Daugherty was my being thrust into the 1924 presidential campaign as an extremely controversial participant. It constituted my first major break with the Democratic Party.

I gave ample warning during the spring of the year that I would not go along with the party leaders unless they went to the country with a progressive program. I felt the leaders were sitting back and counting too much on the Justice Department and Teapot Dome scandals to sweep them back into office.

The Republican National Convention met in Cleveland in June and routinely nominated President Calvin Coolidge for re-election, with the Chicago banker, Charles G. Dawes, as his running mate. This made the Democrats even more overconfident—they happily noted that the GOP platform declared that business would be given a free hand without any government interference. *The New York Times* commented that "the only discordant note was sounded by Burton K. Wheeler, who served notice . . . that unless the New York Democratic convention nominated a progressive candidate on a progressive platform a third party was certain and would sweep the Middle West and Northwest."

When the Democrats met in convention in New York, the major contenders for the nomination were Al Smith, the colorful New York governor, and William G. McAdoo, who had been Secretary of the Treasury under Wilson and was very popular in the West. McAdoo was regarded as a progressive and I was for him, although I was not a delegate. I had contracted with Hearst to write a series of twelve articles on the convention for his syndicate. Frank Vanderlip, the retired New York Republican banker who had assisted me in the Daugherty investigation, gave me his suite in the Hotel Plaza and also arranged for interviews for me there with such would-be presidential candidates as McAdoo, Smith, William Jennings Bryan, and Representative Cordell Hull, then Democratic National Chairman.

Vanderlip told me flatly that John W. Davis would wind up with the nomination. When I expressed disbelief, Vanderlip explained that the Morgan banking interests would play off McAdoo against Smith until the exhausted delegates would be ready to take Davis. I knew that Davis was attorney for both Vanderlip and J. P. Morgan and that Vanderlip wasn't inclined to talk through his hat.

Vanderlip at the same time asked me if I would be interested in running with Davis as the vice presidential nominee. I said no.

In one of my convention articles for Hearst, I predicted that Davis would be the Democratic nominee, thereby scooping the professional journalists (although they didn't realize it until later). The day this article appeared, I met William Randolph Hearst in his suite at the Waldorf. As I walked in, he greeted me with: "Where did you get the idea that John W. Davis will be nominated? The Democrats will never nominate Davis." I disagreed with him. While Hearst didn't say so, I got the impression he thought it was a crazy idea.

At that time, a two-thirds majority was required to win the

Democratic nomination, and in the steamy marathon session at the old Madison Square Garden neither Smith nor McAdoo could muster even a simple majority. On the 103d ballot, the exhausted and exasperated delegates turned to Davis as a compromise.

Previously, Senator Thomas J. Walsh, who was chairman of the convention, had asked me if I would consider running with either Davis or Senator Carter Glass, another prominent dark horse. I said no, because both were ultraconservatives. After Davis was nominated, Walsh left a note for me at my hotel saying he wanted to see me. I went to the apartment of a friend of his with whom he was staying, and there I found Senator Key Pittman of Nevada, former Secretary of the Navy Josephus Daniels, and several other influential Democrats. Walsh was sitting back in his chair, very tired.

"Burt, these people think I should accept the nomination for Vice President, what do you think?" he asked immediately.

"What would you rather be—a defeated candidate for Vice President or a re-elected Senator?" I shot back. Walsh had a problem, in that he was up for re-election to the Senate and could not run for two offices at the same time.

"Of course, I would rather be elected to the Senate," he replied.

"Well, then," I said, "that ought to answer your question."

Walsh then expressed doubt that he could be re-elected if Davis were defeated for President. I assured him that he was popular enough to surmount a Davis defeat—which I felt was certain because of the party-splitting fight between Smith and McAdoo.

Walsh then turned to the circle of Democrats and said, "That ends it." If looks could kill, I would have been a dead man. These party chiefs had hoped to get Walsh on the ticket to take the curse of Wall Street off of it. Reluctantly, they picked up their hats and departed.

Walsh asked me to remain and shortly afterward Mrs. J. Borden Harriman, a prominent Washingtonian and a good friend of his, arrived at the apartment. She urged him to take the vice presidential spot—as did Davis himself, on the telephone. Walsh would not be budged in his decision.

When we got back to the convention floor for the balloting that evening, Walsh asked me to remain on the platform. He had had to adjourn the last session until 6 P.M. because the delegates were roaring their demand from the floor that he be nominated. He had presided over the convention with immense dignity and patience and it was obvious that his presence on the ticket would do much to heal the wounds of the party. He seemed worried that if a stampede for his nomination started he would need all my moral support nearby to resist it.

However, the delegates were prevailed on to nominate as Davis' running mate, the little known Charles W. Bryan, the governor of Nebraska and brother of William Jennings Bryan. This was the best they could do as a sop to the populist vote of the West.

I promptly announced I could not support the Democratic ticket.

"When the Democratic Party goes to Wall Street for a candidate, I must refuse to go with it," I explained. ". . . the nomination of Mr. Davis was brought about in the hope it would make possible a big campaign fund . . . as a result of this nomination the Democratic Party, in my opinion, has forfeited any right it may have had to the support of the progressive Democrats . . . between Davis and Coolidge there is only a choice for the conservatives to make. The uncontrolled, liberal, and progressive forces must look elsewhere for leadership."

Commented the New York *Herald Tribune,* a Republican mouthpiece: "As for Senator Wheeler, while his statement regarding Davis is chiefly claptrap and buncombe, his desertion of the ticket is a serious portent. For a number of months Democratic newspapers all over the country have been seeking to make a hero of him because of his conduct of the Daugherty investigation. Their fulsome praise of him which doubtless they now bitterly regret must have given him a certain prestige with the party."

In Cleveland the newly formed Independent Progressive Party had adjourned its convention after nominating Senator

Robert M. La Follette for President. The selection of La Follette's running mate was left in the hands of an executive committee. My name immediately turned up in the press in speculation over a choice for this spot, along with the names of Supreme Court Justice Brandeis and others.

The following Sunday I received a visit at my home from La Follette, his son, Robert Jr., and son-in-law Ralph Sucher. La Follette asked me to run for Vice President with him, adding: "Either you or I will be elected President of the United States." What he meant was that the election would be deadlocked in the electoral college and thrown into the House of Representatives, where we would have an excellent chance—but that because he was sixty-nine years old and not in robust health he might not survive very long.

I refused. I felt I couldn't make a good national campaign; I had never spoken in large cities like New York, Boston, and Chicago, where audiences were far different than they were out West. La Follette assured me that I could make a good campaign and went on to try to convince me that we could carry many of the large industrial states in the East.

"Senator," I said, "you think of the laboring people in the East as being like those in the West, but I was born and raised in Massachusetts and I think I know them better. The political bosses in those states will take the laboring people away from you like taking candy from a baby."

La Follette insisted that the Progressive ticket could get nine or ten million votes but I argued that it didn't have a chance of doing so. I said he would be lucky to get 5,000,000 votes.

A story was circulated at the Democratic convention that I was to undergo a second indictment as related in the preceeding chapter. It was another reprisal for my investigation of Daugherty. I asked Ray Baker, who had been director of the United States Mint in Wilson's Administration to check this out through his Republican connections. Baker reported back that the administration would not indict me if I did not run with La Follette. (There were a great many progressive Republicans that year, especially in the West, and the Republicans thought a La

Follette-Wheeler ticket would hurt them worse than it would hurt the Democrats.) Immediately after Baker left, I went to see La Follette in his office in the Capitol. I told him I'd changed my mind and would run for Vice President with him.

I changed my mind because I refused to let Daugherty and his crowd blackmail me the rest of my life. I determined not only to run but to make a major issue out of what I knew personally of the crookedness and general corruption in the Justice Department—the very thing, apparently, that the GOP feared. I admired La Follette but he never knew that I changed my mind only because of Baker's report.

In accepting the nomination—which was formally tendered by the Progressive Party's executive committee—I made it clear in a statement that I was not renouncing my affiliation with the Democratic Party.

"I am a Democrat but not a Wall Street Democrat," I explained. "I shall give my support and whatever influence I may possess to those candidates for office who have proven their fidelity to the interests of the people, wherever they may be found, but I shall oppose every man on whatever ticket he may appear who bears the brand of the dollar sign."

I announced my unqualified support for Senator Walsh for re-election and got La Follette to endorse him too.

The executive council of the American Federation of Labor, in an unprecedented action, gave us its "personal and nonpartisan endorsement for election." It declared that "it is no fantastic thing to look for the success of Senator La Follette in the coming election. America is seething with protest against the machinations of big business, the betrayal of the public trust and the lack of patriotic, constructive statesmanship in the two major parties."

La Follette and I issued a strong denunciation of the Ku Klux Klan, then at the peak of its influence with a membership estimated at 5,000,000 in the North, South, and Midwest. The Democratic National Convention had refused, on a hairline vote, to denounce the Klan by name. But Davis followed our lead and denounced the Klan a week later. Coolidge chose to preserve his silence on the question. The Klan thereupon announced it would devote all its energies to defeating the Progressive ticket.

La Follette thought Davis was the man to beat because the Wall Street money was behind him. He wanted me to launch my campaign by attacking him. I disagreed. I felt that Coolidge was the man to beat and, anyway, he and I were New Englanders and I wanted to open against him in Boston—which I did.

A tremendous crowd of 5000 or so gathered at Boston Common after a heavy rainstorm to hear me. The late James Michael Curley, then the golden-throated mayor of the city, introduced me. The crush was so great that the police had to carry me on their shoulders to get me off the platform and out on to Tremont Street.

My next destination was Portland, Maine, with speaking stops in all the Massachusetts cities en route. After the Boston speech, Joseph P. Kennedy's right-hand man, Eddie Moore, came to my hotel and asked me how I was traveling to Maine. I told him I didn't know. The upshot was that Kennedy, the multimillionaire financier, furnished me with his elegant Stevens-Duryea and chauffeur for the trip. When I returned and campaigned from Boston to New York, Kennedy supplied me with his Rolls-Royce and chauffeur. Kennedy enjoyed the irony of the spectacle: in swanky Newport, Rhode Island, and in all the principal towns from there to New York, I denounced Wall Street often from the back seat of a Rolls-Royce owned by a Wall Street operator. It occurred to me later on that Kennedy actually might have been trying to undermine me in this fashion.

Kennedy and I had become quite friendly that summer. I had taken my family for our vacation to Cape Cod. Not far away was the Kennedy place on Nantucket Sound which is still a gathering place for President Kennedy and Joe Kennedy's other sons and daughters.

Joe Kennedy anonymously contributed $1000 to my campaign. Later on in Washington, D.C., he informed me that after the Democrats saw the crowds I drew to Boston Common and other cities throughout New England, they were afraid La

Follette might carry Massachusetts. I asked him what they did to try to hold their normal Democratic vote.

"We scared hell out of them," Kennedy said with a laugh. "We told them that a Progressive Party victory would close all the mills and factories. And in South Boston we told the Irish that the La Follette program would destroy their Church."

In New York I spoke first at the famous Cooper Union, where Abraham Lincoln in 1860 had impressed Easterners that he had the makings of a President. The hall was filled a half hour before the meeting was to start and loudspeakers were set up outside. I was dismayed at the idea of facing this sophisticated audience, especially since I was following such experienced orators as Sidney Hillman and Morris Hillquit. I was so nervous I misplaced my glasses and had to borrow a pair so I could read my speech.

The New York Times reported that I was "clearly tired out" and faltered several times. However, the heartwarming response by the audience erased my fears. By the time I was hitting the upstate New York towns I was back in stride. I was cheered when Oswald G. Villard, editor of *The Nation* who was accompanying me, wrote: "He is doing extremely good work, quiet, modest, and unassuming, yet dramatic to a remarkable degree by his simple straightforward narrative of Teapot Dome and the Daugherty scandals."

After my speech in Syracuse, the Syracuse *Journal* called on all Democrats to support Coolidge because the presidential battle was now clearly between Coolidge and La Follette.

After I drew an overflow crowd in Philadelphia, I was called back to New York to speak at a special fund-raising banquet. It raised $10,000. The money promised by the labor unions was slow in coming in and up to this point the campaign was being financed with the cash collections taken up at our public meetings.

By mid-September, GOP campaign strategy became clear. The Republicans saw the capacity crowds at the Progressive meetings and the AFL endorsement as evidence that a farmer-labor coalition had finally been effected on a national scale. I kept hearing rumors that "Wall Street" had abandoned Davis and was putting its money on Coolidge. Then Frank Kent, the Baltimore *Sun* correspondent, wrote that Coolidge and Dawes had adopted the line of ignoring the Democratic candidates and of warning of the danger to the country if La Follette won.

"Credit for it," Kent continued, "belongs to neither Coolidge nor Dawes but to certain Old Guard Republican leaders who reason . . . [that] every state La Follette carries cuts the electoral votes out of the Coolidge column. He cannot be elected but if he carries more than five states it means either the election of Davis or an election by Congress. The only way to elect Coolidge is to keep the La Follette vote down. The only way to do that is to attack him as a 'Red' and frighten the conservative forces back of Coolidge . . . it avoids a lot of embarrassing subjects such as 'oil' . . . it is good politics if they can get away with it but it is pure humbug."

Republican National Committee Chairman William M. Butler of Massachusetts set the tone of the attack by declaring, "The struggle is not over the methods of government but the abolition of government. The issue is to save the country." Dawes, nicknamed "Hell 'n' Maria" because of his salty tongue, was given the task of carrying the offensive against the Progressives. Coolidge of course kept cool—and silent—in the White House.

Dawes launched the Republican campaign, posing the issue as a fight between those who "favor the constitution of the U.S. and those who would destroy its essential parts." He pictured La Follette as the "master demagogue" and the "leader of a mob of extreme radicals of which the largest part, the Socialists, fly the red flag."

The fear of an inconclusive election—in which Congress would choose the chief executive—became another principal theme of all Republican campaign orators and leading editorial writers. A much-publicized and widely reprinted article in *The Saturday Evening Post* in the final weeks of the campaign entitled "Let X Equal La Follette" expounded this theme. It noted that if the Republican ticket were to receive less than a majority of the electoral votes, the choice of a President would then go to Congress. It was argued that La Follette could and would prevent an election in the House, where the balance of power was held by the Progressives. The contest would then be referred to the Senate, which was limited in choice to the two vice presidential candidates highest on the list. As between Dawes and Bryan, the Democratic-Progressive coalition would choose the man whose brother was thrice denied the presidency by popular vote.

Time magazine summed up the GOP argument: "A vote for La Follette is a vote for Bryan. A vote for Davis is a vote for Bryan. A vote for Coolidge is a vote for Coolidge."

Similarly, the Progressive effort to make the question of monopoly control over the economic life of the country the principal issue was twisted by the Republican spokesmen into a threat to destroy industry and jobs for American workingmen. Coolidge's dictum, "The business of America is business," was shortened simply to "Coolidge or chaos," as the campaign wore on.

As I stumped west to Chicago, I drew heavily on the Teapot Dome and Daugherty investigations for an endless fund of stories on Republican corruption.

"Let's see who is destroying this government of ours," I would ask. "Is it the farmer, the laborers, or the merchants of the country? Or is it the Daughertys, the Falls, and the Dohenys?"

My solution was: "Stop government by special privilege and you stop government by corruption."

While I was in my third day of campaigning in Ohio on the record of the "Ohio Gang," Daugherty released from his home an affidavit from Gaston B. Means, the one-time investigator in the Justice Department, repudiating his damaging testimony before our committee and stating that he, Means, had engaged in a conspiracy with myself, La Follette, and Walsh to frame the Attorney General and the administration. By the time I replied to the effect that Means was trying to curry favor with the administration in the face of pending prosecution, Means repudiated the repudiation.

Davis also made good use of our record of the Daugherty hearings and stated that "common honesty" in government was the issue between the Republicans and the Democrats. In the course of his speeches, Davis also called my indictment by the Justice Department "as black and dastardly a crime as could be committed by any man who held in his control great power over the liberty and honor and reputations of fellow men."

I welcomed Davis' sudden concern about my indictment but noted that in the absence of a clear-cut economic issue between the two old parties mere condemnation of GOP corruption was not enough.

"All the corruption that was unearthed and exposed . . . had its beginnings in the abnormal greed of the interlocking financial interests that controlled the Republican convention of 1920, as they controlled the conventions of both old parties this year," I said. Winning economic freedom for the masses of the people, I argued, was the only guarantee of uncorrupted administration of the law.

To stay on the offensive in the face of the heavy Republican fire, I always bearded the lion in his den. In Massachusetts I had ripped into the myth of Coolidge as a "strong, silent man." In Pittsburgh, I had concentrated on the "help-the-rich tax program" of Andrew Mellon, and in Ohio my target was the "Ohio Gang." In Chicago, I went after Coolidge's running mate Dawes, an Illinois resident. The text was one of my favorite quotations: "Patriotism is the last refuge of a scoundrel." I described the famous "Dawes Plan" for the settlement of the international debt problem as nothing less than a bonanza for the international banking house of J. P. Morgan. I charged that Dawes had once helped another banker-politician, William Lorimer, open a bank with worthless paper and that as a result 4000 Chicago citizens had been robbed of their savings. And I discussed "General Dawes' gallant service as commander of the 'Minute Men of the Constitution' in his war on organized labor."

Even before this speech, the Baltimore *Evening Sun* had commented that Dawes and myself as campaigners were easily overshadowing the other four candidates. "It was a mean fate which put Dawes and Wheeler in opposing camps," this editorial concluded. "Together they would sweep the country."

Dawes and I kept up our running battle. To his charges that

La Follette and I were dangerous radicals, I said: "His idea is that during a campaign the people should listen to one set of men call another set demagogues, anarchists, and Communists and then should march to the polls and vote the way their fathers did. After the campaign is over then the economic problems of the farmer could be taken up by the bankers and the bankers' lawyers sitting as a commission."

I was still not a polished orator—and never became one—but my style kept my audiences awake. The Chicago *Tribune* reported: "John W. Davis spoke here a few days ago. He used meticulous English but didn't hold the crowd. Senator Wheeler spoke here last evening. He murdered the King's English but got the crowd."

Mrs. Wheeler joined the party in late September after getting our five children settled in school. She took over any chores that might relieve the strain on me. To her surprise, in Pittsburgh, she was called on to make the first political speech of her life. After that, she became a scheduled attraction—and made a hit—at every stopping point. Everywhere she called on women to take an active part in politics in order to be of real service to their families. Her speeches were concerned primarily with the question of world peace and the need to abolish war and win a higher standard of living. She discussed particularly the proposed Progressive platform plank calling for a referendum prior to a declaration of war. She also noted that many well-known women—such as Jane Addams—who had fought successfully for woman suffrage were among those actively campaigning for La Follette.

Up to Chicago, our entourage had been obliged to travel by auto and other passengers on the trains. But there, in early October, we boarded a private railroad car, the *Republic*, which was fitted out luxuriously. I enjoyed teasing the staff about their new-found "bed of roses." Some newspapers considered it unseemly for the poor man's candidate to travel in a private railroad car, like other candidates.

WHEELER LIVES IN PRIVATE CAR LIKE POTENTATE, ran the headline in the San Francisco *Chronicle*. *PULLMAN PALACE ON WHEELS BRINGS LA FOLLETTE*

RUNNING MATE. In the accompanying two-column story, the car was said to be "fitted with that luxury which Wheeler sneers at . . . all it lacks to resemble the Hotel Del Monte is the Roman pool . . . there's a luxurious lounge at the rear end where the vice presidential candidate may loll at ease when the campaigning gets tough." Even the chef assigned to our train was attacked—as a "money-spending fool."

Railroad workers all over the country, however, seemed to take pleasure in ensuring my comfort and safety, doubtless because I had championed their cause since my early Montana days. One night I got a chuckle while lying awake in my berth during a brief stop in Texas. I heard the train crews tapping the wheels of the car.

"This is Senator Wheeler's car," one worker said to another. "Be sure you check these wheels carefully and to hell with the rest."

Everywhere, members of our entourage noted, the locomotive engineers were extraordinarily solicitous in picking up our car in such a way that there was only an imperceptible jolt when we were being pushed, pulled, and hooked on. One newspaperman who had just boarded the train told me that, in contrast, it was worth one's life to travel on Dawes' car.

We were heartened by the size and enthusiasm of the crowds in Minnesota and Iowa. A total of more than 25,000 turned out for seven meetings in one day in the Twin Cities.

In Des Moines, Iowa, I hit on an original showmanship gimmick.

The hall was jammed to the rafters. A minute before I was introduced, I whispered to Mrs. Wheeler not to let anyone take my chair when I went to the rostrum. (That had happened often when some of the overflow audience stood on the stage.) After I made a few opening remarks, I said, "You people have a right to know how a candidate for President stands on issues, and so far President Coolidge has not told you where he stands on anything . . . so I'm going to call him before you tonight and ask him to take this chair and tell me where he stands."

People in the audience began to crane their necks to see if

Coolidge really was somewhere on the premises. I pulled the vacant chair out in the center of the stage and addressed it as though it had an occupant.

"President Coolidge," I began, "tell us where you stand on Prohibition." After a pause, I continued: "Mr. President, why was it necessary for Congress to act before you dismissed the Secretary of Navy who had allowed the Navy's oil reserves to be turned over to the Secretary of the Interior, knowing this Secretary of the Interior was frankly in favor of turning over all the nation's natural resources to private exploiters? Tell me, Mr. President, why is it you stood behind Harry Daugherty?"

I went on with rhetorical questions in this vein, pausing after each for a short period. Then I wound up: "There, my friends, is the usual silence that emanates from the White House." The crowd roared in appreciation. Afterward, quite a few members of the audience came up on the platform to talk to me. The president of one of the big banks in Des Moines congratulated me and added, "The only thing is, I wish you were making that speech for John W. Davis." The Denver *Post* described my stunt as "an excellent bit of comedy, and it knocked them out of their seats." *The New York Times* flatteringly described it as a "technique that would have done credit to an actor." That was one term I never expected to hear applied to me.

In my stump speeches, I tried to strengthen the progressive bloc in Congress. In Nebraska, for example, I called for all-out support of Senator George W. Norris, the great independent Republican, on the ground that he was "one of the really big men in the United States Senate. Norris," I said, "has all the attributes of greatness—honesty, courage, ability, and determination." Norris, however, made no endorsement in the three-way presidential race.

La Follette had vigorously opposed any third party tickets for state and local office because it might endanger the election of progressives running on the Republican or Democratic tickets. But we found that in many Western states third-party candidates were entered—in some cases, I suspected, at the instigation of the Republicans.

In Montana, for example, Walsh was opposed by a Republican candidate with acknowledged Ku Klux Klan sympathies. But a local Farmer-Labor party, in defiance of advice from La Follette headquarters, had entered a third candidate as well as a separate slate of La Follette presidential electors. In three major speeches, I told my audiences that "the defeat of Walsh would be looked upon by the country as a repudiation of his magnificent fight against corruption in Washington." In Butte, where the Farmer-Labor ticket would win the most support, I said that Walsh "has aligned himself with the progressives on almost every issue during the last session of Congress."

Walsh did no campaigning for the Davis-Bryan ticket, in contrast to the two previous presidential campaigns in which he had undertaken major responsibilities for the Democrats. As chief prosecutor in the Teapot Dome scandal, he would of course have made an invaluable contribution to his party's ticket.

Elsewhere in the Northwest, I dealt primarily with the burning issue of public power and conservation of natural resources, charging that Dawes, on his record, would abolish all reclamation in the West and hand the power in the Columbia Basin over to private companies. At the same time, Dawes was attacking me as "a smoke screen behind which socialism would advance on the American government."

At most stops, I used examples of Coolidge and Dawes deals to illustrate my point that the Republican candidates "regarded the government of the United States as an instrument for exploiting the people—not an instrument for serving the people." I had many hecklers but I enjoyed jousting with them, and I believe they enlivened our meetings.

Paul Mallon, a United Press correspondent who covered my campaign, wrote from Seattle that I was "a two-fisted fighter . . . at his best when he has someone fighting against him. During his campaign trip across the country his speeches were best when they were delivered to an antagonistic crowd. He was most brilliant when he was heckled. When he met no opposition he lost his fire and his speeches sounded commonplace."

Unfortunately, Coolidge remained as silent as a monk despite my constant needling, and Dawes refused to meet me in debate.

At a luncheon meeting in San Francisco, a man stood up and identified himself as a captain in the British Army and asked me to comment on La Follette's war record. He waved a copy of the resolution passed by the Wisconsin legislature denouncing La Follette in this connection.

After commenting that "we have had too much British interference in our national affairs," I replied that I had no apology to make for La Follette's vote against our entry into the war. I said he had voted with the sentiment of the American people when they elected Woodrow Wilson on the slogan, "He kept us out of war." I said we were not asking for English, Japanese, or any foreigners to vote, but just Americans who believed in America.

This answer met with such wild cheering that I used the story again at an evening meeting and any other place I could figure out a way to drag it in.

In Los Angeles, the Progressives were unable to get a hall in the city large enough to accommodate the expected crowd and so the Hollywood Bowl was chosen for the major area meeting. Although the Bowl is seven miles from the center of the city and transportation in those days was difficult, 10,000 tickets were sold before the meeting at prices ranging from 25 cents to $5.00 each. The Los Angeles *Examiner* estimated the audience at 20,000 and reported: "No prima donna, no golden throated tenor, no orchestra leader with a magic wand has ever known the depths of applause that reverberated through the Hollywood Hills about the Bowl when Senator Wheeler had finished." The Los Angeles *Record* said I was given "the greatest demonstration received by a candidate in the history of California."

R. B. Martin, an ex-preacher and former Non-Partisan League organizer who collected contributions for us, reported that $7500 was taken in when the tin plates were passed in the Bowl to "keep the Wheeler show on the road."

The New York Times reported accurately that the main

problem in California at this time was that the La Follette ticket lacked organization to capitalize on the sentiment of the people—"Wheeler's charges against Dawes and Coolidge are going unanswered." Another problem in California was that the state Supreme Court had barred Independent Progressive electors from the ballot. As a result, La Follette's state committee reluctantly had been forced to accept the offer of the Socialist party to use that place on the ballot. This naturally was widely used by Dawes to bolster his charge that we were socialists in slight disguise.

We rolled on to San Diego and Long Beach, then swung back eastward through Arizona, New Mexico, and Texas. One of my staff members, A. B. Melzner, noted in his diary that on October 16 I made six speeches in New Mexico to crowds running from 150 to 1000 persons. "No notice except a few hours was given," says his diary entry, "and crowds came as far as 30 miles in autos. Some of the towns had only a half dozen houses . . ."

In Omaha, I got word from La Follette announcing his decision to abandon his projected trip to the West Coast and return East. A letter from Mrs. La Follette explained there were predictions that her husband would carry six Western states anyway and that he had been persuaded that if he concentrated on the East it would dramatically emphasize that he was out to win the election, not merely throw the decision into the House of Representatives. "Also there was little money in the till," Mrs. La Follette wrote.

Several political analysts felt this was a serious mistake in strategy, that La Follette should have concentrated on the states from Iowa west where he could have been assured of 120 electoral votes.

Throughout the Southwest I was persistently heckled by bigots. State organizers took great precautions for my safety because of constant Klan threats against the Progressives. At Enid, Oklahoma, the local committee was even afraid to let Mrs. Wheeler and me attend church but I ignored their warnings.

At Kansas City, I cited the lavish funds available to the

Republicans as revealed by the Borah committee. The Republican National Committee treasurer had told Senate investigators that $1,171,317 had been spent up to October 10, 1924, over ten times the amount spent by the La Follette campaign. A few weeks later the GOP figures were raised to over $3,100,000. I used to tell my audiences, "If you're not getting the money, someone is holding out on you."

(According to the final report of the Borah committee, the Republicans raised $4,360,378 against the Democrats' $821,037 and the Progressives' $221,977.)

In one fund-raising letter, Joseph R. Grundy, president of the Pennsylvania Manufacturers Association, warned: "We are confronted by the possibilities of a violent social and industrial revolution. We have in La Follette and Wheeler a Lenin and Trotsky with a formidable band of followers made up of the vicious, ignorant and discontented element, openly organized for battle." T. V. O'Connor, chairman of the Shipping Board, charged that "a large amount of money has been sent from Russia through Mexico to aid the campaign of Senator La Follette." Asked by the Borah committee for the source of his statement, O'Connor replied: "I believe it in my own heart, though I have no way to prove it."

Back in Chicago to address several rallies, I was informed by David K. Niles, then director of our campaign speakers bureau and later an aide to President Roosevelt, that his main problem was how to operate on a budget of $5000 instead of the $50,000 that had been promised.

Arriving in New York City for four meetings, I was greeted with the announcement that the New York City executive committee of the Trades and Labor Council, AFL, had urged its members to switch from La Follette to Davis because "La Follette has no chance to be elected." The widely heralded defection in labor's ranks—coupled with the fact that the AFL had been able to collect only $25,000 for La Follette—was a bitter foretaste of what would happen in the election booths.

I wound up my tour on November 3 in Baltimore, after eight weeks of campaigning that covered 17,000 miles in twenty-six states. Mrs. Wheeler brought our five children over from Washington, D.C., to watch me hurl my questions at the empty chair in the manner they had been reading about.

When the ballots were counted Coolidge had polled 15,725,016 to 8,385,586 for Davis and 4,822,586 for La Follette. La Follette carried only Wisconsin, a disappointing electoral showing, but he ran ahead of Davis in 12 Western states. In Montana, the Progressive ticket received 39 per cent of the vote to 42.5 per cent for Coolidge. (Walsh was re-elected by a plurality of 17,000.) In California, despite the fact we had to run under the Socialist insignia, we polled 33 per cent of the vote to the Democrats' 8 per cent. In the East the only bright spot was the fact that La Follette carried Cleveland, Ohio, due largely to the work of the railroad brotherhoods.

As for the huge crowds I drew, I had long since learned not to be misled by that. In the gubernatorial contest of 1920 I had pulled large crowds too, but I became the worst-defeated candidate in Montana's history. People often come to see and hear a speaker out of curiosity. In 1924, I believe, they came out to see the man who had driven Harry Daugherty from office, who had been indicted by the Justice Department in return, and who had been attacked violently in newspaper editorials.

Despite superficial appearances, it was not a Coolidge landslide. The President received a clear majority only in states with a total electoral vote of 382. He failed to obtain a majority in 26 states.

I felt the greatest factor in the Coolidge vote was the rising tide of prosperity in late 1924, carefully exploited by the Republicans with the slogans, "Coolidge or Chaos" and "A Vote for La Follette Is a Vote for Hard Times." It is always hard to beat the pocketbook as an election issue.

A schoolteacher was one of many who told me after the election that he had fully intended to vote for La Follette up until the last minute, when he began to think that maybe he would lose his job and his home. "If they could scare me that way," he commented, "think what they could do to so many others."

The New York Times commented that the Progressives had

"appealed to the ideals of the American people without money or organization."

I echoed La Follette's view when I said that, in view of the various economic issues posed, "the wonder is not that so many millions were intimidated and voted for Coolidge but that so many millions stood by their convictions and voted the Independent ticket."

Actually, our popular vote of 4,822,586 still stands as nothing to be ashamed of. No third party in America before or since has polled as many votes. Our trouble was that we were ahead of the times. The Progressive Party platform of 1924 became the ideological basis for the New Deal in 1933 and much of it found its way to the statute books by 1935. Unfortunately La Follette never had the satisfaction of knowing this, for he died eight months after the 1924 election.

La Follette and I had known we were taking risks in challenging the regular nominees of our respective parties. After the election, the Republican Party caucus formally ousted La Follette, Smith W. Brookhart, and others who had aligned themselves with the Progressives. (Brookhart, chairman of our Daugherty investigating committee, was re-elected in Iowa although he was repudiated by the entire Republican organization.) This meant they would go to the bottom of the seniority list in the next Congress. La Follette thus lost his position as ranking Republican on the Interstate Commerce Committee.

There was speculation as to how the Democrats would discipline their one rebel. Senator Claude Swanson told me some of the Democrats were talking of throwing me out of the party and stripping me of my committee rank. I replied that it would make little difference, since I was already at the foot of the list as a first-termer. Swanson told me not to pay any attention to these rumors but to keep my mouth shut and keep on smiling. In two years, he predicted, they would be asking me to campaign for them.

I issued a statement that I was returning to my party as Senator Swanson had suggested—but without remorse or apology. I never for an instant had regretted my temporary desertion. I enjoyed the campaign and considered it an unparalleled opportunity for a man so young in national politics.

I had never considered it a permanent break with the Democrats. I had seized on what I thought was the most effective method of protest "against the reactionary control of the Democratic Party." I saw in my candidacy an opportunity to try to force a realignment in the old parties with all the conservative Democrats and Republicans on one side and on the other side an amalgamation of all progressive, forward-looking people of whatever political faith.

Once the election was history, I determined to carry on the fight from within to try to revamp my party along liberal lines. Otherwise, as I warned, it would soon be a sectional party representing only the solid South.

Chapter Thirteen

INSIDE THE SENATE

Shortly after I was sworn into the Senate, Senator Borah took me to lunch and gave me some Dutch uncle advice. He said I could make a reputation. I asked how.

"If you're honest, have ordinary intelligence, and are willing to work," he answered. He explained that most senators were honest but that many wouldn't work.

Senators in the 1920s didn't have the workload that is imposed on them today. The issues, by and large, weren't so complex, and there weren't so many of them. The pressure groups had not yet achieved their great power through ingenious organization. A senator could loaf and get by; from thinly populated Montana I didn't get more than 10 to 13 letters a day.

Yet, this was the era of "giants" in the Senate. It still harbored a large number of rugged individualists and they helped to make the Senate a more interesting and exciting arena than I believe it is today. Debate on the floor was a vital part of the legislative process. The ability to articulate was important. And there were quite a few very able men.

Besides Borah, there were such classic progressives as old Bob La Follette, George Norris, and Hiram Johnson. There was Henry Cabot Lodge; Henry Ashurst of Arizona; Jim Watson of Indiana; Jim Reed of Missouri; Carter Glass and Claude Swanson of Virginia; George Moses of New Hampshire; Henrik Shipstead of Minnesota; Joe Robinson, the Democratic leader; and my Montana colleague, Thomas J. Walsh. There were many others.

The senators of that period were impressive physically as well. Most of them were tall (at an even six feet, I qualified in this respect), and immaculate dressers. And they had a senatorial air about them. Some, like Borah, wore string ties. Some, like Tom Heflin of Alabama, wore frock coats. In the humid, non-air-conditioned chamber during a Washington summer, the Southerners would blossom out in white suits and saunter around like plantation owners.

One of the most skillful and vitriolic debaters at that time was Jim Reed. He was tall and handsome, with steel-gray hair and a rich baritone. Reed had a fine mind but was not given to study. As his words flowed, he seemed to pick things out of the atmosphere. Once, when he was orating in favor of a piece of anti-labor legislation, I slipped over to the seat next to him and said in an aside, "Jim, the Supreme Court has held a similar bill to be unconstitutional." Almost in mid-sentence, Reed glided smoothly into a totally different subject. Afterward, he came over to my desk and asked, "Where did you find that damned decision?"

Old-fashioned oratory, full-blown and gaudily purple, distinguished the "world's greatest deliberative body." Even then, there was talk of putting limits on it. When Congress convened after the election of Coolidge, the first ringing speech came from none other than his running mate, Charles G. Dawes —and it was a crashing failure. No sooner had Dawes been sworn in than he was proving the reason for his nickname, "Hell 'n' Maria." He launched into a lecture on the "outmoded" Senate rules which permit a senator to talk as long as he can stand on his feet.

The new Vice President waved his arms and literally shouted

from the chair. His own party leaders, seated directly in front of him in the well of the chamber, went into a slow burn. From a man who had never been a member of the club, such an attack was unforgivable. The Senate found it easy to ignore Dawes' gratuitous advice to change the rules so that a simple majority of those voting could put a time limit on debate. A majority of two-thirds of those voting was required to shut off talk on a specific bill, as it still is today.

Dawes was a conservative. His view on limiting debate is a perfect example of how political thinking shifts, depending on whose ox is being gored. Since World War II, it has been the liberals who have wanted to make it easier to curb a filibuster; their objective is to circumvent filibustering conservatives who want to block civil rights legislation.

But after World War I it was the progressives, the model liberals of their day, who fought to preserve the right to unlimited debate. Old Bob La Follette, the master of the use of the filibuster to arouse public opinion, warned me never to vote for cloture (which sets a time limit on a debate), arguing that it would destroy the most useful weapon a liberal minority possesses against a conservative coalition. He insisted that cloture must be opposed as a matter of principle; he pointed out that if I voted for it once I could hardly oppose it another time. Actually, cloture was imposed twice during Dawes' four-year term—evidence enough to support the progressives' claims that there was no need to change the rules.

Dawes and I had fiercely assailed each other during the 1924 presidential campaign. Shortly after he became Vice President, I passed him as he was leaving the senators' lavatory. He stopped, stuck out his hand, and said, "Hell, I can get along with anybody." We became good friends. I admired his forthright honesty.

He apparently valued my opinion of him. Not long before his term ended, he called me into the Vice President's room off the Senate floor and locked the door. He recalled that during the 1924 campaign I had questioned the ethics of a business transaction he had had with an Illinois lawyer, William Lorimer. I tried to pass it off but he would not drop the matter.

Even if everyone else had forgotten the charge, Dawes explained, he wanted to satisfy himself that I didn't believe he had done anything wrong. He made me sit there while he dug out an Illinois appellate court decision. Then he put his underslung pipe aside long enough to read aloud the entire lengthy decision in the case. This took over an hour and I was fidgeting to get away.

The decision did convince me the deal had been legal and Dawes was relieved when I said so. The allegation had been passed on to me by Lowell Mellett, a high-class newspaper correspondent covering my campaign. It was an example of the "new material" he said I should provide continually in order to stay on the front pages.

The Senate majority leader during the latter part of the 1920s was James E. Watson of Indiana, a large, good-looking, Old Guard Republican. Watson was an effective orator and an accomplished after-dinner speaker who enjoyed telling stories on himself. He worked hard at politics but not at anything else. He once admitted to me he had signed his name as author of a book that had been ghost-written. When he went to Antioch College on one occasion to deliver an address, the president of the college said, "I read your book and I certainly enjoyed it." Watson told me he replied, "Well, I'm glad to hear that because I never read it."

Watson and I were both on the Interstate Commerce Committee when I was a freshman—but at opposite ends of the seniority list. There was no need for him to pay much attention to me until 1926, when Watson was chairman and Coolidge nominated Thomas Woodlock to be a member of the Interstate Commerce Commission.

Woodlock, who wrote articles for the New York *Sun* and other papers, had been one of the best propagandists for the railroads before he went into the brokerage and investment business. The law said a director or officer of a railroad could not be appointed to the ICC, so Woodlock resigned as a director of two railroads just before he was appointed.

The ICC was then in the midst of a controversy over the method of determining the capital value of the railroads for rate-making purposes, an issue involving several billions of dollars. I cross-examined Woodlock in our committee hearings for several weeks on his views regarding this subject and concluded that he would not be fair in his decisions as a commissioner.

I was well armed with Woodlock's public pronouncements and I inserted them in the committee record as evidence of his bias toward high freight rates and his prejudice against labor. When his nomination came to the voting stage in the committee, I knew I had it licked by one vote.

Under a committee rule, no member could be voted by proxy. Aware that he was facing defeat by a narrow margin, chairman Watson hemmed and hawed. Old Jim looked around the committee table and said, "Now, boys, I know we've got a rule on the committee that no one can vote except by being present but, you know, boys, Simeon Fess asked me—I had forgotten all about it—he asked me as a special favor if the committee wouldn't let him cast his vote because he's been called out of town by an illness."

"Well, if you can do that," I spoke up, "then everybody else who is absent can have their votes cast."

"Well, I'll vote Simeon Fess," Watson insisted.

I noticed that Clarence Dill of Washington was absent. I said, "Well, I'll vote Dill." Watson drummed on the table and then said, "Oh, I forgot all about it, but Guy Goff also asked me to vote him, so I'll vote Goff."

"All right," I rejoined, "I'll vote Howell."

I hadn't previously arranged for these proxy votes but I knew the sentiments of these men and I felt I had as much right as Watson to claim proxies. We kept on voting proxies for other absent members and ended up the way we had started out—I still had the chairman beaten by one vote. The committee reported the Woodlock nomination to the floor adversely.

After the session, Watson put his arm around me and said privately that he could get Woodlock confirmed in the Senate because the minority leadership would support him, but that "Cal"—President Coolidge—would never understand how he was beaten in his own committee.

"I hope you'll go to the floor," Watson said, "and give me the very devil and say that I resorted to every political trick there is to get this man appointed."

"Jim," I said, "that won't be very hard to do."

I made a thunderous speech in which I ripped into Watson for being ruthless in committee. Watson sat at his desk, tapping his fingers as he did when he was nervous.

When I sat down, Watson rose and pointed at me.

"This young man gave the nominee one of the most gruelling cross-examinations that anybody has ever had in this committee," he told the Senate. Then, slapping his leg as he always did for emphasis, he added solemnly, "But he was wrong."

Woodlock was confirmed and afterward Watson put his hand on my arm in the cloakroom and said with a grateful smile, "Well, you squared me with old Cal all right."

On the committee at that time only three of us were regarded as progressives. Soon Watson discovered that some of the most conservative members could be swayed. Senator Hiram Johnson introduced a resolution for an investigation of the prolonged coal miners' strike in Pennsylvania and John L. Lewis came before us to plead for its approval.

In contrast to the status they enjoy today, labor union leaders were the underdogs in those days, but Lewis, always at his best before congressional committees, outdid himself. The committee was literally spellbound by his eloquently emotional force. They asked him only a couple of questions and then quickly voted for the resolution. I was dumfounded because I had never before seen anyone representing the liberal point of view bowl over the reactionaries on our committee.

Watson selected a special committee for the investigation with great cunning. As chairman, he named Frank R. Gooding, an English-born former governor of Idaho and a millionaire sheepman regarded as anti-labor. The other two Republican members were Jesse H. Metcalf of Rhode Island, a millionaire manufacturer of textiles, and William B. Pine of Oklahoma, an oil millionaire. The Democratic members were myself and Robert F. Wagner of New York, who in his pre-New Deal days was looked upon as a conservative. I was the only concession to the cause of labor.

Lowell Limpus, a reporter for the New York *Daily News* who was covering the strike, offered to take me to the scene before the subcommittee got around to making the trip. We went to the Pittsburgh area and Limpus pointed out some of the things the mine owners would be loath to mention. Among other things, they had brought in Negroes in tremendous numbers from the South and had built corrals around them. The Negro miners were forced to sleep in barracks three or four deep.

While I was there, a colored man broke from the barracks in desperation and tried to flee. As he came running down the road, I stopped him. The company police immediately hurried up and told me to move on. I said I wouldn't because I wanted to talk with this miner. When I convinced them I meant it, they moved off. I questioned the runaway and then went to the local police station and began asking questions of several more who were incarcerated there. I did not tell them I was a senator but my manner of questioning made them suspicious and soon no one would talk.

When our subcommittee went to the scene soon after, the owners invited us to go through the mines. I proposed that we be accompanied by a representative of labor, such as Philip Murray. Murray, who had testified before us in Washington, was later to become head of the steelworkers union and the whole CIO. The owners said they wouldn't let Murray into their mines.

"Well, if you won't let Murray or another labor leader go in with us, we won't go," Chairman Gooding told them. Murray was then allowed to go with us under the ground.

The mine owners controlled the stores where the miners had to buy their food and the houses they had to live in. When the strike began, the owners had the miners' furniture thrown into the street. The Miners union had to erect tents to house the strikers and their families.

We held a hearing and Gooding became infuriated at the mine owners' attitude.

"What you're doing is breeding communism," he told them to their faces.

One newspaperman complained that Gooding was too inexperienced to cross-examine witnesses. He urged me to take over. I said I would follow up on Gooding's questioning but would not try to supplant him. I urged the newspaperman to pat the chairman on the back and tell him what a good job he was doing.

The union presented miners and their wives, priests, and community leaders. The union and company attorneys were given the opportunity to question one another's witnesses. This arrangement did not improve the case for the coal operators, many of whom were arrogant or uninformed or both.

Typically, when I urged the coal company officials to resume bargaining with the union and come to some working agreement, an official replied: "We are running an open shop. We have nothing to discuss with them."

I suggested to Richard B. Mellon, brother of Andrew Mellon, that he go in person into the mines and see the conditions for himself. I was just as harsh with John D. Rockefeller, Jr., when he pleaded ignorance of the problems of the coal industry, in which he was a large investor.

The subcommittee filed a unanimous report in which, among other things, we observed that one coal company president "was surprised to learn the committee was shocked by conditions they found on some property where men were housed in buildings that were filthy, poorly ventilated and not fit for human beings . . ." The subcommittee likewise reported it was "impressed with the courage and determination of the miners to stand up for what they believed was their due—an American wage making possible an American standard of living."

Even before our report was drafted, Watson knew what was coming. He came to me and said, "What the hell did you do to Gooding?"

"I didn't do anything to Gooding," I replied.

Shaking his head, Watson continued: "I appointed a millionaire sheepman, a millionaire textile industrialist, a millionaire oilman. I appointed Wagner who, being a Tammany man,

I thought would be all right. And I had to appoint you. But Gooding was worse than you were!"

On another occasion, Watson said: "Why is it you're always in here fighting for the proletariat?"

"Jim," I said, "there's plenty of men on this committee looking after the interests of the big fellows, who also have their lawyers coming down here. Somebody's got to try to at least present the side of the ordinary man and woman who can't afford lawyers."

"You know, Wheeler," he said wryly, "I represent the big interests but sometimes they're damn selfish."

Many of the Old Guard Republicans had no use for President Herbert Hoover. At times, I felt sorry for the President because they actually sabotaged him. Hoover was a very able individual and could have made a great President had he possessed more ability as a politician. Few people seem to recognize that to be a successful President one has to be a politician—to understand the political arts and to get along with the politicians who make up the House and Senate.

After he left office, Hoover seemed to interpret public sentiment much better than he did in the White House, and love and respect for him have grown. Before he became President, his engineering business had kept him out of the country and out of touch with the American people.

Once I came away from a talk with Hoover very angry. I complained to Watson that virtually all through my conversation the President had gazed at the ceiling instead of me.

"I don't talk *to* the President, I talk *at* him," Watson said with a laugh.

Unlike Hoover, Coolidge was a smart politician. I was very much amused at the way he handled Walsh and me when we called on him to try to get the federal government behind a proposed road from Red Lodge, Montana, into Yellowstone National Park. O. H. P. Shelley, then Republican national committeeman in Montana, lived in Red Lodge and was going all out to line up support. Shelley got Watson interested in the project; soon Watson had a friend who wanted to get the contract to build the road. Coolidge got wind of this, and of course he was only too well aware that it was Walsh and I who had embarrassed the Republicans by our twin revelations of the Harding scandals.

So when we went to the White House to discuss the matter, Coolidge didn't pay much attention to Walsh as he talked earnestly about the merits of a new road. The President gazed thoughtfully out the window into the rose garden. When Walsh finished, all Coolidge said, in his extra-dry manner, was: "Well, I don't want to see any scandal about it."

Walsh left the White House with me muttering and fuming. "Did you hear what that fellow said?" he kept asking.

Personally, I thought it was very clever of Coolidge to take a kick at us that way.

A charming and lovable colleague in the Senate was that Virginia gentleman, Claude A. Swanson. Swanson had been governor of his state and he was to become FDR's first Secretary of the Navy. Swanson was no orator and he seldom spoke on the floor, but he was one of the best men to have on your side in a fight. Privately, he could persuade more reluctant senators to go along on a vote than anyone else.

Swanson was a pragmatic political philosopher, or at least he enjoyed pretending to be one. For instance, when I ran for the Senate in 1922 I didn't favor prohibition, but Senator Walsh and Governor Stewart were ardent drys and insisted on a dry platform, even though the Anti-Saloon League had opposed me in the primary. A couple of years later becoming more aware of the bootlegging and other rackets spawned by prohibition and feeling somewhat hypocritical about my position, I came out in favor of repeal of the Eighteenth Amendment.

The day after I came out for repeal, Swanson sat down next to me in the Senate.

"I see the people in Montana have changed their views about prohibition," he remarked.

"How's that?" I asked.

"Well, I see that you've changed your view on prohibition," he said with a chuckle. "You know, the people of Virginia can't change their views any quicker than I can."

I loved to needle George Moses, a charming, sharp-tongued Old Guard Republican leader from New Hampshire. Moses inadvertently left himself wide open during the long debate that followed Hoover's calling of a special session to "do something about agriculture" by increasing the tariff on agricultural products.

The President suggested a "limited revision" of industrial rates. This split the Senate Republicans by uniting the GOP progressives with the Democrats. What eventually resulted was the Smoot-Hawley tariff law, which increased duties on almost all manufactured goods but left wheat and other agricultural products on the free list.

The progressives felt that the tariff aided manufacturers at the expense of the farmer, who sold in a free market and had to buy in a "protected" one. As the bill progressed through the Finance Committee under the chairmanship of the reactionary Reed Smoot of Utah, I issued a stream of statements denouncing various aspects of it. For example, I charged that the powerful producers of an industry were absenting themselves from the hearings and putting forward the least prosperous members "to enter tearful pleas for higher rates to protect them from the old bogey, 'foreign competition.'"

In particular I tried to disprove the hoary argument that the tariff was an act of charity to workingmen. I pointed out that in reality the only connection wage earners had with the tariff was burdensome prices.

The Old Guard grew increasingly exasperated at the progressives' drumfire.

One day I noticed a three-paragraph news item about a dinner speech Senator Moses had made in Boston before the New England Export Club and Commerce Department. Moses had said that the coalition dominating the tariff debate was led by the "sons of the wild jackass." I produced the clipping on the Senate floor the next day—while Moses was presiding—and read it into the record. It was a violent attack on the opponents of the bill and I discussed the implications of it as though Moses had been talking solely of the Western progressives in his own party, although obviously he had been referring to the liberal

Democrats as well. Senator Thaddeus H. Caraway, the Arkansas master of wit and sarcasm, joined in the sport.

The angry Moses was obliged to recognize senator after senator as they rose to speculate on who he had had in mind. What gave an extra-sharp point to our needle was the fact that Moses was due to leave that very evening for Chicago for a conference of Western Republicans on how to win the fall elections. News reports of the debate would go out over the country, we knew, and cause Moses some discomfort at his GOP conference.

When the debate was over, Moses left the rostrum and strode up to my desk.

"God damn you!" he rasped. "You know I meant you—not those Republicans!"

The airing we gave Moses' speech on the floor gave his "sons of the wild jackass" quip nation-wide attention and the phrase gained a place in the lexicon of American politics. Among the progressives, it became a password and a badge of honor.

The tariff debate had just about everything in it—including *Lady Chatterley's Lover*. The customs bureau long had had authority to bar the importation of any book, printed matter, or picture which it considered obscene. Senator Bronson M. Cutting, a liberal Republican from New Mexico, proposed to strike out the whole section of the bill granting this power. He revealed that in 1928 the customs bureau had blacklisted 739 books, all but 114 of which were in foreign languages. He said a point of absurdity was reached in the fact that some books were admissible in one foreign language but not in another!

When Cutting argued that damming the flow of books was arbitrary and unnecessary, he was eagerly joined by Borah, Caraway, myself, and some other progressives.

"It is a question of whether the Congress of the United States thinks the morals of the people of the country are going to be corrupted because a few pieces of literature come in that, in many instances, are classics," I said. "If the morals of the people of the United States are so easily corrupted, then surely the keeping out of a few volumes of classics and works of that kind is not going to save them."

It reminded me of when I ran for governor of Montana in 1920 on the Non-Partisan League ticket, I said, when my opponents spread the canard that the NPL would promote the practice of "free love" if it got into power.

There was a great deal of kidding in the debate about whether the government employed one customs inspector to do nothing but read salacious books. The dignified Smoot, author of the bill, thought the matter of protecting the people from sexy passages was no laughing matter. To try to impress the Senate with what was at stake, Smoot proposed to read to the Senate—in secret session—choice passages from D. H. Lawrence's new novel, *Lady Chatterley's Lover.* Cutting feigned horror at the prospect of the august Senate being exposed to the titillating details of what the lady did with the gamekeeper.

"I tremble to think of the effect of my colleague's proposed performance on the senators' morals," he said.

Unable to get the Senate to vote for a secret session, Smoot showed up in the Senate with an armful of "dangerous" volumes, all helpfully marked for their lascivious passages.

"The reading of these books," he began, "would so disgust senators that they would never dream of agreeing to the amendment of the senator from New Mexico. You need only read a page or two to know how damnable they are!"

Senator after senator marched to the desk and returned to their seats with the blacklisted books and—as the galleries tittered—obviously read more than "a page or two." Cutting riled Smoot by asserting that the Utah senator had talked so much about *Lady Chatterley's Lover* that he had "made a classic out of it." The book at that moment was receiving the rapt attention of Senator Royal S. Copeland, the New York Democrat.

However, Cutting's amendment to wipe out the section of the bill failed by nine votes. It was nearly thirty years before the customs bureau felt the American public was mature enough to have *Lady Chatterley's Lover* imported.

In the days of the giants, senators generally prided themselves on their courtliness. The colorful Robert R. Reynolds of North Carolina was continually testing his power to dazzle women, but he also was confident he could ingratiate himself with men. One man he couldn't impress was Huey P. Long.

I was standing in the cloakroom with Long in early 1933, shortly after Reynolds had been sworn in as a new senator. Reynolds hurried over, stuck out his hand and, ignoring me, said to Huey: "I'm Senator Reynolds of North Carolina."

Long never batted an eye.

"I knew you when you ran an ice-skating rink in New Orleans," he replied. This took the wind out of Reynolds' galleon-like sails—momentarily.

There was only one Huey Long. I first met him when I stopped over in Shreveport, Louisiana, with the Indian Affairs Committee in 1929. Huey, then the thirty-five-year-old governor of the state, was sitting at another table in the hotel dining room. He immediately came over to chat with us. He bragged about how he was going to supplant Senator Joseph E. Ransdell, a conservative who had been in the Senate since 1913, with John H. Overton and later go to the Senate himself. Both these predictions came true.

Huey got himself elected to the Senate for the term starting March 4, 1931, but he preferred to remain as governor for another year before taking his seat in the Senate. I liked him. I think he was sincere in espousing welfare programs—some of them admittedly pretty radical—to do something for the kind of poor people he sprang from. Perhaps he fancied himself a kind of Robin Hood of the bayous.

Also there lurked in Huey a well-concealed sense of chivalry, judging from one episode I happen to know about. It occurred after Senator Caraway died in 1931. His widow, Hattie, was appointed to succeed him. She was the first woman to become a United States senator. She was assigned to a seat in the back row, next to Long. Huey knew she soon had to run in a special election and he asked her about her chances. She said she was worried. Huey volunteered to check into the situation in Arkansas for her.

Long sent some of his men down there and they came back with bad news. In the Senate chamber, he reluctantly told the widow, "You'd better not run because you haven't got a chance." The distressed woman broke down and wept quietly at her desk. Later on, Huey related this to me:

"I went home that night to my hotel and I couldn't sleep. I got thinking about it and the more I thought about it the more I said, 'Hell, we'll go out there and elect her!' So the next morning I said to her, 'I told you yesterday you didn't have a chance, but here's what I'm going to do. I'm going to raise the money and go out there and campaign for you. You'll be elected.'

"I went down to New Orleans," Huey continued. "I got hold of our gang down there and I told them I wanted to raise some money to help Mrs. Caraway. They looked at me and said, 'Huey, you're crazy—it can't be done, and if you go in there and try to elect her, you'll only hurt the whole crowd down here.' I turned to one of them and said, 'You're a lawyer, aren't you?' and he said, 'Yes.' I said 'Well, you don't need a state job, you can make a living.' I turned to a doctor and said the same thing, and to an engineer. I argued with them and they finally said, 'Let's take a vote.'

"'All right,' I told them, 'let's take a vote. I'm the chairman, I vote "aye" and the motion is carried. Now go out and raise some money.' And they did. I went over to Arkansas and sent a van on ahead with a loudspeaker and a sign reading, 'Huey Long will be here!' As we started out campaigning, I said to Mrs. Caraway, 'Now, Mrs. Caraway, you know tonight you haven't got a chance, don't you? But before we wind up this campaign you're going to be elected.' As we went along, the crowds got bigger and bigger and I knew by the time we were pulling into Little Rock she was going to win. And I said to her, 'I want to tell you you will be elected because of the money raised for you by the so-called "notorious New Orleans ring"—but you're going to be the freest member of the Senate because this so-called notorious New Orleans ring is never going to ask you to vote for anything anytime.'"

Huey was at the peak of his influence all through the South that year and Mrs. Caraway was elected. Afterward, she told Mrs. Wheeler and me the substance of this story and called it non-political generosity. She was never for Huey Long or his program, but he kept his promise not to expect her vote.

Huey never lied to me and I had no evidence that he was a crook. Of course, there were a lot of stories about him. But after the way I had been maligned in Montana I knew enough not to believe the worst about a politician just because it was being passed around. One day I said to him, "Huey, if you're crooked and doing all these things, I'd like to know it because I'm not going to have anything to do with you if you are."

"When we raise money we do exactly what the Democratic and the Republican national committees do," he told me.

Once, when I told President Roosevelt he wasn't treating Huey right, FDR said he thought Huey was a crook.

"Well, I don't think so," I replied, "but if he is a crook, he's too smart for you to catch him."

George Norris liked Huey. So did young Bob La Follette. Most of the Southerners didn't like him. Incidentally, Long had far less racial prejudice in him than any other Southerner in the Senate.

Huey was not a debater in a class with Jim Reed; nevertheless no one wanted to take him on. He would talk forever and sometimes would resort to a form of backwoods vilification that would make any victim blanch. The galleries filled up quickly when word got around that he was to take the floor. But if he talked brutally and always put on a good show, he had no wish for physical encounter.

There was a lot of bluff in the "Kingfish." When he introduced his resolution to investigate James A. Farley, then Postmaster General, every senator was outraged. I knew he didn't have a thing on Farley and so I urged Robinson, the majority leader, to let the resolution go through because the ensuing investigation would show up Huey. If the resolution was killed, I argued, it would only make people wonder if Farley had something to conceal. Robinson couldn't see it that way and I was the only senator besides Long who voted for his resolution. I don't believe Farley ever forgave me for that.

Huey's mind was so brilliant he could discourse endlessly on everything from the silver issue to the dunking of cornpone in potlikker. He scorned preparation. When I advised him to study up on the complexities of silver, he cracked: "No, you study it, you tell me about it, and I'll make a better speech than you will."

He had a genius for illustrating a point in vivid barnyard metaphor. On one occasion, a group of visiting Montanans asked him in my presence what he thought of my colleague, Senator Thomas J. Walsh.

Huey startled his listeners by replying:

"You know, Walsh is like a guinea hen. Do you know the habits of a guinea hen? It's a very peculiar bird. If you take a long-handled rake, and rake the eggs out from under the guinea hen's nest, she'll keep on laying eggs. But if you reach your hand in and take the eggs, she'll never lay in that nest again. Now Walsh is like the guinea hen. He lays the ideas, and Joe Robinson takes a long-handled rake and rakes the ideas out. And so Walsh keeps giving Robinson the ideas."

Despite this incisive analysis, Huey respected and liked Walsh.

Huey was never an alcoholic but he gave up drinking because he found he couldn't handle it when he imbibed freely. During a night session, I once saw Jim Watson and George Moses taking Huey into the cloakroom and I suspected they were trying to get him tight. After he had visited their private spa two or three times, I got him aside in the cloakroom and warned him that the two Republicans were out to get him drunk so he'd make a fool of himself. The galleries were filled that night and Huey could never resist a crowd.

"I'm all right," he insisted.

"Listen, you're tight right now," I told him roughly. "Go out and get some coffee and doughnuts and get sobered up."

"Don't talk to me like that!" Huey muttered threateningly.

"I will talk to you like this!" I said. "You're just making a jackass of yourself."

"Well, I'll let you talk to me like that but I won't let any of those other S.O.B.'s in there talk to me like that," he grumbled.

Huey followed my advice about coffee and doughnuts and afterward sat down next to me in the Senate.

"I'm so sober I'm ashamed of myself," he reported.

Huey dressed gaudily but got away with it because he was,

altogether, a very flashy personality. He loved to swagger. Nobody could strut around like he could.

Joe Robinson and Pat Harrison hated Huey like no one was hated in the Senate in my time. They couldn't stand his demagoguery and his clowning, nor the fact that he was one of the most liberal Southerners and opposed them on many issues. His following throughout the South was extensive and had Harrison worried. The fact that Long showed his contempt for these two Democratic elders didn't increase his popularity in the Senate.

FDR feared Huey Long as a dangerous type of liberal. It must be remembered that in the first year of the New Deal Roosevelt was proceeding according to conservative theories. Huey, for his part, openly distrusted Roosevelt and never had any use for him from the start. They were, of course, polar opposites in background, manners, taste, etc.

One day in 1934 Huey was strutting nervously around my office.

"I'm going to beat that S.O.B. at the other end of the Avenue," he said.

I told him he was talking through his hat.

"You've never seen the crowds I get," he told me.

"That's right," I replied, "but, Huey, they come out to see you as a curiosity."

"Yes," he agreed, "but when they get there—I *get* 'em!"

"You know, Huey," I told him, "what Joe Robinson says about you is true—you disgust your own friends with your boasting."

He stopped in his tracks.

"Well, I don't care anything about society," he explained slowly. "I don't care anything about golf. I don't care anything about cards. The only pleasure I get out of life is boasting, and you want to take that away from me! When you stop to think of where I've come from and what I've got to do—don't you think I've got a right to boast?"

Now how could I answer a rationalization like that?

Huey was assassinated about a year after that conversation. He must not have been too surprised when the gun was fired at him in the Louisiana State Capitol. He always had had a bodyguard in Washington and many times I heard him remark, "They'll kill me, they'll kill me."

Roosevelt would never have won the Democratic nomination in 1932, in my opinion, but for Huey Long. And Huey probably would not have backed FDR but for me. Here's what happened.

Early in 1932, after Long took his seat in the Senate, I was determined to line up his potent support in my campaign to get Roosevelt nominated. Huey was then living at the Congressional Country Club, which is several miles outside Washington. I went out there and had dinner with him and talked up Roosevelt. Huey greatly admired George Norris and the only question was how Norris stood on Roosevelt. Norris hadn't told me, but I was sure he would prefer Roosevelt to the other Democrats in the running because he favored public power. So I said I was sure Norris was for the New York governor.

"Well, if Norris will tell me he's for him, I'll be for him," Huey said. He was returning to Louisiana that night and said he would drive me into town. Driving us down a hill on River Road in Maryland, Huey's chauffeur struck a bump and my head hit the roof. Huey asked me if I was hurt and I said no. But he yelled at the chauffeur to stop the car. Then he ordered the man out.

"You can't do this," I protested.

"Listen," Huey replied, "when they bump me, I walk them."

He took the wheel, forced the chauffeur into dark and lonely River Road, and we sped away. The next day I saw the poor fellow in Long's office. He laughed it off, saying, "Oh well, he does those things and afterward he's sorry."

As I suspected, I didn't have to "sell" Roosevelt to Norris. I asked him to let Long know his choice. Later on, Huey came to me and said, "I don't like your ——, but I'll be for him."

Just before the national convention, Huey telephoned me that he had hand-picked his delegates and told them to be for Roosevelt, without bothering with the formality of a state convention. But, he continued, another group, headed by ex-Governor J. Y. Sanders, had held a rump convention and selected another set of delegates—who were anti-Long.

"What should I do about it?" he asked me. I told him the

national convention would frown on his unorthodox methods. So he decided to hold his own state convention—and selected still a third set of delegates.

Three sets of Louisiana delegates rode into Chicago for a contest before the convention Credentials Committee. Sanders made a magnolia-and-molasses speech and got a big hand. Huey took the platform and jeered at it as "a lot of fakery." He launched into as coarse a speech as he could make—which was very coarse indeed. The committee was appalled. It recommended that Sanders' slate be seated. The pro-Roosevelt faction immediately appealed to the convention as a whole to override the recommendation and seat the Long delegates.

I heard that John W. Davis, the high-powered Wall Street lawyer and 1924 Democratic presidential nominee, was planning to talk against Huey on the convention floor. I urged the New Orleans people to substitute a smoother speaker for Huey. They told me not to worry—that Huey could make as fine a legal argument as Davis. Unconvinced, I tried to reason with the Kingfish, but he assured me he would make a noble-sounding argument.

When Long took the dais in the noisy, crowded Chicago Stadium, feeling against him was running high and booing started at once. Huey put his mouth to the microphone and pleaded: "Don't applaud me! Don't applaud me! My time is limited and I don't want applause!"

He plunged into his speech. Gradually the crowd quieted, and eventually it did applaud him. The convention voted to seat Long's second set of delegates. Later, Huey came over to me with a grin and said, "You thought I thought they were applauding me when they were actually booing me, didn't you?" I confessed this was true.

"Well," Long explained, "I knew they were booing but I also knew the people down in Louisiana, hearing all that noise over the radio would take my word for it that it was applause."

During the long night of the balloting, the delegations for John Nance Garner held firm and the Roosevelt drive bogged down. When the Mississippi and Arkansas delegations restlessly threatened to break their lines and jump to Garner,

FDR's manager feared it might start a stampede away from their candidate. They ran for help to the single most influential man in the South—Huey Long. Several times in the months since I had wangled his pledge for Roosevelt, Long had begged me to release him. He actually favored Garner. But now he did more than keep his word. He worked over the two state delegations with all his red-necked eloquence. As a result, Mississippi and Arkansas held fast for FDR. William Randolph Hearst then persuaded Garner to throw his delegates to Roosevelt to keep Al Smith or some other contender like Governor Albert C. Ritchie of Maryland or Newton D. Baker from capitalizing on the deadlock. From this deal Garner emerged as the vice presidential candidate.

During the election campaign, Huey Long continued to work effectively for Roosevelt. I myself labored for him in the Northwest.

In the last day before the election, President Hoover was due to speak in Salt Lake City in behalf of the re-election of Senator Smoot. I was assigned to climax my stumping for Western senators by counteracting Hoover in Salt Lake City later in the day.

Hoover spoke at noon before a tremendous crowd and related "what Smoot has done for Utah." At first, it seemed foolish for me to think I could help bring about the defeat of the well-known Smoot. Then I got talking with a Utah businessman who owned some iron works and had put up money for Smoot's opponent, Elbert Thomas, a schoolteacher. This man urged me to take the hide off Smoot and nail it to the barn wall. I didn't need much urging.

I twisted Hoover's text on Smoot to my own uses:

"I'm here to tell you not what Smoot has done *for* Utah but what he has done *to* Utah." I reviewed how the senator had voted for a high tariff on manufactured articles when Utah had wanted a high tariff on raw materials, and how he had played with the big interests in the East instead of looking to the problems of his own state. I spoke from radio station KSL to virtually the whole Northwest, having been allotted radio time bought by the Democratic National Committee for Election Eve.

Mrs. Wheeler and I began driving east on Election Night,

stopping to buy a few gallons of gasoline so we would hear the returns often. Several filling station attendants asked if I had "heard that fellow Wheeler last night." I finally said to one of them that I was Wheeler. He looked over our little Chevrolet runabout—a car our sons normally used—and replied, "The hell you are!" The next day we had the satisfaction of hearing that Roosevelt had been elected, and that Elbert Thomas had beaten Smoot.

Mrs. Wheeler left me at Albuquerque and took the train to Washington. I continued on, by way of the South, with a friend, A. A. Grorud. One midafternoon we arrived in Shreveport, Louisiana, tired, dusty, and without lunch. I told Grorud I felt like calling Huey Long, which I did from the public telephone in a restaurant.

"How are you traveling?" Huey asked when I got him on the phone. He urged me to come to New Orleans immediately. When I said that was impossible, he replied that he would have someone drive me there. I pointed out that it was completely out of my way to go to New Orleans and, besides, President-elect Roosevelt was expecting me at his retreat in Warm Springs, Georgia.

I hung up and we started to eat lunch. In about fifteen minutes two state policemen came to our table and asked me if I was Senator Wheeler.

"We have orders to take you to New Orleans," they said. I laughed and told them I couldn't go. They looked grim and said, "Senator, we don't know anything about it but we've got to take you to New Orleans."

When I asked them what I was charged with, they repeated their orders. I tried to reason but it was no use. I suspected they were acting on instructions from Huey.

We climbed into their police car and they drove us due south in a drenching rain. Another policeman drove our Chevrolet. We kept driving through the evening and arrived at the Roosevelt Hotel in New Orleans at one o'clock in the morning. There the room clerk said Senator Long had waited up for us until midnight and then had left word that he would call me the first thing in the morning.

Before I was awake the next day, the telephone rang at eight o'clock and I heard a familiar voice announce, "This is the Kingfish. Come on over and have breakfast with me."

Huey met me in green pajamas in his comfortable—but not extravagant-looking—home and ordered our breakfasts. Soon two men came in. Huey didn't introduce them but it was apparent they were newspapermen. One of them asked what I was going to do about the remonetizing of silver now that we had a Democratic President. I said, "I'm still for it." When Huey was asked for his comment, he said, "I don't know a damn thing about it, but if Wheeler's for it, I'm for it."

A few minutes later, two more men came in. One turned out to be Seymour Weiss, the manager of the Roosevelt Hotel and a member of the Long machine. They pleaded with him to stop an investigation of the vote on the newest bond issue. Huey mentioned that the Long group had won and seemed surprised there was an investigation. Weiss said the trouble was that in some of the parishes (counties) they didn't even bother to count the votes. Huey chuckled and said that if they didn't bother to count the votes "they ought to go to jail."

Turning to me, Long added: "The trouble is: some of these people down here are too lazy to count the votes any more." He remained adamant in the face of the pleas of Weiss and his friend that he halt the investigation. Then they left. I noticed in the evening papers that the state attorney general had been substituted for the local prosecutor in the conduct of the investigation.

Huey wanted to talk with me alone.

"You're going to see the President—Roosevelt," he pointed out. "I wish you'd talk to him about stopping some of these investigators from Washington they've got down here in Louisiana."

I asked him what investigators were on the scene.

"Oh, the Treasury Department has quite a few down here," he explained. "They're asking for affidavits from some of our friends about contributions, and things like that. But there's nothing wrong with it. We've taken contributions from people —contractors and others—who had big contracts with the state and others who are friendly with the state administration and we put it in a fund to help elect our candidates to the legislature and statehouse. And that's exactly what the Republicans and Democrats have done. As a matter of fact, some of the money was used to help the election of Roosevelt himself. We donated it."

I told Huey I didn't think it would be appropriate for me to bring up his problem in my visit with FDR.

I said nothing to anyone about the Long investigation but when Huey returned to the Senate for the next session I asked him if anything had come of it.

He laughed, "Oh, that's all forgotten about." Then he gave me the interesting explanation of why it was called off. He said that Ernest Lee Jahncke, the top Assistant Secretary of the Navy under Hoover, had owed a New Orleans bank, I think he said, $250,000, and that the bank suddenly called the loan. Soon Huey got a long-distance call from Washington from Harvey Couch. Harvey was now a director of the new RFC and was very important in the South because he was formerly president of the powerful Arkansas Power and Light Company.

"What about calling this loan on Jahncke?" Huey told me Couch asked him. Huey said he insisted he knew nothing about it.

"Oh, yes, you do," Couch replied. When Huey pointed out that the bank examiner had called the loan, Couch reminded him that Governor O. K. Allen was Huey's man and that the bank examiner was Allen's man.

"Listen, Harvey," Huey said he replied, "I don't have anything more to do with that bank examiner than the Assistant Secretary of the Navy has to do with the Treasury Department."

"Oh, is *that* it?" Couch replied, the light beginning to dawn.

"That's exactly it," Huey told him.

Huey told me the Treasury Department promptly pulled their tax investigators off the Long gang and the bank didn't call Jahncke's loan. I later heard the same explanation from another source, Frank Vanderlip, the retired president of the

National City Bank in New York. Vanderlip said he heard the substance of the story from Herbert Hoover himself.

(The story adds depth to the explanation given by Elmer T. Irey, chief of the Treasury Department's Intelligence Unit during this period, in his book, *The Tax Dodgers.* Irey said that Secretary Ogden L. Mills called him in after the 1932 election and ordered him to suspend his investigation of Long and write a full report. The report, Mills said, would be left on the doorstep of his successor when the Democrats took over in March 1933. After all, Mills was quoted as saying, Huey was one of the Democrats' "babies" so the GOP would "let them decide what to do with him."

(As Irey explained, the Roosevelt Administration did not order him to resume his investigation of the Long gang until nearly a year after it took office. This was the period in which FDR, hating Huey but fearing his power, tried to play along with him. Irey wrote that he was just getting ready to try to indict Huey when he was assassinated in September 1935. The government never did convict the Long clique of tax evasion.)

Another cantankerous but likeable character in the Senate was J. Hamilton Lewis, the pink whiskered, conservative-voting Illinois Democrat. He was visibly upset when Hoover in 1932 proposed the Reconstruction Finance Corporation, which would have wide powers to extend credit to banks and railroads. So was I. Many of the old conservatives were going along with the President on the idea it would cure the depression. Some senators orated that if the RFC lent money to the railroads and banks and insurance companies, smoke would pour from the chimneys and the farmers and workers would regain prosperity.

"When you pass this bill," I argued, "everybody will be down here in Washington wanting money out of the Treasury."

Senator Lewis came over to my desk and said in an aside: "Boy, you're right. Give 'em hell." I turned to him, still holding the floor, and asked him if he would speak against the bill. When he shook his head, I asked him if he would at least vote with me.

"No," Lewis said in a low, intense voice. "I can't, because I represent a damn bunch of thieves—thieves, I tell you!—who want to reach their hands into the public coffers and purloin the money. My God, if I were a free man, I'd tear this thing limb from limb."

The RFC bill passed the Senate, with the liberal vote split. I asked young Bob La Follette why he supported the bill. He said he was afraid there would be a crash. I said, "Yes, and the sooner it's over the better. This will only prolong the depression."

After the vote, I went downstairs to the Senate restaurant and asked Joe Robinson if he thought the bill would solve our economic crisis. He assured me it would.

"After you loan money to railroads and insurance companies and banks," I told him and several others, "the pressure on Congress is going to be too great. Our constituents will say, 'Why can't you loan money to the farmers and everybody else?' "

In my judgment, that was the first step toward a welfare state.

I enjoyed being in a minority party in the Senate, with the opposition party in the White House. It's more fun when you can get up and attack the administration, if you feel like it, and not be charged with disloyalty for doing so. And when constituents write to you for jobs, you can reply truthfully that you haven't any patronage and can't do a thing.

Of course, I had started off by flouting a tradition of the Senate itself. Demanding a roll call on a committee chairman and my own investigation of the Attorney General were the bad manners of an upstart. If I had stubbed my toe, I might have been dismissed as a nuisance and shunted into obscurity. Luckily, my brand of aggressiveness had achieved results and therefore won me not only attention but respect.

Not long after I was in the Senate, my good friend Henry Ashurst took me aside. He said there was a senator—whom he preferred to keep anonymous—who had told him he was going to "take on this brash upstart from Montana and take him apart on the floor."

"Don't try it! Don't try it!" Ashurst told me he replied. He said he pointed out to the senator that he had been a classmate of mine at Michigan Law School and also knew I had survived some lusty battles with powerful enemies in primitive Montana. "He'll cut you to ribbons," Ashurst told me he advised the bloodthirsty senator.

Ashurst then said to me with a wink: "So if you notice some senator being extra nice to you, you'll know who I'm talking about."

Several years later, Ashurst met me on the street with my son, Edward, and repeated the story. Then he disclosed: "The senator was Henry Cabot Lodge."

Vice Presidents Dawes and Garner admired a senator who would stand up and fight for a principle. I believe both many times wished they were down in the well of the chamber where they could sound off. Garner knew, for example, that many senators who agreed completely with me on a bill in the cloakroom went right out on the floor and voted according to the dictates of a popular President.

Shortly before he ended his second and last term, Garner called me into his office and asked me to pour us a drink. Sighting through his glass, he said, "You know, the longer I've lived and the more I've seen of Washington, the more convinced I am that in the Senate it's more important to have guts than brains. And you've got guts."

"You mean—I don't have brains?" I asked.

Garner's eyes twinkled beneath his tufted white eyebrows. "I said—'you've got guts,'" he replied.

Chapter Fourteen

LIFE WITH FDR

My long and bumpy political relationship with Franklin D. Roosevelt began in the Hotel Commodore in New York City in April 1930. I was one of the main speakers at the Democratic Party's Jefferson Day dinner. I had been reluctant to accept the invitation because the dinner was under the auspices of Tammany Hall, which I despised. Senator Robert F. Wagner of New York and Jouett Shouse, executive chairman of the Democratic National Committee, talked me into it.

Wagner warned me that long-winded speeches were not appreciated by the bibulous diners. When I saw the bottles on the massed tables and the rapidly liquefying politicians crowded into the ballroom, I was glad I planned to speak for only fifteen minutes. Also I took the precaution of issuing a press release before the dinner began. I had a serious message—I was coming out for Roosevelt for President. Our speeches were to be carried over the NBC Blue Network and I did not want my message lost in the 100-proof din enveloping the ballroom.

Immediately after I sat down on the speakers' platform, I

was approached by James W. Gerard, who was also seated there. Gerard had been Woodrow Wilson's Ambassador to Germany and was married to the daughter of Marcus Daly, one of Montana's famous "copper barons" before the turn of the century. He asked me if it was true I was about to propose the New York governor for President. I said I had already given such a statement to the press.

"Go to it and God bless you," Gerard commented warmly.

Having been tipped off by Gerard that I would toss his hat into the ring, Roosevelt tactfully left the hall before I spoke.

In my speech, I said: "As I look around for a general to lead the Democratic Party on these two issues, the tariff and control of power and public utilities, I ask to whom can we go? I say that, if the Democratic Party of New York will elect Franklin D. Roosevelt governor, the West will demand his nomination for President and the whole country will elect him."

Political historians have since recorded that I was the first nationally known Democrat to publicly back Roosevelt for the 1932 nomination. *The New York Times* reported the next day that I had "launched a boom for the governor."

My statement helped the governor, for he was fighting Tammany while seeking re-election. When I got back to Washington, I attended a small dinner where Shouse and other Democratic leaders were present. They said I had upset the applecart by mentioning Roosevelt. They thought the nomination should go to Owen D. Young, then head of General Electric, or Myron C. Taylor, then president of United States Steel (and later FDR's envoy to the Vatican).

I was for Roosevelt because I figured he could be elected President; also I wanted to head off another race by Al Smith. I was an admirer of Al and felt he had made a great governor of New York. In 1928 I had been anxious to see him elected—and, for a while, I thought he could be. It was unthinkable that Montana would not vote for a Catholic for President. We had elected Tom Walsh, a Catholic, to the Senate three times.

But when I had campaigned for Smith in Montana I got a shock. I was running for re-election. We had a sign on our car reading, WE'RE ALL FOR AL. Some Democrats asked me to take the sign down. Others said, "I've voted for you before, but never again!" In Scobey, I found our meeting place locked, so I went around the town until I located the key, opened the door of the hall, ushered in the small audience, and introduced myself at the dais.

While I was speaking, I received word that I was billed for a speech at the same hour in Plentywood, fifty miles away. It was then eight o'clock. I sent word to keep the meeting going and that I would get to Plentywood by ten o'clock. I arrived there an hour later than that but found a fair portion of the audience patiently waiting for me.

The botched speaking schedule and the lack of advertising continued the next day and convinced me that my campaign was being sabotaged. Finally, in another little town, I walked into the local telephone exchange and presented the operator with a box of candy. I persuaded her to put in a general call to Froid, twenty-five miles away, announcing that I would make a speech there at 7:30 P.M. This meant that all the subscribers in Froid would get my announcement simultaneously.

A good-sized crowd was waiting for me in Froid and I devoted my entire talk to intolerance.

"You wouldn't be against me because my father was a Quaker," I told my audience. "You wouldn't vote against me because I went to Baptist Sunday school. You wouldn't vote against me because I married a Methodist."

My listeners sat on their hands and grudgingly gave me a smattering of applause when I finished. They gathered in ominous knots of ten or twelve after the meeting while eying us. My driver, "Doc" Cronin, nervously and disgustedly said, "Let's get out of here," although we had planned to spend the night.

I campaigned all over the state for Smith and devoted most of my speeches to plugging him. The Ku Klux Klan, which was very strong in eastern Montana, attacked him and on the Sunday before the election a scurrilous sheet attacking me was circulated through the state by the KKK. Smith lost Montana by 34,800 votes and I carried it by only 12,470—the smallest majority of my senatorial victories. My opponent was Joe

Dixon, a liberal Republican, who had beaten me for the governorship in 1920.

Roosevelt, playing the game cautiously in 1930, did not thank me for my early endorsement for President until June. Then, he wrote:

"I was made very happy by your reference to me at the Democratic club dinner, for the very good reason that I have always thought of you as one of the real leaders of progressive thought and action in this country. Therefore, to be considered as [a] real progressive by you means something to me."

Nonetheless, FDR continued carefully, he had "no personal desire" for the presidency. Then he put this disclaimer in perspective by concluding: ". . . I hope you will keep in touch with the general thought of the mountain states on the power question."

I replied to Roosevelt: "You more nearly typify the progressive thought of this nation than anyone else."

I lined up support for Roosevelt's candidacy before and during the 1932 convention. In the spring of that year Senator David I. Walsh of Massachusetts gave a dinner for me in Boston to which he invited financier Joseph P. Kennedy, whom I had known since 1924. Kennedy came late and said he couldn't stay but asked me to meet him at the Harvard Club before I went back. During an evening with Kennedy at the club and the theater, he asked me who I favored for President. I said, "Roosevelt." He wanted to know if John J. Raskob, then chairman of the Democratic National Committee, was for him and I said no. Kennedy said that "if that so-and-so Raskob is against Roosevelt, I'll be for him."

Later in the spring, Frank C. Walker, whom I had known when he practiced law in Montana, was raising funds for Roosevelt and asked me if I knew anyone who might put up money. I told him about my conversation with Kennedy. He went to Kennedy and got a $5000 contribution to the Roosevelt pre-convention campaign, at a time when it was vital. During the election campaign, Kennedy kicked in $37,500 and I heard that he also loaned the Democratic Party $50,000. As is well known, Kennedy joined the Roosevelt Administration and in

1937 became FDR's Ambassador to the Court of St. James's.

Meanwhile, besides pointing Huey Long toward his support of FDR (as related in the preceding chapter), I traveled all over the West before the Chicago convention advocating the candidacy of Roosevelt. In California, I worked for delegates with Roosevelt's son, Jimmy. I insisted that Montana's delegates go for Roosevelt and I also got half of Minnesota's delegates for him after an intra-party struggle there. Later I stumped the West for Roosevelt during the election campaign.

Right after the election, I met with FDR at his retreat in Warm Springs, Georgia. I told him that my Montana colleague, Senator Walsh, and I wanted him to appoint Ed Keating, editor of *Labor*, as Secretary of Labor. Roosevelt hesitated and then said that he wanted to appoint Walsh as Attorney General, adding: "I've got to appoint Jim Farley as Postmaster General and I can't very well have more than two Catholics in my cabinet" (Keating was also a Catholic). At the same time, he disclosed that he wanted to make George Norris Secretary of Agriculture and Hiram Johnson Secretary of Interior (both these independent Republicans had supported him in the election). I told him I was sure that Norris, Johnson, and Walsh would prefer to remain in the Senate.

The President-elect asked me to talk to Walsh about taking the Attorney Generalship. He didn't know I had already suggested to Walsh he could probably get the post if he wanted it. Walsh had said he wouldn't take it but that I should get it. I told him I wasn't interested—for the simple reason that the Roosevelt Administration undoubtedly would want me to do certain things politically as Attorney General that I would not do.

When I returned from Warm Springs, I relayed to Walsh FDR's desire that he take the job. He repeated that he would refuse it. Shortly after, the President-elect visited the Mayflower Hotel in Washington and was holding court there. I went to him and reported that Walsh wouldn't budge. Roosevelt called in Walsh. Aware of the senator's ambition to go on the Supreme Court, he promised him an appointment to the first vacancy there if he took the post of Attorney General first.

(Considering that Walsh was seventy-four years old, it is worth pointing out that only a few years later FDR was arguing that the "old fogies" on the Supreme Court—those in their sixties and seventies—must be either retired or assisted with extra justices.)

Walsh told me he decided to accept the President's proposition. He was anxious to know who I thought would be appointed by Montana Governor John E. Erickson as his successor in the Senate. I told him I thought the appointment would go to Bruce Kremer, the well-known and well-connected Democratic national committeeman from Montana.

"You can't permit that to be done!" Walsh exclaimed animatedly. I told him I couldn't prevent it. I added that I also thought that if he became Attorney General he would be taking on too strenuous a job for a man of his age. (During the preceding summer Walsh and I had ridden horseback on a fishing trip in the Rockies and I could see that he was mentally not as sharp as he had been.) I also pointed out that the problems of the Justice Department might result in a dim anticlimax to his illustrious Senate career.

"You can turn down one appointment but not two," Walsh replied.

Walsh, who hated very few people, hated Kremer. Kremer, a reactionary and a lobbyist for the Anaconda Copper Mining Company, had opposed both of us politically and I didn't like him any better than Walsh did. Walsh now asked me to telephone the governor and tell him not to appoint Kremer. I refused. I felt it was Walsh's place, not mine, to call the governor.

Shortly afterward, Kremer dropped into my office and smugly told me he expected to be appointed senator. He even suggested that we could work together. I replied that our differences were fundamental and bluntly informed him that I was opposed to his being appointed.

After Congress convened in March, a newspaper reporter told me he heard that Walsh was about to be married. I told him he would be foolish to believe that. Walsh had been a widower for fourteen years. It is true that in the twenties he had gone about town with the socially prominent widow, Mrs. J. Borden Harriman—who had reputedly persuaded him to clip his black handlebar mustache. But he hardly seemed the type to become a late-blooming bridegroom and I was sure he would have told Mrs. Wheeler or me if he planned to do so.

After talking with the reporter, I walked into the Senate chamber and saw Walsh, who instantly motioned me into the cloakroom. There he confided that he was leaving town for a few days and asked me to protect him on any important legislation by "pairing" him in the vote with another absent senator. I told him I had heard a rumor about his getting married but got no reply.

That night I mentioned the rumor to Mrs. Wheeler and she dismissed it as being preposterous. She and the senator long had been good friends and mutual admirers.

A few mornings later we picked up the newspaper and read that Walsh had been married in Cuba to a Cuban widow, Señora P. C. Truffin. The morning after that a news syndicate correspondent telephoned me and said: "Walsh died last night." He had suffered a heart attack aboard the train bringing him back to Washington for the Roosevelt inaugural and his own swearing-in as Attorney General.

I found the news hard to believe. Walsh's personal and political life had been intertwined with mine ever since 1911. My heavy sorrow was expressed in this statement I gave to the press:

"I am grieved beyond words. He has been almost a father to me. Senator Walsh's passing is a real loss to the country. His advice and counsel was so much needed in this time of stress. He was one of America's really great statesmen—intelligent, honest, and courageous. He was devoted to Montana and her people and was ever ready to fight for what he believed to be in the interests of the underprivileged men and women of the country."

As his first Attorney General, Roosevelt then decided to appoint the Democratic national committeeman from Connecticut, Homer S. Cummings, a close friend of Kremer.

On the funeral train en route to Montana, Walsh's daughter,

Mrs. Genevieve Gudger, said almost tearfully: "Burt, you've got to stop the governor from appointing Bruce Kremer." I promised to do what I could.

I went to Erickson with Senator Ed Kendrick of Wyoming. Kendrick said the members of the Senate didn't want Kremer as a colleague; he was not only a corporation lobbyist but the obnoxious kind who slapped them on the back and called them by their first names. The governor said nothing.

After Walsh was buried, Mrs. Gudger went to see Erickson in the statehouse. She was dressed from head to toe in black. Suddenly, she raised the veil above her bereaved face.

"I'm speaking for my dead father," she said in a hushed tone. "He doesn't want Bruce Kremer appointed to the United States Senate."

Describing the scene to me later, Erickson said it was one of the eeriest experiences he ever had.

I next met Frank Kerr, president of the Montana Power Company, in a hotel lobby and told him I understood he was there to get Kremer appointed.

"We have a lot of power in this state," Kerr replied.

"That's right," I said, "and when you have Kremer appointed you'll be serving notice on me that you want a fight. I'm coming up for election in two years and that'd be a good time to test just how much power you really have."

The ultimatum went back to the New York offices of the Anaconda Copper Mining Company, which then worked hand in glove with the power company. The next day representatives of Anaconda informed me it had withdrawn its support for Kremer. I got the two representatives together in my hotel room with Erickson and had them repeat the news, just to make sure he knew about it. That ended Kremer's chances. I then persuaded Erickson to resign as governor and let the lieutenant governor, Frank Cooney, appoint him as Walsh's successor in the Senate.

Speculation by political writers has persisted over the years that I had wanted FDR to appoint me Attorney General after Walsh died and that this led to animosity on my part toward the President. There is no truth in this theory. As explained previously, I had no wish to head up a politically potent department in the Roosevelt Administration. Also, being in line for the chairmanship of the Interstate Commerce Committee, I had much more to gain by remaining in the Senate.

My first rift with the new President was over the question of silver. Most of my early legislative activity under the New Deal was directed toward the coinage of silver at 16 ounces of silver to one of gold. My interest in the subject went all the way back to a debate in Hudson, Massachusetts, High School during the McKinley-Bryan campaign of 1896. I took the side of William Jennings Bryan—and it converted me to the Democratic Party. I had been for the remonetization of silver ever since. Since we were in a depression in 1933, I felt the remonetization of silver would be far better than cutting the gold content of the dollar, or going to paper money, as some were advocating.

True, Montana was a silver-producing state. But its production amounted to only 16 per cent of the entire United States' output and silver was only a by-product in the copper industry. My interest in silver was to add it to our monetary system to offset the severe deflation that was continuing to depress the national economy and to inflict unwarranted hardship on all who owed money.

I offered my 16–1 proposal in the form of an amendment to the Agricultural Adjustment Act. During the roll call, the outcome looked as if it could go either way. Finally, Senator Borah rose and asked majority leader Robinson how the President stood on the issue. Robinson replied that FDR would veto the AAA bill if my amendment was included. Borah promptly announced he would vote against it, although he had always favored the remonetization of silver. My amendment was then defeated 45–43.

After that, Vice President Garner reportedly warned FDR that unless he acted in some way on the money issue, my 16–1 proposal would eventually pass. The President called in Senators Jimmy Byrnes, Key Pittman, and a number of others to discuss possible legislation on money. I was conspicuously not invited.

While the White House conference was in progress, I was

standing in the Mayflower Hotel lobby. A friend asked me if I would like to meet Father Coughlin and we went upstairs.

The Reverend Charles Edward Coughlin, the famous "radio priest" who was then at the height of his popularity, was pacing up and down his room. As he walked, he told me about the money conference. I asked him if the group planned to include the remonetization of silver in the proposed legislation and he said no. Father Coughlin, who had been attacking the money system every Sunday over the radio to an audience of many millions, was quite well informed. He was at that time very close to Joe Kennedy, Postmaster General Jim Farley, White House aide Tommy Corcoran, and the President himself. I told the priest that unless the administration did something about the remonetization of silver I would offer my amendment to any bill that came up. I was quite critical of Roosevelt.

The next morning, Frank Walker, then assistant Democratic chairman and an old Montana friend, telephoned me and said he understood I was on the warpath. I acknowledged that I was.

"You can't break with the President," he said.

"Oh, yes, I can," I replied.

Walker said the President wanted to see me on the silver question. I told him I wouldn't see the President. A little later, Marvin H. McIntyre, Roosevelt's appointments secretary, telephoned me and persuaded me to go to the White House.

(FDR's ability to seduce a caller with his special blend of charm and blarney was formidable. Once, at a time when William Randolph Hearst was editorially blasting Roosevelt, I was visiting him in California. I urged him to have a talk with the President. Hearst admitted frankly that he was "afraid to"—because he might be taken in.)

When I walked into the Oval Room of the White House, FDR greeted me with a wave of his hand and an airy: "Hello, Burt, I want to talk to you about silver."

"Mr. President," I said, "I don't deserve this kind of treatment from you, and I'm not going to take it. You called in all these people, none of whom was sincerely interested in the fight I'm making to remonetize silver."

"Burt," he replied smoothly, "Bryan killed the remonetization of silver in 1896."

"Mr. President," I responded, "if this situation keeps up, you're going to take a lot worse remedies to solve our monetary problem than the remonetization of silver."

At this point, Senator William H. King of Utah arrived and proved to be more tractable in listening to Roosevelt's views. Finally, to ward off my offering my amendment again, the President persuaded King and me to step outside and draft a compromise proposal. We devised one which gave the President the right to remonetize silver at 16–1—but did not make it mandatory. I offered the amendment in the Senate and it was made part of the administration bill which reduced the gold content of the dollar.

While FDR never remonetized silver, he did inflate our currency by cutting the gold content of the dollar and he started a program of buying silver above the market price. The silver purchase program was all the mining companies were interested in. Sometimes the President would call me at my home or at my office and tell me he was buying silver. But I was not interested in raising the price. I was convinced that remonetization would help the people as a whole, but all the big banking houses in New York were against it, on the ground that it would be inflationary. I realized it would be somewhat inflationary. Other countries had inflated their currencies by going off the gold standard. I reasoned that it would be much better to use silver to counter the serious deflation that had taken place than some of the other measures that were being proposed. I felt there wasn't gold enough to form an adequate base for our money.

I believe FDR invited me to the White House on that occasion because he felt guilty for having left me out of the conference on silver. He knew what I'd done to get him nominated and how I had campaigned for him and with him in the Northwest. Indeed, I was considered to be so close to the President in the early days of the New Deal that Senator Tom Connally called me "teacher's pet."

Roosevelt sought to square himself with me in typical fashion. A delegation from Nebraska told me they were anxious to get the government to build a dam for flood control and navigation at the old Fort Peck dam site in Valley County, Montana. I asked if such a dam could produce cheap power and also provide a lake where the people of eastern Montana could at least take a bath. We had had a drought in Montana for seven years; the crops had been so poor many of the farmers had gone bankrupt and couldn't even afford overalls for their boys and girls so they could attend school.

The Nebraskans said the lake could be included in the project and so I took them to the White House. I told FDR the dam would furnish navigation, flood control, and cheap power. He asked me what it would cost. I said, "around seventy-five million dollars." We had been with him only fifteen or twenty minutes when he told me the dam would be built.

The Nebraskans, of course, were overjoyed but they told me afterward they couldn't understand how the President could agree so quickly to spend $75,000,000. (The project cost a lot more than that by the time it was completed in 1940. It is 250 feet high and has the fourth largest storage capacity in the world.) Secretary of Interior Harold L. Ickes told me he never would have approved the Fort Peck dam but that there was nothing he could do about it because "you went over my head." The simple fact was that when FDR wanted to help a senator he built a dam for him. He built one on the Columbia River in Oregon for Republican Senate leader Charles McNary because he needed his support. He did the same thing in the State of Washington for Senator Clarence Dill, a Democrat.

In ordinary times, a senator pushing a dam project must go through the tortuous process of maneuvering it through the authorizing committees of the House and Senate and then, if he gets that far, of wangling funds from the appropriations committees of both houses. If he is successful, it usually takes a couple of congressional sessions. But in the depression, all Roosevelt had to do, if he felt like wooing a legislator, was to dip into the federal treasury on his own and allocate some of the millions granted to him under the Public Works Administration. I'm sure most of these projects have been very useful to the economy of the country. Fort Peck was useful to the people of Montana—as well as to me politically.

For example, when I ran for re-election in 1934 my Republican opponent was none other than former Federal Judge George M. Bourquin, who had backed me from the bench during World War I when I had refused to prosecute sedition cases without evidence. Bourquin was a man of considerable intellect and character and highly respected. But in the campaign he made a speech in Gallatin County in which he referred to the lake created by Fort Peck dam as a "mud pond." All the people along the Great Northern Railroad in northern and eastern Montana were outraged. That one crack finished Bourquin. On Election Day, the voters of Montana gave me the greatest victory ever won in Montana politics. I polled 142,823 votes to Bourquin's 58,519. This was a bigger margin than Walsh won by in 1930 and exceeded Roosevelt's majority in Montana in 1932.

Starting my third six-year term in January 1935, I ascended, through the seniority system, to the chairmanship of the Interstate Commerce Committee. My power as chairman was of vital importance to the President. He knew my sympathies were with the New Deal. I had voted for his liquor repeal law, the AAA, the gold reserve act, the Tydings-McDuffie Act for Philippine independence, the Securities and Exchange Act, the Reciprocal Trade Agreements Act, and the Frazier-Lemke Act. Now my influence and ability was about to be tested in the exceedingly fine art of legislating. No test could have been more severe than the administration's bill to regulate the utility holding companies. The lobby that fought this bill was the biggest, bitterest, and most extravagant during my time in the Senate.

I had been interested in doing something about the holding companies ever since Walsh had introduced a bill to investigate them in 1928. The utility heads feared a Walsh probe because they recalled all too vividly what he had done with the Teapot Dome scandal. I worked for his resolution in our committee but at that time the Republicans were in the majority and they kicked the investigation over to the Federal Trade Commission, as the utility people had urged.

The irony of this supposed sidetracking was that the FTC did a much better job of investigating the holding companies than any congressional committee could have done. The FTC had the facilities, the experts and the time to inquire into the situation thoroughly.

Its report condemned the utilities and the holding companies and aroused the progressives. The holding companies were pictured as parasites. I asked Frank Kerr, president of the Montana Power Company, why he should be paying an enormous sum to Electric Bond and Share, and his parent holding company.

"Well, if you want to raise money," Kerr explained, "you've got to go to New York and join one of them. They're like a lot of damn pawnbrokers."

Later, I said publicly that "the only difference between Jesse James and some of these utility men is that Jesse James had a horse."

The National Power Policy Committee reported that thirteen holding company groups controlled three-quarters of the privately owned electric utility industry and that the three largest —Electric Bond and Share, United Corporation, and Insull— controlled some 40 per cent themselves. I felt that this kind of bloodsucker not only drained the investor but through fraudulent overcapitalization of public utilities also fastened outrageous prices on the light, gas, water, and power consumers. I called the holding groups "unsound scalping operations" which easily became highly detrimental to the operating companies they fed upon.

I had gotten up a bill to regulate the holding companies but a day before I planned to introduce it the President called a conference to discuss a promise in his State of the Union message to abolish their evils. Present with me were the late Sam Rayburn, then chairman of the House Interstate Commerce Committee; Senators Norris and Borah; Tommy Corcoran, and one or two others.

FDR announced at the meeting that Rayburn would introduce the bill. I said, "Well, I've got a little bill I'm going to introduce." He was deliberately turning the job over to Sam and ignoring me. I forget why, but I was not in too good grace with FDR at the time.

However, as soon as I got back to my office, Corcoran and Ben Cohen, the White House bill-drafting specialist, arrived. They urged me to introduce the administration bill instead of my own. They said I wouldn't have to do anything until after the bill passed the House. I agreed to go along; their bill was more carefully drafted than mine.

But over in the House, Rayburn couldn't seem to get started. I felt that Sam himself was a little tepid about the so-called "death sentence"—a provision which was tougher than anything I had had in my own bill. It required all holding companies which were not parts of geographically or economically integrated systems to dissolve or reorganize themselves by January 1, 1938. (As a whole, the ultimate object of the extremely complex bill was to bring reduced rates to consumers by eliminating padded valuations, various schemes for milking subsidiaries by the holding companies, and irregularities in securities corporations.)

The utility lobby rushed to Capitol Hill and threw all its giant resources into defending itself; it also applied pressure in the legislators' home districts. The immediate result was to stall all action in the House.

Corcoran appealed to me to get the bill moving on the Senate side. So I scheduled hearings. I was promptly visited by Bowie Chipman, a well-known representative of Laidlaw and Company, a brokerage firm. Chipman pointed out that we had played bridge together and were friends. Then he continued:

"These utility people feel you're putting a gun at their heads and they're going to destroy anybody that gets in their way."

"Did they tell you to give me that message?" I asked.

"Not exactly," Chipman replied. I asked him to take a message back to them.

"You tell them," I said, "that a lot of experts have tried to destroy me and haven't been able to get away with it. If these people know any new ways, I hope they'll bring them on—I'd like to see what they are."

A few days later, I was visited by the president of UGI, a big utility in Philadelphia, accompanied by a former state senator of New Jersey who represented a public service corporation in his state. I facetiously asked if they had any guns on them and they smilingly said no, that they had been searched by my assistant. Then they got down to serious business. They asked me what I was going to do about the "death sentence." I said I was going to keep it if I could.

"Suppose the committee doesn't go along with you?" they asked.

"Maybe it won't, but I think it will," I said.

They wanted to know how much time the utilities would have to present their case in the hearings. I said I would give them one week and the government another week.

"Oh, we've got to have thirty or forty days."

"Well," I said, "if your lawyers can't tell what's wrong with a bill in a week's time, it's just too bad, because that's all you're going to get . . . and if you come over here and act like gentlemen you'll be treated like gentlemen. But if you try to pull any of the rough stuff you pulled in the House I'll throw you out."

"You're pretty cocky this morning," one of my visitors commented. I concluded the conversation by advising them not to send any of their crooked lobbyists or newspapermen around to see me "because if you do, I won't tell them anything!"

The holding companies did send all kinds of people to me to try to exert pressure and propaganda—including, of course, citizens of my home state. I agreed on one occasion to go to dinner with Cornelius Kelley, chairman of the board of the Anaconda Copper Mining Company; James Hobbins, president of Anaconda; and Ned Grossbeck, head of Electric Bond and Share. Grossbeck talked about the schoolteachers in Montana who were stockholders in his firm and also mentioned that I was believed to be prejudiced against his company. I finally exploded and told them they were wasting their time.

"The President of the United States asked me to handle this bill and I told him I'd do it," I explained. "I'm not going to double-cross the President of the United States and you wouldn't have any respect for me if I did, and I wouldn't have any respect for myself."

That ended the conversation.

In April the lobbying intensified and the fight began to have a national impact. Will Rogers wisecracked that "a holding company is something where you hand an accomplice the goods while the policeman searches you." The big interests brought pressure to bear on the inimitable humorist. Here's the way he "retracted" in his newspaper column:

"Well, I didn't figure that little half-witted remark would upset the whole holding company business. But I forgot that a remark generally hurts in proportion to the truth."

I used Rogers' two quotes to help make my point about the utility lobby in a radio speech over the NBC network on April 3.

"I hope the good people of Philadelphia are listening tonight," I began. "You know, I have an ever-growing warm spot in my heart for Philadelphia. More letters have come out of that metropolis with my name on them in the last month than I have received from my home state of Montana during the last two years . . . nice, chummy letters too. They call me everything from such high class terms as 'rogue' and 'rascal' on down the scale. Most of them show the fine hand of the United Gas Improvement Company. The best of them must have come from Gertrude Stein. It consists of this: 'It makes me sick to think how sick I get when I think about you.'

"There has been more lying propaganda about this bill, and on a larger scale, than about any other bill I have ever seen," I said. "The power trust has tried to make investors believe that the holding company bill imposes what they call a death sentence on all the private companies in the electric light and power industry. That's bunk."

I got the bill approved by my committee without much trouble and it reached the Senate floor late in May. One night early in June I was attending a big party given by Joe Kennedy at his Potomac, Maryland, mansion (which had a gold bathroom on the second floor). Quite a few senators were there. About midnight, Jimmy Byrnes pulled me aside. Like the other

Southerners, he was under heavy pressure from the utilities.

"Burt, you're putting the President on the spot with that so-called 'death sentence,'" he said. I pointed out that I was not putting FDR on the spot because the death sentence was his idea, not mine.

"Well, I've talked with the President and had him talked out of it but he said he was standing behind you," Byrnes replied.

"He isn't standing behind me—I'm standing behind him," I corrected Byrnes. This so annoyed me that I telephoned the President a few days later, said I wanted to see him, and repeated Byrnes' remarks.

"Jimmy didn't have any right to say that," he told me.

"Well, Mr. President," I said, "don't give the impression you're willing to change because this is your bill."

He said he didn't want to change it, but somehow the impression was out that he was being put on the spot. Senator John H. Bankhead of Alabama echoed Byrnes' line to me, and so did a few other Southerners.

This time I went to the White House. FDR was sitting in bed, propped up by pillows, his cigarette and holder jutting up out of his mouth and cigarette ashes dropping on the bedspread. I started right off saying I'd change the bill any way he wanted it changed, but that I was tired of being buttonholed by senators. He turned on the charm and reassured me that he was standing pat. I suggested that he make a public statement to clear the air. The President had no stomach for going that far. He called for a pencil and paper and scrawled a short statement.

"You can show this to them," he said, giving the sheet of paper to me. I don't think he intended for me to make it public because, I suspected, he was being very careful in what he was saying to the utility people privately.

As the debate in the Senate got hot, Senator William H. Dieterich of Illinois rose and insisted that Roosevelt was really willing to amend the bill by striking out the "death sentence" provision in Section 11. This is what I had been waiting for. I drew the President's note from my pocket, where I had been keeping it handy, and read it to the Senate.

"*Dear Burt,*" it ran, "*to verify my talk with you this morning, I am very clear in my own mind that while clarifying or minor amendments to Sec. 11 cannot be objected to, nevertheless any amendment which goes to the heart of major objectives of Sec. 11 would strike at the heart of the bill itself and is wholly contrary to the recommendations of myself. Sincerely, Franklin D. Roosevelt.*"

That knocked the wind out of the opposition. Section 11 was retained by the hairline margin of 45–44 and the bill itself then easily passed the Senate 56–32. The President telephoned me from Hyde Park to congratulate me, sounding very happy about the way the bill had been handled.

It was one of the most difficult assignments I have ever had. The bill was very hard to understand, and harder to explain. Borah was frank about it. When I heard the utility people had gotten him to agree to attack it as being unconstitutional, I asked if this were true.

"How the hell can I make a speech about it?" Borah asked. "There isn't anyone on the Senate floor who understands it but you."

He didn't attack the bill. I was able to learn the bill backward and forward only because every night for one week during the hearings I had been tutored at my home by Corcoran and Cohen, who had done a masterful job of drafting it. During the Senate debate, I had Cohen sit next to me, in case highly technical questions arose.

On the House side, meanwhile, the Commerce Committee struck out the mandatory death sentence, giving the SEC discretionary power to order dissolution instead. When the bill hit the House floor, Rayburn was unable to muster enough strength even to get a roll call on the death sentence. It was rejected on an unrecorded vote.

When the two versions of the bill went into a Senate-House conference for the showdown, a deadlock resulted. After a week of stalemate, the President called me in along with Alben Barkley, another Senate conferee. He told us that Joe Robinson and House Speaker Joe Byrns had reported to him that no compromise was possible in the conference, and that I would have to take the bill back to the Senate for another vote.

I suggested that FDR let the bill die in conference and take the case against the utilities to the people. He said he didn't want to do that—he wanted something to come out of conference. I believed he was weakening under the terrific pressure. I told him I would not take the bill back to the Senate. I pointed out that I had gotten the death sentence provision through by the margin of a single vote and that now the opposition could use the conference deadlock to pick up votes and kill the death sentence outright. I felt the President knew I could not get a vote of confidence out of the Senate but that the bill's fate there would provide him with an escape hatch.

"What should I do?" he asked. I advised him to call in some of the House leaders who professed to be such great friends of his and tell them to make the House conferees go along with us. I also suggested that he write a letter to Rayburn telling him flatly that he wanted the Senate version passed. Roosevelt asked me to compose such a letter. Barkley and I went back to my office and sent for Tommy Corcoran. The three of us drafted the note and the President signed it and had it delivered to Rayburn.

Rayburn must have shown the letter to the House Democratic leaders, who presumably then put the pressure on the House conferees. In any event, shortly after the letter was delivered, the administration's bill emerged from the conference and the President signed it on August 26, 1935.

Until the very last day of the conference, the lobbying never stopped. Senator Hugo L. Black, heading a committee investigating the lobby, reported that on the basis of still incomplete returns the utilities had spent at least $1,500,000 to create a protest against the bill. He estimated they paid for a total of 250,000 telegrams and stimulated 5,000,000 letters that inundated Capitol Hill while the bill was being considered. The Scripps-Howard newspaper chain reported that the utilities had 660 agents busily lobbying the 527 members of Congress.

Apart from the legislative lessons I had learned, I discovered that the only way to deal with Roosevelt was to stand up to him. Ickes once remarked that it was impossible to come to grips with FDR but now I made this note—that you could come to grips with him if you insisted on your point of view. It wasn't easy. In the early days of the new administration, I saw FDR frequently in the White House. He used to invite me there in the evening with Borah, Norris, Hiram Johnson, and young Bob La Follette. He was currying favor with the progressives. But he not only dominated the conversation, he did practically all the talking. Finally, Louis Howe, his alert little aide, began to interrupt him.

"Franklin," Howe would say, "why don't you let some of these men talk and see what they've got to say."

Having passed a great many bills in my time, I have been asked for the secret of being a successful legislator. There is no secret as such. You must acquire experience and skill in the art of timing and maneuvering, of course, but the fundamental rule is still a basic one: you must believe in your bill and then study it until you're prepared for any eventuality when it's up for action on the floor. If someone takes you by surprise with an amendment and you can't discuss its effect on your bill, you may lose the battle right there.

When FDR first came into office and the depression was on, the only question when a bill came before a committee was: What does the President say? If he wanted it, the committee would approve the bill without even finding out what was in it. When I became chairman of the Commerce Committee, I put a stop to that. Even if it was my own bill, I would appoint a subcommittee with a 3–2 Democratic majority and direct it to pick the measure to pieces before reporting back to the full committee. If I considered it a bad bill, though, I admit I would take the precaution of putting it in the hands of a subcommittee chairman I was sure would sink it.

After the fight over the Holding Company bill, Joe Robinson called a meeting of all the committee chairmen and told them to take a leaf from my book. He lectured them on the necessity for knowing their bills inside out before taking them to the floor.

I must confess that there was one bill I was not proud of having enacted. It was drafted under the supervision of John

Collier, the new Commissioner of Indian Affairs, immediately after FDR became President. Roosevelt had wanted to appoint an Indian as commissioner but I convinced him it would be a mistake because I knew of no Indian at that time who was competent to handle the job. So he had appointed Collier, who had headed up an Indian rights organization and had carried on propaganda against the Indian department.

I was then chairman of the Senate Indian Affairs Committee and Collier asked me to introduce the bill in the Senate. (Representative Edgar Howard of Nebraska introduced a companion measure in the House.) I did so without even having read the bill, which was being given a big publicity buildup. Its purpose was to let the Indians govern themselves and it became known as the Wheeler-Howard Indian Rights Act. But when I began looking over the original draft, there were many provisions I didn't like. It set up a special judicial system for the Indians, with a federal judge to try only Indian cases. I thought it was a crazy idea and had it thrown out in committee.

One day Steve Early, the White House press secretary, called me and said the President wanted me to push the bill along.

"Has he read the bill?" I asked, feeling sure he had not.

"Well, I don't suppose he has," Early replied.

"You tell him he ought to read it," I said, "before he puts his stamp of approval on it because there are some things in it I'm sure he wouldn't favor."

The result was that we modified it considerably. Even so, it was not a good bill. It authorized the Indian tribes to elect a group of people as executive officers, instead of relying on the old tribal council.

Many Indians complain it has been a detriment to them rather than a help. The way the Act is administered a small group of mixed-blood Indians elect officers who then completely ignore the older full bloods. The officers can spend the money they control recklessly, pay themselves large salaries for doing little or nothing, and even loan money to their favorites and to themselves. Several of the tribes never put the Act into effect.

There were other things I tried to do for the Indians which

I am proud of. For example, one of the most worthwhile electric power sites in the United States existed at the foot of Flathead Lake in Montana, on the Flathead Indian reservation. The Montana Power Company wanted to build a dam there to produce electric power. Some white settlers and the company maintained that they did not need a license from the Indians, that they could file on it under state law. I insisted that the site belonged to the reservation. Senator Walsh agreed with me, and we obtained an agreement, first executed with the Coolidge Administration, under which the company was required to pay royalties to the Indians. This was the first time in the history of the United States that Indians were indemnified with royalties. The agreement is based on a sliding scale; since 1954, the annual rate paid to the Confederated Salish and Kootenai tribes on the Flathead reservation amounts to $238,-375.

Although as District Attorney in Montana, I had had to prosecute Indians for taking whisky to the reservation, they were among my strongest supporters whenever I ran for office. At times, many of them marked the ballot for me and no one else. As soon as I was in the Senate, I introduced and got approved a bill giving Indians the right to sue the government in the Court of Claims, but it was vetoed by Coolidge.

I introduced and got passed many bills to build hospitals on the reservations. I also insisted the Indian children be sent to public schools, instead of sending them to government-supported boardingschools hundreds of miles away. I felt that if the Indian children were to adjust to the outside world, they should learn to associate with the white children in their communities. At first, the white people objected, but they gradually got used to the integration and many of the Indian children became excellent students.

After I was chairman of the Indian Affairs Committee in 1933, delegations of Blackfeet visited me regularly at my summer cabin on the shore of Lake McDonald in Glacier National Park. The old chiefs were great orators. They would stand for hours, telling me their troubles, while gesturing flamboyantly.

Whole speeches, lasting an hour or more, would have to be translated into English, and then I would reply in kind.

One morning about forty of them came and stayed on until it was close to noon. Mrs. Wheeler called me into the kitchen and worriedly reported that she didn't have enough to feed the tribe. I asked her if she had any spaghetti and she said she'd mix up a big batch. Then it turned out the Indians had brought their own food. They built a big fire on the shore of the lake and did their own cooking, using the spaghetti as a side dish. The mixture of Roman and redskin menus proved a happy one.

The Indian name given to me by the Blackfeet, Assiniboines, and Sioux translates into "Chief Bearshirt."

Once, while our Indian Affairs Committee was taking testimony on a reservation in Montana, an old long-haired chief who was speaking in Indian dialect began whinnying like a horse. I interrupted him long enough to ask the interpreter what he had said. The answer was: "The federal Indian agent has been feeding us horse meat and horse meat until I whinny in my sleep."

When I came to a town near a reservation to investigate conditions, a delegation would immediately call on me. Knowing the long-winded nature of the Indians, I would tell them at the beginning of the day that I could not talk with them until late in the afternoon. I would then proceed to complete the appointments I had made in the town. The entire delegation would follow me throughout the day. As I walked down the streets of a town like Havre, Montana, I would be followed by twenty or thirty Indians. When I stopped, they would stop about twenty or thirty feet behind me. When I went into the office of a friend of mine, they would stand or sit patiently and stoically on the sidewalk outside. When I returned to my hotel in the late afternoon, I would then ask them if they had chosen a spokesman. The designated spokesman then would take up various matters with me. Usually the agenda included their requests for legislation, irrigation matters, the application of the various Indian acts to their particular problems, complaints against the Indian Bureau in Washington, complaints against the local Indian agent and then, equally important in their eyes, the settlement of disputes arising on the reservation.

The latter included not only matters involving the election of the tribal council and its chief but disputes of all kinds, including affairs of the heart. One stands out in my mind. I had had a long day at Havre, and had returned to the hotel in the late afternoon. The hotel had loaned me a room just off the lobby and the Indians were seated in front of me. After discussing various matters through their spokesman, an Indian brave arose in the back of the room and started shouting at another Indian.

When the hubbub quieted down, it became apparent that this Indian was married to a good-looking squaw named Minny Small Calf. It seems that Minny had deserted her husband and was living with another young Indian. When the irate husband finished his harangue, I asked him if Minny hadn't been previously married to another brave of the tribe and whether he hadn't in fact stolen Minny from her first husband and subsequently married her. Having this pointed out to him and realizing that my memory was correct, he lapsed into silence. I then gave Minny a long lecture on marital fidelity and followed it with a lecture to the brave she was then living with, pointing out that if he were successful in the long run he would just be adding his scalp to Minny's collection. I told Minny that if she didn't stop stirring up trouble on the reservation serious punishment would be forthcoming on my next visit. These lectures and judgments were accompanied by the nodding of the heads of most of the Indians present and I passed on to the next problem.

Chapter Fifteen

SAVING THE SUPREME COURT

While I had earlier disagreed with FDR on his veto of the soldiers' bonus, on the silver question, and on the NRA, my first real break with him began on February 5, 1937. In New York on a mission for the Interstate Commerce Committee, I read in a newspaper that FDR had dropped a political bombshell in Washington. He was asking Congress for a revolutionary and sweeping "reorganization of the judiciary," under which he could, among other things, appoint one new Supreme Court justice for every justice who refused to retire after his seventieth birthday. Since there were then six septuagenarians on the Court, FDR would be in a position to pack the Court with six more justices.

I was flabbergasted (as were the President's congressional leaders, none of whom he had bothered to take into his confidence). Here was an unsubtle and anti-Constitution grab for power which would destroy the Court as an institution. I felt I would have to do everything I could to fight the plan.

That the President for some time had been fuming at the

High Court for reversing much of his New Deal legislation was widely known. I was one of the very few persons who knew the administration had toyed with the idea of doing something drastic about it as far back as early 1936. Tommy Corcoran and Ben Cohen, the White House's legislative liaison team, had come to the office of the Senate Interstate Commerce Committee, of which I was chairman, with a speech which they hoped I would deliver. They left the speech with Joe Wright, who was secretary of the committee (and is now president of the Zenith Radio Corporation) because I was out of town. The speech criticized and—by implication—warned the Court to watch its step. When Wright showed it to me, I told him I was not interested in delivering such a speech.

In May, Corcoran came to me and urged me to introduce a bill which would add three members to the Supreme Court. I told Tom, who was one of FDR's closest advisers, that if he wanted to defeat the President in the 1936 election a proposal to tamper with the Court would be the surest way to do it. I argued that the Court was like a religion to the American people. I recalled to him that when I ran for Vice President on old Bob La Follette's Independent Progressive ticket in 1924 our platform had proposed a limitation on the high bench (I found out about the platform only after I accepted a bid to bolt the Democratic ticket and run). It had been used devastatingly against us from one end of the country to the other. Joe Kennedy, for one, had told me how it had been used successfully to take votes away from us in South Boston.

Our 1924 platform plank called for a Constitutional Amendment providing that if the Supreme Court held a law to be unconstitutional Congress could—after the voters had expressed their will at the next election—override the decision on a two-thirds majority vote. And now here was the Roosevelt Administration contemplating a Court "reform" plan which did not even have the virtue of being a Constitutional Amendment! I heard nothing more officially on the subject until I learned of Roosevelt's packing plan that February day in New York.

Back in Washington, I informed Mrs. Wheeler that I intended to oppose the President on the Court-packing and that it would no doubt mean my elimination from politics. I said I was telling her that because it was she who had advised me not to accept an appointment to the Ninth Circuit Court of Appeals when it was offered to me shortly after Roosevelt's election. I recalled she had also dissuaded me when I had the idea of not running for re-election in 1934. I had pointed out that if I started a law firm it would help our two sons who were studying law to get a start in life after college.

Mrs. Wheeler, who was darning socks that afternoon, went right on darning. She said, "We'll educate our sons but after that they must look after themselves." She also said I owed it to the people of Montana to stay in the Senate after the way they had valiantly stood by me in all my fights in the state. I suspect she also felt I would never really be happy outside politics. Then she said: "Do you think you are right?"

I said I was never more right in my life.

"If you feel that way, you should go ahead," she replied.

I was not exaggerating when I told her the risk I would be running in fighting FDR on this issue. He had won a landslide victory only a few months before and was at the height of his popularity. With his overwhelming majorities in the Senate and House he should have a good chance of getting his bill adopted. If he did, it would leave me out in left field, politically.

The next day I got a telephone call from Charley Michelson, publicity director of the Democratic National Committee and an old friend. Michelson was a key man in the lobbying strategy for the Court bill and I didn't want to see him just yet because I suspected why he wanted to see me. I stalled off an appointment with him while I worked over a statement on the bill for the press.

I released the statement and then had Michelson come to my office. He said the President wanted to have dinner with me to discuss the Court issue.

"Charley," I said, "I've just given out a statement opposing the packing of the Court, so the President ought to save the plate for someone who persuades more easily. He should get some of those weak-kneed boys and go after them because he can't do anything with me."

I heard no more about dinner at the White House.

Once my statement was in the press, however, Corcoran asked me to lunch with him at the old Grace Dodge Hotel on E Street at the foot of Capitol Hill. Tommy opened the conversation by saying the President wanted to see me to give me some background on the Court issue.

"He doesn't care about those Tories being against it," he explained, "but he doesn't want you to be against it."

Corcoran then made it plain that if I went along with the Court plan I could sit in on the naming of some of the new justices. Pressing his case, he said: "You want to see a liberal Court, don't you?"

"Of course," I said.

"If you don't go along," Corcoran continued, "he'll make a deal with Tammany and the Southerners and he'll put their people on the Court." I replied that Corcoran was probably right about that but I wasn't going along. When Corcoran angrily warned me that the bill would pass, I pounded the table and replied just as angrily, "Well, Tommy, he *isn't* going to get it!"

The bill split the Senate into hostile camps. The conservative Democrats, opposing it to a man, decided it would be wisest to have the opposition led by a Democrat whose liberal credentials were impeccable. They chose me. I was officially recognized as their leader at a dinner at the home of Senator Millard E. Tydings of Maryland. Present, among others, were Harry F. Byrd of Virginia, Walter F. George of Georgia, Kenneth D. McKellar of Tennessee, Royal S. Copeland of New York, and Edward R. Burke of Nebraska.

"Burt, we can't lick it but we'll fight it," Byrd remarked.

"Harry, why are you against it?" I asked him.

"Because it's wrong in principle," he said.

"Well," I replied, "most of the members of the Senate are lawyers. Deep down, they agree with you and me, but they're like a lot of mercenaries. They want patronage. A small army that believes in principle can lick a bunch of mercenaries, and we'll lick them!"

Byrd said he was glad I felt that way.

We selected a steering committee composed of Frederick Van Nuys of Indiana, Peter G. Gerry of Rhode Island, Josiah W. Bailey of North Carolina, Bennett Champ Clark of Missouri, Tom Connally of Texas, Byrd, Burke, Tydings, and myself. We devised a plan for intensive lobbying of our fellow senators. Our bloc then numbered 18 but it grew to 30 as time went on.

Each member of the bloc was assigned to keep after certain senators who were either for the bill or uncommitted; he was assigned on the basis of his personal acquaintance with those senators. Each day news about waverers was reported back to Gerry, our whip, and each waverer was pursued thereafter by members of the bloc in the Senate chamber, the cloakroom, the Office Building, or at social gatherings.

Our steering committee met secretly every day in a Capitol hideaway to alter strategy in the light of shifting events. Our intelligence network was unexpectedly reinforced by reports from inside the administration forces. Leslie Biffle, an officer of the Senate who was ostensibly working for the other side, informed me nightly by telephone who was weak on their side and who seemed to be weakening on our side. I never knew for certain why he chose to tip us off. It could even have been done with the approval of Senator Joe Robinson, the majority leader, in the hope that building up the opposition to the bill would force the President to back down and compromise. Actually, Robinson had no more stomach for the Court-packing scheme than we did; he dutifully led the fight for it because he was Senate Democratic leader and—it was believed—FDR had promised him a seat on the Supreme Court. Many of us seriously doubted that the President would appoint Robinson to the Court even if he won. He was a conservative.

One of my problems was trying to keep people on our side from making statements that would play into Roosevelt's hands. When the fight was just getting underway, I was invited to New York to meet with the president of the New York Bar Association. When I arrived at his office, I found lawyers from eight or ten of the top New York law firms there, including John W. Davis, the 1924 Democratic presidential nominee.

They asked me what they could do to help defeat the Court-packing bill.

"Do you really want to help?" I asked. They assured me they would do whatever they could.

"Have you any influence with any farm organizations?" I asked.

They didn't think so.

"Have you any influence with any labor organizations?"

Definitely not.

"Have you any influence with church organizations?"

Perhaps some.

"Women's organizations?"

They thought they might be able to do some good with women's clubs.

"There's one other way you can help," I added. "That is, to keep your clients out of this. I think we can win—but only if you keep your clients out."

Once, when I returned to Washington from a trip in which I made speeches against the bill, Mrs. Wheeler told me that Orman Ewing, the former Democratic national committeeman from Utah, was telling people in New York he represented me. She said he had announced that I would address a large luncheon group in Pine Street, in the very heart of the Wall Street financial center.

"I'm not going," I said immediately. She pointed out that the meeting already had been scheduled. The more I thought about it, the more I felt I should go to New York and find out what representation had been made on my behalf. I met the group at one of the downtown hotels. They explained that the luncheon meeting was all set up at some place in Pine Street. I told them flatly I would not go. They said many prominent people would be present. I repeated that I would not go.

"Roosevelt would like nothing better than to have me speak to a Wall Street crowd," I explained.

Then they told me they were getting up a group of young people who would organize in the various states. I asked if they intended to organize in Montana. They said yes. I told them I could guess who they would organize—the Anaconda Copper

Mining Company, the Montana Power Company, the bankers, etc. I said, "I want you to keep out of Montana, or any other state . . . if we have to convince those people that the packing of the Court is wrong, then we are really in for a fight."

When it became obvious that the bill would have to be "sold" to the country, FDR himself opened up on the airwaves. On March 14, he plugged his Court scheme in an address to the Democratic Party's $100-a-plate "Victory Dinner" at the Mayflower Hotel in Washington. His words were carried over the radio to 1100 other such dinners all over the United States. Five days later he pleaded for his bill again in a "fireside chat."

In his dinner speech the President made a direct appeal to all those groups which could expect to get something from the New Deal if the Court was packed. FDR, impassioned, spoke these now famous words:

"Here is one third of a nation ill nourished, ill clad, ill housed —now! . . . if we keep faith with those who had faith in us, if we would make democracy succeed, I say we must act—now!" Etc.

I had heard a good many demagogic speeches, and had undoubtedly made some myself that were looked on as such, but I thought this was the most demagogic I had ever heard, and it was coming from the President of the United States!

Replying to the speech, I warned in a radio address:

"Create now a political Court to echo the ideas of the executive and you have created a weapon; a weapon which in the hands of another President could well be the instrument of destruction; a weapon that can cut down those guarantees of liberty written into your great doctrine by the blood of your forefathers and that can extinguish your right of liberty of speech, or thought, or action, or of religion; a weapon whose use is only dictated by the conscience of the wielder."

In the "fireside chat," FDR, in his rich, ringing, aristocratic voice, pleaded with the American people to trust him as their old friend and leader. This line was echoed to me by that great independent liberal, Senator George Norris. Norris had been instinctively opposed to the administration's approach to reforming the Court but he had succumbed to the blandishments of Roosevelt and his emissaries on Capitol Hill.

"You don't trust the President," Norris said reprovingly to me.

I told him that, like Thomas Jefferson, I put my trust in laws rather than in men.

In his magical ability to rally the nation over the airwaves, FDR was truly masterful and nobody admired this quality of leadership in him more than I did. Yet his two addresses on the Court issue failed to bring as much support from the people as the administration had hoped for.

Not only did FDR "go to the people" but he directed most of his cabinet members to do likewise. When they took to the air, the broadcasting networks saw to it that their voices went into every home in America with a radio. It was a "must" for every affiliate of the chains to carry the speeches.

After the Democrats chose me as the leader of the opposition—it was soon ratified by the Republican senators—I insisted that the networks give us air time to answer. The networks acceded and I picked out the senators who would carry the radio speaking load with me. Soon, however, I discovered that we were not being given a national audience. For example, a radio debate I had in Chicago with Dean James M. Landis was blacked out everywhere but in Washington, D.C., and my home state. The network officials doubtless figured I would never know the difference.

Fortunately, I was then chairman of the Interstate Commerce Committee, which has jurisdiction over laws affecting the communications industry. I made it plain to the heads of the networks that we expected the same treatment as the administration, and I demanded that they furnish me with a list of the stations that carried our speeches to make certain of it. Even so, we did not receive equal treatment because all networks carried the President's speeches simultaneously as they did some of the cabinet members'.

The President forced into line farm leaders and labor leaders and brought to bear every other pressure he could think of to influence senators in favor of the Court bill. I have never seen such pressure put on legislators. Even some of my good friends in Montana, including men I had gotten appointed to federal office, wrote me letters protesting my stand. Labor and farm leaders in Montana were 100 per cent against me; they threatened me with political oblivion if I didn't switch and go along with the President.

On March 10, the Senate Judiciary Committee opened hearings on S. 1392, "a bill to reorganize the judicial branch of the government." The first witness was Attorney General Homer S. Cummings, the man who had dreamed up the scheme to pack the Court via the old-age excuse. Cummings bore down on FDR's original argument—that the bill was necessary because of the crowded conditions of the dockets and because there were so many "aged and infirm judges" in our federal courts.

FDR's covert argument, gradually forced into the open, was that more justices should be added to put the Court in tune with the times. This argument was cogently advanced by the second witness, Assistant Attorney General Robert H. Jackson. Jackson cited the long history of the Supreme Court in usurping or frustrating legislative functions.

Years later, when he was a member of the Supreme Court, Jackson told me he did not agree with the bill, but pointed out that he was part of the administration and felt he had to go along with it.

I was scheduled to be the first witness in opposition to the bill and I wanted an opinion from some of the justices so as to start off with a resounding bang for our side. I knew they would be reluctant to testify on a matter affecting their own integrity; I was trying to figure out some way to get round this problem. Then, on Saturday, March 20, just two days before I was due to appear, I got some encouragement.

Mrs. Brandeis, wife of my good friend, Justice Louis Brandeis, drove across the Potomac and into Virginia to see the new baby born to my daughter, Mrs. Elizabeth Colman. I was surprised she did this until Elizabeth told me on the telephone that when Mrs. Brandeis was departing, she had remarked: "Tell your father I think he's right about the Court bill."

I interpreted this as a tipoff that Brandeis was strongly against the bill—and that I should do something about it. I telephoned him for an appointment and he suggested I come to see him at once.

The Brandeises and the Wheelers had been warm friends since the justice had sought my acquaintance immediately after I came to the Senate in March 1923. Our relationship began with an amusing misunderstanding. The first time we were invited to dinner at the Brandeis' apartment, we arrived in dinner clothes, only to discover that our hosts were dressed informally. Perhaps they assumed that people in the wild and woolly West didn't maintain a formal wardrobe. Then, the second time we went to the Brandeis' for dinner, we were informal while they were attired formally!

After I hastened to the Brandeis' apartment about the Court bill, I said I hoped he and the Chief Justice would testify against the claims by Roosevelt and Cummings that the federal courts were behind in their work, as well as the other charges. Brandeis said he would not appear and would not advise the Chief Justice to appear. He said it was his practice not to write or speak publicly about the Court, that all his disagreements were contained in his dissenting opinions.

But, the justice continued, "You call up the Chief Justice and he'll give you a letter." This took me by surprise. I was not eager to take so bold a step, nor could I be sure that Brandeis had already paved the way.

"I won't call him up," I demurred. "I don't know him."

"Well, he knows you," Brandeis said.

Well, the Chief Justice certainly must have been aware that I was outspoken in opposing his appointment as Chief Justice by President Hoover back in 1930. I had taken this position because Hughes had left the Supreme Court in 1916 to run for President. I felt that reappointing him might encourage other justices to mix into politics.

When I again refused to telephone Hughes, Brandeis led me by the hand to the phone and called the Chief Justice himself. He told Hughes I wanted to see him. Hughes suggested I come to his house immediately.

The imposingly bearded Chief Justice greeted me warmly when I arrived. I told him Brandeis said he would give me a letter.

He said, "Did Brandeis tell you that?" I said yes.

"When do you want it?" he asked.

"Monday morning," I replied. He asked why.

"They've circulated a story that I will not testify after all," I explained. "If I put it off Monday, they'll say I never will take the stand."

The Chief Justice looked at his watch.

"It is now five-thirty," he said. "The library is closed, my secretary is gone. I won't have to call Brandeis or Stone and I won't have to call some other justices, but I will have to call some. Can you come by early Monday morning?"

"Certainly," I said.

Then he asked what I was doing Sunday afternoon. I said, "Nothing."

On Sunday afternoon Hughes telephoned my home and asked me to drop by his house. As I walked in, he handed me the letter and said solemnly, "The baby is born." I read the letter and he asked, "Does that answer your question?"

"Yes, it does," I said happily. "It certainly does."

I thanked him and started to leave, when he said, "Sit down."

"I think I am as disinterested in this matter—from a political standpoint—as anyone in the United States," the Chief Justice began when we were seated, "because the people of the United States have been far more generous to me than I deserve. I am not interested in who are to be the members of the Court. I am interested in the Court as an institution. And this proposed bill would destroy the Court as an institution."

"If we had had an Attorney General in whom the President had confidence," he continued, "and in whom the Court had confidence, and in whom the people had confidence, the story might have been different. But the laws have been poorly drafted, the briefs have been badly drawn and the arguments have been poorly presented. We've had to be not only the Court but we've had to do the work that should have been done by the Attorney General.

I thought to myself, "What a condemnation of Attorney General Cummings!"

Hughes went on: "I could have brought down lawyers from Wall Street who would have been glad to come here out of patriotic motives and correct some of the abuses that have been complained of. They would have been able to do it, because they would know what their clients had been doing. When I was a young governor of New York and I was in a fight with Wall Street and the insurance groups, Elihu Root, who represented many of the Wall Street interests, wrote me a note in longhand which said, 'Keep up the fight. You are right.' Think of what that meant to a young governor!

"You know," Hughes also disclosed, "when Roosevelt was first elected, he called me down to the White House and told me he would like to cooperate with the Supreme Court. I said to him, 'Mr. President, the Supreme Court is an independent branch of the government.' He replied that he had always cooperated with the courts in New York and I said, 'Well, that may be, but this is an independent branch of the government.'"

When I left, the Chief Justice said, "I hope you'll see that this gets wide publicity." I almost laughed.

"You don't need to worry about that," I assured him.

At 10:30 next morning I took the stand as the first opposition witness before the committee in the famous marble-walled, ornate caucus room of the Senate Office Building where so many historic hearings have been staged. The room was packed. The chairman of the committee was my good friend, the courtly and humorously eloquent Henry Ashurst of Arizona, who was opposed to the bill at heart but had been dragooned into going along with the White House because he was chairman. As I seated myself in the witness chair, Ashurst told me later, he noticed the smug look on the face of Mrs. Wheeler, sitting in the overflow audience.

"I don't know what he's going to spring but it'll blow us out of the water," Ashurst said he whispered to the senator next to him.

Ashurst was even more graciously grandiose than usual in introducing me. He said: "Senators, we are signally honored this morning. We have before us one of the most, if not the most distinguished member of the United States Senate, Senator Burton K. Wheeler of Montana."

"Mr. Chairman and members of the Committee on the Judiciary," I began, "it is with some reluctance that I appear here this morning. I have only appeared because of the insistence of many of my colleagues who are opposed to the bill which is pending before you to increase the Supreme Court membership by six. I want it to be understood at the outset that anything I may say is not because of the fact that I have any unfriendly feeling toward the President. On the contrary, my relations with the President of the United States during his term of office have been exceedingly friendly, perhaps more friendly than those of some other members of this committee. I supported him when he was first a candidate. I supported him in his preprimary campaign. I was one of the first members of the United States Senate to openly come out for his nomination. I traveled from one end of the country to the other making speeches for him in his preprimary campaign. I went to the city of Chicago ten days in advance of the convention and worked for his nomination. There has never at any time been anything but the most cordial relations between us."

I then noted the several instances in which I had disagreed with FDR on issues since he came into office. But I added: "Notwithstanding these disagreements, I have always had and have at the present time a very high regard for the President."

(Every word of that statement was true. Over the years, political observers and writers have sought to find some cause for personal bitterness in my motivation. They would not concede me the motivation of principle. Perhaps they expected that as a long-time liberal I should have followed the President blindly because he claimed that his Court plan was a liberal move. But to me the bill was illiberal in its very essence. If a President could make both branches of government subservient, I feared totalitarianism could happen here as well as anywhere else. I was by no means the only liberal who felt this way. Many of them said so only privately and went along publicly, so as not to offend the administration. One who did take a strong stand against the Court plan was that apostle of liberalism, then Governor Herbert H. Lehman of New York.)

In my testimony before the Judiciary Committee, I said I was opposed to this type of tinkering on principle and I was sure "the American people would never stand for it."

I noted that I disagreed with the Supreme Court on many of its decisions on New Deal legislation. But, I said, "I do not believe that age has anything to do with liberalism." Also, I said it was a serious reflection on the Court to say it was behind in its work.

Senator William H. Dieterich, a committee member and a supporter of the Kelly-Nash Democratic machine in Chicago, was dutifully defending the administration bill. I knew how much he detested me and so at the start, I said, "I know the Senator from Illinois will not agree with me." I said it again in connection with two other statements about the work of the Court. The third time Dieterich replied, "Of course not." He finally came through with what I wanted.

"Well," I said, "I have a statement from a man who knows more about the Court than the President of the United States, than the Attorney General, than I do or any member of this committee."

Slowly drawing the letter from my inside coat pocket, I continued: "I have a letter by the Chief Justice of the Supreme Court, Mr. Charles Evans Hughes, dated March 21, 1937, written by him and approved by Mr. Justice Brandeis and Mr. Justice Van Devanter."

You could have heard a comma drop in the caucus room while I read the letter aloud. It struck down, one by one, every point raised by Roosevelt and Cummings in maintaining that the Court had been unable to keep up with its workload.

After demolishing the administration's position with a masterful marshaling of fact and argument, the Hughes letter concluded: "I understand that it has been suggested that with more justices the Court could hear cases in divisions. It is believed that such a plan would be impracticable . . . I may also call attention to the provisions of Article III, Section 1, of the Constitution that the judicial power of the United States shall be vested 'in one Supreme Court' and in such inferior courts as the Congress may from time to time ordain and establish. The Constitution does not appear to authorize two or more Supreme Courts functioning in effect as separate courts."

The letter had a sensational effect. The newsreels photographed it, newspaper reporters clamored for copies, and it was all I could do to keep it from being snatched from my hands when the session was recessed. The administration and its supporters were disconcerted by the unexpected counterattack from the eminent leader of the so-called "nine old men." We heard with amusement that FDR and his strategists were furious at the Chief Justice for "playing politics." The letter put the bill's backers on the defensive.

Assistant Attorney General Jackson's opinion afterward was that the Hughes letter "did more than any one thing to turn the tide in the Court struggle." Secretary Ickes commented later: "The whole world knows that, while at first it appeared that the President would be strong enough to carry his reform through Congress, he was outmaneuvered in the end, largely by Chief Justice Charles Evans Hughes."

It was said that after I produced the letter, Vice President Garner telephoned FDR, who was in Warm Springs, and reported, "We're licked." But the President put up a show of serene confidence. For one thing, he still thought he could win me over. He sent labor leaders to try to influence me. Among them was Sidney Hillman of the Amalgamated Clothing Workers, who had always been friendly to me, but was never an intimate.

During the height of the Court fight I got an amusing White House reaction relayed through the late Frank Walker who was then treasurer of the Democratic National Committee and close to Roosevelt.

"The President says you and a lot of others on 'the Hill' are prima donnas," Walker said.

"Of course we're prima donnas," I replied with a laugh, "that's the reason we're here. He wants to be the only prima donna but we're going to show him there are three branches of government and he can't be the only one."

On May 18 the Judiciary Committee voted, 10–8, to report his bill unfavorably. The stinging report—to which I contributed material, though I was not a member of the committee—concluded with this sentence:

"It is a measure which should be so emphatically rejected that its parallel will never again be presented to the free representatives of the free people of America."

On the morning before debate on the bill was to open in the Senate, I took a phone call from Senator Homer T. Bone of Washington, who was in the White House at the time. He asked me if I would come down to see the President at noon. I pointed out that Joe Robinson, the majority leader, was scheduled to begin the debate after the Senate convened at noon and that I planned to be on hand to answer him. Bone apparently was in the room with FDR. "Well, can you jump in a cab and come right now?" pursued Bone. I said, "Certainly," and hung up. I was at the White House in a few minutes.

"Burt, I just want to give you a little background on the Court matter," the President said as I was ushered in. He continued:

"There was a justice of the Supreme Court of Missouri who was visiting in London and was invited to sit on the Appellate Court as a guest. A case was presented where two boys were convicted of a crime in the lower court and had not been permitted to put in the defense of an alibi. When the argument was over, the presiding justice turned to the Missouri judge and said, 'What do you think we ought to do about the case?' The Missouri judge said he thought it ought to be reversed. Whereupon the presiding judge said, 'We do,' and reversed the case and turned the boys loose."

FDR looked at me keenly and said, "This is the sort of thing we ought to have over here."

"That's what we've got here," I told him. "It is so elementary in our jurisprudence that if it is necessary for a party to be present at the time of the commission of the crime that no justice of the peace, state judge, or federal judge would think of not allowing the defendant to put in the defense of an alibi."

The President shifted his ground.

"Look at all those delays in these criminal cases," he said.

"That's not the fault of the judges," I told him, speaking from firsthand experience. "That's the fault of your district attorneys. It's always the defense that wants to delay the case as long as possible, hoping that some of the witnesses may die or leave town, or public sentiment will die down. You get the files of the time when I was district attorney in Montana and you'll find no delays in criminal cases."

"Why didn't the Chief Justice tell the judge in Pittsburgh that he shouldn't issue an injunction against the judge in New York in the Mellon case?" he next asked.

"Mr. President," I said, "the Chief Justice has no right to tell the judge in advance how he should decide a case. The only thing he can do is decide questions of law when they're appealed to the Supreme Court."

FDR asked me to let the Republicans lead the fight. I told him I had been selected and I would carry on as leader.

"Well, let's keep the bitterness out," the President urged.

"The Supreme Court and the Constitution are a religion with a great many people in this country," I told him, "and you can't keep bitterness out of a religious fight."

Roosevelt turned the conversation to the liberals who were supporting him. I mentioned that the bill was opposed by octogenarian Justice Brandeis, who was a liberal before the President and I had ever heard the word.

"Justice Brandeis was all in favor of it, at first," FDR replied wryly, "but the old lady—the nice old lady—kept dropping little drops of water on his head until he changed his mind."

"Whoever told you that was mistaken," I insisted. Mrs. Brandeis dominated the justice in some ways but I was positive that on questions of law and legislation he certainly made up his own mind. The President was very suspicious about the influence of wives. He was reported to have called Mrs. Wheeler the "Lady Macbeth of the Court fight." There was no basis for that crack. But I believe he sensed correctly that Mrs. Wheeler distrusted him.

I told the President that if he dropped the Court bill he could have at least two resignations on the Court.

"How can I be sure?" he asked, showing a flicker of interest.

"You can be just as sure as Senator Borah and I giving our word," I replied. I had never talked with any of the justices on this question but I understood Borah had done so.

Roosevelt insisted that he wanted the bill passed, and I repeated that I was sorry but I couldn't go along with him. We parted without hostility on either side.

I returned to the Senate chamber at noon and found Robinson in his seat waiting to start the debate.

"How did you get along down there?" he asked.

"Not very well," I replied.

"You keep after him, I can't do anything with him," said the majority leader, plainly unhappy about his lieutenant's chore. "You know, you and I could settle this thing in no time," he added. By the end of May, our steering committee had concluded that, as a result of its incessant wheedling, threatening, cajoling, we commanded an absolute majority of the Senate. Robinson, who had his own spies, must have known this.

By now, ironically enough, the Court was voting along the liberal lines FDR had been seeking to bring about by other means. While the fight had raged all spring, the Court had handed down a series of decisions sustaining important New Deal measures; only recently it had upheld the far-reaching Wagner Labor Relations Act. Everyone but the President admitted privately that this seriously weakened his argument. Never having lost a major battle with Congress, he was determined to bend it to his will. But he did finally and reluctantly concede that it might be better to try to do that with a softer bill. A bill sponsored by Senator Carl A. Hatch of New Mexico was selected for the compromise. It would have authorized the President to appoint a coadjutor justice for any justice who had passed the age of seventy-five and failed to retire, but the President was forbidden to make more than one such appointment in one year. Robinson was hard pressed to muster a majority in its favor. On top of this, he well knew, we had more than a score of senators ready to filibuster the bill to death if it became necessary.

When the majority leader rose to open the debate, he could

see every seat in the gallery filled; there were senators' wives, diplomats, shirt-sleeved sightseers, and whole platoons of Boy Scouts on hand for a forthcoming jamboree. He gave them a good show from his leader's seat on the corner of the front row. Nine years before, Robinson had been Al Smith's running mate in the presidential race. He was always impressive—a large, heavy-set, fine-looking man, sawing the air with his right hand, his voice loud, angry and threatening.

But Robinson was also sixty-five years old, and he had a touchy temper and a heart condition. For many weeks, he had been laboring day and night for the President. As he thundered for the Court bill, he grew so red in the face that Senator Royal S. Copeland of New York, who was a physician, became alarmed and moved over to the seat next to him.

"Joe, the cause you're fighting for isn't worth your life!" Copeland whispered. "For God's sake, slow down!"

"The doctor tells me I should be careful but I'm in just as good health as Burt Wheeler!" Robinson said, turning around and looking directly at me. I was sitting behind him.

"I'm in training," I said, just loud enough for him to hear me.

"Oh," Robinson went on testily, "he's in training, he's in training!"

As a matter of fact, I *was* in training during the Court fight. Every morning Mrs. Wheeler and I got up at six o'clock. We went straight to the golf course and played seven holes, after which we went home, where I showered, breakfasted, and set out for my daily battle on the Hill. Every night Borah would telephone me to say, "Old man, how are you feeling?" (I was fifty-five years old.) Hiram Johnson also called me up occasionally to remind me to be sure to take care of my health.

The ordeal proved too much for Robinson. On July 14, five days after I fired the first broadside for us, Robinson was found dead in his apartment near the Senate Office Building.

I was so emotionally upset by this development I urged that the President withdraw the bill "lest he appear to be fighting God." I was widely criticized for this remark but the fact was that the impossible burden placed on the majority leader by FDR undoubtedly hastened his demise.

With their forceful old leader dead, the President's reluctant army was thrown into confusion. Returning on the train from the Robinson funeral in Little Rock, Arkansas, Vice President Garner learned this fact quickly in chats with senators. Back in the Capitol, Garner came to me.

"Will you give us two?" he asked, meaning a compromise that would allow the President to appoint two new justices instead of six. An erroneous impression had gone around that I would settle for two. It was absurd, because we knew we had the votes to win.

"Jack," I said, "I won't give you two, I won't give you one."

"Well, that's out," Garner said philosophically. "What about this idea of a roving judge?"

"You don't want a roving judge, Jack," I told him. "If the Department of Justice wanted to convict someone and they had a roving judge they could depend on, they'd send him out to hear the case and he'd hear only one side. Harry Daugherty would have loved to have a roving judge of that kind, and if he had one he would have sent him out to Montana to try me."

"That's out," Garner went on. "What about a proctor?"

When I told him he wouldn't want that, he asked me what a proctor was. I said in old English law a proctor was one who managed or administered the handling of cases; that he would be used to go out and check into cases before the court decided to hear them.

"Well," the Vice President finally said, "go to it and God bless you. Write your own ticket."

My opposition colleagues and I thereupon worked out the interment rites for the dying bill. Senator Marvel M. Logan of Kentucky, an administration wheelhorse, agreed to move that the Senate send the bill back to the Judiciary Committee. The motion would include instructions to the committee to report back a substitute bill making innocuous procedural changes in the lower courts only.

Hiram Johnson rose to make dramatically clear what the recommittal motion signified.

"The Supreme Court is out of the way?" he asked.

"The Supreme Court is out of the way," Logan responded.

"Glory be to God!" exclaimed Johnson. The galleries burst into applause and Garner made no attempt to gavel them into order. The bill was then consigned to its mercy death on a vote of 70–20.

And thus ended the fiercest battle in American history between two branches of our government over a third. If it seemed unnecessary and unfortunate, it also had some wholesome effects, in my judgment. Several lessons had been learned. The President found out that the mandate given him by the people in November was not something to play with as he pleased. The Democratic Party itself had been educated to the will of the people. And the independence of our judiciary had been reaffirmed.

"All in all," I said in an interview published in *The New York Times,* "the Court bill fight has been a wonderful thing. The agitation brought the people to a study of the fundamentals of their government, gave them a veritable lesson in elemental civics. The fight has done the judiciary good too. Courts had become arrogant, and sometimes disrespectful to the rights of the public—particularly the federal courts. Can anyone look at the record already available and say that what has happened recently has not been beneficial to the courts themselves?"

For my part, I retained no bitterness against the President or those who had followed his lead. This attitude was not always reciprocated. I was puzzled when some senators stopped speaking to me after our victory. I finally approached one and said, "Say, what's the matter with you, anyway? These fights are just like lawyers trying a case. When it's over we shake hands and forget about it."

Senator Hugo Black, who was one of the most ardent supporters of the President on nearly all issues, as a reward for his loyalty, was appointed to the first vacancy on the Court after the fight when Justice Willis Van Devanter retired that same year. Senator Sherman Minton of Indiana later was rewarded in the same fashion and for the same reason.

As for me—the so-called "man who whipped Roosevelt"—I was showered with a new spate of national publicity. For example, *The Saturday Evening Post* ran an article on me titled "President-Tamer."

If I had alienated some devout New Dealers by my stand, I had made some converts in highly unlikely quarters. Conservatives who had previously seen horns sprouting from my head now saw me crowned with a hero's laurel instead. This reversal of attitude was summed up very frankly by one good lady who represented that citadel of patriotism, the Daughters of the American Revolution.

"Oh, Senator Wheeler!" she gushed. "I used to think you were a dangerous radical, but now I believe you love our country the same as I do!"

I thought that was mighty handsome of her.

My own feeling was that the Charles Evans Hughes letter had broken the back of the administration plan but that the senators who fought so hard with me were not given enough credit. The group I have mentioned that met first at Senator Tydings' house, as well as others who joined us later, were gallant men. Without the combined efforts of those who believed in three independent branches of government and in Constitutional government, the fight would have failed. Had we lost, it is hard to tell how far FDR would have taken us down the road overriding the Constitution. That he wanted power, and more power, even his friends cannot gainsay.

Chapter Sixteen

REPRISALS AND RECONCILIATION

Would there be reprisals against those of us who had fought the President on his Court bill? Alben Barkley, elected Senate majority leader after the death of Joe Robinson, said he wanted none. However, his hope was not shared by Senator Joseph F. Guffey of Pennsylvania, who followed Roosevelt one hundred per cent.

Guffey, then chairman of the Democratic Senatorial Campaign Committee, castigated some of the principal opponents of the Court plan as "ingrates". He predicted political doom for two of them—Joe O'Mahoney and Ed Burke—for fighting the bill. The next day I opened an attack on Guffey, joined in by Burke and O'Mahoney. As *The New York Times* reported it in its lead story, the three of us "struck back at the Pennsylvanian on the floor . . . with a fury seldom witnessed in the Senate."

I started the attack immediately after the roll was called. In part, I said: "I am glad that the senator did not include me among those who he said were ingrates to the President of the United States, because I am sure that no matter how much I have disagreed with the President he would never for a moment suggest that I had been ungrateful to him or that he was responsible for my election or that he ever contributed anything to my election or that the Democratic National Committee ever contributed anything to my election either directly or indirectly.

"I think likewise everyone knows that I did not need any contribution from them and that I did not need any help and that I did not need to ride in on the coattails of the President of the United States."

I then expressed the hope that if I ran for re-election in 1940 Guffey would come into Montana with his Senatorial Campaign Committee fund and back my opponent. If Guffey ran for governor of Pennsylvania, I added, "I shall go there at my own expense and with my own money and I shall make some speeches in Pennsylvania."

The *Times* reported the conclusion of my remarks as follows:

"'If you want to wash any dirty linen, you may wash it, either upon this floor or upon the public platform,' Mr. Wheeler shouted, shaking his long finger at Senator Guffey. 'And I say to you: "Lay on Macduff, and damned be he that first cries, Hold! Enough!"'"

Guffey sat in the last row, red in the face and with a half-smile, throughout the long tongue-lashing we administered. He made no reply.

With respect to O'Mahoney and me, the President restricted himself almost wholly to that negative political slap, the royal snub. In September, after Congress adjourned, he was scheduled to make a swing through the West, home grounds of some of his recent opponents. Customarily on such occasions, the flower of the local Democracy was invited to ride with him through each state. O'Mahoney was in Chicago to make a speech when he got word that his name was not on the invitation list for the ride through Wyoming. In a you-can't-do-this-to-me mood, Joe canceled the speech and drove fast enough to catch up with the train when it reached his home town of Cheyenne. He climbed aboard the train with his hand outstretched and a hopeful smile.

I had no desire to hop aboard a train where I was not welcome. I had been tipped off by Harry Butcher, then with the Columbia Broadcasting System and later an aide to General Eisenhower in Europe, that when his entourage arrived in Montana, FDR planned to invite my colleague, Senator James E. Murray, and Montana's two Democratic congressmen, Jerry J. O'Connell and James F. O'Connor—but not me—to join him. I decided to have some fun by making a game of it. I had just had a long-distance telephone call from an attorney for Norman Church, a retired industrialist and owner of a racing stable in Los Angeles, asking me to try a case for him there. With this excuse, I shot off a tongue-in-cheek telegram to FDR in Washington, telling him that, very regretfully, I would be unable to be in the state to greet him but that I hoped he would stop at Billings, Butte, and Great Falls. I gave a copy of the wire to the press.

Later, while I was handling the case in California, I learned that the President was to return from the West Coast also via Montana and would stop at the Fort Peck dam. I sent him another needling wire, which I also made public, saying I hoped that at the dam site he would tell the people he intended to put a power plant there to give them cheap electricity. I knew this would irritate him just a bit. I was putting him on the spot in regard to the long-delayed electric power project which he had promised me when Fort Peck dam was built.

On my way back home, I stopped off in Tacoma, Washington, and heard that my first telegram had hit the mark. Senator Homer T. Bone of Washington told me that when FDR had paused in Seattle he had remarked to him with a chuckle: "I got a kind of mushy wire from Burt about not being able to be in Montana." Bone said the President then had asked him seriously what he thought might be the political effect in Montana of his visiting the state without me at his side.

The President didn't seem to appreciate my second telegram. I heard that he got it while he was on the train at Great Falls and showed it to a friend of mine who was aboard—without making any comment. Then, at Fort Peck dam—which was built at my request, before Murray was even in the Senate—he praised Murray and did not mention my name.

(In the primaries of 1938, Roosevelt went far beyond snub punishment by openly attempting to purge four stalwart but generally conservative Democrats who had opposed him on the Court bill—Walter George of Georgia, Millard Tydings of Maryland, Pat McCarran of Nevada, and "Cotton Ed" Smith of South Carolina. All four senators were renominated easily.)

The California trip in 1937 involved me in gubernatorial politics there. The millionaire Church had been in a long battle with the owners of the Santa Anita race track; the controversy stemmed primarily from Church's agitation for a second track in Los Angeles County (it ended with the building of the Hollywood Park track). In the winter of 1936, the stewards at Santa Anita had claimed that one of Church's horses had been artificially "stimulated" before a race he had won.

Church's assistant trainer, Tom Carroll, was suspended. The stewards said they had established the "stimulation" through a saliva test, but Church hired a chemist from the California Institute of Technology to examine the remainder of the saliva and he found no evidence of a stimulant. No hearing was granted to Church and he thus had no opportunity to examine any of the reports or present his evidence.

Church asked the racing board to overrule the stewards but it refused. Strong-minded and outspoken, he told me he was convinced he had been framed. When I arrived there in late August, he was trying to have the matter handled politically through Republican Governor Frank Merriam. Church was a long-time Republican and had contributed to Merriam's election campaign.

I called on the governor, in Church's behalf, but he declined to intervene with the racing board. Church complained that he could not get his side of the story into the newspapers, so I next went to see William Randolph Hearst, who had been a friend of mine for some years. He was then living at the home he had built for Marion Davies. Hearst said he would give us all the publicity we wanted to get our side before the public, and he did give us some.

Church meanwhile filed an action against the racing board in the Superior Court in Sacramento asking that the suspension of his trainer be set aside. My son, John, a lawyer practicing in Los Angeles, and I argued the case in Sacramento and the Superior Court threw out the suspension. The California Supreme Court later upheld this decision, on the ground that the racing board had acted improperly in not granting Church a hearing.

During my visits with Church, he asked what he could do to change the racing board. I suggested that the surest way would be to bring about a change in the state administration. I urged him to do what he could to defeat the governor who had been so ungrateful about his support. Church doubted that any Democrat could beat Merriam in the 1938 election but I said I would see for myself.

After scouting the political prospects in the Democratic primary, I told Church that I felt Cuthbert Olson, a Los Angeles lawyer, would wind up with the Democratic nomination for governor.

"What do you know about California politics?" Church asked.

"I don't know much about it," I replied, "but when there are five Irishmen and one Swede running in a primary, the Swede will be nominated."

Church said he had heard Olson was a "wild man" but I suggested that nothing could be lost by having a talk with him. We arranged a meeting with Olson and afterward Church asked me what I thought. "He looks like a governor," I replied.

Church backed Olson, worked for him, took part in the fund-raising, and contributed personally around $40,000. My son, John, helped in the Olson campaign and I was able to get some help from Tom Corcoran of the White House and some other influential Democrats in Washington. Olson was nominated and elected.

I'm sorry to say that Olson did not make as good a governor as I had hoped.

Back in Montana, I was feeling some further slights for having fought the President on the Court bill. He tried to discipline me by routing patronage through Montana's two Democratic congressmen, O'Connell and O'Connor. The effect on me was minor. The Roosevelt Administration had never made any secret of its policy of rewarding its friends and punishing its enemies.

Right after the first election of FDR, in fact, Jim Farley gave out a statement that unless members of Congress went along with the New Deal they could expect no patronage. I told Jim that he shouldn't say things like that; I reminded him that he was dealing with United States Senators, not members of a city council. If he ever threatened me like that, I said I would tell him what he could do with his patronage. Farley said he wouldn't do that to me but that patronage meant a lot to some senators.

Soon there was plenty of evidence that he was right. It was not that the legislators wanted to succumb to what almost amounted to taking a bribe. They were well aware that constituents unfortunately too often judge their senators and congressmen on their ability to wangle federal "pork" for their state, or to have a say in the appointment of a federal marshal, district attorney, customs collector, etc.

Therefore, in the years after the Court fight the people of Montana stopped coming to me looking for favors, assuming that I was getting none from Roosevelt.

However, one day in the spring of 1942 I was visited by three leading citizens of Great Falls, Montana—the mayor, the secretary of the chamber of commerce, and the head of the American Legion. An Army air base was to be built in the Northwest and they were anxious to have Great Falls selected as the site. They had been buttonholing officials in Washington for nearly two weeks and had got nowhere. Among others, they had seen the other members of the Montana delegation; Wayne Johnson, a former Montanan who was then treasurer of the Democratic National Committee; and a colonel and a major at the War Department.

I asked them if they would like to talk with Major General Henry H. (Hap) Arnold, head of the U. S. Army Air Corps. They asked whether that could be arranged. I picked up the phone and put in a call to Arnold—whom I had met only once—and made an appointment for them.

I escorted the Great Falls civic leaders to Arnold's office and introduced them.

"General," I began, "they think the Army will do nothing for me because I disagree with the President on the war issue."

"That's silly," Arnold said. He pressed a button and called in two generals, explained the situation, and asked them to look into the matter.

Within a few weeks, there was an announcement that the new air base would be located at Great Falls, in preference to the numerous other cities which had been actively in competition. Of course, this was a tremendous break for the development of Great Falls, which now ranks first in size in Montana. The Great Falls Air Force Base at the same time proved to be a strategic way station for the Air Force during the war and since.

This incident is a good illustration of another point: that, regardless of the attitude of the White House, a department usually is anxious to go out of its way to help an influential senator, for obvious reasons. It doesn't matter whether the senator represents the party then in power, as long as he is an effective friend to have on "the Hill." The department quite properly is willing to accommodate a good fighter; if it thinks he has a good case, it will insist that his constituents get fair treatment.

Despite Farley's pragmatic attitude, I have reason to know that FDR himself had little respect for senators he could lead around by the nose simply by holding out the favor of patronage. Knowing he could keep them in his hip pocket, he concentrated on wooing the support of the independents.

Actually, my relations with Roosevelt beginning in 1938 were much better than was generally supposed. He needed my help. Something had to be done to prevent more of the railroads from going into bankruptcy, and I was chairman of the Interstate Commerce Committee, which had jurisdiction over railroad legislation.

The President appointed a committee of six men to work out legislative remedies and told them he would go along with their ideas. They were Carl R. Gray, president of the Union Pacific;

Martin W. Clement, president of the Pennsylvania; Ernest Norris, of the Southern; George Harrison, president of the railway clerks union; Dave Robertson, of the firemen's union; and Bert Jewell, president of the International Brotherhood of Boilermakers. They came up with their recommendations, FDR approved them, and they then discussed who should introduce the bill.

Harrison and Gray asked me to dinner in their suite at the Carlton Hotel. They read their proposals to me and asked for my opinion. Some months earlier, I had started to work on some legislative ideas of my own on the subject. I told Harrison and Gray I liked some of their ideas and couldn't go along with others. One proposal I agreed with was their idea of putting the water carriers under the Interstate Commerce Commission. Unless all forms of transportation were brought under the same agency, there would be a conflict in decisions which would be bad for the carriers and bad for the public.

But I told Harrison and Gray that their recommendations would mean the rewriting of the entire Interstate Commerce Act, together with all the amendments that had been added since its adoption in 1887. Bringing the water carriers under the act would mean the inclusion of 24 chapters covering a complete set of rules and regulations for them.

I wanted to stress the dimensions of what they were getting into because I recalled vividly the long, bitter fight I had led in 1935 to bring buses and trucks under the ICC. Most of the truckers had opposed any substantial regulation and when that was inevitable they had fought being placed under the ICC, which they felt was railroad-minded. The teamsters union also had threatened to fight the amendment unless it included a provision protecting its interests. Remembering my troubles at that time, I was not eager to take on another one that promised to be even bigger.

Gray stressed to me that both the railroad executives and the railroad brotherhoods wanted me to handle the bill. When I refused, Gray and Harrison said, "The President wants you to do it." I still refused, explaining that ever since the Court-packing fight I didn't think the President had any confidence in me and that I would not handle the legislation. Gray looked surprised and asked me what he should tell FDR.

"Tell him what I said," I told Gray, "and say he can give it to Truman, Minton, or Schwellenbach"—all of whom were one hundred per cent New Dealers—"to handle. I won't put anything in their way."

In a few days, Gray came to my office, reported that he had relayed my message to the President and had "made it good and strong," and that the President was going to send for me.

When Roosevelt sent for me, and I walked into his office, he said, "Hello," waving his arm as usual, and asked, "How's the missus?" Then he said he wanted to talk to me about railroads. I interrupted and said, "Before you go any further, let me tell you what I told Carl Gray and George Harrison, so you can get it straight." I repeated what I had said to them, with a little emphasis.

"Burt," he began, when I had finished, "you and I disagreed on the Court issue—we agreed in principle but disagreed on the method. Now that's water over the dam and I want you to handle this legislation."

I immediately said no, but in his most persuasive way, with a little flattery thrown in, he kept on talking. I finally said, "This is tough legislation—there's no glory in this for anyone, but if you have someone from the ICC, the RFC, the SEC, or if there is anyone else in whom you have confidence, I'll sit down with them and see what we can work out."

Roosevelt hesitated for what seemed like several minutes.

"Isn't there someone you have confidence in?" I prompted.

"To be frank with you, I haven't anyone," he answered.

I felt sorry for him when he said that. After all he had been President for seven years, and confidence begets confidence.

"I'll tell you what I'll do," I finally said. "I'll undertake this under one condition—that whatever I work out you'll go along with, since I don't agree with the railroads on some of their suggestions."

"I'll do anything you want me to," he replied.

I worked on the railroad bill to the exclusion of almost everything else. Senator Harry Truman was a member of the committee and welcomed my offer to list him as a co-sponsor of the bill. I knew that Senator Joe Guffey and some other New Deal senators would oppose anything I sponsored because of the Court fight, but they were friends of Truman. Truman was conscientious and loyal in working for the passage of the bill.

The groups that would be affected by the legislation could not get together on the remedies, the hearings soon revealed. The owners of freight-carrying ships—known in the industry as "water carriers"—organized an extensive lobby which lined up most of the senators along the Mississippi River against my proposals. The mail was full of letters every day insisting that the water carriers be left out of the bill. I went on a nation-wide radio hookup to defend the bill by debating my opponents.

Soon the bill was opposed by Secretary of Agriculture Henry A. Wallace, Secretary of War Harry H. Woodring, and Admiral Emory S. Land, chairman of the Maritime Commission. The pro-New Deal newspaper columnists didn't help either. They said the President had gotten me out on a limb on this bill, just to embarrass me. Many of these pundits were mad at me because of the Court fight.

Suspicious about the growing opposition, I telephoned the President and asked if he had lost interest in the legislation. "If you have," I said bluntly, "I won't go ahead with it. I undertook it at your urging."

I pointed out that the two cabinet members, Admiral Land, and his pet columnists were lambasting the bill. I said he ought to put a stop to that. He said he had been in Warm Springs and so was not familiar with what they had done, but he promised to put a stop to it. He did. There was no more opposition from these quarters, though the lobbying by the water carriers continued.

Some of the representatives of the railroads tried to get Roosevelt to make changes in the bill. He called them to the White House one evening with me present. We went over their complaints and he asked me for my opinion. I told him I didn't agree with their ideas.

"Well, gentlemen," Roosevelt told the executives, "I told Burt Wheeler I'd go along with him."

That ended this type of pressure.

When I was just about ready to have the bill reported out of committee, I was visited by a representative of the railroad brotherhoods and Carter Fort, an attorney for the Association of American Railroads. They said if I didn't make certain changes, the brotherhoods would fight the bill when it reached the Senate floor.

I had worked hard to get the warring factions together, with the exception of the water carriers, and I was getting tired. So I told the union leader angrily that if the brotherhoods fought it on the floor by as much as one raised eyebrow, I'd throw the bill into the wastebasket. I turned to the association's attorney and added, "That goes for you too."

They didn't fight the bill on the floor and Roosevelt kept his word with me. However, when the fight waxed hot in the Senate, some senators grew weak in the knees. The President apparently became worried and he sent for me.

"Burt, I don't think you can get that bill through the Senate," he said.

I told him I was pretty sure I could, and I subsequently did so, by a 17-vote majority. But it was one of the most exasperating and wearying victories of my career. I never at any time had a great deal of strong support and in the final debate I had to stand on my feet for five and a half hours explaining the complex provisions of the bill repeatedly to my doubting and confused colleagues. Some of the most able debaters in the Senate were on the other side, including Arthur H. Vandenberg, Bennett Champ Clark, and Henrik Shipstead.

The bill was finally passed by the Senate in August 1940—three years after I had begun work on it—and it was soon passed by the House in slightly different form. The resulting compromise bill as signed by the President was called the Transportation Act of 1940.

Writing legislation to regulate industry necessarily must be rather broad, giving the regulatory agency wide latitude in interpreting it, and also giving it the power to make rules of its own. It is impossible for Congress to lay out all the rules in detail. As a result, the commissions and the courts sometimes construe the legislation in a way never intended by the author of the bill or by Congress. Too often, the commissions forget that they are arms of Congress, set up to carry out the will of Congress, and not instruments of the executive branch (from whence they receive their appointments, and reappointments).

Another problem is that the President too often appoints to the commissions men who serve a purely political purpose and are lacking in the knowledge, training, ability, and industry which make first-class commission members.

The regulatory agencies have been investigated a great deal by Congress in recent years—and some have had scandals—but there is nothing wrong with the commissions that can't be cured by the appointment of honest, intelligent, and efficient commissioners.

I don't always agree with the Interstate Commerce Commission but it has a fine tradition of competence and independence, and has had a number of outstanding members. Joseph B. Eastman, a commissioner from Boston who had been appointed by President Wilson in 1919 and served for twenty-five years and was looked upon as one of the great authorities on transportation of all times, is just one example of a fine public servant. Eastman told me that Roosevelt once called him to the White House and made a suggestion regarding a decision in a certain case. Eastman said he replied to the President that the ICC was an arm of Congress and not of the executive branch. Eastman's appointment to a new term was afterward held up for some time but was finally made by the President after many persons, including myself, wrote strong letters in his behalf.

Chapter Seventeen

THIRD TERM AND FOURTH TERM

In the summer of 1939, speculation over whether FDR would run for a third term was already rife. On August 4, when Congress was preparing to adjourn, I had a long chat with him in the Oval Room of the White House. The Court fight was two years past and our relations, despite what most people thought, had become friendly again because of our frequent discussions about the railroad legislation.

Our talk on August 4 covered railroads and a good many other topics, including politics and candidates, past and future. As soon as I returned to my office I dictated a memorandum of what was said, so I have an accurate record of the conversation.

I said to the President I wanted to talk with him before I went back to Montana, and that I knew he had been very, very busy, as I had been also. I remarked that columnists and others might say various things about my attitude toward him, and so I wanted him to know firsthand just exactly how I felt.

I told him that Senator George Norris had come to me recently and said he had a question to ask. Making it clear that he was speaking entirely for himself, Norris had asked, "Would you run for Vice President with President Roosevelt?" I said my response to Norris was, "No, I wouldn't run for Vice President with anyone," adding that he should not encourage the President to run in 1940.

I then told FDR I thought it would be a mistake for him to seek a third term. He immediately interrupted me by saying casually, "Of course, it would be a mistake." I explained that it would be a mistake for him personally, and for the Democratic Party as well; that all the New Deal legislation would be jeopardized by his fight over the third-term issue—because if he lost his defeat would be interpreted as a repudiation of the New Deal legislation which he had put on the statute books.

I added, "Mr. President, I am worried about the future of this country, and I am worried for fear some reactionary Republican, or some reactionary Democrat will come into power.

"While I feel you would make a mistake running for a third term, nevertheless, if you are nominated, I will take off my coat and work for your re-election."

I also told him that I would not be a stooge for the reactionaries or for the big interests.

"Many of them believe because I was against you on the Court issue, I will be against you on everything else. Of course, that is not so," I said.

"I am for seeing the Democratic Party nominate a liberal candidate, and it is the only way we can win," I added.

The President replied, "I don't want to see a reactionary Democrat nominated. I love Jack Garner personally. He is a lovable man. But he couldn't get the Negro vote, and he couldn't get the labor vote."

I expressed my fondness for Jack Garner but I doubted he could get the Irish vote. I called attention to the fact that a friend of mine from Boston, when I suggested to him that Garner might be nominated, had said, "It would be a mistake." I had asked him if Garner could carry Boston, and he answered by saying that even if the Pope came over here and made a speech for him, "I doubt that he could carry Massachusetts."

Then Roosevelt remarked that Jim Cox, the 1920 Democratic presidential nominee on whose ticket he had run for Vice President, had "played with reactionaries." He next mentioned John W. Davis, conservative 1924 Democratic presidential nominee, and said he didn't want anyone of that type to be nominated or to get control of the Democratic Party. "I'm getting too old to go out and fight for a ticket that cannot win, and I want to see a ticket that can win," FDR mused.

"I supported Bryan," he went on reminiscently. "I was young and got into the Bryan campaign for the experience. I supported Wilson, and he won. After Wilson, I ran with Cox. I said to Cox, 'Of course, we've got to go along with Wilson's League of Nations. We've got to be good sports. If we do go along with it, the anti-Leaguers are going to be sore, and if we don't go along with it, all the Wilson forces are going to be sore.' So I said to Cox, 'We'll go along and be good sports, and after it's over, you'll go back to Ohio, and I'll go back and practice law in New York, because we cannot win.'"

When I pointed out during this talk with Roosevelt that I had gone along with him on all of his legislation that I considered "liberal," he interrupted me by saying, "Burt, I would like to have you do one thing for me. I'd like to have you make a speech or a statement and say that while you disagreed with me on the method of reforming the Supreme Court, you agreed with me on the objective and that the Court has now been liberalized and that I have won my objective." I was somewhat shocked at how deeply he felt about his defeat. I told him I had made a speech—I think it was in Baltimore—in which I said I had agreed with him that some of the decisions of the Court had been wrong, but had disagreed on the way he wanted to correct the situation.

The President said, "This will help you and it would help me." (He had previously asked Secretary of Agriculture Wallace to ask me to make the same statement. Secretary Wallace had written down what the President wanted him to ask me and had seen me a few days later in his office to tell me the President's wishes. I had refused to make the speech.)

FDR and I then discussed the political situation. He said, "Burt, I think we can win and I want to win in 1940." He added: "We will go along until January, February, or March. We will get together then. We will sit around and take up different combinations, and try and pick out one that will win."

He talked about labor and John L. Lewis. He said John was an able fellow, and that if he would do something (I forget the language he used) he would be an excellent labor leader. He said, "If Sidney Hillman was the leader of the CIO, I could settle all differences in the labor movement in a very short time, but we took $600,000 from Lewis in 1936, and he has never gotten through boasting about it. We made a mistake. We never should have taken the money.

"Now," he said, "Lewis made a mistake. It was a mistake for him to say what he did about Garner." Lewis had called Garner a "labor-baiting, poker-playing, whisky-drinking evil old man." (I later told John Lewis what he had said about him and the $600,000 campaign contribution; John's only comment was that the Democrats had kept asking for the money and the President knew it.)

The President continued: "You are strong in eastern Montana, and the endorsement of you by Lewis would not help you in eastern Montana because there are no strong labor unions over there." (This bore out what I already knew—that after the Court fight he had someone make a very careful check on Montana to find out whether I could be beaten in the 1940 election. One congressman from Washington interviewed the postmaster in Billings and at least one or two other places and was told that while the people would vote for the President, they would also vote for me.)

The President next told me he planned to be in Montana around October 12 and hoped I would be there at the time. I told him I had a long-standing engagement to be in Hudson, Massachusetts, at that time; my home town folks, reinforced by leading Massachusetts politicos, were planning a big celebration in my honor. Roosevelt asked me to see if I could have the date changed. (I couldn't.)

In our conversation I also told FDR that Jim Farley, the last time I talked with him, "never mentioned a third term, nor did he say anything which was in the slightest disrespectful of you." I related that Farley did say the one person who would not get the 1940 nomination if he had anything to say about it was Paul V. McNutt, then Federal Security Administrator, and that Farley had also complained about Tom (Tommy the Cork) Corcoran, the President's able agent on Capitol Hill.

"I know that Jim is very bitter against McNutt," the President commented, "and I know he doesn't like Tommy Corcoran. But I never see Corcoran more than once a month, and I told him that a lot of things Tommy might say I didn't know anything about, and that the newspapers gave Tommy credit for a lot of things that were not so."

(I knew for a fact that FDR was not being candid here. He saw Corcoran quite often and to my knowledge Tommy's key role in the President's legislative program was not exaggerated in the newspapers.)

"I had a very fine talk with Jim," Roosevelt continued, in regard to Farley. "He wants to run for Vice President, and because of his large acquaintance over the country he feels he could have the nomination. But a Hull-Farley ticket could not be elected." (The supposition here was that Farley might conceivably be the running mate of Cordell Hull, in the event that the Secretary of State ever achieved his ambition to be nominated for President.)

Roosevelt then quoted his good friend, George Cardinal Mundelein, of the Archdiocese of Chicago, as saying that "some day we're going to have a Catholic President; but he should not come in the back door. They could not nominate Farley or Frank Murphy"—then the Attorney General—"for Vice President with the idea that either could become President that way. The Catholic they would elect would have to come out of the West and not from the sidewalks of New York."

Roosevelt added his own thought that if there were an outstanding Catholic Democrat available—someone like my Montana colleague, the late Thomas J. Walsh, when he was "a young man and vigorous"—he could possibly be elected in 1940.

When I left, the President remarked, "Well, I'll see you in October."

FDR was no doubt sincere when he said that seeking a third term was a mistake—under ordinary conditions. (Corcoran has since told me the President had him put out feelers—on his own —on the third-term issue; he believes that FDR never really put the idea out of his mind.) The war that erupted in Europe three weeks after our conversation upset all calculations and gave Roosevelt the excuse that he needed to break the two-term tradition.

Nonetheless, no one for the next ten months could be absolutely sure that he would not run, for the President delighted in keeping his own counsel. Into this vacuum eagerly stepped Farley, McNutt, and Vice President Jack Garner. Also Hull did nothing to discourage his supporters.

None of them looked like a winner to the powerful liberal-labor groups which dominate Democratic conventions. Soon I began to get a buildup in the newspapers and national magazines as "the man to watch." I was pictured as a fighting campaigner and as a liberal of long-standing who could swing many conservative votes.

I refused to think I had a chance for the nomination but I had a keen interest in who the nominee might be. In the fall of 1939, I raised the question of FDR's intentions while lunching at the Capitol with David K. Niles, the White House assistant in charge of minority groups and a friend of mine since he had worked for the La Follette-Wheeler ticket in 1924.

"He doesn't want to run and he won't if he can find someone to succeed him who will look upon him as the elder statesman and send him to the peace conference," Niles told me.

"Who've you got?" was my next question.

"Nobody," said Niles. When I mentioned Senator James F. Byrnes of South Carolina, an FDR favorite, Niles replied that Byrnes couldn't be elected because he was an ex-Catholic. When I named Farley, McNutt, and Senate majority leader Barkley, Niles said none of them would do.

Then he said, "You could be elected." I replied that the big city bosses in the party would never stand for me because of my independence. He pointed out that the bosses wanted to win. When I said Roosevelt would never stand for me because I had broken with him on the Court fight, Niles answered: "I've never heard him say anything against you—cross my heart."

A little later, when I was in Boston, Governor Charles F. Hurley remarked that he was sure I could have second place on a Roosevelt ticket if I wanted it. Hurley, a friend of mine, urged me to take it.

My relations with the White House staff continued to be close. When I was writing my address for the National Association of Manufacturers dinner in New York in early December, Niles asked me for a copy of the speech and carried it back to the White House for study. He returned it with some suggestions for changes—made by whom he did not say.

The theme of my speech was that big business must learn to cooperate with both labor and government—or face more regulation and less profit. My correspondence file, as I review it now, shows that this advice was surprisingly well received by the NAM tycoons; many of them dropped me laudatory notes. This reaction encouraged those who were chafing to get a go-ahead from me to work for my nomination in 1940.

Press comment on my chances stepped up in January, after John L. Lewis, by that time violently anti-Roosevelt, gave me an unsolicited endorsement, and George Norris said I was his choice in the event FDR did not choose to run. Columnist Ernest K. Lindley wrote that Lewis' support put me "on the left of Roosevelt."

The theory of my double-edged appeal as a candidate was summed up this way in the Washington *Star* by Charles G. Ross, who later became President Truman's press secretary:

"Senator Wheeler will be offered as a liberal who appeals to the conservative wing of the party, with whom he fought shoulder to shoulder in the Court fight, and who at the same time, because of his progressive record, can be counted on to hold in line the labor vote which the party must have to win."

During the following five months virtually every national

magazine took a crack at analyzing my assets and liabilities. Assessing the developing situation, Robert Moses, the tart-tongued New Yorker, concluded in *The Saturday Evening Post* that if FDR would give his blessing to a ticket composed of Wheeler for President and Senator Harry Byrd for Vice President "it would be no easy ticket to beat."

My record for being an independent-minded Democrat led to contradictory conclusions on the same page in the March 1940 issue of *Current History*. Robert S. Allen, the syndicated columnist, theorized that if I had "remained true" to the liberals on the Court-packing bill I would by 1940 have been either a Supreme Court justice or the "undeniable successor to Franklin D. Roosevelt . . . today, neither the liberals nor the conservatives trust him."

However, Ludwell Denny, New York *World-Telegram* columnist, wrote: "The reason for Burt Wheeler's growing strength as a compromise candidate (if the third term is out) is not money or organization—he has neither. It is because he is trusted by both liberals and conservatives, labor and capital."

I was "Man of the Week" on the cover of the April 15, 1940, issue of *Time* magazine over the caption, "The Democratic Party Has a Great Future." *The Christian Science Monitor* called me a "left-wing Coolidge." Even the *American Astrology* magazine got into the act; its crystal ball disclosed that if Roosevelt did not run, Wheeler would be the Democratic nominee!

My relations with the Roosevelts were friendly. Mrs. Eleanor Roosevelt wrote asking me to come to the White House on February 5 for a discussion with some young people who she said were planning a Citizenship Institute of the American Youth Congress:

"I suggested you might be willing to come here and hold a meeting at which everyone present would have an opportunity to find out about the purposes and objectives which they hope to achieve by holding this institute in Washington . . . I hope very much you will be able to make this sacrifice of your time."

I attended the meeting and talked to quite a few youngsters, some of whom I felt were obviously under the influence of the Communists—as the American Youth Congress was later proved to be. I have had an instinct for spotting red sympathizers ever since I associated with radical labor leaders and the IWW in Montana.

I have two amusing recollections of Eleanor Roosevelt, and I will digress to relate them here. After the 1932 Democratic convention, I had been summoned to the Roosevelt home at Hyde Park to discuss campaign strategy. We sat up until after midnight talking over possible appointees. Roosevelt said he wasn't interested in big names for his Cabinet, because most of them had been built up by the newspapers. We went over various issues to be discussed in the campaign. The next morning, breakfasting with Mrs. Roosevelt, she confided ruefully that "they won't let me campaign because I'm considered too liberal." (I left Hyde Park somewhat disillusioned. When I got back to our summer camp in the Rockies, Mrs. Wheeler asked me what I thought of FDR. I said I was disappointed, that I didn't believe he had any deep-seated convictions about anything.)

In 1934, I was aboard the Roosevelt train when the President returned through Montana from a trip to Hawaii. Mrs. Roosevelt was sitting with us one day when we were discussing the drought.

"Franklin, what are you going to do about unemployment?" she suddenly asked. FDR went right on talking about something else.

"Franklin, what are you going to do about unemployment?" she persisted. Still her husband ignored her. Finally, when she repeated the question a third time, FDR replied: "My dear, if I knew I would have told you a long time ago. I'm going to try a little of this and a little of that and see what we come out with."

In 1937 I related this conversation to a White House aide and his comment surprised me. "Did it ever occur to you that there is no unemployment in wartime?" he asked.

Late in April 1940 the newspapers carried a press association report that the President was about to invite me to the White House to offer me the vice presidential nomination. The story was not true and when I scotched the rumor I could not help quipping: "Anyhow, I'm not old enough to be Vice President"—I was fifty-eight. "A man ought to be sixty to hold that office."

One evening in June 1940 Mrs. Wheeler and I were invited to dinner at the home of Robert E. Kintner, then a columnist partner of Joseph Alsop and later successively the president of the American Broadcasting Company and the National Broadcasting Company. Kintner was close to the White House and the other guests were practicing New Dealers—Leon Henderson, head of the Office of Price Stabilization; Ben Cohen, FDR's able legal draftsman; and Edward Foley, general counsel for the Treasury Department.

After dinner, Henderson leaned back in his chair, removed a big cigar from his mouth, and said, "The convention is going to nominate you for Vice President and you're going to have to take it."

A hush fell over the Kintner living room. The four couples waited to hear my reaction.

"No," I said.

"Why not?" Henderson asked.

"Because the President is going to get us into the war and I won't go out and campaign and say he won't," I explained. This was not long after I had been visited, as related in Chapter One, by an admiral and an Army officer, both of whom warned me that Roosevelt would finagle us into the war.

When Henderson frowned, I continued: "He shouldn't want me, anyway. I couldn't be a Vice President like Garner. Whenever I disagreed with him, I'd come right out and say so. You know me well enough to know that."

Henderson said that I ought to take the vice presidency under the condition that when the emergency was over, FDR would resign and I would become President. I thought it was a joke.

"Will he let me decide 'when the emergency is over'?" I asked, beginning to enjoy myself.

At this point, it was pointed out to Mrs. Wheeler—in a typically Washington gambit—that "you'd be the Vice President's wife."

"I'd rather have my husband in the Senate," replied Mrs. Wheeler truthfully.

Henderson said: "Here is Bob Kintner, here is Ben Cohen, here is Ed Foley, Tom Corcoran's friend, and you know how we stand," intimating that they were speaking with the authority of the White House.

Before the party broke up at about eleven o'clock, the other three men present joined in urging me not to close my mind to the vice presidential candidacy.

The President played the sphinx on the third-term question. In November 1939 I had allowed a Wheeler-for-President organization to be set up, while making it clear at that time I would support FDR if he should choose to run. The organization was a modest one, relatively small in funds and extending into few states outside Montana. But a number of volunteers worked enthusiastically in my interest. One of them was the late Senator Richard Neuberger, then a free-lance writer. His extensive correspondence with my supporters shows that he unsuccessfully tried to get the liberals in Oregon to withdraw the President's name in the Oregon primary and substitute my own.

In December 1939 I had received a letter from Roy Howard, head of the Scripps-Howard newspaper chain, asking if he could set up a luncheon in New York so that I could meet "a dozen or so people in key positions . . . whose acquaintance with you might be worth while." Howard went on to say that "on firsthand acquaintance you're a rather pleasant surprise to a lot of people whose impressions are based, conscientiously or otherwise, on the efforts of individuals who have done a rather artistic job of presenting you in a false light."

There was nothing back of the invitation, Howard wrote slyly, except that "I know of no man I'd rather see as the next occupant of the White House than yourself." He added that he had no illusions that he and I would always see "eye to eye" on every subject.

Thanking Howard, I replied:

"The charge was made against me that when I disagreed with the President, that I disliked him personally. No one who knows him can dislike him personally. I said to an audience in Montana that I disagreed with my wife sometimes, and she sometimes violently disgrees with me, because she is Scotch, but that does not mean that we are not one of the most congenial married couples in the United States. If you cannot disagree with a party and still be friends, he really was not much of a friend in the first place."

The Democratic National Convention was due to open in Chicago on July 15, 1940. On the train bound for the Windy City, my son, Edward, was buttonholed in the vestibule of a Pullman by David Niles.

"Don't let your father get in a fight with Roosevelt before the voting starts," he urged. It was not clear to Edward whether Niles was thinking of first or second place on the ticket. Nobody professed to know Roosevelt's intentions, and so I had consented to let my name be placed in nomination. While Montana had only eight delegates, the assumption was that I would start as the candidate of the West and, if FDR didn't run, my Supreme Court and anti-war fights plus my general liberalism would appeal to the delegations from most states. Edward and the others working for my nomination never pretended to have more than a handful of delegates committed to me but no other candidate could count on many delegates either. Almost every delegate was waiting for the word on FDR before sticking his neck out.

I still didn't take my candidacy very seriously. If FDR didn't choose to run, he could just about name his successor and I felt he must have been irked at my recent attacks on his war policies.

The suspense evaporated on July 9, with the arrival in Chicago of Secretary of Commerce Harry Hopkins, FDR's confidant who lived right in the White House; and Senator Byrnes, FDR's right-hand man in the Senate. They were there to stage-manage the President's nomination.

Hopkins logically set himself up in the Blackstone Hotel suite that included the notorious "smoke-filled room" where Warren G. Harding's nomination had been master-minded in 1920 by my old friend, Harry Daugherty. There Hopkins began dealing with the city bosses and the labor leaders. Across the street in the Stevens Hotel, Byrnes began passing the word among key politicians that the President was "available." Hopkins and Byrnes made no bones about wanting to avoid the traditional poky roll call—nomination by acclamation would look better.

Having spent time and money to build themselves up, Farley and Garner refused to be blocked off. They wanted a roll call. Senator Barkley, the convention's permanent chairman and an agent of the White House group, tried to outsmart them by stimulating the apathetic delegates. He read a message from the President to the effect that while he "never had any desire" to run again "all the delegates are free to vote for any candidate," obviously including a man named Roosevelt. Some of the delegates did not immediately get the significance of the clever wording. But the leaders did—it was clearly an "invitation to the draft," as they put it.

The reading of the President's message touched off a pandemonium that could only have been manufactured by the efficient organization of Chicago Mayor Edward J. Kelly. The key instrument—since famous in political annals—was a microphone in the basement of the Chicago Stadium hooked into the loudspeaker system. Pressed close to the microphone was the mouth of Tom Garry, Superintendent of Sewers.

"We want Roosevelt!" Garry bellowed, and the amplified words re-echoed around the huge hall like thunderclaps of doom for the avowed candidates. In the galleries as well as on the floor, thousands of the mayor's ward heelers took up the chant. There followed a screaming demonstration for FDR which, under Garry's invisible chant-prompting, continued for 53 minutes. To the radio listeners, it must have sounded as if the delegates couldn't wait until the balloting session to nominate the President. Actually, as has been written elsewhere, the delegates were far from enthusiastic about having traveled all the way to Chicago to be cast in the role of puppets.

Just off the convention floor, my sons John and Edward were trying to organize the Wheeler-for-President standard bearers for the time when my name would be placed in nomination.

But once the commanding "voice from the sewers" gushed forth, Kelly's goons snatched the placards away from my sons' group and broke them. Standard bearers for other candidates suffered a similar fate—and were roughly handled if they resisted.

Once the word got around that FDR would run, it was all over. The steamroller began to move. A roll call was ordered but I decided not to let my name go before the convention. I told Senator D. Worth Clark of Idaho, who was scheduled to offer my name, that I would not subject him to the catcalling punishment on the floor that was the lot of those who were nominating candidates other than FDR. Clark wanted to nominate me anyway but I wouldn't let him.

Roosevelt got 946 out of a total of 1100 delegates' votes, Farley got 72 and Garner got 61, with Senator Tydings and Cordell Hull sharing the handful that remained.

Within 24 hours, it became known that FDR's choice for running mate was Henry A. Wallace, his Secretary of Agriculture. In Chicago, I had been sounded out for second place twice, in a roundabout way, and both times I had rejected the idea.

Before the convention opened, Mose Cohen, a Los Angeles lawyer originally from my own town of Butte, Montana, had come to my suite in the Congress Hotel. He breathlessly announced that he had just come from a session with Hopkins; Frank Walker, then treasurer of the Democratic National Committee and later its chairman; and Edward J. Flynn, the boss from the Bronx.

"You can have the nomination for Vice President," Cohen said.

"They're not serious," I assured him. When he insisted that they were serious, I told him I would accept the offer "only if the President calls and asks me." I heard no more from Cohen.

On the opening day of the convention, I had decided to pass up the routine formalities at the Chicago Stadium and take a nap in my suite. I left word that I didn't want to be disturbed. Shortly afterward, Edward, who was standing guard outside my door, was brushed aside roughly by William H. Hutchinson, the large and colorful Washington bureau chief of the International News Service and a good friend of mine.

"Hutch" barged into my room and told me he had been talking long-distance with Supreme Court Justice Frank Murphy.

"Murphy has just left the White House and says that if you will agree to take the vice presidential nomination, the President will call you and ask you to," he said.

"I can't do it," I told Hutch. "He's going to get us into the war and I can't tell the people he's going to keep us out."

"You're the biggest damn fool in the world!" Hutch exploded. "You'll be President of the United States if you agree to this!"

I added that Mrs. Wheeler would divorce me if I became FDR's running mate. After further upbraiding me for what he called shortsighted stubbornness, Hutchinson stomped out of my suite. During the next several years, he kidded me publicly about passing up a chance to be President. He expected Roosevelt to die in office, though perhaps sooner than it happened.

I could well believe that Murphy had discussed the matter at the White House, for he had told me much earlier I was his choice for Vice President. I had known him well when he was governor of Michigan and United States Attorney General.

Despite what the public may think about the remoteness of the Supreme Court, the justices in my time were frequently consulted by the President of the United States on non-judicial matters, such as executive appointments and party candidates. Men like Murphy and former Senators Sherman Minton, Hugo Black and Harold Burton were politicians to begin with and did not completely lose their taste for or interest in politics just because they were elevated to the high bench.

Those who remember me now primarily as "the man who fought Roosevelt," may be surprised that I was within reach of second place on the ticket in 1940. Tom Corcoran has since confirmed to me that this was indeed the situation as viewed from the inside. He explains that FDR ever since the Court fight considered me an opponent to be reckoned with and doubtless felt that relegating me to vice presidential "limbo" would neutralize me, so to speak. I can well imagine he would like to have shut me up on the red-hot intervention issue, and this is precisely why I could not in good conscience run with him, as I have said. Corcoran also points out that in picking a running mate FDR didn't really think he was choosing a successor—he simply could not imagine himself dying!

Surprising as it may be to many, again in 1944 White House aides talked all around the edges of the question of my being a possible vice presidential candidate, although the situation was not clear-cut as it was in 1940.

Early in 1944, Dave Niles asked my son, Edward, to have dinner with him at the Carlton Hotel. Edward reported back to me that Niles had said that if I would call on the President and try to patch up our old differences Roosevelt would "throw up his hands with glee." The President was represented as believing that Mrs. Wheeler hated him and influenced me against him. (I believe Roosevelt's feeling about Mrs. Wheeler's attitude dated from the day in 1934 when he invited us and a few others for a cruise down the Potomac on the presidential yacht. The President and Mrs. Wheeler rode alone together to the dock in his limousine, while the rest of us followed. FDR tried several times to engage her in conversation but she all but ignored him. She had a strong antipathy to Roosevelt from this date.) Then the conversation went around, in Niles' circuitous fashion, to the question of FDR's running mate.

Niles gave Edward the impression that he and other liberals either didn't want Vice President Wallace renominated or knew FDR wouldn't take him again; also that as a substitute for Wallace their choice boiled down to Senator Harry Truman and me. They were mainly concerned with getting a "true liberal." Niles knew I was a vigorous campaigner. Truman passed the test for liberalism but his ability to wage a fighting campaign was not known (ironical as this may seem now in view of his "give 'em hell" campaign in 1948). The forcefulness of the vice presidential candidate was important because none of the White House insiders could be sure how much campaigning FDR's alarming decline in health would permit.

Thus, as Edward reported his impression to me, the group of

liberals for which Niles spoke preferred me but weren't sure they could "sell" me to the President unless there was a reconciliation first. They knew that Truman was acceptable to Roosevelt and also to the potent CIO group.

I called Niles the next day and said that Edward had told me of their talk. I told him that I was not sore at the President but did not want to embarrass him (Niles), otherwise I would talk to him. He said it wouldn't embarrass him but might help him. I said, "If you feel that way, come up and have lunch." He did and again said the President didn't want to run but felt he might have to. Niles did not offer me the vice presidency but did say that the President would rather have me as a successor than some of those "tories." I told him if I ever had any desire to run for President I didn't have any more, as I felt the man who followed the President might be shot and I didn't want to be a dead hero.

He then asked me about Senator Truman. He said, "Can he make a speech?" I told him he could, though he had not made many in the Senate.

He then said, "If the President doesn't run, it will probably be Truman."

In the spring of 1944 Judge Sam Rosenman, who was FDR's confidant and speech writer, called me up and then came to the Interstate Commerce Committee room at the Capitol. Sam had always been on friendly terms with me and I considered him one of the able men around the President. He not only wrote the speeches for FDR but a good many of Truman's after he became President. He said he wanted to bring about better relations between the President and me. We spent three hours together discussing various possibilities for the national ticket. He mentioned that if the President ran for a fourth term they were having difficulty in finding the right person for Vice President. He said that people were going to the President carrying tales of what I said about him and people were coming to me telling me what the President said about me. I then told him I understood that when the Court fight was going on the President had said, "Wheeler's all right but that wife of his is Lady Macbeth." The next day he called me on the phone and said the President "vehemently denies that Shakespearean quotation."

Sam came to see me again at my office later and we spent over an hour talking generally about legislation. Again he said he wanted me and the President to get along better.

I did have a long visit with FDR in the White House in the spring of 1944 but the vice presidency was not mentioned. Nevertheless, the story was circulated that this meant I was going to run for Vice President. Constantine Brown, columnist for the Washington *Star*, was one of several who told me he had heard the story.

Frank Walker, Postmaster General and an old friend of mine from Butte, Montana, called my house one morning and asked me to pick him up on the way to the office. He wanted to discuss the political situation and especially vice presidential candidates. He sought my opinion of Truman, Byrnes, and Supreme Court Justice William O. Douglas. He wanted to know if I thought the Catholics would fight Byrnes because he had left the Church as a younger man. I told him that he ought to know more about that than I did, since he was a good and prominent Catholic.

I told Walker with a chuckle what happened after I had been to the White House and the story got started that I had been offered the number two spot on the ticket. Taking a table in the Senate restaurant, I was immediately approached by Gregory, a veteran waiter I had known for years.

"If you're going to ride a horse," Gregory advised me, "ride him yourself." Then, shifting to another metaphor, he had added seriously, "Don't play second fiddle."

"All right," I told Walker I had replied to Gregory, "if you don't want me to run for Vice President I won't do it."

This caused Walker to comment, "You're just as ornery as ever."

"As I grow older, I get more mellow," I replied with a laugh.

Alighting at the Post Office Building, Walker grunted, "Just on the surface."

Another who came to me with worries about the choice of FDR's 1944 running mate was James V. Forrestal, then Secretary of the Navy and privy to many White House matters. At lunch, Forrestal remarked that if Wallace were renominated many influential persons would refuse to support the ticket. He was wondering if Douglas would do.

In September 1944 Tommy Corcoran was visiting me in my office and we discussed the Democratic convention of that summer.

"Why didn't you take the vice presidential nomination?" he asked.

"It wasn't offered to me," I replied.

"Didn't Dave Niles offer it to you?" Corcoran said. "He was supposed to."

Corcoran, who was no longer in the government, had worked to get the vice presidential nomination for Douglas and he had no use for Niles.

Whether I was ever considered for second place by the President in 1944 I do not know, but I could hardly help feeling that the talks I had with Niles, Rosenman, Walker, and Forrestal were attempts to sound me out on the idea. At any rate, I couldn't have accepted if it had been offered because in supporting the President in the campaign I would have had to repudiate much of what I had said previously about his foreign policies. Besides, the job of Vice President never appealed to me. It had been a terrible bore for me to sit in the presiding officer's chair whenever I had been "drafted" for it. I ducked it whenever I could. There is no excitement wielding a gavel.

I liked it down on the floor of the Senate. You can have a real debate there. I also liked the committee work, particularly the investigations, where a man could show his initiative and imagination. Altogether, I felt then and I feel now that the office of United States Senator is the finest there is—if you are a free man. By this I mean free from dictation by political bosses and control by corporations, labor or other pressure groups. A senator as fortunately situated as I was in Montana could disagree with a President who was in his own party when he believed the President was wrong. To be beholden to any individual or group would have made the Senate a stultifying experience for me.

Of course, there was a time in Montana, as in many other Western states, when the large corporations and their retainers completely dominated both political parties. As I have related in an earlier chapter, Montana politics had been corrupted by the lavish outlays of money during the fight of the "copper barons." That day has long passed. My erstwhile enemies, the Anaconda Copper Mining Company, while still interested in legislation in Washington that affects them and their relations with organized labor, have long since abandoned the political tactics they once practiced.

I didn't realize how free I was in the Senate until I had a few words one day in the 1920s with Senator Edward I. Edwards, a Democrat from New Jersey. Edwards was a former governor of his state and very likeable. One morning he came to me and said he was going to vote with me and the elder La Follette on a bill. In the afternoon, he said he was sorry but that he couldn't go along. When I asked why, he said his "boss," Frank Hague of Jersey City, had called him up and told him not to.

"Do you have someone call you up and tell you what to do?" I asked, perhaps naïvely.

"You have to do what the boss says or you don't get re-elected," he replied. "Who's your boss?"

I said I had none.

Edwards didn't believe this. He suggested that Tom Walsh must be my boss. I was a great admirer of Walsh's ability and integrity, and we generally agreed on our votes, but neither of us ever tried to tell the other how to vote.

Even my good friend, Harry Truman, remarked once that he had to go along with Roosevelt on a vote because he had ridden in on FDR's coattails. "You're in a different position," he noted.

When Truman was tapped for the vice presidential nomination at the 1944 convention in Chicago, it angered Byrnes, Alben Barkley, and a few others who had been led to believe in one way or another that they had had FDR's blessing. I heartily approved. I felt I had a special interest in Truman's career, having played a role in his rise in the Senate.

Truman acknowledged this fact in a letter he wrote me from the winter White House at Key West, Florida, on November 17, 1951.

Thanking me for a note I had dropped on another subject, the President went on to say: "I think you and I have always understood each other. I've always believed in your honesty and integrity, and your statements about my reputation and truthfulness are highly appreciated. People do not always have to see exactly eye to eye to be good friends. As far as I'm concerned, you and I will continue to understand each other. I'll never forget the fact that you recognized the junior senator from Missouri and gave him something to do when he came to the Senate in 1935."

Truman's reference to my help went back to the time when he was a new appointee to the Interstate Commerce Committee which I headed. One day after I opened hearings on an important investigation of railroad financing, I noticed Truman had slipped into the audience and was paying close attention to the testimony. Later, I asked him if he was interested in the subject. He said he was. I appointed him to the subcommittee. When the Utility Holding Company bill came up, my time was wholly occupied with that and I made Truman the acting chairman of the railroad financing subcommittee. He proved to be very diligent and capable.

When the Democratic boss of Kansas City, Tom Pendergast, was convicted of defrauding the federal government of income taxes in 1939, Truman asked me whether I thought the senators would feel he should resign from the Senate. He said he owed his election to Pendergast. I asked him if he was involved in any way in the scandal. Truman said he was not. I said there was no reason for him to resign and advised him to go about his business as if nothing had happened.

Early in World War II, I introduced a resolution to investigate reports of scandalous transactions in munitions contracts. I had reports of inexcusable wasting—if not worse—of government funds by businessmen who were on cost-plus contracts and didn't care how much they spent.

My resolution was recommended for passage by my committee but I knew that even if I got the Senate to approve it I would have trouble getting money from the Rules Committee to conduct a thorough probe. The Roosevelt Administration would block me there by passing the word that I was out to discredit the war effort. Anticipating this, I had intended to appoint Truman as chairman of the committee if my resolution went through. The administration took no chances on my taking the chairmanship myself. They asked Truman to introduce a similar resolution. I did not press my resolution and Truman's passed. Over several years, Truman did an excellent job with his special committee and it did more than anything else to propel him into nation-wide prominence and the vice presidency.

During the campaign in 1944, Truman came through Butte and stopped to make a speech. I was not notified of his appearance, although I was at my summer home on Lake McDonald. In that speech he berated the isolationists. I read about it and was ready to issue a blast against Truman when friends of mine talked me out of it.

I was still angry about it after the election and I did not congratulate him on the victory. Shortly after he had taken his seat as Vice President, he dropped into a seat in the Senate next to mine. I told him I didn't like the speech and had no notice of it, and I recalled that I had made speeches in Missouri and praised him when he needed it. He told me that he at first had refused to go into Montana, because the Democratic National Committee had wanted him to talk against me. But he said they had pleaded with him on his way back from Seattle and he finally agreed to make that one stop.

He then said to me: "If you ever see me doing anything wrong, I hope you'll come and tell me."

I always felt that Harry Truman was honest and that he wanted to do the right thing, notwithstanding that I didn't always agree with him.

Not long after our conversation a picture appeared on the front pages showing a beaming Vice President tinkling the piano at the National Press Club with a movie star sitting on top of the piano displaying her lovely legs. I went into the Vice President's room off the Senate floor.

"You told me to tell you whenever I saw you doing something wrong," I said to Truman. "Now don't have your picture taken playing the piano with some girl sitting on the piano. You are going to be President of the United States and the people want someone whom they can look up to; they don't want a professor in a sporting house for President."

Truman laughed heartily and replied, "Don't worry, that won't happen again." He explained that "some of my friends asked me to go there and I didn't think there was to be any publicity."

I then said, "Now that you're Vice President some friends will want to use you, and so remember—you can protect yourself against your enemies but you can't always protect yourself against your friends." He seemed to be very grateful for our talk. He was a sincere friend and I always wanted to help him.

On April 11, 1945, the day before President Roosevelt died, Senator Bennett Champ Clark and Vice President Truman gave a luncheon for Robert E. Hannegan, the new Chairman of the Democratic National Committee, in the office of Leslie Biffle, Secretary of the Senate. There were fourteen or fifteen Democrats present. As the luncheon was breaking up, I went up to Truman and told him I didn't think he ought to attend a dinner we had all been invited to that was being given for the labor delegates from England, Russia, and several other countries. The delegates were on their way to San Francisco to attend the meeting of the group working on the formation of what became the United Nations.

"They're friends of yours and mine," Truman said.

"I am afraid there's a bunch of Communists among them and something might occur that would embarrass you later," I advised. "You're going to be President."

He said he had already accepted and I said, "Tell them you had forgotten you had another engagement." Just then Bob Hannegan came up and I told him what I had said. Hannegan agreed with me.

The next day President Roosevelt died and Truman was

sworn in as President. The day after that Lowell Mason, a friend of Truman's and afterward a member of the Federal Trade Commission, called Matt Connelly at the White House from my office in the Senate Office Building. Matt, who was Truman's appointments secretary, was not there but in a short time he telephoned me. Truman got on the phone, and said he was coming up for lunch at the Secretary of the Senate's office and wanted me to be there. One of my assistants called up Biffle's office and was told they knew nothing of the luncheon. I then called Biffle and told him I knew nothing about it but that the President wanted me there. He said they would be glad to have me.

It was a non-partisan affair. Senators Warren R. Austin of Vermont, Arthur H. Vandenberg of Michigan, Claude D. Pepper of Florida, Barkley—all of them internationally minded—were present. They told Truman what they thought about the international picture. After listening to them, he turned to me and asked what I thought about it. For once I felt it was no time to get into an argument and said I didn't know.

The President then told them that a day and a half previously I had said he was going to be President and he didn't believe it. I told him I thought I had more knowledge of FDR's failing health than some others—which was true.

It was not long afterward that President Truman asked me to come over and see him. He paid me a fine compliment by saying he wanted my advice—which incidentally he never followed on foreign policy. At this meeting in the White House, I told him I wanted to see him make a good President—first because it was so necessary for the country and secondly because I liked him.

I told him he should pick out a Cabinet that owed its allegiance to him—that the present Cabinet owed its allegiance to FDR. "Give me time," he replied. "I'll pick out a Democratic Cabinet but they'll be Truman Democrats." He added that he was going to get rid of Attorney General Francis Biddle for one. I advised Truman during our talk not to try to take on all of FDR's enemies because not all of FDR's friends would stay with him. I pointed out that some of FDR's newspaper enemies hated FDR, but they didn't hate him. He then paid his respects to Robert R. McCormick, publisher of the Chicago *Tribune* and William Randolph Hearst—in his usual colorful four-letter language.

Chapter Eighteen

LIBERAL WITH A NEW LABEL

Long ago I learned not to take political labeling seriously. Because every shade of political tag was hung on me (while I knew I had not changed my basic thinking), the phrases became meaningless. Thus, by the time I was assailed as an "isolationist," I didn't care one way or the other. But I will say now that I think the term was inaccurate or at least misleading if it was meant to describe me as one who felt Uncle Sam should have the very minimum of relations with the rest of the world.

While I have always advocated doing everything possible to stay out of a war in which we were not attacked, I have always believed my country should do everything possible to promote peace and I went abroad as often as possible, at my own expense, to learn conditions.

My journeys took me to Europe and Latin America a number of times, to the Orient twice, and around the world once. On the trip Mrs. Wheeler and I took to Europe in 1923, I got acquainted in Vienna with Adolph Igra, an Austrian-born American representative of an American firm. Igra knew European history better than almost anyone I have known. He introduced me to Arthur Kuffler, a Viennese textile manufacturer. I told Kuffler I could not understand why the Austrians, Germans, French, Italians, Irish, Norwegians, and Russians could get along together in the United States while in Europe they constantly quarreled among themselves.

"It isn't the people, it's the politicians," Kuffler explained. "Whether they're kings or czars or emperors, or whatever they are, for political reasons they appeal to the prejudice of the people in their particular communities, states, or nations. They stir up old hatreds along racial lines against other countries. And that brings on war."

"Do you realize what your people have done to Europe?" Kuffler continued. "We used to have factories in Hungary, Austria, and what is now Czechoslovakia, but today if you want to ship a piece of machinery from Austria or Czechoslovakia over to Hungary, you have to pay tariffs and have all sorts of border difficulties. They have destroyed the economy of Europe—that's what you did at Versailles. In addition, by dividing up Europe you have created more jealousies that can only cause more wars."

I felt at the time that Kuffler was right about the pernicious effects of the Versailles Treaty. It was almost forty years before the western European nations got around to forming the sensible common market, which eliminates the irksome tariff barriers.

Though I had been opposed to getting into the First World War, I admired Woodrow Wilson. Many other young Progressives also would have been glad to support Theodore Roosevelt for President on his Progressive ticket of 1912 if Wilson had not been nominated. But Wilson was looked upon in the West as a true Progressive and we supported him. Like most of my friends in Montana, I was for Wilson's League of Nations before I went to Europe. After talking with a great number of people on my European trip, I became convinced that the League would have to maintain the status quo of a divided central Europe and a wholly unsound economic situation which could only result in a collapse and war.

It was then I came to favor a United States of Europe—which I later found had first been suggested by George Washington. When I returned from Europe in 1923, I gave out a statement that unless such a federation was created there would be another war.

I injected myself into Senate debates on foreign affairs for the first time in 1926. I favored Uncle Sam's participating in peace conferences and arms-limitation agreements but strongly opposed what we then called "dollar diplomacy." A dramatic example of this policy was Calvin Coolidge's decision to send the United States Marines into Nicaragua in late 1926. The Leathernecks landed to protect the forcible overthrow of the U.S.-backed Nicaraguan government—and thus retain control for some New York bankers of that little country's national bank and railroad.

I attacked our Nicaraguan policy as "a war waged privately by President Coolidge in defiance of the Constitution, without the consent of Congress or the approval of the American people."

I introduced a resolution calling on Coolidge to withdraw the Marines and I requested an investigation into the entire field of concessions held by American citizens and corporations abroad. I said these concessions "produce tension which frequently has led to armed intervention and may lead to war." The Senate Foreign Relations Committee rejected the resolution, on the ground that their presence in Nicaragua was necessary to enforce an agreement made by then Secretary of State Henry L. Stimson in the world war that Uncle Sam would be the final arbiter of any dispute arising there.

However, the opposition led by myself and others did bear some fruit. Coolidge sent Stimson to Nicaragua as a special representative and he worked out another agreement which disarmed both sides pending another election to be held the next year, with the United States Marines acting as poll watchers.

The Constitutional provision giving Congress the right to declare war has become almost meaningless today because of the foreign policy moves of Presidents Roosevelt, Truman, Eisenhower, and Kennedy. Sending military missions all over the world, and taking sides in internal controversies is war by whatever name you call it. The President's right to do this has become so much a part of our "one world" philosophy that he does not even have to justify it by saying we are over there to protect American property or citizens.

An election was held in Nicaragua in 1928 and the so-called "progressive" group won. In March 1929, I went to Nicaragua to see for myself how things were working out. I was lavishly entertained by General José María Moncada, the new "liberal" President. On the basis of statements made about the President by our American Ambassador at a dinner in my honor I began to worry about the kind of crowd I had supported.

I was even more worried when Moncada told me blandly he would like the U. S. Marines to stay down there to prevent a coup d'état by the defeated party. I told Moncada that if the Marines were left down there very long there would be a gradual change in the color of the population. The President replied that that might not be such a bad idea.

I was disillusioned with the party leaders in general in Nicaragua. They were quite obviously more concerned with power and jobs than with the welfare of the people. I found that the word "liberal" in Latin America had no similarity to its meaning in the United States. At the same time, my visit made it clear to me that the people of Nicaragua were being exploited by American financial interests who collected their profits and taxes while using the Marines as a club. I came home more than ever unhappy about "dollar diplomacy."

There was no justification to my mind for our interfering in the affairs of another nation. In 1927 I violently disagreed with Senator Jim Reed of Missouri and others who wanted us to go to war with Mexico when its left-wing government expropriated some American oil properties and some property belonging to the Catholic Church. Catholic organizations were supporting a congressional resolution to sever relations with Mexico and I was strongly criticized for my stand by some of my good Catholic friends in Butte and Great Falls. My position was that every country had to work out its church-state relationship in its own way, without outside intervention. If we went to war because some country was persecuting a religious group, I argued, we would be at war with every country in the world sooner or later. I pointed out that we had mistreated our own Indians but we would have resented it if England or any other country had tried to tell us what to do.

In 1927 I became concerned about our policies in the Far East. The question of Philippine independence was being hotly debated in Congress and there was a civil war going on in China, a country which Congress knew little about. The British had dispatched a division of troops and additional naval forces to Shanghai to protect its nationals against further outbreaks of anti-foreign rioting. While U. S. Marines and gunboats were stationed at numerous points in China, American business interests were seeking active intervention on our part.

To learn something about the Orient, I sailed in March 1927 with Mrs. Wheeler and our three oldest children, John, Elizabeth, and Edward, on a trip that was to last four months. We were royally entertained by the Filipinos, who were well aware of my stand in favor of their independence.

We brought back with us from the Philippines a seventeen-year-old boy, Simeon Arboleda, who was working on a wealthy estate. He was anxious to join us as a servant and we picked him up on our return from China. All his worldly possessions were on his back—a silk shirt and duck trousers. Back in the United States, we sent him to public school and ever since he has been our indispensable cook, handyman, and devoted friend. He has one of the finest characters I have ever known.

In Hong Kong, I began to hear some interesting things about the Chinese Kuomintang leader, Generalissimo Chiang Kai-shek. In the United States, Chiang had been portrayed as a Communist but, by March 1927, I found he had broken with the leftist forces and I heard in Hong Kong more and more about his new base of power in south China. Some American business concerns were supporting Chiang by paying their taxes in advance.

With my oldest son, John, I traveled up to Nanking, seat of Chiang's government. Chiang and his foreign minister, C. C.

Wu, assured me they were willing to accept responsibility and make reparations for damage suffered by the Americans in the Nanking disorders of a few months past. In a series I was doing for the North American Newspaper Alliance, I wrote that Chiang "did not seem big enough for the stupendous tasks he had before him."

We sailed on the American troop transport *Henderson* to Tientsin with Major General Smedley D. Butler and were fascinated by that famous Marine veteran's personal stories of international trouble-shooting by the Leathernecks. General Butler took a very materialistic view of American foreign policy and was cynical about its fine phrases and idealism. I could understand this feeling by a man with his experience.

From Tientsin we drove with General Butler to Peking, armed for the journey with $300 in gold, and a gun, just in case we were waylaid by bandits. Our car was the only one on the road all the way to the capital but we ran into no difficulty.

In the course of our visit to Peking, the U.S. minister took me to meet Chang Tso-lin, the wealthy Manchurian war lord who ruled north China. As I wrote in an article, he reminded me of a Western "tin-horn gambler—slick, suave, cunning, and insincere." He appealed for support from the United States government on the ground that he alone could save China from the Bolsheviks. I suggested, by way of reply, that he stop fighting with the Nationalists and spend the time, money, and energy building roads, schools, etc. His reply was: "Who are you to tell us what to do about China—we had a civilization over here when your ancestors were roving the plains of Europe clad only in the skins of wild animals."

After a trip through Japan, we sailed for home. In my series for NANA, I vigorously opposed American military intervention in Shanghai as suggested by American business interests there.

"England's strong-armed policy in the Orient has failed," I wrote. "If the United States follows the advice of some of her pro-British citizens in the Orient, she will also fail. The issue is militarism, graft, and special privilege against national sovereignty and democracy."

I argued that the United States should help the Chinese help themselves to become educated and to raise their standard of living. I pointed out that the Russians worked with them and talked with them. Occidentals only spoke to the Chinese when they wanted something; more usually they cursed them. I predicted that Chiang's "new democratic movement will go on . . ."

"Take your choice," I summed up, "help a Chinese moderate government in China or be forced to take a Bolshevik China."

In 1930, I took another trip to Russia. Seeing the Soviets in action seven years after my first Russian trip was an eye-opener. This time my companions were Senators Alben Barkley and Bronson Cutting. Barkley was the likeable, storytelling Kentuckian who became Truman's Vice President. Cutting was a promising newcomer to the Senate, a handsome, polished young liberal from New Mexico who sprang from a socially prominent New York family. He was tragically killed in an airplane crash in Missouri in 1935.

We accompanied a group which was touring England, France, and Germany as well as the Soviet Union, and we came in contact with the leaders of all those countries.

In the seven years since I had been there, new office buildings and apartment houses had risen in Moscow. But we discovered that the farmers were farming in exactly the same way they had been before—cutting their grain with a sickle and threshing it by pounding it the way they had for hundreds of years. True, we saw some cooperative farms where there was more up-to-date machinery, but nothing comparable in the slightest to what we had in America.

We had lunch with the head of what would be our Department of Commerce. He stressed the Soviets' desire to trade with the United States. He talked about competition and said it would be fifty years before they would be capable of making steel knives and forks enough for the people—the vast majority of whom had never seen such implements.

When we interviewed the heads of the Soviet Foreign Office, they told us they could take over China any time they wanted to. But, they added: "Why should we want to? China would be a liability to us, not an asset, because of the uncounted millions of people and the economic conditions there."

In a town about seventy miles outside Moscow, once an old religious center, there were two magnificent churches and a great cathedral. We persuaded a Russian to take us through the abandoned cathedral. He took us into a section of it made up solely of crypts. Opening up one crypt, he let out a hideous yell. Inside was a mummified man. I asked him if he thought it was a Communist. "*Nyet! Nyet! Nyet!*" he cried, literally shaking in his boots.

Our nights in Russia were less enjoyable for me. I was extremely allergic to bedbugs. In the town where we visited the cathedral, our landlady assured us the bedbugs had been cleaned out of the room only two days before—but asked us how I thought a Russian bedbug would like the taste of an American senator! This is a sample of how informally friendly all the Russians were toward us.

As soon as I climbed into one of the iron cots assigned to us, I found that the bedbugs had returned in force. Cutting had a can of bedbug powder in his grip and I shook it all over my bed. The powder failed to discourage them from biting and when I opened my eyes in the morning literally thousands of bedbugs were marching up the wall. Barkley said it reminded him of Napoleon's retreat from Moscow.

In another city, I was amazed to run into an American who had built the wire mill for the Anaconda Copper Mining Company in Great Falls, Montana. He was an adviser and consultant to the Soviet government. He introduced us to a group of Russian workers, who promptly plied us with questions. During the discussion, I got a chance to ask the interpreter: "Why are you just building heavy machinery—why not have light machinery, so you could furnish shoes and clothes and things that your people need so badly?"

"We're building it for war—for defense," he replied.

When I said nobody wanted to attack Russia, he said they feared attack by "the capitalist nations and the Pope." I pointed out that the Pope had nothing to attack Russia with and I asked why the capitalist nations should want to do so.

"Because this has become an industrial nation," he answered.

When I stressed that my country certainly had no aggressive designs on the Soviet Union, he asked why we had built so many big battleships and why we had attacked Nicaragua and Haiti. In the small towns and small cities, there were no newspapers and the citizens depended for news on the government propaganda emanating from loudspeakers. In these towns, our entourage was usually surrounded by gaping crowds. I was told they had never seen either an American or an automobile before.

In the 1930s I became increasingly concerned about both the totalitarian evils rising in Europe. I first saw the blackshirts marching in Italy in 1923. Back in the United States in 1937, I attacked Hitler and Nazism in a speech in Butte, Montana; again, in a Constitution Day speech before an audience of 20,000 in the Chicago Stadium, I assailed the philosophy of the totalitarians, whether red, brown, or black.

"In Germany," I said in my Chicago speech, "the power was first given to a man well meaning and sympathetic with the people [von Hindenburg] but it was wrested from his hands by a leader who, it would seem, owes allegiance not even to his God."

By June of 1940, as I related in the first chapter, my inside information from Admiral Hooper led me to warn publicly that if Roosevelt were allowed to continue on his present course it would surely involve us in the war. I was immediately assailed on grounds that I was not sufficiently anti-Nazi and was even a questionable Democrat. In a statement issued on June 26, I replied that "unlike some, I was a Democrat before 1933, and I am a Democrat in 1940. I have voted for every appropriation for defense of this country, and have agreed with nearly all of President Roosevelt's reform measures."

I went on to say that "everyone in this nation has been shocked by the aggressor nations in Europe and Asia, and our sympathies are wholeheartedly with those nations that have been attacked. We want to see this nation fully prepared to defend our shores against any nation, but the people of this country are overwhelmingly opposed to our entering into the European conflict."

I also stated that "I am opposed to this administration bringing into key positions in this government two of the most active proponents of intervention"—Henry L. Stimson, the new Secretary of War, and Frank Knox, the new Secretary of the Navy.

My statement continued: "President Roosevelt in his message to Congress on September 21, 1939, in speaking of his attempt to avert war in Europe, said: 'Having thus striven and failed, this government must lose no time or effort to keep this nation from being drawn into the war. Our acts must be guided by a single hardheaded thought—keeping America out of this war!'

"I agree with what the President said in this message to Congress . . ."

I wound up with the hope that both parties at their national conventions would nominate candidates who were not captives of that "little handful of international bankers in New York who seemingly want to get us into the war."

Once the Democratic convention and Roosevelt's re-election in November were out of the way, we non-interventionists were fighting an uphill battle. After the attack on Pearl Harbor, when I said "Let's lick hell out of 'em," I supported the war effort. Like many other senators, I also reserved the right to criticize specific policies in the conduct of the war when I felt such criticism was justified.

Of course, I was denounced in some quarters for exercising my right to free speech but by this time I was used to such reactions. For example, before we were at war officially, I was castigated for having said in the early summer of 1941 that we were sending American boys to Iceland to relieve some 15,000 British soldiers garrisoned there. As a result of the furor, Roosevelt notified Congress of the troop movement but made it appear to be a matter of defense for the Western Hemisphere!

Stimson some time afterward said in all candor that this was considered "a more palatable argument to the people." It also came out later that immediately after the troop movement to Iceland Admiral Harold R. Stark, chief of naval operations, wrote in a letter to Captain (later Admiral) Charles M. Cooke

Jr.: "The Iceland situation may produce an incident . . . whether or not we will get such an incident I do not know. Only Hitler can answer."

Since such supporting evidence was unknown to the public at the time, it was easy for some persons to condemn me for intimating that the President was consciously flirting with hostilities.

Throughout the war, I felt that our biggest mistake was in helping to build up one totalitarian menace—communism—in order to conquer the other, Nazism. I had said that if Hitler and Stalin fought it out, one would end in his grave, the other in the hospital, and the United States and the world would be rid of two menacing tyrants. The passage of the lend-lease bill in March 1941 was followed swiftly by aid to the Soviet Union on a scale probably not dreamed of even by Soviet dictator Joseph Stalin.

While we non-interventionists realized that our cause was probably a lost one, I did not think this was any reason to keep quiet about what I felt was the shape of things to come. In 1940, I said at one point: "The United States will undoubtedly enter the war against Germany and win. But mark my word, within ten years we will be asking Germany to assist the West in controlling Russia."

In no sense do I wish to present myself as a rare prophet. All one had to do was to take the openly announced program of the Communist International at face value. It boasted that its intention was to subjugate the world. Many, many others, including specialists in history, read the signs as I did and spoke out. To cite just one, Professor Nicholas J. Spykman of Yale warned in a book shortly before Pearl Harbor: "We must not annihilate either Germany or Japan, lest we leave Europe or the Far East open to domination by Russia."

The Roosevelt policy foolishly closed its eyes to this ancient balance-of-power concept, as well as to the stated aims of Russian communism. An overconfident President, aided by a Russophile agent-in-charge, Harry Hopkins, lavished supplies and equipment on Stalin and followed his wishes in the strategy of invading Europe through France rather than the Balkans.

(Hopkins' influence can hardly be overestimated. By playing up to Stalin and Churchill and by making trips to the Soviet Union and England, he became the eyes and ears of the President and thus the most important person around him. He lived right in the White House and even boasted to one of FDR's advisers that every evening he was the last man to see the lonely President—in other words, in a position to undo what others had done.)

In his postwar writings, the wise and far-seeing Churchill reveals how astonished he was that FDR was eager to get into the war—and at the same time was blind to Stalin's plans for empire.

Like many of my colleagues, I was sickened and frustrated during the war by the fawning of some prominent Americans on the Russians, who overnight had become advocates of peace and friendship. Today, liberals of all shades vie with one another to denounce the Kremlin as a colossal threat to world peace. But some of us can share the attitude of the New York *Daily News* when it noted in a postwar editorial: "Begging nobody's pardon, this newspaper never did get suckered into believing that Bloody Joe was fighting for anything but eventual Communist domination of the world."

During World War II, the practice of pasting on political labels became ridiculous. To the "liberals," it didn't matter how reactionary you were on domestic issues. If you were an "interventionist," that is, pro-war, you were automatically welcomed with open arms as a "liberal." And if you were anti-interventionist, you were *ipso facto* considered a reactionary, and probably pro-Hitler or a Nazi or Fascist as well.

Some of the most conservative senators embraced FDR's policies—and immediately were called liberals. Then there was Wendell Willkie, the Wall Street private power advocate, who had fought against the Utility Holding Company Act of 1935; he joined Roosevelt when he couldn't lick him, and was hailed for his "liberal" views. On the other hand, when lifelong progressives like myself opposed intervention, as we always had previously, we were denounced for having deserted liberalism. It was the great liberals like Norris, La Follette, and Congresswoman Jeannette Rankin of Montana, to mention only a few, who fought against our involvement in the First World War. La Follette at the time was hung in effigy in his own state. But on his death his state placed his statue in the Hall of Fame at the Capitol.

Never before had the question of whether one was a liberal or conservative turned on his view of foreign policy.

FDR and Secretary of War Stimson denounced me many times in extreme language for criticizing their war policies. Yet, once again, my break with the President was not irreconcilable. We had a long conversation on May 16, 1944. Congress planned to celebrate the centennial of Samuel F. B. Morse's invention of the telegraph and, as chairman of the Senate Interstate Commerce Committee, I called at the White House to invite the President to make the anniversary address.

Roosevelt said he had known Morse but that he didn't want to make a joint address to Congress soon. He seemed to want to chat with me about other matters and so I decided to bring up some things that were on my mind.

In the course of our disjointed conversation, I asked, "How are you going to keep Europe from going Communist?" FDR replied that he didn't think Stalin wanted to take over Europe. I asked if it had ever occurred to him that "he doesn't need to 'take it over'—it will fall into his hands because of the economic chaos and near starvation?"

"Burt," he said with a smile, by way of reply, "you'd like Stalin."

"Do you trust him?" I asked.

FDR hesitated a moment and then said, "Up to this time, yes."

"Let me tell you, Mr. President," I replied earnestly, "when I was a young man in a fight with the Anaconda Company in Montana I defended the American Federation of Labor, the railroad brotherhoods, the Socialists, and the IWW's—because every time they got into a mess they came to me. Now I think I know the Communists. They want to channel your mind and unless they can do so, one hundred per cent, they'll cut your heart out!"

"Well, Burt," he replied casually, "as long as we *know* them."

He didn't know them. But he was not alone in this as many other experienced politicians and businessmen agreed with him at the time.

I was there for about forty-five minutes, far longer than the time ordinarily allotted a presidential caller. During the first fifteen minutes Roosevelt's mind seemed perfectly clear but during the last fifteen minutes he seemed very tired and his mind drifted from subject to subject.

During the conversation I told FDR that feeling in the United States was better toward Russia than it had ever been since the Communist revolution. But, I added that "if they keep part of Finland and part of Poland and the Baltic and Balkan states, the public sentiment in this country will change very rapidly.

"Why don't you tell those Germans what you want?" I asked. "Tell them to get rid of Hitler and all his gang and set up a United States of Europe?"

I recalled that when I came back from Europe in 1923 I had advocated a United States of Europe to avoid another war and that I had been naïve enough to think it was an original idea.

I mentioned to the President the idea of negotiating with the anti-Hitler Germans because I was worried about the casualties in an invasion of Nazi-held France.

"Jimmy Byrnes has said that if we cross the Channel we'll lose half a million men," I remarked, of the man who was then War Mobilizer.

"Jim hasn't any right to say that," Roosevelt answered.

"Well," I continued, "why don't you tell the Germans what you want before you cross the Channel. They undoubtedly won't accept it, but you'll have placed yourself in a much stronger position with the people of the world for having tried."

I told him I felt that Woodrow Wilson, by offering his Fourteen Points to the Germans in the First World War, had made a very good impression on world opinion.

At this point, the President astounded me by remarking casually: "We're going to cross the Channel on June 5, depending upon the weather." This was of course the most secret date in the world at the time. I was disturbed he had told me because I assumed it meant he had told others.

During the latter part of our talk, Roosevelt rambled on about a Hanseatic state and other extraneous ideas in a way that convinced me his mind was wandering. His appointments secretary, Marvin McIntyre, came in twice to remind him that the Chinese Ambassador was waiting. Another time, McIntyre popped in to announce that "the Governor of Mississippi is here."

Each time, FDR would wave him away with, "Three minutes more! Three minutes more!" Several times I tried to excuse myself.

I left the White House worried most about the fact that the President had told me the date for D-Day. (Weather was to force postponement of the invasion for twenty-four hours so D-Day actually turned out to be June 6, 1944.) I decided not to breathe the secret even to my wife, for I was well aware that if it leaked my enemies would blame me and not the President. While I was flattered at his faith in my integrity, implied by the disclosure, I still couldn't get over the fact that during wartime Roosevelt had revealed a date which was of crucial importance to the Germans.

My forty-five-minute meeting with FDR gave me great concern about his alarming physical decline. To me he seemed a very sick man who was in no condition to carry on as President. Some of his friends indicated to me that they were equally worried.

In January 1945, when Roosevelt returned from the Yalta conference and addressed a joint session of Congress, his failing health could no longer be kept secret from Congress. He was a proud man and preferred to walk—with the aid of canes and leg braces. This time he walked into the House chamber on the arm of his son, Jimmy, after being wheeled to the entrance in a chair. Then, for the first time, he sat in a chair in the well of the House instead of standing at the rostrum in front of the Vice President and Speaker. When he left the House after the speech in a wheel chair, he looked like he was in a state of collapse.

The President's appearance deeply shocked his friends and critics alike and was the subject of much private discussion among the senators. Everyone realized that the end could not be far off. To me it was a tragedy indeed that a person in this critical condition had attempted to cope with a creature like Stalin at Yalta.

After Truman was inaugurated as President, James V. Forrestal, then Secretary of the Navy, wrote me that it would be helpful to the armed forces if the Senate Interstate Commerce Committee made an on-the-spot study of international communications problems in Europe. Four members of the committee made the trip: Republicans Homer E. Capehart of Indiana and Albert W. Hawkes of New Jersey; Democrat Ernest W. McFarland of Arizona, later the Senate majority leader; and myself.

We went first to England, where Prime Minister Winston Churchill invited us to meet him at No. 10 Downing Street. Previously, I had had one introduction to Churchill—at a reception in the Capitol after he addressed a joint session of Congress in 1941. At the risk of sounding immodest, I will relate how he flattered me at that time.

Our meeting was described as follows in a column by Drew Pearson and Robert S. Allen, who were not exactly admirers of mine:

". . . when Wheeler was presented, Churchill stopped him, shook his hand warmly, and said, 'This is a genuine pleasure to me, sir. I've long wanted to meet you. This is one of the pleasantest moments of this very happy occasion.'

"Smiling broadly, Wheeler thanked Churchill cordially and moved on. Later, during the congressional luncheon at which Wheeler was not present, the Prime Minister again referred to his delight in meeting the Montana senator.

"'I liked him,' Churchill said. 'He is a fighting man. I have been in 14 political fights, won eight and lost six. Once I was beaten three times in 18 months. I respect and admire fighting men even if they are against me. In these troubled times we should welcome good fighters, regardless of the differences of the past.'"

Charley McNary, the Senate Republican leader who attended the luncheon, later told me Churchill had brought up my name substantially as Pearson and Allen had reported it. I had not been invited to attend this luncheon some of the senators gave Churchill, apparently for fear I might sound an inharmonious note.

At that time nobody wanted to hurt the rugged old British leader's feelings. For example, the night before Churchill was to address the joint session, Bernard Baruch telephoned me to put in a plug for him.

"I've never been a warmonger and I haven't stood too well at the White House," he told me, "but the Prime Minister is a great fellow and a good friend of mine."

Although Mrs. Wheeler and I had been guests of Baruch at his North Carolina estate and I knew him well, he had never telephoned me before. I was puzzled about this call until I learned that there was some nervousness that the isolationist senators might boycott the chamber when he addressed the joint session. None of us had any thought of doing that.

I realize that in praising me Churchill may have simply been trying to line up all the senatorial help he could get for his country. But I liked and admired him as a fighter and especially because he was not fooled for one minute about what the Communists were up to. When we sat down with him on our stop in London in 1945, I asked him how he liked Stalin. Pausing to puff on his cigar, he replied: "When I'm with him, I like him." I then asked how he could keep Europe from going Communist. He puffed hard a couple of times and replied thoughtfully, "Mr. Senator, that is a very serious question."

We next met the members of Churchill's cabinet. Several came around the table to shake hands with me, but some pointedly did not. Slightly miffed, I left the other senators and went outside to the car. Churchill came out as we were leaving and said he understood we were going to Germany, Italy, Greece, and Egypt. He said he hoped we would come back through London and report on what we found.

The following day, the newspaper publisher, Lord Beaverbrook, came to my suite at the Dorchester Hotel while Senator

Hawkes was there. Beaverbrook said "the PM"—meaning the Prime Minister—"had said some nice things about me to the cabinet members," and then added: "You better look out—he'll take you over!" I told Beaverbrook he need not worry about that.

As for being "taken over," it seemed to me that whereas FDR thought he was using Churchill—and he did to some extent because he was in a position of power—he never for one minute fooled Churchill, and Churchill, after all, got what he wanted: United States intervention in the war.

From England, we went to France, Germany, Italy, and Greece. In Greece I said I wanted to go to Malta because I'd never been there. We sent word ahead, but the Malta authorities replied they didn't have any accommodations fit for senators. I said at the time I had campaigned in Montana many years before and put up with anything.

When we got there, the governor general of Malta put us up at his palace. We had heard that the island was one of the most bombed places in the world but we found that only in the port had there been any serious bombing.

While we stopped in Malta, the daughter of the governor general remarked to Senator Hawkes that "Senator Wheeler is anti-British."

"No," Hawkes told her, "he's not anti-British, he's just pro-American."

Paul Porter, then chairman of the Federal Communications Commission, accompanied us on the trip. In Paris and in Rome, he suggested that we ought to meet the heads of the Communist Party in those countries. I told Porter we would talk to them if they wanted to come and see us but that I had no intention of looking them up.

The four of us senators were greatly concerned about the spread of Communist forces in Europe. At Rheims, in a conversation with General Dwight D. Eisenhower, then Supreme Allied Commander, we voiced that concern, and warned of the danger of getting too intimately involved with the reds.

Eisenhower surprised us by commenting, "Well, gentlemen, there are Communists and there are Communists. For instance,

I have a very dear friendship with General Zhukov"—Marshal Georgi Zhukov, the Soviet commander—"and I would trust him as far as I would trust any friend in America or elsewhere."

"But, General, he *is* a Communist, isn't he?" I asked.

Eisenhower hesitated for a few seconds and then said to us, "Yes, he is, but what I said goes anyway."

Although Senator Hawkes has since confirmed the accuracy of what was said in this conversation (which he had taken the trouble to record in a memo for his files), I do not for one moment want to leave an impression from this chat that Ike was pro-Communist or pro-Russian. He had come in contact with Zhukov near the end of the war, they had become friends as well as brothers-in-arms, and I am sure Eisenhower came to admire him. As Eisenhower said in a television interview in 1962, Zhukov was too independent-minded for the Communists and eventually was demoted into obscurity.

We flew from SHAPE headquarters with General Eisenhower to inspect a camp where our boys who had been German prisoners of war were being maintained before being sent home. There had been complaints about the food being served there. Flying back to SHAPE in Ike's private plane, I had become airsick and so went immediately to the unoccupied quarters of Lieutenant General Walter Bedell ("Beedle") Smith and lay down on his couch.

Smith, who was Ike's Chief of Staff (and later his Undersecretary of State), soon turned up and I had a chat with him. When I asked him how strong the Russians were, he said: "They haven't anything except what we've given them. We could go through them like a dose of salts."

I heard substantially the same thing from other American generals in Germany. At Augsburg, Lieutenant General Alexander M. Patch, who had commanded the U. S. Seventh Army, was so frank that he finally told us: "If you tell"—back in the states—"what I've told you, they could court-martial me."

Like other generals, Patch was frustrated by the fact that his forces had been inexplicably ordered not to cross the Rhine and continue on to Berlin. He said SHAPE had taken two divisions away from him at the crucial time—before the Battle of the Bulge—and "turned me around the other way." Patch said the Germans knew what was being done and couldn't understand why we didn't go right through to the capital.

Patch now realized that we had deliberately held back in order to allow the Soviet Army to get to Berlin. His anger obviously has proved justifiable. There is hardly need to recall the many serious international crises caused afterward by the joint occupation of that city.

Incidentally, Patch also expressed himself as being disgusted with the lack of fighting spirit of the French.

As soon as our subcommittee returned to Washington, we called on President Truman. He was due to leave the next day for the important Potsdam conference with Stalin and we were eager to report on the conditions we had found in Europe.

"Mr. President," I told him, speaking for the four of us, "you'd better stand up to Russia."

Truman replied that he wasn't afraid of Russia, that he was more afraid of England and France. I was shocked. I told him to get out his little memorandum book and write this down: "You'd better stand up to Russia."

When the President returned from Potsdam, where he had sat across the bargaining table from Stalin, I had another talk with him. His feeling was that Stalin was "all right," that the problem for us was the Politboro. There was an echo of this later when Truman, on a trip through the Far West, astounded virtually everyone by off-handedly referring to the Russian dictator as "good old Joe."

This is not intended to try to embarrass Eisenhower or Truman. Both are honest, patriotic men. But we are all human beings and as such we sometimes misjudge people. Truman soon became well aware of the imperialist aims of Russian Communism and he reacted by getting Congress to put through some bold anti-Communist programs, first the Greek-Turkish aid bill and then the Marshall Plan. As President, Ike too moved to checkmate Communist advances.

I have cited these firsthand experiences merely to underline how skillfully the Communists were able to sell themselves as peace-lovers to intelligent Americans before the red leaders began to show their hand boldly. And it was not only Roosevelt, Truman, and Eisenhower who trusted the Communists during World War II but a great many other influential Americans as well.

I have been called an isolationist because I opposed getting into World War I and World War II and because I voiced skepticism of Russia's aims and that the United Nations or foreign aid would solve all international problems. If such positions warrant the badge of isolationist, I wear it proudly. I still believe America would have been better off by remaining out of the two world-wide holocausts. We went to war twice to save democracy. At the end of both wars there was less democracy in the world, millions of Americans were killed or wounded, the peace "settlements" created far more serious problems for the United States and the world than had existed before, and our national debt was skyrocketing.

No one will gainsay that the Communist menace we face today is the most critical in our history. Our aid to Russia during and after the war and our commitments to her at Teheran, Yalta, and Potsdam are responsible for the postwar challenge to us. Our moral, economic, and political influence in the world has never been less in this century. We try to "buy" with foreign aid the friendship of nations we seek as allies, and like all friendships that are bought they are ephemeral. I think most of the money we spend in the vain pursuit of friends is wasted. To a high degree it goes into the pockets of the dictators, princes, ruling families, or generals that control the countries we seek to aid. The plain people never see it and never benefit from our gifts of millions of dollars. We continue to pay excessive taxes and to lose our national supply of gold to line the pockets of corrupt foreign officials. I abhor this as much as I abhorred the corruption of Harry M. Daugherty and the "Ohio Gang." I would rather see Uncle Sam rely less on dollars that often corrupt, and more on his moral influence that uplifts.

Just as Winston Churchill's first concern was for England and Stalin's first concern was for Russia, so I have no regrets or apologies to make for placing the welfare of America ahead of that of any other country. This does not mean that I think we should crawl into our shell like a turtle and ignore what is going on in the rest of the world. There is no easy panacea. The "preventive war" urged by the "radical right" recommends itself to me even less than intervention in prior wars. In the conduct of our foreign relations in the future, I would urge that it should be a "must" to consider first and foremost the effect of every proposal on the United States and its people. We must be realistic in the conduct of our foreign affairs, as all other major powers are. Intervention in foreign wars, civil or otherwise, is fraught with grave danger. It should not be undertaken unless a serious threat to the security of our country is involved. Similarly, the maintenance of U.S. military forces in foreign countries is a serious mistake in most instances.

While we may not be able to extricate ourselves immediately from our heavy military and financial global commitments, we should make a beginning at once, if we are to avoid an atomic or economic catastrophe.

Also I think the Congress and the people should be kept better informed on the activities of the President and the Department of State in the field of foreign affairs. And the guiding light of our policy should be, "What's best for America?"

Chapter Nineteen

DEFEAT AND RENAISSANCE

One warm morning in early June of 1946 I arrived in the little village of Fairview, Montana, to deliver the major kick-off speech of my campaign to be renominated in the Democratic primary. Fairview, which is located in the far eastern part of the state, was celebrating the installation of a new electrical cooperative. As a long-time champion of public power, I had been invited to make the dedicatory address.

Several thousand farmers and their wives were on hand early to inspect the exhibits and enjoy the picnic spirit of the occasion. At noon, I started circulating among them. I shook hands and chatted briefly with several hundred persons in the course of about two hours. Then Edward Cooper, a campaign aide who had accompanied me from Washington, suggested I take a nap in order to be fresh for my speech late in the afternoon. We repaired to a friend's home where I could lie down.

When I stretched out, Cooper drew the blinds and began to leave the room, but I asked him to sit down for a minute.

"Ed," I said, "we've got a tough fight on our hands."

Cooper scoffed. He asked what in the world I was talking about.

"We're in deep trouble," I went on. "The worst I've ever had in a campaign."

Perhaps to conceal his own apprehension, Cooper insisted that things were "going well."

"I know better," I told him quietly. "I've been around a lot longer than you have."

I explained that during the noon period I realized that something was wrong. The old outgoing enthusiasm the people had always demonstrated was missing. Those who took my hand had been politely pleasant but that was all. I had absolute confidence in my sixth sense which detects that shade of warmth which makes all the difference to a candidate. In a few hours of talking to people in Butte, I could gauge slight shifts in voter sentiment and predict the outcome of an election within a very few thousand votes, even when I was not involved in the race myself. Now there was no reason my political antenna shouldn't work just as accurately in agricultural eastern Montana, where I had always run well.

After delivering my speech in Fairview, I drove westward with Cooper, pausing in small towns along the way to speak from the stump. Within twenty-four hours Cooper too was picking up some of the danger signals. With the primary facing us on July 16—little more than five weeks off—we buckled down to plans for making the belated campaign a whirlwind effort.

The situation was even worse when we got to Butte, my home town and traditional stronghold. The wives of copper miners who had always volunteered to help out in my campaigns—by tacking up signs and doing other chores—now asked Cooper how much they would be paid for their work!

I felt discouraged but far from licked. After all, I had been elected to the Senate four times, the last two times by record-breaking majorities which carried every city and county in the state.

But a primary presents special problems. A Democratic primary in a state with a population as small as Montana's is usually dominated by the number of voters shepherded to the polls by the labor unions and the Farmers Union. These organizations had worked hard for me in the past, but now their leadership was opposing me in favor of their hand-picked candidate, Leif Erickson, a Sidney, Montana, lawyer and a former member of the state Supreme Court who had been defeated as a candidate for governor in 1944.

Fighting my renomination was not only the Farmers Union but the Mine, Mill and Smelter Union which was now Communist-controlled (as congressional committees later revealed) and some of the Montana locals of the railroad brotherhoods, which had previously been my most loyal supporters. I had had trouble with Alvanly Whitney, national president of the Railway Trainmen, because I had blocked his choice for an appointment to the Railway Mediation Board. I told him I opposed his nominee because I felt the man would be a partisan for the brotherhoods; I had helped pass the legislation which set up the board and was anxious to have impartial members appointed to it. Whitney made no secret of the fact that he was bitter about this.

But aside from Whitney, why had the labor leaders turned against me? It was easy to see why the Communists did. They had hailed me when I had opposed our intervention in the war —up to the time Hitler attacked Russia. Then, according to the upside down doctrines of Stalin, it became a "people's war." Bill Mason, a leader of the Mine, Mill and Smelter Union, had wired me from Butte to change my views about the war. I replied that I was just as much opposed to our getting into it after the attack on the Soviet Union as I was before.

Since then, I had warned that while Russia was fighting on our side at the moment it would never abandon the Stalin-Lenin aims for world domination. The stand I took on the United Nations in 1945 had further alienated me from the Communists, fellow travelers, and even many well-meaning liberals. I had voted for the UN charter because a lot of internationalists had said the reason the League of Nations was unsuccessful was because the United States had not joined. I didn't want them to have the same alibi about the UN. So I voted for it but made a Senate speech in which I warned that the UN wouldn't work because Russia wouldn't permit it to work. I believe that Russia's actions in the UN have vindicated my prediction. The UN has practically become a debating society. Most important international disputes are handled by the major powers at meetings outside the UN, by regional groups such as the Organization of American States, conferences called by interested nations to resolve specific problems through traditional diplomatic channels. My stand on the UN was unpopular at the time. Most people saw the UN as the last hope of the world to prevent another terrible war and many people still had very friendly feelings toward Communist Russia.

A barber in Butte—an old-country Irish-Catholic, of all people—gave me a friendly tip. He said if I would get up at just one meeting and say something nice about Russia it would help my campaign. Of course, I couldn't do that.

The noisy liberals and the Montana labor leaders—most of whom were certainly not Communists—harbored a grudge against me not only because of what I said about the UN and Russia but also because I had broken with Roosevelt twice on major issues. True, both breaks had come before the 1940 election, in which I was re-elected overwhelmingly. But after we were in the war, and the people rallied around their President, my independence was construed by some as disloyalty.

In time of war, as I had discovered in 1916–18, the feelings of the citizens are whipped to such a pitch that they are ready to believe almost anything. The image of the isolationist in World War II was distorted into something sinister. For example, I found that many members of the Farmers Union believed a charge on the radio that we non-interventionist senators had voted against the fortification of Guam in the late 1930s. I explained that we never had a chance to vote on the issue because the President and the State Department were against the fortification of Guam and so it had never come up in the Senate. Although this was a simple, indisputable fact, it is hard to counteract the effects of a big lie once it has been widely planted.

I had been painted as a symbol of isolationism and as such

I was the target nationally. A Senate committee which investigated the 1946 Montana primary found that substantial funds were funneled into the state for Erickson from well-heeled internationalists in New York and Hollywood. Even my Democratic colleague, the late Senator Murray, worked with "interventionists" in the Montana primary. He collected $2000 from Albert Lasker, the advertising magnate, for Erickson. Bernard Baruch told me that someone from the Murray group solicited an anti-Wheeler contribution from him, on the ground that I was anti-Semitic. Baruch said he told the emissary that this charge was false. That was the kind of campaign I was up against.

Billboards and radio time advertising Erickson and castigating Wheeler saturated the state. My own campaign did not lack contributions—in fact, I had more than I ever had before—but obviously much more was being spent for Erickson—who needed an expensive buildup because he was less well known.

Even before the campaign began, I had not been overconfident. Anyone who has been a senator for twenty-four years would be a fool to take renomination and re-election for granted. The longer one stays in the Senate the more enemies one makes. If the senator acquires a national reputation, the risks become even greater. Many constituents assume the publicized senator has become more preoccupied with national or international affairs, to the detriment of his state.

In 1946 my opposition successfully planted the big lie that my break with Roosevelt made it impossible for me to win any favors for Montana. When I moved Montana projects along in the Senate, many people were ready to believe that some other legislator deserved the credit for it.

Take the case of Hungry Horse Dam. Ever since I had entered the Senate, I had urged construction of a dam on the south fork of the Flathead River, which flows into the Columbia. The project was opposed by the Montana Power Company and for two decades it got nowhere. But in 1946 it got through the House, after I and others had testified for it there, and I was determined to get it through the Senate.

Early in the year, Senator Carl Hayden, a highly influential senior member of the Appropriations Committee, advised me that the bill's future was dim because all the Republicans and some of the southern Democrats on the committee were against it. I asked which Republicans, and he named Senators Styles Bridges and Wayland Brooks. Well, ever since the Court fight, I felt I had as many friends among the Republicans as among the Democrats. I went to Brooks and he told me to see Bridges, the ranking Republican on the committee.

By working hard behind closed doors, Senator Bridges had become one of the most effective men in the Senate. Many of his fellow Republicans felt they were too busy to sit through the "marking-up" (the actual voting of a bill in committee, section by section) of an appropriations bill. They gave Bridges their proxies and he used them shrewdly. When he had first come to the Senate in 1937, he was continually on his feet, popping off. I gave him this advice: "You can kill yourself off quicker by talking too much than in any other way." Whether or not it was because of this tip, Bridges soon concentrated his time and energy behind-the-scenes, where most of the real work of the Senate is done. Bridges and I became good friends; also, the fact that I had relatives in his home state of New Hampshire didn't hurt our relationship.

When I approached Bridges on the Hungry Horse project, I said simply, "Styles, I've *got* to have it."

"What is the minimum you need?" he asked. I mentioned the sum and he said, "Well, I'll do it for you but I won't do it for that colleague of yours." (The colleague he meant, of course, was Senator Murray.)

The next time the committee met it voted the appropriation I requested for the dam and the funds in time were voted by Congress. Nonetheless, the credit for the project somehow accrued to Murray.

The hardest obstacle for me to cope with was the feeling by rank and file union members that when I won friends among the conservatives in bucking Roosevelt I also changed my political philosophy. Cooper, who had worked in the mines of Butte as a young man, was appalled to hear his old buddies in the mines in 1946 telling him I was no longer fighting for them. Most damning to my cause was the fact that I was being given a break for the first time in the pages of the Montana *Standard,* the paper which dominates the Butte area and is owned by the Anaconda Copper Mining Company. Every politician needs newspaper space, but in this case it was embarrassing. When I was running for governor back in 1920 against Company-picked candidates, I had quipped that if my photograph ever appeared in a Company-owned newspaper I would search my pockets to see if I had picked them overnight.

After I filed for the 1946 primary, the *Standard* not only ran my picture but carried a front-page story lauding me for my service on some of the "most important Senate committees" and for my "vigorous sponsorship of measures for the welfare of Montanans and Americans from every other state."

Whether the Company was trying to help or hurt me by this sudden attention is still unclear; it did not endorse a candidate in the senatorial primary. But this publicity was used to full advantage by the Erickson forces to try to bolster the charge that I had become a "Company man"—the worst canard that could be circulated among the workingmen of Butte, Anaconda, and Great Falls.

For decades I had been anathema to the Company because I had refused to take orders as a state legislator and afterward had acted contrary to their concept of a conservative. In 1946, however, they obviously would have preferred me to a left-winger—Erickson. At the same time, it must have been apparent to the Company that in the fall election I would stand a much better chance than a left-winger of whipping Zales N. Ecton, a rancher who was their hand-picked Republican candidate. Several Republicans told me that "the word has gone out to nominate Erickson and elect Ecton." But I had no evidence that the Company was working actively to defeat me in the primary.

While an issue was made of my "disloyalty" to the President, there was no attempt to make an issue of the fact that I had always been independent of party discipline. Party loyalty doesn't mean very much in the Western states. It meant something to the first settlers of Montana because many of them were stanch Democrats from Virginia and Missouri. But with the influx of homesteaders from the Midwest, the emergence of the Non-Partisan League, and the depressions in the farm areas, the Montana farmers came to believe that both parties were dominated by the same groups.

I made a number of mistakes in the 1946 primary. Instead of tending to legislation in the Senate, I should have gone out to Montana several times early in the year to campaign. I had heard the first disquieting notes sounded in 1945. Friends wrote to report that they had seen people in the post offices throwing to the floor speeches I had mailed to Montana on lend-lease and other controversial issues. They were angry at me for speaking out against the Roosevelt Administration in wartime.

Whether to go back home and campaign early or stay on the job in Washington always poses a dilemma for a senator in an election year. If you go home, you are subject to criticism for neglecting your senatorial duties. If you tend to your knitting in the Senate, you may be criticized for not showing yourself to your constituents and meeting the charges of your opponent. My decision was to remain in Washington. It was a year of many bitter fights over postwar legislation and there was plenty for me to do as chairman of Interstate Commerce and as a senior member of the Agriculture, Judiciary, and Interior committees. I was very much interested in amending the bill to extend the OPA; the Montana stockmen, meat packers, and others were fiercely opposed to some of its provisions. There was also a railroad retirement bill which I was pushing in Interstate Commerce.

Some of my friends urged me to forget about lawmaking and go home and campaign. When I finally did go to Montana, I spent too much of my time stumping sparsely populated eastern Montana and too little time in densely populated Butte, Great Falls, and Anaconda. But I had made those dates in eastern Montana early—when I was being assured by many persons back home that "everything's all right."

I am making no complaints about the quantity or quality of the work by my diligent campaign staff headed by the late

Bailey Stortz. They were loyal workers—perhaps *too* loyal to believe the trouble that was brewing.

President Truman wrote a letter of endorsement, and that was a help. Normally a President stays out of a primary fight in his own party, but Truman is a man of intense loyalty and he not only came out for me but defended my labor record—which for the first time in my career was questioned.

I felt right up to the end that the race would be close and could go either way. Non-Montanans were laboring feverishly and expensively to beat me. The left-wing Independent Citizens Committee for the Arts, Sciences, and Professions had Jimmy Roosevelt make a radio speech from Southern California that was broadcast across Montana. He insisted he knew his dead father wanted me defeated.

Not long before primary day, a book was thrown into the offensive against me. Even by the low standards of campaign books, this was an incredible volume. The title was: *The Plot Against America; Senator Wheeler and the Forces Behind Him.* The author was David George Kin, alias Plotkin, a New Yorker. This 394-page, hard-cover diatribe was published in Missoula, Montana, by John E. Kennedy, a former secretary of former Congressman Jerry O'Connell, the left-wing Montana Democrat who had contributed to the Communist *New Masses.* Who coughed up the funds to underwrite this project is anybody's guess; it could have come from a number of sources which were furnishing anti-Wheeler money for the primary.

Two samples suffice to indicate its style and political outlook. The preface said: "The workers and farmers and the middle-class of America must rally round Russia, for the defense of America and the preservation of our democratic way of life, which our fascists in Washington are about to choke to death through an all-out atomic war against the Soviet Union." Here is another Plotkin sentence: "Truman and Wheeler see eye to eye—they are leading the American retreat from Reason, into the safe, ventilated hell of Nazi-Fascism."

Senator Edwin C. Johnson of Colorado, a member of the committee which investigated this campaign, said both the author and publisher should be "publicly horsewhipped." The chief counsel of the committee, Robert E. Barker, called the book "a mixture of smear, of Marxism, communism, and sex." The book was so laughably trashy I doubt if it could have done me any harm. In any event, it was introduced too late in the campaign for us to counteract it.

On the eve of the primary, the gamblers in Butte were giving 3–1 odds against Erickson winning. On the basis of form displayed over the preceding twenty-four years, they simply could not believe that Wheeler could be beaten in Montana. I was afraid my campaign staff felt the same way. Stortz gave out a statement that the next day's balloting would be "one of the closest in the senator's career"—I would win by only 15,000 votes!

Erickson took an early lead and held it. I swept small towns of eastern Montana but for the first time in my life I lost my home town of Butte. Erickson carried the state by 6000 votes out of some 92,000 cast.

People have asked if this was the biggest blow of my life. It was not. The only time I was on the ropes—temporarily—was when I was indicted in 1924 after my investigation of Attorney General Harry M. Daugherty. This was because, as I mentioned earlier, I had never before been accused of breaking the law and while I was entirely innocent of the "conflict-of-interest" charge I could not be certain I could survive a frame-up arranged by the powerful United States Department of Justice.

Earlier, I had had a number of political disappointments, but all of them had turned out to be blessings in disguise. Each setback led to another step forward in my career. If I had been elected Attorney General of the state of Montana in 1911, I would not have been appointed United States District Attorney by Senator Walsh in 1913 and involved in attention-winning cases for five years. If I had not resigned as District Attorney in 1918 to avoid hampering Walsh's re-election, I would not have delivered an angry speech before the Non-Partisan League and gained invaluable political experience by becoming the League's candidate for governor in 1920. If I had not lost the gubernatorial race, I would have become governor just in time for the 1920 panic—which would have finished me politically. This chain of events made me the logical Democratic candidate for the Senate in 1922. The defeat of the La Follette-Wheeler Independent Progressive ticket in 1924 helped establish me as a national political figure in 1924.

In 1929 I was also shaken when I lost rather heavily in the stock market crash. This put me in debt at a time when senators earned only $7500 a year, and at a time when I was paying for the education of our six children. We faced years of paying off the debt by living at a reduced standard of living. Mrs. Wheeler was quite worried about the future but I assured her that, come what may politically and financially, "I'll earn you a living as Senator, practicing law, or as a railroad section hand."

But I hate to lose and, in July 1946, I was not happy about losing or of the tactics used by the anti-Wheeler forces to defeat me. Still, I certainly did not see this as the end of my world and I was not bitter toward the people of Montana. When George Norris was at last defeated in the 1942 election in Nebraska, he complained that the voters were "ungrateful" after his lifetime of service and had repudiated his great fight for progressive causes. I didn't feel that way. It always has seemed to me that the person who is elected to public office owes an obligation to his constituents, rather than vice versa. I made it clear to the voters that it was their privilege to kick me out of office if they believed I was doing a poor job. When I received a letter complaining about a vote I had cast or a statement I had made, I never tried to placate the complainer. I would reply by telling the writer to "go ahead and elect someone else if you feel he can represent you better."

After my defeat in the 1946 primary, I said in a statement that while I felt the voters had been misled by propaganda I wanted to thank them for having been so good to me for so long. I felt strongly about that. Forty-one years before, I had been stranded in Butte, owning little more than the clothes on my back. Montana and I took to each other and its people had elected me four times to the highest office within their power to bestow.

My statement also noted that my constituents had relieved me of some "heavy responsibilities." In place of public duty there was now private opportunity. I had always boasted that I didn't need public office to make a living.

Falling into this mood immediately, Mrs. Wheeler and the six children joked about my being jobless. Actually, they suspected that a new life at sixty-four would be stimulating for me. And possibly they looked forward to a change of pace for themselves too. The demands of a politician's life had not made their home life easy. But if it bothered them to have to live in two places and have a father who was away much of the time, they never showed it. Quite the contrary. They had plunged into the complexities of politics and government the same way they jumped into the cool waters of Lake McDonald, where we built our summer cabins, and climbed the snowcapped Rockies of Glacier Park which surrounds it. After each day in the Senate, I made it a point to have dinner with members of my family. Sometimes they proved to be tougher debaters than senators. The burning issues of any particular day passed around the table faster than the meat and potatoes. Mrs. Wheeler was always outspoken and the children were encouraged to form and express opinions of their own.

Priding myself on being independent, I am likewise proud of the integrity of my children. They have all been "free-Wheelers." Our youngest child, Marion, began to speak her mind at age six. Huey Long came to dinner with the family one Sunday and insisted on pushing all the flowers back into the corners because they distracted his vision from the person he was talking to. At the dinner table, he told our servant to take the floral centerpiece to the kitchen because it kept him from having a full view of me across the table. Little Marion's mouth fell open and her eyes stared in astonishment. She asked the much-feared "Kingfish" if he did that at home. Huey replied that he always made Mrs. Long take the flowers away.

"Well!" exclaimed Marion. "I'd sure hate to be *your* wife!"

For once in his life, Huey was speechless.

In 1932 my brilliant and aggressive daughter Elizabeth (now Mrs. Edwin W. Coleman of Milwaukee) became the "moving spirit," as one newspaper put it, in a drive to organize a national organization of Young Democrats. In November, they held a national convention at which Tyre Taylor of North Carolina was elected president, Elizabeth was elected secretary and Jimmy Roosevelt was elected treasurer. (Jimmy was elected out of deference to his father and did not bother to attend the convention.) A constitution was drafted for proposed ratification at a convention to be held in Kansas City, Missouri, in September 1933.

Jim Farley, the Democratic National Chairman, wanted the constitution changed in such a way as to put it under the control of his national committee. The prospect of turning the Young Democrats into errand boys and girls for Farley did not appeal to Elizabeth. She got busy (without of course consulting me) and circularized the delegates, urging them to vote against Farleyism at the convention. In August, when we were resting at Lake McDonald, she asked me for the car so she could drive to Kansas City for the convention with Frances, another headstrong daughter who was a fervent Young Democrat. I demurred at the thought of these two girls motoring across the plains by themselves but Elizabeth said they would hitchhike to Kansas City if the answer was no. Knowing that Elizabeth could be taken at her word, I gave them the car.

The two sisters picked up fellow convention delegates at stops in Salt Lake City and Denver, and in both cities they made headlines. They were interviewed by reporters on their opinion of Farley, and they replied in unequivocal language. The idea of Senator Wheeler's daughters leading an anti-Farley offensive into Kansas City seemed to tickle editors generally.

Of course, Farley, being Farley, adroitly whipped the young party members into line at the convention. Elizabeth and a fellow delegate immediately called on the national chairman in his hotel room to let him know what they felt he was doing to their organization. Someone telephoned me at Lake McDonald to report on what Elizabeth was up to, and I phoned her to ask her if she was acting too hastily. We ended the conversation with my advising her to stand by her principles and disregard any possible political effects it might have on me.

Elizabeth did stick to her guns but it was a disillusioning experience. One by one, she saw her fellow delegates called into Farley's room and told to vote his way under threat of "no federal patronage." One by one, the delegates agreed to vote for the change in the constitution as Farley demanded. The result was that the Young Democrats never became the vital, creative group Elizabeth had visualized; later she married a Republican and became one herself!

In 1937 Frances again was news. When I took my stand against Roosevelt on the Court-packing bill, she was attending Connecticut College for Women. Asked by a reporter where she stood, she said she sided with the President—and thus made the newspapers.

After the 1946 primary, quite a few friends urged me to run as an independent against Ecton and Erickson in the fall election. Senator Clyde M. Reed, a Kansas Republican, offered to put up $1000 for my campaign if I would run. Senator John G. Townsend, Jr., of Delaware, the money-raiser for the Republican Party, told me he would raise funds for me—and none for Ecton—if I would run.

I never gave a thought to running as an independent. To me an election in one sense is like a lawsuit—once the verdict is in, you've either won or lost, and that's that. In the election, Erickson ran poorly and Ecton, an extreme conservative, was sent to my seat in the Senate. In 1952 he was defeated by Democratic Representative Mike Mansfield, who later became Senate majority leader.

The late Mrs. Eleanor ("Cissie") Patterson, publisher of the Washington *Times-Herald*, wanted me to enter the 1952 Montana primary against Mansfield. I sought to put her off by pointing out that it would cost some money; she asked "how much?" "About $50,000," I told her. She said that while she had never before financed a candidate she would be willing to put up that sum. I was abashed at this generosity and it was not easy for me to turn "Cissie" down.

She had been a loyal friend ever since 1924, when I was a bumptious freshman senator and she was one of Washington's leading hostesses. I will never forget the fact that immediately after I was indicted by the Daugherty clique she invited me to a big dinner party at her mansion. Nicholas Longworth, soon-to-be Republican Speaker of the House, and other reigning Washington big shots were present, but "Cissie" seated me in the place of honor at her right. She enjoyed flaunting her loyalty to the controversial upstart, and it gave me a big lift when I needed it most.

In 1958 I was again asked to run for the Senate against Mansfield, this time by J. Wellington Rankin, the Republican national committeeman from Montana, who personally called on me at my office in Washington to ask me to run on the Republican ticket. His request was followed by calls from GOP Governor J. Hugo Aronson of Montana, the Republican state chairman, and several other GOP leaders in the state. While I felt a deep sense of gratitude to these men who, although of the opposite party, "wanted me back in the Senate to serve Montana," I declined to resume an active political life.

Enjoying a successful law practice, I was content to remain in the role of a highly interested political observer. In 1946, defeat had again turned out to be a blessing in disguise. At first, I had considered returning to Montana to hang out my shingle; it had been so long since I'd closed my office there in the early 1920s that I wondered if I would be successful in my home bailiwick. But Mrs. Wheeler pointed out that most of my contemporaries had either died or left Montana. I took the suggestion of Edward, my son, a Harvard Law graduate, and opened a law office in Washington.

At about this time, I was offered a job by Herbert Bayard Swope. He said the liquor industry wanted to retain me as its "czar" at $75,000 a year. When I said no, the offer was raised to $100,000. But I had no interest in the position at any price because I felt the liquor interests wanted me for whatever influence my name carried.

Early in 1948 the executive council of the American Federation of Labor offered me $20,000 a year to direct its campaign against congressional supporters of the Taft-Hartley Act. I rejected the offer because it would have required me to work for the defeat of many of my old colleagues who had voted against the law passed the year before.

I have done very little lobbying. Most of the work in my law practice has been with the regulatory agencies, or arguing cases before the Circuit Court of Appeals and the Supreme Court.

After I began to practice law with Edward, I determined not to tie myself to one client. Fortunately, we soon had many and diverse clients. Some were powerful industrialists who had been on the other side of issues from me during my Senate career. Now they wanted the advice and knowledge of one who had helped write many of the transportation acts and many of the other regulatory statutes. Our clients have included both large and small companies in the radio, television and communications industries, railroads, trucking firms, unions, Indian tribes, and trade associations. Within ten years after my defeat in the Montana primary, I had earned more money than I had in the entire previous period of my life.

After my defeat, President Truman asked me if there was anything I wanted. I said no, that I was "out of politics for good."

"Burt," the President replied with a laugh, "you wouldn't be out of politics even if you could make a million dollars."

While Truman and I disagreed on foreign policy, it made no difference in our friendship. I have been told he won't let anyone criticize me in his presence.

In 1948 Truman asked me why I didn't jump into the Montana senatorial primary against my old Democratic colleague, Jim Murray, who had worked for my defeat in 1946. Truman said I was needed in the Senate.

There were rumors in Washington in 1947 and again in 1952 that President Truman would appoint me as Attorney General. In 1947 Tom C. Clark, his Attorney General, was under attack for alleged laxity in prosecuting the Democratic vote frauds in Kansas City. Mrs. Patterson's *Times-Herald* came out with a ringing editorial in favor of my succeeding Clark, but at no time did Truman ever make the suggestion to me.

When Truman later elevated Clark to the Supreme Court, he replaced him with Senator J. Howard McGrath. When Mc-

Grath resigned in 1952 during a furor over new evidence of corruption in the executive branch, reports again circulated that Truman wanted me as a "clean-up" Attorney General. Quite a few people telephoned me to find out if it was true. Truman never mentioned it to me and I never entertained the idea seriously. I knew there would be a great deal of opposition to my appointment—not from the Senate but from those editors, columnists, and professional liberals who had never got over their bitterness toward me on the war-intervention issue.

As for my many encounters with corrupted office holders and their corrupters, I must add that I have not become discouraged. There are always plenty of good men on the scene too and I believe our system in the long run triumphs over human weakness. I am certain that most members of the Senate, for example, are honest, as are most of our government servants. If most of our lawmakers could be bought, Uncle Sam's democracy would have been finished long ago—and we would have a dictatorship.

Often members of Congress are sold down the river by their "friends" and lobbyists who earn their living by purported "influence." For example, I once introduced a resolution to have the Federal Communications Commission investigate the long-distance charges of the American Telephone & Telegraph Company. Later that day I was followed into my office by two men. One of them, a hanger-on and some-time lobbyist around town, introduced the other to me as a lawyer from Chicago.

"This man knows all about the telephone business and can give you facts that would let you make a speech tearing the companies to pieces," the lobbyist explained.

I replied that if I needed him I would get in touch with him, but that I didn't think I would need his help. A few days later, some representatives of the telephone company came to see me and wanted to know whether I intended to make a speech on the resolution. I said I didn't see any need for it, unless they fought the resolution. A few days after that, Bowie Chipman, a Washington businessman who was in touch with the utilities, asked Mrs. Wheeler and me to dinner. During dinner, Chipman told me that the two men who called on me had gone to the telephone companies and told them I was going to make a "vicious speech" against them on the Senate floor. They said they could stop me from making the speech—for $5000.

Later, the two men came back to my office at the Interstate Commerce Committee and it was all I could do to contain myself. I told them if they didn't get out immediately I'd kick them down the stairs.

(This is not the only case I know of where large sums were asked for "stopping" something on Capitol Hill which was not going to happen anyway. A member of Congress never knows what sins are being committed in his name.)

The resolution passed and the FCC investigation resulted in cutting the long-distance rates.

For me this book will be worthwhile if it serves no other purpose than to make the reader appreciate more fully that the bulwark of our freedom is Congress. In recent years, it has become fashionable to make fun of Congress and to decry its inability to act expeditiously. In fact, many of those who style themselves "liberals" are loudest in their demands that we vest ever more power in the executive branch. Indeed, these scoffers give only lip service to our tradition of separation of powers between three branches.

Like Presidents Lincoln, Jackson, and Theodore Roosevelt before him, Franklin Roosevelt greatly expanded the power of the presidency at the expense of Congress. The defeat of the Court-packing bill and the administrative reorganization bill which followed it stopped the trend toward autocratic presidential power, but the Second World War gave it new momentum. I greatly fear this trend; it could all too easily lead to dictatorship. We must have as much faith in Congress and the courts as we do in the President.

Everyone agrees that one-man government is more efficient than a democracy, but the price in terms of individual liberty is excessive. Don't forget it when you read an editorial or hear a commentator ridicule Congress. Congress is an essential part of our tradition and it alone can keep us free. If you don't approve of your senator or congressman, do something about it by working in a party or simply by voting, but don't undermine

Congress and don't countenance anyone else doing such a wrecking job, whether it is your neighbor, the smart aleck, know-it-all magazine editor, or the President of the United States. If you do so, you may well lose your freedom.

Another word about tradition. A very wise and well-informed friend of mine who was formerly high in the Foreign Service of a Latin American country told me in 1962 that the basic difference between our government and those of Latin America is tradition.

"Never scoff at your traditions," he urged me. "Never do the slightest thing to undermine them. Do everything to build them up."

He continued: "The reason many of the Latin American countries have dictatorships is the lack of tradition which demands that when a President ends his four-year term he stands for re-election, and if he's defeated, he steps aside. In South America they have what is called the *caudillo* tradition. *Caudillo* means leader. They look to the man rather than to the office of the presidency. Once a man is elected, he immediately starts building himself up with the various factions and tries to solidify his position with the Army so he can either suspend elections or, if he is not re-elected, set aside the constitution and remain in office by force.

"In your country such a thing is unthinkable," my friend said. "No President would entertain the idea of not holding an election or attempting to get the Army to maintain him in office if he were defeated. But, even more important, if he tried to do so, I am sure the Army officers would laugh at him because they would not expect to be, and would not permit themselves to be, used for such a purpose."

Similarly, he pointed out that in the United States if Congress fails to pass legislation requested by the President, the President does not call out the Army and disband Congress and force its leaders into exile or worse. This is not because many Presidents may not sometimes feel like doing that but because our tradition prevents it.

So when you hear or read statements debunking our traditions or the great men in our history who established them or helped uphold them, don't fall for it. Such statements are usually made by someone who wants to appear either learned or clever. Acceptance of them would undermine our greatest heritage.

It is a chronic complaint of the latter-day "liberals" that Congress is not "carrying out" the President's program. What they really want is for Congress to be a rubber stamp, although they use the term, "party discipline." Too strict party discipline is not compatible with our democratic system; it cannot be enforced without intellectual or financial dishonesty. On the presidential train in 1934, Eleanor Roosevelt brought up the subject of party discipline and the President said he would like to see a great deal more of it in the Democratic Party. My comment was: "Show me an efficient, disciplined party organization in any big city and I will show you a corrupt organization."

I certainly never felt I had to touch my forelock to the executive branch. My zest for making full use of a senator's powers plunged me into most of the major issues of my time and made me a principal protagonist in such blazing episodes as the Harding Administration scandals, the Court-packing fight, and our fateful tumble into World War II. When one survives in the Senate for twenty-four years, his seniority usually makes him someone to be reckoned with. If he uses that power responsibly, he can have the satisfaction of playing a constructive role in his country's history.

As chairman of a major committee, I felt I could make my contribution by blocking bad bills as well as pushing good ones. Twice during my chairmanship the House approved bills to legalize wire-tapping, under certain conditions. Twice I saw to it that the House-passed bill was referred to our Interstate Commerce Committee—rather than to Judiciary, where it might have gone—and twice I sat on the bill, that is, never let it come up for a vote.

At first hand, I had seen how the "dirty business" of listening in on a person's privacy could lead to blackmail back in Montana, and so I did everything I could to keep it from being condoned in any fashion by the federal government. To me such spying is indefensible and I felt that it would set a very bad example for the country if the highest officials of the government officially resorted to it.

On other occasions, I would refer what I regarded as a bad bill to a hand-picked subcommittee, and the bill would be held there. This earned me the term, "dictator," and there was some justification for it. But I knew that if certain bills ever came up for a vote in the full committee the powerful lobbies behind them would fall on the committee members and the bills would be voted out. Perhaps this was high-handed on my part, but there is no necessity for voting on every bill introduced and, rightly or wrongly, I felt in those cases I was doing what was best for my country.

On the positive side, the most satisfaction I got as a committee chairman came from helping to shape not only railroad legislation, which I have already mentioned, but in using my influence in the exciting new field of communications.

Some of the uproar over quality and competition in radio and television in the 1960s are almost reruns of my experience with the two industries during their birth and formative years. Even before I became chairman of the Interstate Commerce Committee in 1934, I was concerned about the future of radio, as were other members of the committee. Incredible as it now seems, some people were blind to the potential of broadcasting and were unconcerned about how it was developing.

Like a few of my colleagues on the committee, I felt that since the air space was owned by the public those who used it had responsibilities to the public and should not look upon it as a private preserve to be exploited solely for profit.

The National Broadcasting Company originally had two networks, the Red and the Blue. David Sarnoff, head of RCA, the parent company of NBC, wanted a radio monopoly, as he later did in TV. Senator Clarence Dill, my predecessor as chairman of the committee, and I believed competition would be healthy and we encouraged the development of the Columbia Broadcasting System.

As chairman, I repeatedly warned the network heads at public hearings that they were indulging themselves in too many "soap operas" and too much jazz music. The excuse was always the same: "We're giving the public what it wants." In private interviews and public hearings, I warned them that they should use the airwaves for which they had been licensed to elevate the taste of the public, not to degrade it.

What I said about radio in its developing years goes double for TV. The pandering to the lowest common denominator of a mass audience of many millions is what led to the rigged quiz shows and payola scandals. Today television is making heroes out of gunmen and lighting the picture tubes of a nation night after night with sexy and glamorous murder-detective stories which I feel certain have a bad effect on many youngsters. It is undoubtedly part of the cause of the teen-age crime waves that crop up periodically.

When in 1961 Newton Minow, the new chairman of the Federal Communications Commission, decried the overdose of violence in what he called TV's "vast wasteland," I congratulated him. He was trying to alert the industry, as I had done two decades earlier. Unless the industry improves the quality of its programing, the people of the United States will demand censorship of both radio and television.

When TV was ripe for launching, the Radio Corporation of America wanted the FCC to adopt standards which would compel the use of equipment blanketed by RCA patents. Had this been done, RCA would have commanded a virtual monopoly in the manufacture of sets. FCC's refusal to adopt the standards urged by RCA kicked off a furor with charges that the federal agency was needlessly delaying the bringing of television to the American public. On our committee fell the burden of investigating the charges and countercharges.

At the hearings, one of the witnesses was Sarnoff. I was opposed to giving a monopoly to RCA in this field and I told Sarnoff that if it had the best system RCA would get the most business anyway. After the hearings Sarnoff asked me to lunch with him.

"I'm in trouble," he told me as we sat down. He related that when James Lawrence Fly was appointed chairman of the FCC in 1939 he had told Sarnoff that he understood that RCA had the best television engineers. This was something Sarnoff said he had never heard from an FCC chairman before; he was delighted to learn that Fly felt so kindly toward RCA. He explained that he had also been assured by certain people "close to the President" that "everything was all right" for his firm.

Sarnoff lamented, "I called Sam Rosenman [FDR's counsel] and Anna Rosenberg [also close to the President]. They told me everything was all right. But it's not all right. Fly has changed his mind about using the RCA TV standards.

"You know who's keeping Fly on as chairman of the commission?" Sarnoff asked me. I said no and he replied: "Burton K. Wheeler." I asked where he got that idea and he explained that Roosevelt told him he was keeping Fly there "because Fly knows how to handle Wheeler." This was news to me. I hadn't known that Fly could "handle" Wheeler. (Actually, I suspected that FDR, typically, was using this as an alibi to Sarnoff, who was pressing him to get rid of Fly.)

This struggle over television standards was one of two very severe struggles which the controversial and able Fly had with the dominant figures in broadcasting, principally RCA. This second controversy involved charges that a few powerful networks, centered in New York, were unduly dominating all broadcasting throughout the country. We then had only radio broadcasting in which three reasonably strong networks were engaged—with Mutual a struggling fourth. Of these three the RCA's subsidiary, the National Broadcasting Company, operated two, its so-called Red and Blue networks. It is obviously unhealthy in a democracy to have two out of three such powerful opinion-forming organizations in the hands of a single company.

There were other complaints about undue monopolization in broadcasting. The networks occupied positions of great power and they would serve local stations only if the local stations agreed to submit themselves almost fully to network control. Thus, a network could command all the time of its affiliated stations. It could compel a local station to carry a network soap opera or dance band even though the local station might prefer to broadcast an event of great local importance or interest.

FCC, at my prodding, had undertaken a study of the problems involved. In 1941, it announced a series of rules which were designed to introduce more competition into broadcasting and to free local stations from the degree of dominance exercised over them. Most importantly it would have compelled RCA to yield up one of the two networks which it was operating. These rules kicked off another great uproar, with both RCA and CBS asserting that irresponsible bureaucrats in Washington were destroying the basis for all network broadcasting. The inevitable forum for such a controversy is the congressional committee, and hearings on the subject were held before the Senate Interstate Commerce Committee. The broadcasting industry has always been able to command very powerful lobbies in Washington since senators and congressmen necessarily pay great attention to the complaints of those who control access to the microphones of the country. The affiliates of RCA and Columbia constituted the most powerful lobby for the networks. The networks always called upon them to intercede with their senators and congressmen.

Again I backed Fly fully and FCC's rules, with some minor modifications, became effective. Despite the calamitous predictions, they have not destroyed network broadcasting and the country has undoubtedly benefited from their adoption. RCA was finally forced to give up its Blue Network, which became the American Broadcasting Company.

When Fly began his term in 1939, he told me he was in favor of granting licenses for ten or twelve "super-power" radio stations, carrying some 500,000 watts each. I opposed the idea. I pointed out that the super-power stations would have all the best programs and thus get all the business. A little station serving a community could not compete. I also told Fly that only a rich political candidate could afford to buy time on a super-power station.

I introduced and got passed a resolution stating it was the "sense of the Senate" that a radio station should be limited to 50,000 watts. Though the resolution has never had the force of law, or even become a stated FCC policy, the FCC has followed its intent ever since. In my judgment, it is one of the reasons we have so many thriving radio stations serving small communities today.

The networks had first intended to broadcast only from the populous areas of the East and Midwest. When they decided to go West, they planned to accept as affiliates only stations in Denver and Salt Lake City. I told M. H. (Deke) Aylesworth, then president of NBC: "You just can't skim off the cream in the West." Later, Aylesworth informed me: "We're going east from Spokane to St. Paul, and we'll connect the stations in Montana with our network." I subsequently convinced William S. Paley, then CBS president (later chairman of the board) that his network had to follow suit in offering their programs and services to smaller stations throughout the West.

I also made clear my concern about "equal time" in a conversation with Aylesworth and Ed Craney, owner of a Butte, Montana, station. I said a station which gave free time to one political candidate should give the same amount of time to all his rivals who had legally qualified themselves as candidates. This posed the question of whether a Communist was entitled to the same degree of fairness. Aylesworth recalled that in 1932 NBC had broadcast both the Republican and Democratic conventions. The Communist Party then demanded that its convention should be aired. Aylesworth said they solved the problem by broadcasting the speech of William Z. Foster, one of the better-known Commie leaders, but not those of all his comrades. I agreed with this decision.

Aylesworth turned to Craney and remarked that while he didn't always agree with me he felt all station owners should abide by this practice or face government ownership. When the basic act setting up the FCC was written and passed in 1934, the "equal time" concept was incorporated and it has been in the law ever since.

Another provision I worked into the basic FCC act required any company convicted of violating the anti-trust laws to forfeit its radio license. After I left the Senate, this provision was repealed.

In most countries, broadcasting is a government function and of course has an unlimited potential for disseminating propaganda. I want to avoid that in the United States and that's why I am so anxious for the chosen few who are licensed to operate our airwaves to live up to their responsibilities to the public. It is the only way to preserve private ownership.

The achievement which gave me the most satisfaction in my career was being selected by both Republicans and Democrats to lead the fight against the Court bill. It also was the most significant in relation to our governmental system of checks and balances. I must confess it gave me quite a thrill when we defeated the President. We could not have had a smarter or more powerful antagonist. Roosevelt was a fighter and for this and other reasons I liked him—as a personality. Some people find this hard to believe. But, as I said in an earlier chapter, I harbored no bitterness after a scrap was over. Bitterness only hurts the person who indulges in it. I attribute much of my success in politics to this philosophy.

Roosevelt was a great personality, a man whose charm you couldn't help enjoy—even when you knew it was being used against you. Oliver Wendell Holmes said that FDR had "a second-class intellect but a first-class temperament." I agree with that. Roosevelt was not well read and he had no profound knowledge of any subject. But he had a superficial knowledge of a great many things, and he supplemented it with inexhaustible brain-picking. He understood people, and he admired people who disagreed with him if he felt they were honest.

I used to be amused by the way the President revealed his feeling toward me. Before the Court fight, he always began his letters to me with "Dear Burt." During the Court fight it was always, "My dear senator." When I handled the railroad legislation for him, he went back to "Dear Burt," but it was "My dear senator" again when we broke on the war issue. In May 1944 he returned to the "Dear Burt" salutation and it remained that way until he died.

His finest talent was his superlative use of the radio to reach the masses. The "country squire" with the upper-class upstate New York accent was able to make the people feel he was against the rich and for the poor. In my time, no other person could influence public opinion as effectively as he could. He was the first—but not the last—President to make separate and special pleas to all the minorities, racial, religious, farm, labor, etc. I always doubted his sincerity when he played on the feelings of the minorities like a musician fingers the keys of a piano. But it gave him the aura of being a strong and truly national leader.

I doubt whether Roosevelt could have been elected to a third term if the radio had not been invented. The newspapers were virtually unanimous in their opposition to him. True, in Montana I had been able to overcome a hostile press—which had amounted to a news blackout. I did this by literally covering a state which is 600 miles wide and speaking directly to the voters, sometimes to groups as small as ten or fifteen persons. But a President cannot cover forty-eight or fifty states unless he has electronic help. People will believe what they read in the papers, in the absence of contrary information.

I admired FDR as you admire a clever magician or showman. He had such great personal magnetism and warmth that it projected immediately to his audience when he mounted a platform or spoke his first sentence over the radio. Even vigorous opponents were at least momentarily swept along by his dynamism. This is an indispensable quality of leadership. It is also a gift. FDR reminded me, on a larger scale, of Arthur Townley, the dynamic leader of the old Non-Partisan League. All Townley had to do was stand on a soapbox and smile at the farmers; before he uttered a word, he had them in his hip pocket.

Showmanship in a politician is not to be scorned. It is the means through which he can reach the voter and educate him in the important issues. It is not easy to capture and hold the public's attention, but it must be done before education can begin. When I made speeches about the corruption of the Daugherty crowd, I used to suggest the dimensions and the drama of the scandal by saying that it had "reached right up to the White House door." You could have heard a pin drop in the hall following this statement.

FDR's showmanship sometimes slid into demagoguery, of course. I was furious when he went on the radio in the Court fight and talked about "one third of the nation" being "ill nourished, ill clad, and ill housed." This had nothing to do with the merits of the issue. But I had to admit to myself that on occasion I myself had used these arts to make a point in Montana when I was in a heated fight against the powerful companies ranged against me.

Roosevelt relied on rhetoric and was constantly searching for vivid metaphors that stick in the mind. When I campaigned with him through the West in 1936, I occasionally helped him play with words. In Denver, he asked me for some ideas on water resources, and I told him to repeat what he had said on the subject in Montana in 1934, on the site of the Fort Peck dam project. Although I had made a great many talks myself on irrigation, I had never heard that dull subject so lyrically and inspiringly extolled as it was on that occasion. That audience in 1934 must have felt they were looking at a latter-day Moses, ready to strike a rock and make the waters gush forth.

When we reached Colorado Springs in that 1936 campaign, Roosevelt again asked me for a speech and idea. I proposed the kind of simple image that appealed to him. I suggested he remind his listeners that when he had first campaigned for President in 1932 they were wearing overalls and traveling in freight cars. But now, after four years of the New Deal, they were wearing good clothes and riding in Cadillacs. FDR pulled out all the stops with this comparison at Colorado Springs and it was effective. He liked it so much that I heard him using it later in Pittsburgh when I caught his speech over the radio.

Of course, some of Roosevelt's best lines were contributed by Sam Rosenman, the adroit ghost writer. When speech drafts were discussed, you could never be sure what Sam had contributed. When we were on the train en route to St. Paul, Minnesota, in the 1936 campaign, Sam read the draft of a speech FDR was to deliver there on farm cooperatives. I told him it was "terrible." It was a dull explanation of co-ops—with which his audience would be much more familiar than the

President. I didn't learn until later that Rosenman had written the text!

Roosevelt's extreme popularity actually was an extra source of satisfaction to me. For I never used or needed the benefit of his coattails to ride into office and therefore I was not afraid to stand up to him. That my refusal to go along with the Roosevelt Administration on every issue eventually contributed to my defeat only underscored the fact that I had followed what I believed to be principle rather than expediency.

My refusal to go along with my party's leadership when I felt it was wrong has confused some observers about my political philosophy. One pundit had concluded that in the course of my Senate career I made the "classic swing from left to right." My own feeling is that while the times, the issues, and the leaders have changed, my basic outlook has remained the same. I don't know if there is a label for this philosophy; I never felt one was necessary. In the generally accepted groupings today, I agree with the "liberals" when they are on the side of justice for the individual and against the concentration of economic power. I agree with the "conservatives" in their opposition to the buildup of centralized power in the federal government.

What bothers me about today's "liberals" is this: through the ages, those called liberal fought to take the power away from the kings and the emperors and to give it to the parliaments; now it is the "liberals" who are anxious to give more and more power to the executive, at the expense of the legislative branch. We must not forget that Hitler was able to become a dictator because he persuaded the Reichstag to vote away their powers—"temporarily," so they thought!

Too, the modern "liberals" preach tolerance but in some ways are extremely intolerant themselves. They would cast into outer darkness anyone who does not go along with them one hundred per cent. And some of our labor leaders have become so powerful they try to tell legislators how to vote not only on union legislation but on foreign policy and civil rights issues as well.

On May 24, 1941, Joe Kennedy delivered a commencement

address at Oglethorpe University in Atlanta, Georgia. The former Ambassador to Great Britain counseled the graduates against slogans and words that have been "counterfeited."

"For example," he told them, "the word 'liberal' has become entirely suspect because of the grossest sins committed in its name. Today many so-called leaders are professional liberals. They would rather be known as liberal than to be right. They have tortured a great word to cover a false philosophy, to wit, that the end justifies the means. Liberalism, your studies here at Oglethorpe have taught you, has never meant a slavish devotion to a program, but rather did liberalism connote a state of the spirit, a tolerance for the views of others, an attitude of respect for others and a willingness to learn by experience, no less in social fields than in the physical sciences. Basically, liberalism predicates that man is a spirit and out of Godlike qualities can come the triumph over the basic instincts that have made him so many times 'vile.'"

I agree with that statement.

If my career has brought me more than one man's share of fights, I regret none of them. Incessant conflict made me live life more deeply. On my 80th birthday, February 27, 1962, I realized just how fully I had lived. My children gave me a huge reception which 450 of my friends attended. They included many busy persons—Chief Justice Warren and a majority of the Supreme Court plus many prominent members of Congress. The affection evident in that turnout brought tears to my eyes, and a flood of memories. The party stirred other persons' memories too. Accepting the invitation, Supreme Court Justice Felix Frankfurter had dashed off this note in longhand: *What! Eighty? Old Time is indeed a liar. Why, it's only yesterday—so vivid is my recollection of it—since you first swam into my ken as the fearless U. S. Attorney in Judge Bourquin's court* (a judge deserving to be remembered) *and then those glorious battles in the Senate . . . was all that 40 years ago?*

A wealthy industrialist once told me that I was a "very rich man" because, regardless of what happened to my politics or my pocketbook, I had a wonderful wife and family. There is no greater reward than seeing all your children turn out well, as mine have. Frances, who for years devotedly did much of the research in preparation for this book, died in 1957 but the other five are well, successful, and happily married. John, the oldest, went West and became general counsel for Sears Roebuck in the Far Western states. Edward is my law partner. Richard runs, and is part owner of, radio stations in Denver and Phoenix. Marion, our youngest, is married to Robert Scott, a Washington lawyer. Elizabeth, as I have noted, lives in Milwaukee with her husband, Edwin, a successful businessman. The main credit for rearing these sons and daughters goes to Mrs. Wheeler, who has been a sensible, farsighted, and strong-minded mother.

Growing up in the West and being educated in the East, our children have had the advantage of getting to know—and therefore, better love—their country. After being elected to the Senate, I bought a house in Washington but we always spent our summers in Montana. The hunting lodge I acquired back in 1912 on the wooded shores of Lake McDonald (in what has since become Glacier National Park) was expanded to three cabins, with the help of my strong sons. There three generations of Wheelers go boating, fishing, horseback riding, and swimming together.

Life for me in Washington is as full as I could wish it. Every morning I go to my law office and then lunch at my club with old friends or clients. When I feel like it, I play cards after lunch at the club, or take the afternoon off and play eighteen holes of golf.

The skinny, towheaded young fellow who headed West, without friends or money, certainly never dreamed of a future with such excitement and rewards as were in store for him. If I seem to have done everything the hard way, I have no regrets—I would do it the same way again. As Mrs. Wheeler says, our life has never been very simple and never dull. What more can a man ask?

INDEX